# BURIAL RECORDS 1811 – 1980
## of the
# WESTERN CEMETERY
## in
# PORTLAND, MAINE

Transcribed By

William B. Jordan, Jr.

D1446428

Delta County Genealogical Society

HERITAGE BOOKS, INC.

Other Titles By William B. Jordan, Jr.

History of Cape Elizabeth, Maine

Published 1987 By

HERITAGE BOOKS, INC.
3602 Maureen Lane, Bowie, MD 20715

ISBN 1-55613-060-0

# TABLE OF CONTENTS

# INTRODUCTION

As the 18th century drew to a close it was increasingly evident that the Eastern Cemetery, despite enlargement, must be supplemented by a new cemetery on the western end of the peninsula. Not only was there over-crowding and multiple internments in single graves but there was also little or no provision for an orderly arrangement of family lots.

In June 1788 a committiee of three was appointed to investigate the availability of a suitable location. Apparently their search was conducted at a leisurely pace. On 26 October 1789 Capt. Joseph McLellan, Richard Codman, and Thomas Robinson, were empowered by the town to continue the search. Their efforts were notcrowned with success.

Finally, in April, 1805, the town appropriated $2000 for the purchase of land. Near the present site of the Maine Medical Center a tract of land was obtained from David Ross. Over the next ten years little or nothing was accomplished. In June of 1812 it was reported that the site was of doubtful suitability inasmuch as the soil was filled with large stones and coarse gravel; an annoying obstacle to grave digging. However, it was suggested that surface preparation be carried out by the Keeper of the Alms House and the site used as a garden or hay field.

The Ross tract must have been eventually rejected for use as a cemetery. In December of 1828 it was recommended by the Committee on Burying Grounds that the city purchase another site. The new tract, containing approximately ten acres was located at the junction of Vaughan and Bridge (Danforth) Streets. The land in question was purchased late in 1829 from the heirs of William Vaughan and others at a price of two hundred dollars an acre.

The tract already contained a small private cemetery that was retained by the Vaughan family along with a right of way to Vaughan Street. Without waiting for the laying out of lots burials were immediately initiated in the central area, now designated as Section E.

In the spring of 1836 the City Council ordered that lots, with suitable avenues, be laid out and the cemetery graded. The services of James Hall, a civil engineer, were engaged and a suitable plan drafted in 1840 at a cost of fifteen dollars. It was specified that the lots must be a minimum of 15'x 15' and the avenues at least six feet wide. The ranges were alphabetically arranged and each lot designated by number. The lots were made available to any citizen of Portland free of charge.

A year prior to Hall's survey, in the spring of 1839, an additional two acres of land was purchased from the heirs of Elias Merrill at a cost of six hundred dollars. At the same time the City Council authorized the construction of a fence to completely enclose the cemetery and the planting of shade trees.

The Committee on Burying Grounds in 1847 bestowed appropriate names on the avenues and paths. The central area, Section E, was designated Woodbine Grove. The avenues were named Cyprus, Laurel, Cedar, Poplar, Chesnut, Willow, Maple, Citron, Oak, Fir, Walnut, Pine, Spruce, Magnolia, Beech, Hemlock, Elm, Almond, Locust, and Olive. The paths were identified as Hawthorne, Hazel, Tulip, Columbine, Hyacinth, Rose, Jasmine, and Myrtle. Inasmuch as the only copy of Hall's plan was destroyed in the fire of 1866, it is now impossible to determine where most were located.

It is apparent from the records of the Superintendent of Burials, imperfect though they may be, that the Western Cemetery immediately became Portland's primary burying ground. From 1829 until 1852, when Evergreen Cemetery was established, it received a majority of the city's dead. In that period it fulfilled the needs that Forest City Cemetery and Evergreen now serve.

After 1829 most of those individuals who were homeless, friendless, or indigent, were buried in Western Cemetery, largely in Section L, originally identified as the "Strangers' Ground." The overwhelming majority do not have a gravestone or marker of any kind. After Forest City Cemetery was established in 1858 a section therein was set aside for that purpose.

Prior to the establishment of Calvary Cemetery in 1861 a section of Western Cemetery was designated as the "Catholic Ground." In years to come it was usually refered to as the "Old Catholic Ground." The first recorded burial was that of Mary Dickey who died 25 May 1843 at the age of twenty days. Like most in that section she has no stone. The area can be located on the Goodwin map of 1889 as lots 1 thru 61 in Section I. There was eventually an overflow into the eastern extremities of Section J. The majority of those intered in the "Old Catholic Ground" are Irish. There is no evidence that more than a tiny number were moved to Calvary in later years.

In 1854 the City Council authorized the Superintendent of Burials to grant lots in Evergreen Cemetery to any lot owner in Western Cemetery on an even exchange basis with the understanding that all bodies would be transfered. Under these terms a few exchanges were forthcoming. Although the records are incomplete it is known that William Pitt Preble, William Willis, Thomas B. Reed, William Pitt Fessenden, Nathan Clifford, Luther Dana, Henry Goddard, Horatio N. Jose, and Neal Dow, availed themselves of the opportunity to find eternal rest in Portland's "Valley of the Kings." Apparently they thought that Evergreen would be a "garden cemetery"on a scale with Greenwood Cemetery of Brooklyn, New York, and Mt. Auburn of Cambridge, Massachusetts. The lots they vacated in Western Cemetery are for the most part unrecorded.

By 1880 it was painfully evident that Western Cemetery must be phased out as a place of burial. The fire of 1866 had destroyed Hall's map and inasmuch as the burial records seldom indicated the specific location of the grave, plus the fact that less than half the graves were marked in any way, made empty grave sites very much a matter of conjecture. As early as 1853 parts of avenues were pressed into use for single unmarked burial plots and in many other areas more than one body rested in a single grave.

In 1888 the City Council halted indiscriminate burial in Western Cemetery. Interment was now limited to family lots or tombs. Although burials have continued, very few have been made since 1910.

As its active life faded into the past each passing year brought less and less maintenance by the city of Portland. Over the last fifty years uninterrupted vandalism has taken its toll. Despite the fact that twenty-one lots are identified as having perpetual care the cemetery is seldom visited by city employees. On one occasion a city bureaucrat publicly advocated that Section E be converted to a baseball field! As of this moment Western Cemeterv is a desolate wasteland covered by deep grass littered with rubbish an# hundreds of tombstone fragments. The destructive hand of the vandal reigns supreme. It competes strongly with the Eastern Cemetery as Portland's dreariest example of conscienceless and callous public neglect.

In conclusion, it must be noted that the tombs present a special problem. Apparently, some of the hillside tombs were frequently utilized as receiving tombs and the Superintendent of Burials never recorded a subsequent removal. In some of the tombs the existing body count is much too large to be accomadated. Two of the tombs, i.e. Longfellow (A:12) and Cummings (A:13), were opened for repairs to the entryways on 26 June 1986. At that time both were found empty! No clue has been discovered as to when the bodies were removed or where they were taken. The city burial records are devoid of information.

William B. Jordan, Jr.
Westbrook College
Portland, Maine
30 March 1982

# ABBREVIATIONS

Capt. - Captain
Co - Company
Col. - Colonel
Cpl. - Corporal
d - died or day(s)
d/o - daughter of
gr - grand
GSL - Grave Site Lost
h/o - husband of
Inf - Infantry or Infant
KIA - Killed In Action
LME - Ledger Monument
  Eroded
1Lt - 1st Lieutenant
2Lt - 2nd Lieutenant
m - month(s)
Maj. - Major
MB - Monument Broken
MBE - Monument Badly
  Eroded

MD - Monument Destroyed
ME - Monument Eroded
MEB - Monument Eroded &
  Broken
Mnt - Monument
nd - no date(s)
NM - No Monument
NS - No Stone
s/o - son of
SB - Stone Broken
SBE - Stone Badly Eroded
SD - Stone Destroyed
sis/o - sister of
TM - Two Monuments
USN - United States Navy
w - week(s)
w/o - wife of
wid/o - widow of
y - year(s)

# CEMETERY INSCRIPTIONS

Child found in a vault buried 29 May 1850 Catholic GSL

Body/o man found in Cape Elizabeth, unknown ae: c40y buried 27 Nov 1863 Strangers' Ground GSL

Child found, unknown, buried 4 July 1854 Strangers' Ground GSL

Child found near West Promenade buried 20 Nov 1870 GSL

Child fr Lewiston Falls buried 29 May 1848 ae: 2y GSL

Inf child murdered buried 30 June 1878 GSL

**ABBOTT,** Abigail w/o Stephen d 28 Aug 1846 ae: 59y G:75

Andrew d 8 Aug 1847 ae: 41y GSL

Andrew J s/o Andrew J d 12 June 1894 ae: 54y 7m 20d Civ/War: 1st Reg ME Inf SD D:65

Charlotte Emery no burial record SD E:1

Dorothy w/o Andrew d 22 Dec 1832 ae: 24y D:65

Elizabeth Taylor Daveis d/o John TG & Frances E Daveis b 20 May 1854 d 20 Dec 1937 Tyron, North Carolina E:2

Etta d/o Andrew d 11 July 1869 ae: 10m SD D:65

George d 3 Oct 1910 ae: 65y 7m 16d Pendleton, Oregon suicide E:2

Louisa D w/o Andrew J d 10 Sep 1881 ae: 36y SD D:65

Mary J d 12 Sep 1881 ae: 50y GSL

Mary S w/o Thomas S d 16 Mar 1859 ae: 61y Hilborn Tomb

**ABBOTT** (continued) A:10

Nathaniel d 20 May 1842 ae: 52y GSL

Susan L d/o Andrew d 29 July 1866 ae: 3y 8m SD D:65

Woodbury s/o Andrew & Dorothy d 12 Mar 1833 ae: 10m D:65

**ABRAMS,** Mehitable w/o Ralph d 3 Sept 1849 ae: 78y GSL

**ADAMS,** Inf ch d 1 Nov 1853 ae: 5m Hagget tomb A:18

Abba W d/o Capt William & Eliza A d 25 Nov 1853 ae: 5m 18d B:3

Aletha W d/o Amos & Catherine d 3 Jan 1850 ae: 20y I:106

Alfred A s/o Amos d 15 Sept 1864 ae: 48y I:106

Amos d 12 Nov 1857 ae: 48y SD G:38

Amos d 13 Oct 1849 ae: 73y I:106

Avis b 24 June 1787 in Castine Maine d 20 May 1871. H:95

Catherine d/o Amos d 24 Oct 1854 ae: 41y SD I:106

Eliza A d/o Isaac & Lydia R Fuller w/o Capt William H d 6 June 1913 ae: 86y B:3

Eliza A w/o A d 4 Nov 1881 in South Boston MA ae: 66y G:69

Emma O d/o William H & Eliza N d 7 Nov 1931 ae: 79y 7m 21d SD B:3

George W s/o William & Eliza F d 29 Aug 1909 ae: 47y SD B:3

Hannah D wid/o Horace D d 6 Dec 1846 ae: 26y "enclosed by an iron fence" GSL

**ADAMS** (continued)

Henry s/o John P d 17 Aug 1858 ae: 5m GSL

Horace d 12 Sep 1843 ae: 27y GSL

Isabella w/o Amos d 19 Aug 1851 ae: 10m GSL

James d 27 Oct 1843 ae: 74y F:86

John s/o George H d 5 Sep 1857 ae: 2y GSL

Joseph d 23 Aug 1850 in Providence, Rhode Island ae: 70y I:105

Mary Frances d/o Amos & Sarah A d 23 Nov 1844 ae: 2y 9m SD G:38

Moses d 26 Nov 1859 ae: 87y Haggett tomb A:18

Sarah w/o Moses d 4 Feb 1852 ae: 80y Hagget tomb A:18

Sarah Ann w/o Amos d 6 July 1856 ae: 40y SD G:38

Sarah B wid/o Joseph d 31 Mar 1868 ae: 80y I:105

Capt William H d 8 Aug 1890 ae: 68y Civ/War: 7th Reg Maine Inf USN B:3

**AEGLE,** Mary d 8 Dec 1848 ae: 28y GSL

**AHUA,** Mary d/o John d 4 Dec 1850 ae: 9m GSL

**AIKEN,** James d 7 July 1847 ae: 54y GSL

Millicent w/o James d 13 June 1843 ae: 55y GSL

**ALEXANDER,** Charles d 21 May 1872 ae: 17y GSL

Charles S s/o William W d 19 Sep 1851 ae: 9m SBE J:122

Electra B w/o William W d 15 Aug 1865 ae: 45y 6m SD J:122

2Lt Reuben wounded Cedar Mt Virginia 10 Aug 1862 d 17 Jan 1864 ae: 24y Civ/War: 10th Reg Maine Inf, Co B SBE J:122

Sarah w/o Samuel d 30 Sep 1857 ae: 83y GSL

William W no burial record SD J:122

William H s/o William W d 16

**ALEXANDER** (continued)

Jan 1865 ae: 21y 8m 11d Civ/War: 5th Reg Maine Inf, Co C J:122

**ALLEN,** ---- w/o Parker d 14 July 1855 ae: 55y GSL

Inf s/o Moses & Hannah d 27 Aug 1855 SBE F:43

Inf d/o William & Mary Ann d 3 July 1846 SBE H:36

Alfred s/o Joel d 30 Apr 1843 ae: 7m GSL

Anna E d/o Daniel W & Olive d 29 Mar 1867 ae: 3y 15d SBE G:33

Betsy F w/o Joel d 20 Apr 1837 ae: 27y SBE F:89

Charles H d 8 Oct 1861 GSL

Charles M s/o Parker d 29 Apr 1851 ae: 17y GSL

Cornelius s/o William d 22 Mar 1853 ae: 20y Catholic SB J:276

David d 12 May 1862 ae: 69y GSL

Elizabeth w/o Joel d 28 Nov 1842 ae: 33y SBE F:89

Elizabeth w/o Joseph d 28 Nov 1842 ae: 33y GSL

Ellen d 20 Feb 1855 ae: 26 GSL

Ernest D s/o Nathaniel P d 15 Nov 1870 ae: 3y 10m GSL

Ferdinando C s/o Daniel W & Mary d 14 Aug 1851 ae: 14y 6m SD G:33

Fernald C s/o Daniel W & Olive d 13 Aug 1853 ae: 14y SBE G:33

Francis M L d/o F C d 7 Nov 1860 ae: 1y GSL

Frederick L s/o Elias B d 12 Jan 1865 ae: 4m GSL

Helen R d/o late William d 22 Sept 1861 ae: 22y H:36

Herbert J s/o Jacob P d 2 Sept 1872 ae: 10m GSL

James s/o Hiram d 15 Mar 1842 ae: 13y GSL

Joel d 15 July 1873 ae: 74y F:89

Justus s/o Hiram d 15 Mar 1842 ae: 21y GSL

Lydia w/o Jacob d 19 Dec 1845 ae: 77y F:139

ALLEN (continued)
Martha d/o Joel d 19 Sept 1841 ae: 18m GSL
Mary d/o William d 7 Oct 1849 ae: 2y H:36
Mary w/o Solomon d 30 Aug 1878 ae: 78y H:58
Mary Ann w/o William d 6 Oct 1856 ae: 50y SD H:36
Mary B d/o Dr Solomon & Mary b 6 June 1825 d 16 Apr 1864 H:58
Mary E w/o Jacob d 23 Oct 1872 ae: 31y GSL
Mary L d/o William & Mary Ann d 30 Sept 1849 ae: 20m H36
Nancy T w/o Robert d 11 Aug 1846 SD B:29
Nathaniel B d 29 Apr 1852 ae: 36y I:86
Parker d 26 Aug 1859 ae: 63y GSL
Robert Jr d 27 July 1862 ae: 21y Civ/War: 1Lt, 1st Reg US Cav, wounded Richmond, Virginia SD B:29
Sarah A w/o Nathaniel d 30 June 1871 ae: 60y 7m SBE I:86
Sarah E d/o Charles d 5 Aug 1852 ae: 9m GSL
Solomon, M D d 5 Feb 1859 ae: 64y H:58
William d 6 July 1850 ae: 40y 4m H:36
William d 27 Mar 1854 ae: 56y Catholic Native of Glanmira Parish, County Cork, Ireland J:195
William d 13 Oct 1860 ae: 59y SB J:276
AMES, Cynthia M w/o Daniel W d/o Matthew A & Sarah L Cobb d 31 Aug 1914 ae: 80y D:77
Marietta F d/o Franklin J d 24 Nov 1860 ae: 5y 6m GSL
ANDERSON, John F s/o John d 3 Nov 1844 ae: 16m GSL
ANDREWS, Elizabeth w/o Charles d 20 Oct 1858 ae: 22y Buried head of Capt T Kallard's grave GSL
Grace L d/o William d 19

ANDREWS (continued)
May 1859 ae: 11m H:102
Martha L w/o Edward Jr d 9 Apr 1850 Lisbon, Maine ae: 31y 6m GSL
Sarah Ann w/o William d/o George Clark d 14 Dec 1873 ae: 59y H:102
William d 30 Apr 1872 ae: 56y H:102
William s/o William d 5 May 1848 ae: 1y 6m SD H:102
ANGLER, Margaret d/o Timothy d 29 July 1846 ae: 16m Catholic GSL
ANGUS, Ann w/o Dennis H d 25 Dec 1871 ae: 74y 6m SB C:55
Dennis H d 31 Aug 1855 ae: 76y SB C:55
Maria d/o Dennis d 14 Oct 1888 ae: 66y SD C:55
ANNIS, Jesse d 26 Jan 1864 ae: 55y SBE on D:19 C:76
APPLETON, Frances C d/o John W d 15 June 1856 ae: 38y SD B:22
Frederick Augustus s/o E W & Martha d 14 Mar 1845 ae: 6y 4m C:33
Gardner d 12 Oct 1875 ae: 88y GSL
John W d 27 Mar 1862 Baltimore Maryland ae: 81y SB B:22
Nancy d/o Asa Woodbury d 3 Feb 1871 ae: 83y GSL
Sophia W w/o John W d 16 Jan 1860 ae: 73y SB B:22
ARCHAMBEAU, George H H s/o Alfred d 7 May 1865 ae: 8m SD F:84
Mary B Heard w/o Alfred b1836 d1869 F:84
Mary Etta d/o Alfred d 8 Aug 1863 ae: 4w SD F:84
ARCHIBALD, Adeline d/o George W & Elizabeth b 4 July 1852 d 1 June 1872 SBE F:124
Augustus s/o George W & Elizabeth b 27 Oct 1855 d 24 June 1885 Greely Hosp SBE F:124
Elizabeth H w/o George W b

3

ARCHIBALD (continued)
4 Nov 1819 d 23 Dec 1885
F:124
Ellen S d/o Benjamin d 18 Sept
1848 ae: 14m GSL
Emma d/o George W d 1 Oct
1855 ae: 14m SD F:124
Everline d/o George W d 1 Nov
1862 ae: 10m SD F:124
Frances E d/o Benjamin d 12
Aug 1849 ae: 1y GSL
George W d 21 Oct 1898 ae: 81y
5m SD F:124
Washington s/o George W d 12
June 1851 ae: 11m SD F:124
AREY, Isabella d/o James d 10
Oct 1853 ae: 4y 4m GSL
ARMSTRONG, Ann d/o William
d 1 Aug 1856 ae: 22y GSL
Jacob L d 27 Jan 1873 ae: 28y
GSL
Margaret d 10 May 1881 ae: 80y
GSL
Samuel G s/o John R d 27 Oct
1865 ae: 5y GSL
Thomas w/o William d 6 Aug
1854 ae: 18y GSL
William d 13 Aug 1854 ae: 54y
GSL
ARNAULT, Anna Maria w/o
Andre d 4 Apr 1859 ae: 23y
GSL
AROSEMENA, Angelica Isabel
d/o Don Eduard d 24 Mar 1858
ae: 11y 4m Native of Panama
Hilborn tomb A:10
ARTELS, Rebecca w/o John OB
no burial record SD D:52
ASKIN, Charles H d 19 July 1856
ae: 3m SB J:58
ATKINS, Mary Louisa d/o Joshua
d 21 Sept 1846 ae: 15y GSL
Melvin A s/o Joshua d 22 Mar
1859 ae: 39y 7m GSL
ATKINSON, A G d 17 Feb 1859
ae: 20y Trowbridge tomb Site
unknown
ATWELL, Dolly w/o John d 19
Feb 1854 ae: 73y C:10
John d 2 Feb 1821 Native of Ben-
ton, New Hampshire C:10
ATWICK, Thomas C d 25 Nov

ATWICK (continued)
1849 ae: 46y GSL
AUGUSTINE, Lydia d 27 Apr 1855
ae: 35y GSL
AVERILL, John d 24 Aug 1863
ae: 74y GSL
Mary w/o David d 24 June 1851
ae: 57y GSL
Sophia wid/o John d 11 Sept 1863
ae: 70y GSL
AYERS, Abigail D w/o John d 11
Nov 1862 ae: 70y SD A:6
Allen s/o Rufus A d 4 June 1893
ae: 6m 28d SD A:6
David P d 30 Aug 1889 Boston,
Massachusetts ae: 46y GSL
George A s/o George d 14 July
1841 ae: 8y GSL
Georgianna d/o John & Joanna d
11 July 1857 ae: 14y 4m A:6
Harriet F wid/o Joseph N d 24
Feb 1865 ae: 41y GSL
Joanna H d 11 July 1896 Charles-
town, Massachusetts ae: 80y
4m SD A:6
John d 6 July 1866 ae: 80y 6m
SD A:6
John Jr d 2 Dec 1859 ae: 47y A:6
John Jr d 1 July 1865 ae: 24y
Civ/War: 16th Reg Maine Inf
Co H SD A:6
John F d 6 July 1866 ae: 86y
War of 1812 veteran A:6
Margaret M d/o Moses G d 22
Dec 1849 ae: 1y Catholic GSL
Mary wid/o Joseph d 17 Mar
1869 ae: 87y 11m GSL
Sarah w/o John Jr d 20 June 1869
ae: 30y SD A:6
Stephen D s/o Rufus A d 6 Sept
1895 Gorham, Maine ae: 1y 6m
SD A:6
Walter A s/o John d 10 Dec 1865
ae: 10w A:6
AYLING, Cornelius d 23 Mar 1853
ae: 20y Catholic GSL
BABB, Bathsheba w/o Daniel d 5
May 1859 ae: 72y SB D:73
Edgar s/o Peter d 11 Sept 1847
ae: 6m GSL
Emily d/o John d 2 Nov 1842 ae:
20y GSL

**BABB** (continued)

Peter d 14 Sept 1848 ae: 31y GSL

**BAGLEY,** George s/o John d 13 Nov 1871 ae 22y GSL

Johanna d/o Michael d 20 July 1847 ae: 1y Strangers' Ground GSL

John B d 8 Nov 1889 Old Men's Home ae: 88y 3m SD J:58

Mary H w/o John B d 30 Nov 1843 ae: 49y J:58

**BAGSIGANS,** John w/o Thomas d 22 Aug 1850 ae: 3w Catholic GSL

**BAILEY,** Anna Maria d/o Frank J & Nancy d 22 Aug 1862 ae: 5w B:50

Annie Elizabeth d/o George G & ME d 2 Sept 1855 ae: 5m SD B:47

Annie K d 22 Oct 1952 Sawyer tomb A:14

Arthur s/o Luvier d 14 Aug 1886 ae: 6m GSL

Augusta Ann d/o J d 3 Mar 1870 ae: 1y 6m GSL

Lebbeus d 15 Nov 1849 ae: 58y GSL

Nancy s w/o Frank J d 16 Aug 1862 ae: 28y 2m B:50

Nelly A Fry w/o Charles L d 31 Mar 1857 ae: 19y 6m GSL

Peter d 15 Dec 1857 ae: 58y GSL

Rebecca B w/o Daniel d 26 Aug 1842 ae: 94y F:1

**BAIN,** Alvin T s/o Capt James d 2 Aug 1857 ae: 3y 5m GSL

**BAKER,** inf s/o CW d 19 Aug 1855 ae: 7w GSL

Caroline A d/o Charles d 7 Dec 1864 ae: 20y alias Decker Strangers' Ground GSL

Charles s/o Edward W & Clarissa Folsom d 8 May 1836 New York City ae: 2y D:40

Charles E P L s/o Edward d 14 July 1868 ae: 4m GSL

Charles P no burial record Civ/War: 29th Reg Maine Inf Co C SD D:40

Clarissa Folsom d/o Edward W b1800 d1890 D:40

**BAKER** (continued)

Edward W b 11 July 1796 d 1 Aug 1880 D:40

Eunice M Kellogg w/o William J b1829 d1915 J:108

Frances E d/o Charles H & Helen AV d 18 July 1852 ae: 7y 7m SBE B:65

Frederick F s/o James H d 14 Oct 1851 ae: 4w GSL

George Folsom s/o Edward W & Clarissa Folsom d 13 July 1843 ae: 2y 9m D:40

George H s/o Edward P d 14 Sept 1863 ae: 2y 19d GSL

Henry W s/o Alfred B d 10 Sept 1856 Boston, Massachusetts ae: 6m GSL

John W Chickering s/o Edward W d 1 Feb 1871 ae: 33y D:40

Joseph no burial record Civ/War: USN SD D:40

Joseph Dana s/o Edward W & CLarissa Folsom d 13 Apr 1834 ae: 9y 5m D:40

Joseph McLellan s/o Edward P d 14 Aug 1871 ae: 10m 3d GSL

Louisa A d 7 Nov 1888 ae: 75y Sawyer tomb A:14

Sarah C w/o JH d/o John & Sarah A Edmunds d 2 Oct 1872 ae: 20y C:74

Sarah Chase d/o Charles H d 19 Apr 1849 ae: 5y 8m SBE B:65

W A d1871 SBE D:40

William Jay b1829 d1856 J:108

**BALDWIN,** Cornelius w/o William d 27 Oct 1856 ae: 21y Catholic GSL

James w/o William d 27 Sept 1850 ae: 1y Catholic GSL

**BALKAM,** Hannah A d/o John A & Mary J d 22 June 1843 ae: 28y J:233

John A d 1 Mar 1863 ae: 65y J:233

Mary J w/o John A d 5 Feb 1884 ae: 80y 6m J:233

**BALL,** Eva d/o James M d 28 May 1855 ae: 3y 6m Black buried Charles Barrett lot GSL

John M d1 Dec 1857 ae: 66y GSL

BALL (continued)
Phebe M d 29 Apr 1863 ae: 56y GSL

BANCROFT, Susan H w/o Lucius L d 18 Apr 1851 ae: 30y GSL

BANKS, Ivory H s/o John T d 26 Nov 1894 ae: 49y Civ/War: 23rd Reg Maine Inf Co C Sawyer tomb A:14

BANNON, Ann w/o John d 19 June 1874 ae: 74y Catholic D:83

Ellen d/o John d 31 Oct 1855 ae: 9m Catholic SD D:83

Rose d 31 Aug 1878 ae: 34y Catholic D:83

BARBARICK, Ann w/o Capt Theophilus d 17 May 1865 ae: 65y 5m SBE F:53

Eddie s/o Theophilus d 26 Apr 1881 ae: 2y SD F:53

Ellen T wid/o Theophilus T d 1 Feb 1907 ae: 58y 1m 5d SD F:53

Emeline M w/o Theophilus Jr d 19 May 1862 ae: 32y F:53

Emeline M d/o Theophilus & Emeline M d 21 Sept 1853 ae: 1y 8m 11d SD F:53

George M s/o Theophilus & Emeline M no burial record SD F:53

Hamner s/o Theophilus d 10 June 1850 ae: 17y SD F:53

Margaret d/o Theophilus & Emeline M d 12 Sept 1842 ae: 6y 3m F:53

Sumner s/o Capt Theophilus & Ann d 10 June 1850 ae: 16y 10m F:53

Theophilus d 1 Aug 1899 Revere, Massachusetts ae: 73y 8m 6d SD F:53

Capt Theophilus d 23 Jan 1879 ae: 87y 6m F:53

BARBOUR, Charles Allen s/o James P d 22 July 1863 ae: 1y 3m Hossack tomb A:17

Mary d/o Seward d 23 Mar 1843 ae: 3y GSL

Mehitable K w/o Alexander d 2 Aug 1848 ae: 43y GSL

BARKER, Anne E d/o Thomas d 17 Jan 1853 ae: 13m GSL

Jennie A d/o Wilbur L & Althea L d 19 July 1898 ae: 16y 11m SD J:136

BARNARD, Mary G w/o Edward d 27 Apr 1850 ae: 27y G:71

Mary H d/o Edward S & Mary G d 7 Aug 1850 ae: 3m 25d G:71

BARNES, Helen M wid/o Washington d 11 Dec 1897 ae: 62y SD G:9

James d 29 May 1856 ae: 79y GSL

James Augustus s/o James & Harriet d 18 June 1847 ae: 7y D:63

Jane, d/o William d 22 Sept 1854 ae: 18m 25d GSL

Jane Bell w/o Joseph d 8 Mar 1853 ae: 62y 6m D:1

John W s/o Nathan & Louisa d 18 Sept 1847 at sea ae: 35y D:26

Joseph d 13 June 1864 ae: 77y 7m Native of Ostend D:1

Joseph s/o Joseph & Jane Bell d 16 July 1843 Point Peter, Georgia ae: 21y 3m SD D:1

Joseph W s/o William H d 28 Sept 1861 ae: 4y GSL

Lois w/o Nathan d 14 July 1885 ae: 94y 6m D:26

Mary Ann d/o Nathan & Louisa d 7 July 1826 ae: 15m D:26

Mary E d 29 Oct 1873 ae: 15y GSL

Nathan d 18 Dec 1864 ae: 88y D:26

Samuel L J s/o Nathan & Louisa d 29 Jan 1850 ae: 22y D:26

Sumner E C s/o Nathan & Louisa d 29 Mar 1847 ae: 17y D:26

Thaddeus Percival s/o Nathan & Louisa d 5 Feb 1841 ae: 2y 8m D:26

BARNETT, Benjamin D d 14 Oct 1897 ae: 72y 9m B:48

Isabella Carter d 16 May 1850 ae: 16y B:48

John s/o William d 16 Aug 1854 ae: 4y GSL

**BARNETT** (continued)
John M s/o Charles F no burial record SD B:48
Julia Shanks w/o Benjamin D d 14 May 1868 ae: 40y B:48
Mary A d 4 July 1822 ae: 84y B:48
Silas d 28 Jan 1890 Greely Hosp ae: 1y SD B:48
William G s/o William B d 30 Apr 1883 ae: 8d Black GSL
**BARRELL**, Samuel H s/o George H d 6 June 1861 ae: 5m Dyer tomb A:15
**BARRETT**, ---- d/o Edward d 12 Sept 1854 GSL
Edward s/o Edward d 5 Oct 1856 ae: 8m Strangers' Ground GSL
Hinory d/o Edward d 4 July 1850 ae: 7m Catholic GSL
John d 15 Dec 1847 ae: 27y GSL
John d 23 June 1849 ae: 30y Catholic GSL
**BARROWS**, Robert s/o Robert d 22 Mar 1855 ae: 4y GSL
**BARRY**, Catherine d/o Andrew d 14 Dec 1850 ae: 15m Catholic GSL
John s/o John d 6 June 1857 GSL
Patrick d 28 Aug 1853 ae: 40y Old Catholic Yard GSL
**BARSTOW**, Abby Frances d/o Hetherly & Abigail A d 12 Nov 1838 ae: 11m H:76
Abigail A w/o Hetherly b1812 d1859 H:76
D Franklin d 16 May 1901 ae: 58y Civ/War: USN H:76
George R s/o Hetherly & Abigail A d 12 Mar 1837 ae: 19m H:76
Hetherly d 11 June 1871 ae: 60y H:76
Joshua W d 22 Mar 1857 ae: 76y GSL
Sarah R d/o Hetherly d 29 Jan 1849 ae: 1y H:76
**BARTEL**, Rebecca C w/o John O d 2 July 1842 ae: 24y SD D:52
**BARTELLS**, George d 8 Apr 1855 ae: 76y Means-Cummings tomb A:13
**BARTLETT**, Abby P w/o Allen d

**BARTLETT** (continued)
23 July 1864 ae: 74y GSL
Adah May d/o C W & S E d 15 Mar 1872 ae: 8y 10m SBE I:84
Allen d 2 Mar 1836 ae: 48y SD D:75
Charles F d 20 Dec 1854 ae: 22y SD B:48
Charles W s/o Alexander P d 24 Dec 1903 ae: 60y 1m 26d Civ/War: 14th Reg Maine Inf I:84
Charles W Jr d 17 July 1904 Kansas City, Missouri ae: 34y 2m SD I:84
Eva Bell d/o CW & SE d 17 Apr 1876 SBE I:84
Flavel P d 22 Feb 1836 ae: 25y SD D:75
Harriet E d 13 Aug 1831 ae: 8m SD D:75
John s/o William d 19 June 1855 ae: 7m GSL
Sarah E w/o Charles W d 11 Nov 1906 City Hosp ae: 58y 2m 28d I:84
**BARTOL**, Lydia w/o Solomon d 16 Mar 1852 ae: 56y J:122
Solomon d 7 Nov 1860 ae: 70y 6m J:122
**BASFORD**, Abigail d 12 Sept 1848 ae: 62y SD F:88 (See Addendum)
**BASSINGTON**, Mirinor A d 3 July 1851 ae: 21y GSL
**BATES**, Elnora J d/o Nathaniel & Cynthia d 24 July 1850 ae: 8y J:74
Minnie L d/o Levi L d 27 Aug 1867 ae: 6m GSL
Nathaniel B d 4 July 1854 ae: 44y SBE J:74
**BAXTER**, Edward s/o Edward d 17 Aug 1855 ae: 2y GSL
Elizabeth w/o Henry d 13 Oct 1880 Chelsea, Massachusetts ae: 90y SD J:250
Henry d 22 Oct 1862 ae: 76y J:250
Robert s/o Robert d 23 Apr 1842 ae: 3y GSL
**BEACH**, Matilda E s/o Charles d

**BEACH** (continued)

6 May 1852 ae: 6y 10m GSL

**BEALE**, Martha Ann w/o Samuel N d 1 July 1844 ae: 40y GSL

**BEALS**, Alfred s/o William & Hannah d 18 Oct 1852 ae: 25y H:65

Hannah w/o William d 31 July 1870 ae: 74y H:65

William d 8 June 1853 ae: 51y H:65

William Jr w/o William & Hannah d 3 June 1853 ae: 22y H:65

**BEAN**, Albert W s/o Levi & Frances d 14 Jan 1941 ae: 65y 9m 15d No stone I:98

Carrie E d/o George M d 29 Oct 1886 ae: 2y 3m GSL

Carrie I w/o Levi A d 27 Dec 1912 ae: 54y G:72

Eveline F s/o John D d 29 Sept 1874 ae: 17y GSL

Georgia w/o Alfred d 23 Oct 1873 ae: 29y GSL

John H s/o Alfred d 12 Mar 1850 ae: 2y GSL

Joseph A s/o William A d 4 Sept 1846 ae: 13m GSL

Mary Ann w/o Capt Alfred W d 20 July 1901 ae: 82y 1m 18d SD G:71

Rebecca w/o James d 1 June 1867 ae: 82 GSL

Lt William A S d 20 Dec 1864 ae: 28y Civ/War: 13th Reg Maine Inf SBE G:72

**BEARCE**, Mary d/o George d 15 May 1843 ae: 6m GSL

**BEECHER**, Ann w/o Richard d 15 Sept 1856 ae: 34y GSL

Joseph William s/o Richard d 22 Aug 1854 ae: 7y GSL

**BELL**, Sarah d 5 Sept 1849 Boston, Maine ae: 71y GSL

**BENNETT**, Francis d 19 Oct 1876 ae: 65y Hilborn tomb A:10

Hannah M wid/o Benjamin d 5 Mar 1848 ae: 62y H:100

Harriet d 12 Apr 1883 ae: 67y Hilborn tomb A:10

**BENSEN**, Isaac B d 30 Mar 1864 ae: 69y 20d War/1812 vet D:81

**BERRY**, Ann d/o Andrew d 31 Jan 1852 ae: 8w Catholic GSL

Charlotte d/o Edward d 13 Oct 1856 ae: 16m GSL

Edward s/o Edward d 27 Feb 1859 ae: 1w GSL

Hannah w/o William d 1 Feb 1858 ae: 27y Catholic GSL

James H s/o James d 5 Oct 1856 ae: 11m GSL

John s/o William d 20 Mar 1857 ae: 9m Old Catholic Ground GSL

Mary d/o Michael d 4 Apr 1850 ae: 16y Catholic GSL

Mary d/o Patrick d 30 Sept 1855 ae: 10m Catholic GSL

Mary w/o Andrew d 19 Dec 1854 ae: 42y Catholic GSL

Mary E d/o William d 28 May 1855 ae: 6m Catholic GSL

Michael d 11 Sept 1857 ae: 52y Catholic GSL

Michael s/o Andrew d 16 Nov 1852 ae: 7y Catholic GSL

Richard s/o Patrick d 20 Sept 1856 ae: 2w Catholic GSL

Samuel H d 19 Nov 1860 Havana, Cuba ae 24y Buried Ira Berry lot GSL

**BESSE**, Martha d/o George d 29 Aug 1846 ae: 10m GSL

**BIBBER**, Thomas P d 4 Dec 1890 Boston, Maine ae: 70y 1m 4d SD F:127

**BICKENTON**, Circia D d/o Thomas d 30 July 1854 ae: 10m Buried in mother's grave GSL

**BICKFORD**, Ada Frances d/o Joseph H d 22 Aug 1853 ae: 1y SD C:15

Charles H s/o Joseph H & Mary A d 14 Dec 1852 ae: 3y 1m SD C:15

**BIGELOW**, Ruth A w/o William H d 28 Feb 1887 ae: 62y 11m B:5

William H s/o Samuel b 1827 d 1895 Mex/War: vet Civ/War: 16th Reg Maine Inf Co G B:5

**BINNEY**, Hannah d/o Michael S

8

**BINNEY** (continued)
26 Nov 1852 ae: 3m Catholic GSL
BIRCH, Esther P w/o James d 16 Dec 1865 ae: 52y GSL
BIRD, Mary w/o Seth d 25 May 1852 ae: 75y GSL
Seth d 23 June 1852 ae: 79y GSL
BIRNEY, Mary d/o Thomas d 10 Apr 1857 ae: 2y 2m 14d Strangers' Ground GSL
BISBEE, Henry s/o Rufus d 30 Sept 1844 ae: 4d GSL
B L A C K, Elizabeth T d/o Ira d 9 Oct 1847 ae: 8y GSL
Harriet E d/o Josiah & Laura d 24 Jan 1849 ae: 4y 24d SBE D:9
Harriet J d/o Ira d 1 Sept 1845 ae: 22m GSL
Ira d 4 July 1860 ae: 48y 10m GSL
Jane d/o Thomas d 17 Aug 1856 ae: 5y GSL
Josiah b 1802 d 1876 D:9
Lavina, wid/o Josiah b1809 d1891 D:9
Mary d/o George d 12 Apr 1863 ae: 5y GSL
Mary wid/o James d 22 Apr 1859 ae: 65y GSL
BLACKSTONE, George H w/o William d 14 Sept 1848 ae: 2y GSL
Margaret P w/o Driver d 18 Apr 1853 ae: 72y Black GSL
B L A I R, Isabella d/o William John d 7 Sept 1861 ae: 1y GSL
Martha d/o William J d 3 Oct 1856 ae: 7m GSL
BLAISDELL, John s/o Levi d 3 Oct 1848 ae: 18m GSL
Nelly D d/o Edward R d 11 Mar 1861 ae: 19m GSL
B L A K E, Albert s/o Samuel & Caroline M b1843 d1843 B:64
Caroline E d/o Samuel d 3 June 1861 ae: 24y SD B:64
Caroline M w/o Samuel b1804 d1893 B:64
Clarence s/o Mary d 15 Oct 1851 ae: 17m GSL

**BLAKE** (continued)
Eliza d 2 Dec 1853 ae: 17y GSL
Evis Maria d/o Samuel & Caroline M b1838 d1861 B:64
George s/o Samuel d 2 July 1864 ae: 22y SD B:64
George A s/o Charles H d 6 Feb 1853 ae: 2y 4m Cummins tomb A:13
Harry Lewis s/o Samuel & Caroline M b1840 d1871 B:64
John d 20 Dec 1854 ae: 58y GSL
Marie C wid/o Marcellus H d/o William A & Mary Ann Bean d 15 Dec 1939 Roxbury, Massachusetts ae: 86y 8m 3d G:72
Mary Caroline d/o Samuel & Caroline M b1826 d1839 B:64
Olive d/o Samuel & Caroline M b1830 d1831 B:64
Richard M s/o Samuel & Caroline M b1828 d1854 B:64
Samuel b1794 d1859 B:64
Susan E d/o Samuel & Caroline M b1830 d1900 B:64
Sarah H d/o Samuel & Caroline M b1835 d1841 B:64
Willie w/o Samuel & Caroline M d1846 d1847 B:64
BLANCHARD, Olive S w/o John D d 22 Aug 1847 at sea ae: 32y GSL
Capt Samuel d 31 May 1864 ae: 70y SD B:15
Sarah w/o Capt Samuel d 20 June 1872 ae: 79y 5m B:15
Sarah T d/o Samuel d 12 July 1844 ae: 12y SD B:15
B L U E F I E L D, Emmette d/o Simon d 24 Apr 1857 ae: 2y 4m GSL
BOLDING, Elizabeth d 3 Jan 1857 ae: 40y GSL
BOLTON, Albert s/o Nathaniel d 16 Feb 1870 ae: 28y GSL
Anna d ae: 9d no dates on stone no burial record H:98
Caddy M d 18 Feb 1868 ae: 28y GSL
Clarence no burial record SD H:98
Cynthia A w/o Peter b1825 d1907

**BOLTON** (continued)
C:11

Daniel d 4 July 1858 ae: 65y 3m C:11

Edward A s/o Levi & Sabrina d 9 Apr 1858 ae: 21y 4m F:127

Elbridge G s/o Horace d 14 Aug 1852 ae: 3m GSL

Freddie d ae: 2y no dates on stone no burial record H:98

Frederick E s/o Charles d 28 July 1849 ae: 5w GSL

Freeman d 24 Aug 1856 ae: 23y 8m H:98

Jerusha w/o Peter d 24 Nov 1861 ae: 53y SBE C:11

John A s/o Levi d 10 Apr 1859 ae: 22y SD F:127

Johnnie d ae: 10m no dates on stone no burial record H:98

Levi d 6 Aug 1864 ae: 66y SD F:127

Levi G s/o Levi & Sabrina d 1 Mar 1843 ae: 3y 7m F:127

Lewis s/o Peter & Jerusha d 30 July 1853 ae: 19y SD C:11

Louisa A d/o Levi & Sabrina d 23 Nov 1846 ae: 18m SD F:127

Louisa F d/o Levi & Sabrina d 8 Jan 1828 ae: 5m F:127

M W s/o Sabine d 14 July 1852 ae: 2y GSL

Peter d 17 Sept 1872 ae: 63y C:11

Sabrina w/o Levi d 9 May 1857 ae: 51y F:127

Thankful w/o Daniel d 8 Feb 1871 ae: 74y 4m SD C:11

Thomas d 21 Jan 1864 ae: 27y GSL

Thomas C s/o Thomas C d 23 Aug 1864 ae: 7m 7d GSL

Willie d ae: 2y no dates on stone no burial record H:98

**BOLWIN,** Henry s/o William d 2 Nov 1860 Thomaston, Maine ae: 23y GSL

**BONAYNE,** Ellen w/o Bartholomew d 29 Jan 1884 ae: 67y Native of Ireland Catholic J:41 (See Addendum)

**BOND,** Charles F s/o John d 12 Oct 1847 ae: 15m GSL

Clara Berry w/o Samuel d 7 May 1893 ae: 61y 25d SD J:246

Cora Fd 26 Jan 1881 ae: 15y GSL

Sgt Edwin F d 29 May 1867 ae: 46y Civ/War: 1st ME Batt Lt Art G:9

Ella d/o Samuel d 12 Nov 1857 ae: 9y GSL

George F d 11 Feb 1881 ae: 26y GSL

Harriet E d/o John d 12 July 1846 ae: 1y 10m GSL

Ida M H d/o Joseph H d 10 Nov 1874 ae: 19y GSL

John E s/o John d 30 June 1846 ae: 3y 6m. GSL

Mary E d/o Samuel & Clara B d 10 Nov 1857 ae: 8y 11m 2d J:246

Mary H w/o Samuel d 22 Aug 1860 ae: 38y SD J:246

Samuel d 4 Aug 1875 Augusta ME ae: 54y Civ/War: 4th Batt US Lt Art SD J:246

**BOONEY,** Frederick D s/o Marshall d 19 June 1853 ae: 5y. GSL

Marshall d 23 Nov 1859 ae: 64y GSL

**BOOTHBAY,** Abby Louisa d/o Samuel & Julia Ann d 5 Aug 1844 ae: 22d SD I:133

Julia Ann w/o Samuel d 22 July 1850 ae: 32y SD I:133

Samuel b 1820 d 1889 I:133

Samuel Alton s/o Samuel & Julia Ann d 30 Aug 1850 ae: 4m 22d. SD I:133

**BOSEK,** Edward s/o Mannus d 8 Sept 1850 ae: 5m GSL

**BOSWORTH,** Stacey d/o George F d 30 Apr 1890 Malden MA ae: 26d Cummings tomb A:13

**BOURNE,** Catherine wid/o Melitiah d 10 July 1854 ae: 68y GSL

Melethia d 8 May 1853 ae: 72y GSL

**BOUTELLE,** Esther d 16 June 1905 Poland, Maine ae: 80y SD

BOUTELLE (continued)
H:92
BOWE, Adeline S w/o Abel d 6
Feb 1857 ae: 21y 7m Hilborn
tomb A:10
Henry C s/o Alexander d 25 Apr
1865 ae: 5y 6m GSL
Wesley P s/o Alexander d 14
Aug 1856 ae: 8y GSL
Willie M s/o Alexander d 23 OCt
1856 ae: 14m GSL
BOWEN, Dennis d 27 Aug 1850
ae: 45y Catholic GSL
BOWERS, Annie E d/o Henry &
Helen d 18 Nov 1945 Auburn,
Maine ae: 82y 1m 14d F:62
Ephraim d 5 Jan 1872 ae: 78y 8m
GSL
Helen K d 5 Jan 1902 ae: 64y 4m
24d F:62
Martha w/o E H d 17 Oct 1862
ae: 58y GSL
BOWIE, Charles D s/o E H d 1
Sept 1867 ae: 5m 20d GSL
Minnie J d/o E H d 12 Sept 1868
ae: 4m GSL
BOWKER, Hannah H b 23 Jan
1826 d 8 Apr 1909 Malden,
Massachusetts I:65
BOWMAN, Bartholomew s/o Bar-
tholomew d 6 Aug 1855 ae: 5m
15d GSL
BOYCE, Ann Maria w/o Patrick
Henry d 17 Feb 1892 ae: 56y
10m Catholic I:150
Charles A d 30 June 1906 Chel-
sea MA ae: 36y 23d B:36
Edward s/o Manus d 22 Sept
1853 ae: 2y 2m GSL
Ellen V d 4 Dec 1909 Chelsea,
Massachusetts ae: 63y SD
B:36
Fanny C w/o Patrick Henry no
dates on stone; no burial
record Catholic I:150
Fernessa d/o Michael d 30 Nov
1854 ae: 11m Catholic GSL
George H s/o Patrick H & Ann
Maria d 9 Nov 1871 ae: 4y 3m
Catholic I:150
James A s/o Patrick H & Ann
Maria d 31 Oct 1865 ae: 6y

BOYCE (continued)
Catholic I:150
James H d 19 Apr 1909 Chelsea,
Massachusetts ae: 67y 10m
12d SD B:37
Mary A d/o Patrick H & Ann
Maria d 28 Oct 1865 ae: 3y
10m Catholic I:150
Maud E d/o James A d 12 Sept
1872 ae: 2m GSL
Patrick Henry s/o Neil & Mary d
9 Dec 1895 ae: 68y 7m Cath-
olic Civ/War: 1st ME Batt Lt
Art I:150
BOYD, David F s/o James L &
Sarah D d 28 May 1854 ae: 39y
D:47
Fannie P d/o James L d 29 July
1876 ae: 24y SD D:47
Frances Adelaide d/o James L &
Sarah D d 19 July 1845 ae: 3y
6m SB D:47
Fred L s/o James L & Sarah D d
11 Apr 1858 ae: 22y D:47
George Abbott s/o N E & K PS d
26 Aug 1866 ae: 4m 18d SB
H:53
Hannah wid/o Robert d 22 Jan
1846 ae: 80y SD E:1
Henry Scott s/o N E & K P S b
11 Oct 1864 d 11 Jan 1869
H:53
James d 19 Apr 1909 ae: 67y
Civ/War: 5th Reg Maine Inf
Co I SD B:36
James A s/o James L & Sarah D
d 25 June 1838 ae: 2y 8m D:47
James L d 28 May 1854 ae: 40y
SD D:47
James L s/o James L & Sarah D
d 25 May 1846 ae: 6y 7m D:47
James L s/o James L d 13 July
1855 ae: 17m SD D:47
James Osgood s/o James L &
Sarah d 19 Apr 1838 ae: 6w
D:47
James Osgood s/o James L d 23
May 1846 ae: 6y 7m SD D:47
Joel Hall s/o Robert S b 9 Dec
1836 d 15 Jan 1894 C:44
John B s/o James L & Sarah D d
12 Apr 1913 Boston, Mass-

11

**BOYD** (continued)
achusetts ae: 50y SD D:47
John P s/o James L & Sarah D b 23 May 1850 d 1902 D:47
Lendall G S b 17 Feb 1805 d 18 Feb 1881 SB H:53
Margaret Ann wid/o Robert Southgate b 10 Dec 1810 d 1 May 1881 SBE C:44
Mary B Scott w/o Robert d 8 Feb 1852 ae: 46y GSL
Mary C w/o Joel Hall b 29 Dec 1840 d 20 Aug 1888 C:44
Robert Southgate b 24 Oct 1804 d 11 Dec 1877 C:44
Sarah D wid/o James L d 5 Dec 1855 ae: 40y SD D:47
Susan C d/o Robert d 6 July 1854 ae: 58y GSL
Theresa Orne w/o Lendall G S, d/o Nicholas & Ann T Emery b 18 May 1813 d 12 Nov 1890 H:53
**BOYLE**, Catherine d/o Patrick d 26 May 1849 ae: 5y Catholic GSL
Catherine d/o Patrick d 3 May 1852 ae: 10m Catholic GSL
Ellen M d 22 Nov 1849 ae: 46y Catholic GSL
James s/o Patrick d 23 Aug 1851 ae: 3m Catholic GSL
Patrick d 16May 1853 ae: 45y Catholic GSL
**BRACKETT**, A M no burial record SD H:97
Almira W w/o Isaac d 19 Sept 1861 ae: 33y 10m D:13
Catherine J d/o George & Emily d 15 Feb 1865 ae: 21y I:93
Charles E d 25 Apr 1865 ae: 38y Civ/War: 17th Reg Maine Inf Co C H:97
Charlie no dates on stone; no burial record C:56
Dana s/o Isaac & Almira W d 30 Aug 1861 ae: 6w SD D:13
Dexter W b 15 Sept 1825 d 5 Dec 1878 C:56
George E s/o George & Emily d 30 Jan 1852 ae: 4y 29d I:93
George W b 1841 d 28 Feb 1862;

**BRACKETT** (continued)
no burial record Civ/War: 7th Reg Maine Inf Co G H:97
Isaac b 18 July 1821 d 22 Feb 1900 D:13
Isaac s/o Isaac & Almira no burial record SD D:13
Lydia d 12 Sept 1849 ae: 48y GSL
Rebecca H w/o Dexter W, d/o Dennis H & Ann Angus d 28 Mar 1912 ae: 78y 6m 21d C:56
Sarah M w/o Isaac, d/o Nathaniel & Sarah C Brackett b 22 Feb 1836 d 25 Nov 1919 D:13
Sophia c w/o Samuel M, d/o Rev Noah & Sophia S Cressy d 17 Dec 1899 ae: 85y F:131
**BRACY**, Mary J d/o William & Elizabeth d 8 Mar 1852 ae: 8m SBE J:133
**BRADBURY**, Harriet w/o Rev Horace J, d/o John & Sally Ulrick d 12 Apr 1849 ae: 33y 5m SD I:63
Mary wid d 26 Aug 1843 ae: 60y GSL
**BRADFORD**, Dorcas w/o John d 3 Sept 1846 ae: 26y GSL
Eddie s/o John E d 21 June 1871 ae: 1y 4m GSL
Elizabeth d/o John d 28 Apr 1852 ae: 16y GSL
Frederick B s/o John E d 17 Feb 1858 ae: 14m GSL
Mary d/o John d 3 Oct 1843 ae: 28y GSL
William s/o John d 12 Oct 1843 ae: 6w GSL
**BRADISH**, Maj David d 3 July 1853 ae: 67y War/1812: veteran I:173
Emelia Maria w/o Maj David d 6 Oct 1835 ae: 41y I:173
Fannie d 17 Feb 1861 ae: 19y I:173
Fanny w/o David d 18 Mar 1882 ae: 80y SD I:173
George M d 17 July 1881 ae: 59y Civ/War: US Navy I:173
Henrietta d/o Henry C d 17 June

BRADISH (continued)
1862 ae: 18m GSL
Mary E d 21 Dec 1909 ae: 62y SD
I:173
BRADLEY, Anna Mrs d 13 Oct
1845 ae: 81y Buried William
Evans' lot GSL
Cornelius s/o Dennis d 24 Apr
1858 ae: 5y Catholic Strangers'
Ground GSL
Edward s/o John & Margaret d 14
Jan 1851 ae: 12y Catholic
J:172
Edward s/o William d 15 May
1842 ae: 5y 9m GSL
Frances E w/o Leonard W d 8
Apr 1858 ae: 31y GSL
James d 19 Dec 1848 ae: 65y
Catholic GSL
James d 2 May 1850 ae: 27y
Catholic Native of Co London-
derry, Ireland SB J:26
John J s/o James d 18 Sept 1852
ae 2y Catholic GSL
Mary Ann d/o John & Margaret d
8 Jan 1849 ae: 15y Catholic
J:172
Sarah d/o William C d 29 Oct
1847 ae: 7y GSL
Thomas s/o James d 1 Sept 1854
ae: 15m SD J:26
BRADY, Clara A d/o Josiah R d 3
Nov 1853 ae: 4y 4m Hilborn
tomb A:10
Josiah R s/o Josiah R d 5 Nov
1853 ae: 5y 4m Hilborn tomb
A:10
Lelia A d/o Josiah R d 1 Oct
1853 ae: 1y 4m Hilborn tomb
A:10
Mary Ann d/o John d 7 Feb 1870
ae: 2y 7m GSL
BRAGDON, Ella S d/o Samuel H
d 3 Nov 1857 ae: 8y GSL
Jane C wid/o John G b 1824 d
1881 G:96
John G b 1818 d 1875 G:96
Royal L s/o John G & Jane C d
19 Sept 1845 ae: 13m SD G:96
Royal L s/o John G & Jane C b
1849 d 1856 G:96

BRANNIGAN, James F s/o Henry
d 8 May 1864 ae: 2y 4m Cath-
olic GSL
James H s/o John d 23 Apr 1849
ae: 5y Catholic GSL
Mary E d/o Henry d 29 Aug 1867
ae: 2y Catholic GSL
Matilda d/o John d 24 Sept 1846
ae: 6d Catholic GSL
BRANO, Joanna d/o John d 13
Sept 1848 ae: 1y Catholic GSL
BRANSCOM, Clarence Arthur s/o
Arthur H d 7 Aug 1846 GSL
BRASSINGTON, Mirmorah w/o
Joseph, d/o John R Huckins d
3 July 1851 ae: 21y 7m SD
J:52
BRAZIER, Capt Daniel d 26 Jan
1826 ae: 61y H:59
Daniel Jr s/o Daniel & Dorcas d
15 May 1800 Havana, Cuba ae:
19y H:59
Dorcas w/o Capt Daniel d 26 Oct
1839 ae: 72y H:59
Enoch d Feb 1856 Cuba SD H:59
Harrison C s/o Daniel & Dorcas
d 24 Sept ---- ae: 2y no burial
record H:59
Phebe H w/o Enoch d 22 Jan
1852 ae: 44y SD H:59
BRESLIN, inf c/o Thomas d 20
Aug 1853 ae: 1d Catholic GSL
Jerry d 24 Aug 1850 ae: 28y
Catholic Strangers' Ground
GSL
Manassah d 7 Apr 1855 ae: 4y
GSL
Mary d/o Thomas d 30 Mar 1847
ae: 2y Catholic GSL
Thomas s/o James d 10 July
1858 ae: 22y Drownded Salem,
Massachusetts Catholic GSL
BREWER, Frances d/o late
Thomas Esq, Boston, Mass-
achusetts d 5 Apr 1857 ae: 62y
J:233
Georgianna d/o Thomas d 9 Dec
1877 ae: 68y SD J:233
BRIDGES, Clara Ellen d/o Wil-
son H d 18 Aug 1858 ae: 4y 7m
18d Hilborn tomb A:10
BRIGGS, Abner d 4 Feb 1833 ae:

BRIGGS (continued)
75y G:68
Anna E wid d/o Thomas & Grace
Pratt b 2 June 1875 d 23 Mar
1963 Freeport ME NS H:46
Charles buried 24 Oct 1931 no
burial record NS H:46
Mary w/o William d 10 May
1874 ae: 65y G:68
Minnie d/o George N d 10 July
1877 Charlestown, Massa-
chusetts ae: 9m GSL
Sarah w/o Anber d 19 Mar 1840
ae: 73y G:68
Sarah A d 21 Nov 1884 ae: 44y
SD G:83
Sarah D w/o William d 5 Jan
1838 ae: 32y G:68
William d 19 Oct 1852 ae: 55y
G:68
William E d 7 May 1863 ae: 37y
SD G:68
BRION, John s/o John d 1 Dec
1852 ae: 22m Catholic GSL
BRISTOW, George d 1 Sept 1850
ae: 45y GSL
BROAD, Mary E Libby w/o Her-
bert A b 1 Nov 1872 d 10 Feb
1904 H:52
BROCK, Amanda M d/o Benjamin
d 11 Dec 1850 ae: 2y GSL
Benjamin d 28 Aug 1875 ae: 69y
GSL
Charles d 6 Oct 1859 ae: 36y
GSL
Edward s/o George d 28 Nov
1862 ae: 1y 2m Cummings
tomb A:13
Grace M d/o William f d 3 Sept
1878 ae: 5m GSL
Isaac s/o Nehemiah & Mary A d
6 Dec 1918 ae: 73y G:22
Lucy w/o Otis d 26 Aug 1854 ae:
48y GSL
Mary A Fuller w/o Nehemiah b
1810 d 1851 G:22
Mary J w/o Benjamin d 25 Jan
1873 ae: 64y GSL
Nehemiah b 1804 d 1887 G:22
BRONE, Catherine d/o Patrick d
14 Mar 1849 ae: 18m Catholic
GSL

BROOKE, John d 4 Nov 1865 ae:
30y Strangers' Ground GSL
BROOKS, Aida Gertrude d/o
James S & Huldah d 21 July
1850 ae: 8m 11d F:51
Betsy d 21 Sept 1851 ae: 67y
GSL
Clarence Edwin s/o James S &
Huldah d 17 ?Sept 1858 ae: 5y
3m F:51
Daniel d 14 June 1831 ae: 48y
F:51
E Corser s/o James d 17 Sept
1858 ae: 5y 1m 2d Dyer tomb
A:15
Elizabeth w/o Daniel d 21 Sept
1851 ae: 67y F:51
Georgianna F d/o Hiram d 23
Feb 1845 ae: 19y GSL
Huldah w/o James S b 16 Nov
1818 d 10 Sept 1896 F:51
James B s/o James S & Huldah
d 17 Oct 1843 ae: 13m 22d
F:51
James Shepard b 20 Oct 1818 d
16 June 1895 Chicago, Illinois
F:51
Roscoe F s/o James S & Huldah
d 22 July 1846 ae: 19m 17d
F:51
BROSS, Eunice M B d 29 May
1915 Mt Vernon, New York ae:
85y 6m 23d SD J:108
BROWN, Abby E w/o James d 13
Nov 1854 ae: 27y J:243
Abigail w/o Daniel H d 17 Feb
1868 ae: 50y Buried "near the
pump" GSL
Angeline L d 1 Feb 1848 ae: 27y
D:64
Ann Elisa, d/o William M d 20
Jan 1864 ae: 1y 10m GSL
Ann M d/o James d 2 June 1852
ae: 11m Catholic GSL
Anna d/o James M d 1 Aug 1867
ae: 6m GSL
Annie E d/o William N d 3 Jan
1866 ae: 1y 2m GSL
Arthur Wallace s/o Stephen D &
Mary J d 3 Jan 1892 ae: 21y
H:20
Benjamin d 2 Feb 1867 ae: 63y

**BROWN** (continued)
6m GSL

Bridget w/o James d 19 Nov 1853 ae: 43y Catholic GSL

Charles Coffin s/o Rev Charles M & S d 23 July 1837 ae: 2y 6m SD F:94

Day d 4 Sept 1837 ae: 19y SBE D:64

Eddie s/o James & Abby E no dates on stone; no burial record J:243

Elizabeth E d/o Thomas B & Jane A d 20 Mar 1855 ae: 7m SBE I:94

Ella E d/o Rev S E d 29 Nov 1852 ae: 1y 4m GSL

Ellen K w/o William Jr, d/o Simeon & Hannah Skilings d 2 July 1861 ae: 24y 4m J:95

George d 20 Dec 1864 ae: 79y GSL

James d 13 Oct 1851 ae: 24y J:243

James s/o Parker d 2 Nov 1846 ae: 13m Catholic GSL

James E d 25 Nov 1859 ae: 46y GSL

Lt James M killed in action Locust Grove, Virginia 27 Nov 1863 ae: 23y Civ/War: 17th Reg Maine Inf Co A SD J:243

James Jr b 1825 d ---- no burial record Civ/War: Corp 5th Reg Maine Inf Co D SD H:20

Jane A w/o Thomas d 22 Oct 1855 ae: 28y SBE I:94

John d 19 Feb 1844 ae: 45y Catholic GSL

John O s/o Jeremiah O d 23 Aug 1849 ae: 3y GSL

John Q A d 9 Nov 1849 ae: 24y 2m I:164

John W s/o William N d 24 Sept 1861 ae: 1y GSL

Mary d/o Benjamin d 21 Oct 1842 ae: 2y GSL

Mary w/o Nathaniel d 25 Mar 1850 ae: 48y GSL

Mary Ann w/o James S d 5 Dec 1854 ae 25y 6m GSL

Mary F wid/o James d 19 Nov

**BROWN** (continued)
1854 ae: 27y GSL

Mary J w/o Stephen D d 31 Dec 1900 ae: 65y H:20

Patrick s/o Patrick d 10 June 1852 ae: 12y 6m Catholic GSL

Rebecca d 28 Nov 1864 ae: 64y GSL

Ruth M w/o Charles d 7 Mar 1857 ae: 22y GSL

Stephen D d 14 Oct 1890 ae: 54y Civ/War: 17th Reg Maine Inf Co H H:20

Susan Ann w/o Cornelius d 6 Nov 1856 ae: 54y SD C:65

Thomas B b 1843 d ---- no burial record Civ/War: US Navy SD I:94

Rev William McNutt d 11 Dec 1864 Winchester, Virginia ae: 55y Civ/War: Chaplain 12th Reg Maine Inf SD H:20

William Jr d 5 Mar 1871 ae: 38y H:20

**BROWNE**, Henry F s/o Samuel d 7 Aug 1858 ae: 7y 3m GSL

Julia A d 24 Mar 1862 ae: 48y SB D:64

**BRUCE**, Thomas s/o Thomas d 11 Sept 1853 ae: 1y GSL

**BRUCY**, Mary J d/o William & Elizabeth W d 8 Mar 1852 ae: 8m SD J:132 (See Addendum)

**BRUNELLE**, Franklin A s/o Alphonso d 12 Aug 1855 ae: 1y GSL

inf s/o Alphonso d 7 Sept 1861 ae: 3w GSL

**BRUNS**, Line d/o Charles N d 27 July 1865 ae: 1d GSL

**BRAVAD**, Mary E w/o Hubert A d 10 Feb 1904 ae: 31y 3m 9d SD H:52 (See Addendum)

**BRYAN**, Frank s/o Moses d 16 Feb 1866 Alms House ae: 19y. GSL

Orville no burial record SD H:24

**BRYANT**, Elizabeth wid/o Samuel d 25 Jan 1895 ae: 84y SD B:39

Harriet w/o Samuel d 30 Aug 1850 ae: 47y B:39

**BRYANT** (continued)

Harriet Amanda d/o Samuel d 11 Oct 1855 ae: 28y 9m SD B:39

Samuel d 6 Nov 1856 ae: 56y B:39

Samuel s/o Samuel & Harriet d 27 June 1826 ae: 1y B:39

**BRYCE**, Nina d/o James d 10 Sept 1868 ae: 10m GSL

**BRYSON**, Andrew d 12 Apr 1859 ae: 37y Catholic SD J:24

John s/o Andrew d 9 Aug 1858 ae: 4y Catholic SD J:24

John s/o James d 7 June 1853 ae: 14m Old Catholic Ground GSL

Mary J Hone w/o Andrew b 1826 d 1850 Catholic Native Co Tyrone, Ireland J:24

Wiliam A s/o Andrew d 8 Dec 1860 Dover, New Hampshire ae: 27y Catholic SD J:24

**BUCK**, Henry s/o James d 3 Dec 1868 ae: 30y SD D:84

James W w/o Martin d 13 Nov 1915 ae: 86y SD D:84

Sarah A w/o James W d 16 Nov 1895 Augusta, Maine SD D:84

**BUCKLEY**, Lorenzo s/o Lorenzo d 13 Aug 1841 ae: 2y Catholic GSL

**BUDD**, Mary Ann w/o William d 31 July 1839 ae: 32y C:7

**BUDDEN**, Julia d/o Jabez d 16 Ag 1860 ae: 10d Haggett tomb A:18

**BULL**, James M s/o Joeph W d 4 Mar 1870 ae: 27y 9m GSL

**BURBANK**, Sarah M w/o E P d/o William & Sarah B Graves d 14 Nov 1839 ae: 26y SD C:59

**BURCH**, Esther P w/o James d 15 Dec 1865 ae: 52y 3m SBE I:174

James d 6 Apr 1894 ae: 80y 9m SD I:174

Georgianna d/o James & Esther d 24 June 1846 ae: 1y I:174

James H s/o James & Esther d 17 Feb 1862 ae: 19y 11m 11d SD I:174

**BURDICK**, Zilpha d 5 Sept 1871

**BURDICK** (continued)

ae: 70y GSL

**BURGTON**, Sarah wid/o John d 8 Aug 1856 ae: 60y GSL

**BURIS**, Joseph H s/o Robert d 30 Nov 1864 ae: 2m GSL

**BURKE**, Chester V s/o Stephen & Mary d 15 Apr 1910 ae: 21y 7m 18d GSL

Edward s/o John d 30 Aug 1847 ae: 7m Catholic GSL

Ellen d/o Richard d 12 May 1856 ae: 2w GSL

Hannah d/o John d 21 Feb 1855 ae: 1y 9m GSL

Hannah d/o John d 14 Aug 1857 ae: 2y 4m GSL

John s/o Richard d 14 July 1856 ae: 2y 6m 14d GSL

John H s/o John d 18 Sept 1855 ae: 10y 18d Catholic GSL

John H s/o John d 22 July 1857 ae: 7m 6d Catholic GSL

Margaret Ellen d/o John d 17 Sept 1859 ae: 2m 16d Catholic GSL

Mary d/o John d 1 June 1851 ae: 3d Catholic GSL

Sarah Elizabeth d/o John d 12 Sept 1849 ae: 1y Catholic GSL

Thomas d 21 June 1865 ae: 55y Strangers' Ground GSL

William d 19 Sept 1854 Strangers' Ground GSL

**BURNETT**, Julia P w/o Benjamin d d 14 May 1868 ae: 49y GSL

**BURNHAM**, Abigail d 12 July 1883 ae: 85y GSL

Aice W d/o Henry A & Catherine McD d 13 Feb 1885 ae: 16y F:59

Arthur W s/o George A d 1 Nov 1884 ae: 7m SD F:59

Caroline M w/o Ira d 12 Sept 1874 ae: 40y SD I:86

Catherine McDonald w/o Henry A b 1 Sept 1829 d 9 July 1905 F:59

Clara M d/o Henry A & Catherine McD d 14 Oct 1876 ae: 21m F:59

**BURNHAM** (continued)

George A s/o Henry A & Catherine McD d 28 Feb 1886 ae: 30y F:59

George M s/o Thomas J & Hepsabeth L d 28 Dec 1842 ae: 5y F:47

Sgt Henry A d 16 Jan 1884 ae: 53y Civ/War: 10th Reg Maine Inf Co C F:59

James H b 15 July 1846 d 17 June 1865 Civ/War: 10th Reg Maine Inf Co E C:38

Lizzie A d/o Henry A & Catherine McD d 24 Oct 1887 ae: 29y F:59

Lucy M d/o Henry A & Catherine McD d 23 Aug 1881 ae: 21y F:59

Mary d 26 Oct 1858 ae: 54y J:245

Mary wid/o Ames d 26 Oct 1858 ae: 73y GSL

Minerva D Chapman w/o Ira d 8 June 1858 ae: 27y 2m SD I:86

Minnie D d/o Henry A & Catherine McD d 16 Mar 1887 ae: 20y F:59

Miranda A d/o Thomas d 17 Oct 1853 ae: 18y SD F:59

Simeon d 3 Nov 1854 ae: 21y 5m Buried Weston lot GSL

Thomas M s/o Henry A & Catherine McD d 11 Apr 1870 ae: 6y F:59

**BURNS**, Albert d 24 Dec 1885 ae: 62y 3m B:53

Albert s/o Michael d 7 Oct 1856 ae: 2y GSL

Albert E s/o Albert & Sarah S d 9 Mar 1854 ae: 2y 7m SBE B:53

Bertha A d/o Albert & Sarah S d 30 Mar 1931 Freeport, Maine ae: 70y 5d NS B:53

Caroline d/o Richard d 6 Sept 1861 ae: 1y GSL

Hannah w/o James d 26 Oct 1881 ae: 46y SD C:38

Hugh s/o Matthew d 20 Aug 1841 ae: 2y GSL

Ida May d/o Albert & Sarah S d 24 July 1861 ae: 4y 1m 23d B:53

**BURNS** (continued)

Mary A d/o James d 29 July 1850 ae: 7y Catholic GSL

Sarah S w/o Albert d 15 Feb 1887 ae: 54y B:53

Thomas d 24 Feb 1854 ae: 14y Catholic GSL

William s/o Edward d 21 June 1858 ae: 5y GSL

**BURROWS**, Eleanor d/o James G d 12 July 1853 ae: 7y GSL

Philip s/o Robert d 23 OCt 1858 ae: 1w GSL

Robert E s/o Robert d 11 Mar 1861 ae: 18m GSL

Robert Thomas s/o Robert d 17 May 1857 ae: 4m GSL

**BURSON**, Sarah d 22 June 1862 ae: 38y GSL

**BURTON**, Julia A d/o Burleigh d 9 Dec 1870 New York City ae: 28y SBE D:26

**BUTLER**, Abbie H d 21 May 1867 ae: 59y I:116

Ann d 28 Oct 1848 ae: 17y Native St John, New Brunswick GSL

Ann M d/o Cornelius d 30 June 1857 ae: 8y 8m SD I:116

Catherine d/o Patrick d 20 Nov 1864 ae: 14y 8m Catholic GSL

Edward d 4 Nov 1848 ae: 59y SD H:11

Edward d 2 Dec 1869 ae: 5y 7m GSL

Frederick A s/o C B d 28 June 1857 ae: 5y 4m GSL

James s/o Patrick d 31 June 1858 ae: 6m Catholic GSL

Jane W d 2 Aug 1893 ae: 83y I:116

John d 11 Sept 1849 ae: 42y Catholic GSL

John s/o Mary R d 29 Apr 1851 ae: 14m Catholic GSL

John Storer s/o M M d 22 June 1853 ae: 9m Frost tomb GSL D:31

Nancy A d/o Patrick d 13 July 1857 ae: 5y 10m Catholic. GSL

Patrick d 9 Mar 1848 ae: 33y Catholic GSL

Sally w/o Cornelius d 5 Jan 1869

BUTLER (continued)
ae: 82y I:116
Thomas d 25 Apr 1857 ae: 34y
Old Catholic Ground
Willie d s/o A d 6 Oct 1857 ae:
1y 2w GSL
BUTMAN, Nancy d 5 Sept 1864
ae: 70y 6m G:59
BUTRICK, Ada d/o Charles F d
31 July 1873 ae: 2m GSL
BUXTON, David d 1 June 1870
ae: 78y 5m C:72
Mary wid/o Samuel d 25 May
1855 ae: 66y I:141
Mary A d 28 Jan 1883 ae: 43y SD
I:141
Rhoda wid/o David d 28 Feb
1862 ae: 75y C:72
Sauel d 21 Aug 1853 ae: 69y
I:141
BUZZELL, Charles Henry s/o G
W & M J d 17 Mar 1855 ae:
2m 14d SD I:141
Eliza Jane d/o G W & M J d 28
Mar 1854 ae: 1m SD I:141
George F s/o George W d 6 July
1863 ae: 19y Civ/War: 10th
Reg Maine Inf Co B SD I:141
Mary C d/o George & Mary J d 4
June 1900 ae: 58y 11d SD I:141
Mary J w/o George W d 12 May
1865 ae: 47y 5m SD I:141
BYRAM, Ermina d/o Orville d 24
July 1847 ae: 11y SD H:24
Oliver d 23 Apr 1849 ae: 36y GSL
Orville d 23 Apr 1849 ae: 34y SD
H:24
William s/o Orville d 9 Sept
1847 ae: 5m SD H:24
BYRON, Charles W d 3 Oct 1871
Fitchburg, Massachusetts ae:
5m GSL
CADY, Martin d 10 Sept 1854 ae:
60y Strangers' Ground GSL
Mary w/o Martin d 10 Sept 1854
ae: 58y Strangers' Ground GSL
Patrick s/o John d 26 Mar 1858
ae: 3y 6m Catholic GSL
CAIN, Elizabeth d/o John d 4 Apr
1857 ae: 5w GSL
Ellen d/o Patrick d 9 Nov 1854
ae: 5m Old Catholic Ground

CAIN (continued)
GSL
John s/o Howes d 30 Sept 1856
ae: 16m GSL
Margaret w/o Michael d 14 June
1853 ae: 26y Old Catholic
Ground GSL
Mary Ann d/o Patrick d 29 May
1856 ae: 1y 6m Catholic GSL
Michael d 12 July 1850 ae: 52y
Catholic GSL
Stephen s/o Michael d 5 Oct
1853 ae: 10m Old Catholic
Ground GSL
CALDWELL, Anna c d/o late
Prof Merritt d 15 Oct 1849 ae:
9y GSL
Eva May d/o William & Ella b
17 June 1871 d 23 Sept 1875
H:6
Prof Merritt d 7 June 1848 ae:
41y GSL
CALEB, Charles A s/o Capt John
O & Lydia d 11 July 1843 ae:
2y G:6
George a s/o John & Lydia d 1
Dec 1904 Greely Hospital ae:
58y Civ/War: 12th Reg Maine
Inf Co H G:6
John s/o Daniel d 4 Sept 1859
ae: 5w GSL
Lydia w/o John O d 6 Jan 1868
ae: 60y SD G:6
CALLAGAN, Catherine w/o Pat-
rick d 18 Mar 1857 ae: 50y
Catholic GSL
Sarah d/o Hugh d 22 Nov 1857
ae: 6y 2m Catholic Strangers'
Ground GSL
CALLAN, James s/o Patrick d 23
Mar 1848 ae: 3m Catholic GSL
Thomas s/o Patrick d 16 May
1860 ae: 29y Drowned Cuba
GSL
CALLOWAY, Timothy d 21 Feb
1847 ae: 35y Casualty on the
rail road Catholic GSL
CALTON, Phebe d 22 June 1853
ae: 60y GSL
CALVIN, Mary d/o Martin d 25
Dec 1855 ae: 16y Strangers'
Ground GSL

CAMELHED, George W s/o William d 13 Oct 1848 ae: 14m Strangers' Ground GSL
CAMPBELL, Alexander D s/o William & Jannett d 7 June 1858 ae: 9m F:65
Benjamin d 2 Sept 1856 ae: 25y GSL
Catherine d 13 Jan 1858 ae: 17y 5m GSL
John s/o Catherine d 24 May 1852 ae: 10y Catholic GSL
John W s/o William & Jannett d 9 June 1858 ae: 5y 1m F:65
Mary d/o John d 7 Feb 1853 ae: 5y Catholic GSL
Mary A d/o Michael d 9 Dec 1856 ae: 15m GSL
Mary B d/o William & Jannett d 6 June 1858 ae: 2y 5m F:65
Michael d 18 Sept 1856 ae: 28y Native Dunnismack Parish, Co Donnegal, Ireland Catholic SBE J:150
CANALES, Carrie E d/o Frank W d 27 Apr 1894 ae: 11y 9m 2d SD J:232
Francis E s/o Samuel d 13 May 1894 ae: 9d SD J:232
Frank W s/o Francis & Sarah d 25 Jan 1909 ae: 54y 9m 16d J:232
Gracie d/o Frank W & Ella M d 9 Feb 1896 ae: 1m SD J:232
Josephine d/o Frank W & Ella M d 26 Apr 1900 ae: 5m 20d SD J:232
Nathan C s/o Frank W d 4 Jan 1886 ae: 1y 14d SD J:232
CANARY, Richard s/o William d 5 Sept 1859 ae: 8m GSL
CANAVAN, James d 11 Sept 1847 ae: 54y GSL
CANELLIS, Charles A s/o Francis P d 25 Apr 185 ae: 13m GSL
CANN, Mary w/o Thomas d 18 July 1856 ae: 55y GSL
CANNADY, Bridget w/o John d 17 Nov 1851 ae: 35y Catholic GSL
Edmund d 28 Nov 1851 ae: 70y GSL

CANNEY, John d 20 Sept 1854 ae: 30y GSL
CANNUS, Thomas d 20 Aug 1851 ae: 40y Catholic GSL
CAPEN, Mary w/o Thomas d 9 Dec 1839 ae: 80y SBE F:67
CAREY, Bridget d/o John d 3 Sept 1856 ae: 1y 10m Catholic GSL
Ellen d/o James d 18 Aug 1856 ae: 1y Catholic GSL
CARKES, William s/o Matthew d 16 Apr 1857 ae: 15m GSL
CARL, Barney d 13 Sept 1842 ae: 47y Catholic GSL
Elizabeth d/o Cahrles d 18 Sept 1848 ae: 11m Catholic GSL
Mary d/o Michael d 19 Dec 1856 ae: 4m Catholic GSL
CARLETON, Jeremiah s/o James d 31 Oct 1855 ae: 14m SGL
Phebe d/o Edward & Phebe d 24 June 1853 ae: 60y SD F:56
Phebe A w/o Deacon Edward d 30 Apr 1852 ae: 83y SD F:56
Warren s/o William d 31 June 1851 ae: 15d GSL
CARLIN, Eliza w/o Michael d 5 Feb 1848 ae: 40y Catholic GSL
Robert s/o James d 23 Sept 1857 ae: 1d GSL
CARLORAN, Elizabeth w/o Michael d 5 Feb 1848 ae: 44y Catholic Native of Ardee, Co Louth, Ireland SBE J:16
CARLTON, Kitty d/o James d 4 Aug 1859 ae: 1y GSL
CARMICHAEL, George d 6 May 1850 ae: 36y GSL
George d 25 Oct 1854 ae: 61y I:152
George Jr d 6 May 1850 ae: 24y 2m I:152
Mary d 20 Nov 1886 Greely Hospital ae: 84y GSL
Mary d/o George d 21 Nov 1851 ae: 24y 9m I:152
CARPENTER, Mary Stuart d/o Stephen D d 14 July 1848 ae: 3y 6m Native of Bangor, Maine E:1

CARRAGAN, Ann d/o William d 13 Jan 1857 ae: 15m GSL

Catherine w/o Owen d 13 Mar 1857 ae: 33y GSL

Hannah d/o Martin d 7 Nov 1854 ae: 2y 4m Old Catholic Ground GSL

Rosanna G d/o James d 9 Nov 1856 ae: 1d GSL

CARRINO, Maria d/o Patrick d 27 July 1857 ae: 2y 11m 22d Old Catholic Ground GSL

Mary d/o John d 3 Oct 1857 ae: 4m 12d GSL

CARRL, Michael s/o Edward d 8 Jan 1851 ae: 11m Catholic GSL

CARROLL, Martha d/o Edward d 2 Sept 1846 ae: 2w Catholic GSL

Mary d/o Michael d 22 Aug 1857 ae: 13m Catholic GSL

Patrick d 13 July 1857 ae: 17y 6m Killed by fall into hold of Bark *Saxon* Native of Halifax, Nova Scotia Catholic A:1

Rosanna d/o James d 18 May 1856 ae: 3w Catholic GSL

CARRUTHERS, Charles E d 10 July 1863 ae: 24y 4m Mortally wounded 2 July 1863 Gettysburg, Pennsylvania Civ/War: Corp 17th Reg Maine Inf Co B D:72

Charles H d 10 Apr 1889 ae: 76y D:72

Freddie s/o Charles H & Greta R d 17 Oct 1860 ae: 17w D:72

Greta R Edwards w/o Charles H d 28 Dec 1863 ae: 46y D:72

Harold s/o Charles & M J d 16 June 1862 ae: 5m SD D:72

Helen M d 18 Mar 1882 ae: 38y D:72

James d 28 Nov 1857 ae: 85y SD D:72

CARTEN, Mary d/o James d 5 Aug 1853 ae: 14m GSL

CARTER, Artemus Jr d 9 May 1862 GSL

Caleb S d 18 Dec 1855 ae: 53y GSL

CARTER (continued)

Charlotte B d/o Edward R & Isabella d 8 Sept 1856 ae: 16m SBE B:48

Edward s/o Edward d 26 Feb 1860 ae: 4y 11m GSL

Ezra d 11 May 1887 ae: 83y SD B:30

Jane A wid/o Caleb S d 23 Aug 1865 ae: 55y GSL

Judith Augusta d/o Ezra d 23 Aug 1849 ae: 10m SD B:30

Judith W wid/o Ezra d 18 Nov 1889 Worcester, Massachusetts ae: 81y SD B:30

Michael s/o Edward d 10 Oct 1849 ae: 3w Catholic GSL

CARTIN, William d 28 Sept 1847 ae: 43y Catholic GSL

CARTY, Thomas s/o John d 21 Aug 1855 ae: 14m GSL

CARWIN, Michael d 19 Feb 1858 ae: 6m GSL

CARY, Daniel Jr d 9 June 1852 ae: 32y 6m GSL

CASEY, Bridget d/o Michael d 14 Oct 1854 ae: 27y Catholic GSL

Ellen Mary d/o Luke d 8 Sept 1853 ae: 10m Catholic GSL

Frank d 26 July 1882 ae: 10d Catholic GSL

James d 20 Mar 1857 ae: 71y Catholic Strangers' Ground GSL

John s/o Henry d 15 Sept 1846 ae: 6m Catholic GSL

Maurice d 2 Mar 1853 ae: 47y Catholic GSL

CASH, Betsy Mrs d 2 Nov 1860 ae: 79y SD H:78

Jane w/o Michael d 20 Feb 1848 ae: 30y Catholic GSL

Jeremiah d 8 Jan 1856 ae: 53y GSL

Jeremiah s/o John d 7 May 1852 ae: 9y Catholic GSL

Margaret d/o John d 19 May 1853 ae: 6y GSL

CASSIDY, Ellen d/o Francis d 8 Mar 1850 ae: 3y Catholic GSL

Jane d/o Francis d 15 Mar 1850 ae: 2y Catholic GSL

CASTLAW, Thomas d 12 Dec 1847 ae: 28y Casualty near Lewiston Falls, Maine Catholic GSL

CATES, Mary E d/o James d 20 May 1864 ae: 1y 1m GSL

CAVERKEE, Eunice J B d/o John d 1 Aug 1856 ae: 15m GSL

CAWLEY, Timothy d 8 Sept 1854 ae: 40y Catholic Strangers' Ground GSL

CHADBOURNE, Betsy d 17 Nov 1848 ae: 53y D:48

Sarah L d 21 Dec 1867 ae: 15y GSL

CHAFFIN, Lydia J w/o Adoniram d 9 May 1870 ae: 47y GSL

CHAMBERLAIN, Daniel W s/o John & Phebe R b 1826 d 1831 I:143

George s/o James d 13 Dec 1869 ae: 31y GSL

John W s/o John & Phebe R b 1847 d 1851 I:143

Lois B d/o John & Phebe R d 17 June 1853 ae: 17y 10m I:143

Louisa U d/o John & Phebe R b 1840 d 1852 I:143

Rebecca E d/o John & Phebe R b 1827 d 1851 I:143

CHANEY, Josiah d 21 Apr 1853 ae: 58y SD J:257

Marcia G w/o Benjamin d 30 July 1858 ae: 38y 4m GSL

CHAPMAN, Isaiah M d 24 Dec 1857 ae: 56y 5m GSL

CHASE, inf d/o Caleb & Susan d 23 Feb 1831 ae: 10d J:77

Caleb d 20 Sept 1850 ae: 67y 7m J:77

Charles C A s/o Caleb & Susan d 5 Aug 1865 ae: 41y J:77

Daniel d 8 Feb 1843 ae: 55y GSL

Daniel Poor s/o Caleb & Susan d 21 Nov 1851 ae: 33y 9m J:77

Frederick M s/o Lorenzo d 11 Oct 1864 ae: 2m GSL

George H s/o Edward & Sarah J d 11 Jan 1858 ae: 8m D:76

George H s/o William A d 22 Aug 1859 ae: 6m SD D:76

George W s/o William A d 15

CHASE (continued)
July 1862 ae: 15y 10m SD D:76

Hattie J d/o Robert d 1 Apr 1871 ae: 5m 25d GSL

James s/o George d 28 Apr 1846 ae: 17y GSL

Josephine A w/o Quincy A d 24 July 1876 Clifton Springs, New York ae: 39y Cummings tomb A:13

L Genniss s/o William C d 15 July 1855 ae: 18m GSL

Moses H s/o Jacob L d 7 Apr 1854 ae: 21m Hilborn tomb A:10

Olive G w/o William A d 3 May 1861 ae: 31y SD D:76

Owen Murdock s/o Caleb & Susan d 6 Oct 1838 ae: 12y 8m J:77

Sarah Moulton d/o Caleb & Susan b 1835 d 1903 J:77

Susan w/o Caleb d 28 Sept 1856 ae: 62y J:77

Dr Warren E d 21 Jan 1852 ae: 45y Hilborn tomb A:10

Willie W s/o William A & Olive G d 3 Dec 1856 ae: 3y 6m SD D:76

CHATMAN, Edwin s/o late Nathan d 23 Feb 1855 ae: 20y Chatman tomb    Location unknown

CHEEVER, Geroge B s/o John S & Sarah M d 30 Nov 1857 ae: 5y 10m 23d I:65

J Augustine s/o John S & Sarah M d 13 Aug 1851 ae: 11y. SBE I:65

John E s/o John S & Sarah M d 18 Apr 1857 ae: 3y 4m 15d I:65

John S b 6 May 1827 Dracut, Massachusetts d 31 May 1886 Sagua LaGrand, Cuba I:65

Sarah M w/o John S b 23 July 1831 d 14 Feb 1908 I:65

CHESLEY, Deborah B w/o Clinton H d/o Arnold & Jane Bowie d 23 Aug 1911 ae: 73y 9m 26d SD D:70

Freddie E s/o Samuel d 27 Aug 1872 ae: 2y SD D:70

**CHESLEY** (continued)

Frederick E s/o Samuel & Rebecca H d 4 Feb 1855 ae: 18y 1m 18d SD D:70

George B s/o Samuel A d 30 Nov 1873 Hyde Park, Massachusetts ae: 6y SD D:70

Rebecca H w/o Samuel d 15 Feb 1834 Bangor, Maine ae: 20y SD D:70

Rebecca Howell d/o Samuel & Rebecca H d 26 Apr 1835 ae: 14m SD D:70

Samuel d 21 Apr 1866 ae: 54y 7m SD D:70

Sarah E d/o Samuel & Sophia M d 18 Mar 1873 ae: 23y 5m SD D:70

Sophia E d/o Samuel & Sophia M d 31 Aug 1847 ae: 3y 7m Stone on C:17 D:70

Sophia M w/o Samuel d/o John Morrison d 27 Apr 1870 ae: 58y 6m SD D:70

**CHESTERLOW**, Thomas d 30 Apr 1857 ae: 35y Strangers' Ground GSL

**CHICK**, Amos d 18 Jan 1878 ae: 77y 7m Warrent Officer USN D:61

Amy d/o Amos d 11 Aug 1874 Worcester, Maine ae: 31y SD D:61

Aurelia w/o Joseph C d 7 Sept 1848 ae: 27y Strangers' Ground GSL

Charlotte Locke d/o Amos & Elizabeth H d 10 May 1833 ae: 3m D:61

Elizabeth H w/o Amos d 26 May 1880 ae: 76y 3m D:61

**CHIPMAN**, George H s/o Isaiah & Ruth d 3 May 1864 ae: 28y SB I:86

Isaiah d 24 Dec 1855 ae: 56y 5m I:86

Martha D no burial record SBE I:86

Ruth w/o Isaiah d 14 Sept 1877 ae: 71y 10m I:86

Thankful d/o Isaiah & Ruth d 4 Jan 1852 ae: 22y 3m I:86

**CHIVIS**, Eliza L w/o George d 18 Sept 1862 ae: 23y GSL

**CHRISTIE**, Frederick A s/o Mary d 12 Aug 1847 ae: 17m Catholic GSL

**CHRISTIANSON**, Christopher adopted s/o Christian d 27 Sept 1863 ae: 7w SD H:94

George H s/o Christian & Margaret d 25 July 1853 ae: 6m SD H:94

**CHUB**, Jabez B s/o Jabez d 19 Mar 1853 ae: 6m GSL

**CHURCHILL**, Henry H B d 5 May 1854 ae: 30y GSL

James C d 20 Nov 1865 ae: 78y GSL

Mary P w/o Edwin d 3 May 1863 ae: 51y GSL

**CHUTE**, Walter S s/o George d 10 Feb 1870 ae: 2m SD F:5

**CILBAN**, Patrick s/o Patrick d 17 May 1856 ae: 4m 17d Catholic GSL

**CLAHANE**, Edward d 14 Feb 1844 ae: 21y Catholic I:4A

**CLAHERTY**, Anna d/o Peter d 14 Aug 1854 ae: 2y Old Catholic Ground GSL

James d 29 May 1854 ae: 24y Old Catholic Ground GSL

Patrick s/o Peter d 26 Aug 1854 ae: 4y 3m Catholic GSL

**CLANCEY**, Eleanor w/o James d 24 Feb 1849 ae: 45y Catholic GSL

Ellen d/o Morris d 27 July 1854 ae: 5m Catholic GSL

James d 3 Sept 1849 ae: 42y Catholic GSL

James d 4 Mar 1858 ae: 51y Old Catholic Ground

John C s/o Morris d 30 June 1854 ae: 9m Catholic Strangers' Ground GSL

Martin d 20 Jan 1855 ae: 22y Catholic Strangers' Ground GSL

Mary d/o Morris d 14 Aug 1854 ae: 6m Catholic Strangers' Ground GSL

Patrick d 25 July 1856 ae: 32y

22

CLANCEY (continued)
Casualty on the railroad
Catholic GSL
CLAPP, Hannah wid/o Jabez d 17
Feb 1864 ae: 76y GSL
Harriet E d/o James S d 9 Oct
1853 ae: 1y GSL
Jabez d 31 Dec 1849 ae: 64y
Trowbridge tomb Location
unknown
Mary E d/o JS d 5 Sept 1857 ae:
3y 6m GSL
Oliver S s/o James S d 6 Mar
1857 ae: 8m 16d GSL
CLARIDGE, Albert S d 15 Nov
1921 ae: 77y Sawyer tomb
A:14
Georgie A s/o William A d 12
Oct 1875 Haverhill, Maine ae:
3m SD D:10
Hannah w/o William Jr d 1 June
1855 ae: 49y SD D:10
Lindly T s/o William A d 14
Sept 1868 ae: 5y 6m SD D:10
Louisa d 22 June 1855 ae: 51y
SD D:10
Mary F d/o William d 14 July
1877 Haverhill, Maine ae: 9y
SD D:10
Ursula wid/o William d 29 Oct
1840 ae: 68y D:10
William s/o William d 23 Nov
1871 ae: 62y SD D:10
CLARK, Almira d 15 Oct 1859 ae:
41y H:93
Catherine E d 15 June 1898 ae:
72y 11m GSL
Catherine M w/o Francis d 18
Aug 1870 ae: 82y SD G:51
Dorothy w/o Samuel W d 30 July
1866 ae: 77y H:93
Eleanor P w/o Freeman d 5 May
1863 ae: 43y 8m Frost tomb
D:31
Frank M d 8 May 1862 ae: 1y
GSL
Frank W s/o William C d 24
Aug 1861 ae: 1y GSL
Holly Ann d 21 Sept 1841 ae: 8m
GSL
Jedediah B d 16 Aug 1862 ae:
26y GSL

CLARK (continued)
Lois d/o Samuel W & Dorothy d
13 Oct 1839 ae: 45y H:93
Mary M d/o DW d 1 Sept 1854
Chicago, Illinois ae: 3y 6m
GSL
Nancy J d 10 Sept 1877 ae: 49y
GSL
Nellie M d/o FS d 17 Sept 1862
ae: 24y Frost tomb D:31
Samuel S s/o Samuel d 12 May
1851 ae: 4y GSL
Samuel W d 28 July 1848 ae: 64y
H:93
Sarah M d/o Francis & Catherine
d 12 Oct 1838 ae: 20y 7m G:51
CLARKE, Adelaide, d/o John d 8
Nov 1847 ae: 4y GSL
Augustus T s/o Elliot F d 15
Sept 1847 ae: 11m GSL
CLARMER, Mary d/o John d 2
Apr 1855 ae: 2m GSL
CLARRY, Mary w/o Martin d 5
Apr 1866 ae: 42y GSL
CLARY, Jeremiah w/o William d
13 Aug 1849 ae: 19m Catholic
GSL
Mary Alice d/o John d 5 Sept
1862 ae: 4y 9m GSL
CLEARY, Timothy s/o William d
24 Nov 1854 ae: 2y 2m 26d
GSL
CLEON, Michael s/o Edward d 18
July 1856 ae: 6y 6m GSL
CLOMUTY, Bridge d/o Peter d 1
Apr 1849 ae: 3y Catholic GSL
CLOONEY, Mary d/o Patrick d 8
Feb 1852 ae: 5y Catholic GSL
CLORTY, James s/o James d 5
Mar 1852 ae: 13m Catholic
GSL
CLOTHERTY, Mary d/o late
Patrick d 3 Dec 1849 ae: 2m
Catholic J:175
Patrick d 11 Nov 1848 ae: 28y
Native of Clifden, Co Galway,
Ireland Catholic SB J:175
CLOUDMAN, Catherine d/o
David P d 26 Dec 1855 ae: 42y
Hilborn tomb A:10
Sarah M d/o David P d 10 Dec
1848 ae: 21y Trowbridge tomb

CLOUDMAN (continued)
Location unknown
Susan D w/o David P d 22 Mar 1858 ae: 66y Hosack tomb A:17
Warren d 13 Sept 1852 South Berwick, Maine ae: 28y Trowbridge tomb Location unknown
CLOUGH, Elizabeth S w/o David d 2 June 1901 Boston, Massachusetts ae: 74y SD G:31
Martha d 28 July 1871 ae: 96y 5m GSL
CLUSKEY, Henry d 18 Dec 1857 ae: 38y Catholic GSL
James d 18 Nov 1847 ae: 27y Native of Fairhill Dundalk, Co Louth, Ireland Catholic SBE J:14
COAD, Clara w/o Edward d 5 Sept 1842 ae: 66y GSL
COATLEY, Michael s/o William d 28 Oct 1851 ae: 3y 4m GSL
COBB, Abigail B d/o Elijah d 13 Feb 1849 ae: 28y GSL
Alice J d/o Alvin d 30 Apr 1887 ae: 24y 6m GSL
Alonzo S s/o Merritt B & Louisa d 17 Jan 1917 ae: 56y SD F:39
Anna d/o late Lemuel d 7 Jan 1856 ae: 49y Cummings tomb A:13
Benjamin B d 17 Apr 1893 ae: 66y 3m 5d Civ/War: 1st Reg Maine Inf Co D SD I:157
Bridget d/o Edward d 17 Sept 1848 ae: 3y Catholic GSL
Catherine S d/o Cyrus D d 9 Aug 1857 ae: 2y 9m GSL
Chitman d 26 Dec 1852 ae: 81y GSL
Edwin A s/y Cyrus D d 28 Oct 1858 ae: 8y 10m SBE A:8
Eleanor d/o Thomas d 17 Apr 1845 ae: 7y 9m GSL
Harriet w/o Alonzo S no burial record SBE F:39
Hiram s/o Matthew & Sarah d 17 Nov 1845 ae: 23y SD D:77
Capt Jacob Adams s/o Matthew d 28 Oct 1865 ae: 46y 10m

COBB (continued)
D:77
Jonathan d 23 Aug 1843 ae: 62y 7m D:73
Lavinia w/o Thomas d 27 Oct 1844 ae: 38y GSL
Lewis d 22 Nov 1844 ae: 63y Buried beside J Smith's child GSL
Mary A d 10 Nov 1857 ae: 58y GSL
Mary A d/o Cyrus d 28 Apr 1857 ae: 7m Hilborn tomb A:10
Mary A d/o Matthew d 1 Apr 1904 ae: 76y 4m D:77
Mary Augusta d/o Samuel F & Sarah M d 10 Sept 1840 ae: 4y SD D:69
Mary E w/o Albion d 24 May 1875 ae: 41y GSL
Mary Louisa d/o Frederick M d 24 Apr 1850 ae: 18m GSL
Matthew s/o Isaac d 6 Mar 1865 ae: 68y 9m SD D:77
Merritt d 8 Nov 1840 ae: 39y SD F:39
Reuben d 28 Nov 1877 ae: 77y GSL
Sally w/o Samuel d 15 Apr 1859 ae: 47y Buried near Jackson Mmt SD D:69
Samuel D d 22 Nov 1853 ae: 41y Hilborn tomb A:10
Samuel F d 24 Dec 1891 Bangor, Maine ae: 83y SD D:69
Sarah w/o Matthew d 27 Feb 1870 ae: 75y D:77
Sarah w/o Nathaniel d 23 July 1851 ae: 40y GSL
Sarah Abba d/o Benjamin & Joanna d 4 May 1850 ae: 14m I:157
Sarah M d/o Matthew & Sarah d 28 Sept 1841 ae: 5y 8m SD D:77
Sarah M w/o Samuel F d 11 Feb 1867 ae: 52y 10m SD D:69
Syble d/o Albion d 10 Aug 1872 ae: 15y GSL
COBURN, Anna P d 21 Sept 1872 ae: 15y GSL
Sumner s/o John d 3 Oct 1852

COBURN (continued)
ae: 6y GSL
Thomas d 22 Feb 1864 ae: 47y
GSL
COCHRAN, Ann w/o Hugh d 11
Oct 1850 ae: 33y Catholic GSL
Georgeianna adopted d/o John F
& MA d 16 June 1861 ae: 2y
6m G:21
Hugh d 26 May 1860 ae: 55y
Catholic GSL
John b1833 d---- no burial
record Civ/War: 12th Reg
Maine Inf Co A SD G:21
Patrick d 20 July 1848 ae: 28y
Killed by the cars at South
Berwick, Maine Catholic GSL
COCKLEY, John s/o Timothy d 8
Aug 1859 ae: 5m Catholic GSL
Michael s/o Timothy d 19 Dec
1849 ae: 3m Catholic GSL
CODMAN, Caroline P w/o RAL d
16 Sept 1852 Roxbury, Mas-
sachusetts ae: 38y GSL
R A L d 28 Oct 1853 ae: 57y GSL
COFFIN, Albert B s/o Walter F
& Sarah E d 17 Oct 1938 Tam-
worth, New Hampshire ae: 52y
10m 21d B:37
Amelia w/o Albert B d/o Otto &
Thilda Peterson d 27 Apr 1926
ae: 39y 8m 2d B:37
Betsy E w/o Isaiah H d 14 Dec
1879 ae: 75y 5m D:59
Charles s/o Rev Charles M & S
Brown d 23 July 1837 ae: 2y
B:37
Isaiah H d 25 Dec 1869 ae: 65y
16d D:59
Sarah E w/o Walter F d 7 May
1900 ae: 46y 5m 16d B:37
Walter F s/o Ivory M & Mary C
d 7 July 1914 ae: 64y 6m 5d
B:37
COLBY, Ambrose d 30 Jan 1872
ae: 58y GSL
Atlanta V w/o Albert W d 10 Aug
1870 ae: 20y 6m GSL
Esther b 12 Apr 1804 d 6 Feb
1888 F:139
Esther w/o William d 30 May
1851 ae: 62y GSL

COLBY (continued)
Jane M d 4 Jan 1878 Revere,
Massachusetts ae: 69y GSL
John d 9 Sept 1867 ae: 59y F:139
COLE, Annie S d/o Lorenzo &
Hannah d 22 Sept 1854 ae: 2y
7m H:69
Charles E P s/o Lorenzo & Han-
nah d 19 Mar 1868 ae: 24y 5m
SBE H:69
Charles O d 14 Feb 1858 ae: 40y
Artiste SD F:42
Daniel d 15 Mar 1864 ae: 45y
Civ/War: 24th Reg Maine Inf
Co A F:117
Daniel A s/o Daniel d 18 Sept
1849 ae: 2y 3m F:117
Eliza A d/o John Greene d 10
July 1872 ae: 54y SD F:117
Eunice d 20 Oct 1851 ae: 65y
GSL
George A s/o Harrison G d 29
June 1876 Augusta, Maine ae:
27y GSL
Hannah D wid/o Lorenzo D d 28
Dec 1891 ae: 82y SD H:69
Helena A d/o Lorenzo & Hannah
d 21 Feb 1853 ae: 2y 2m SBE
H:69
James D d 21 Aug 1879
Washington, DC ae: 29y GSL
Kittie d 21 Mar 1859 ae: 19y
F:42
Lorenzo A s/o Lorenzo & Hannah
D d 1 Jan 1853 ae: 21y 6m
H:69
Lorenzo D d 1 May 1882 Brook-
lyn, New York ae: 76y SD
H:69
Mary d/o Daniel d 26 May 1843
ae: 7y SD F:117
Mary F d/o Charles O d 21 Mar
1859 New York City ae: 19y
GSL
Thomas G C d 25 Apr 1857 ae:
1y Strangers' Ground GSL
William Woodbury s/o Lorenzo
& Hannah D d 5 Sept 1860 ae:
14y 6m H:69
COLEMAN, Artemas d 27 Nov
1854 ae: 33y GSL
David s/o Thomas & Bridget d

25

**COLEMAN** (continued)
13 Nov 1835 ae: 18m SD I:23
Eliza d/o Thomas d 7 Aug 1850 ae: 2y Catholic I:23
Elizabeth d 5 Apr 1850 ae: 28y GSL
John d 8 Aug 1851 ae: 40y Catholic GSL
Julia d/o William d 14 May 1854 ae: 11y 10m Old Catholic Ground GSL
Stephen d 10 Jan 1848 ae: 25y Erected as the only token of an affectionate sister/Bridget Coleman Catholic L:12
Thomas s/o Thomas d 16 Sept 1841 ae: 6m Catholic GSL
William s/o Thomas & Bridget d 3 Nov 1835 ae: 2y 6m Catholic SD I:23
**COLLEY**, Anna E d/o Charles H d 8 Nov 1874 ae: 23y GSL
Elizabeth S d/o Charles S & Eunice d 9 Dec 1847 ae: 9y H:70
Eugene A s/o Albert d 2 Jan 1868 ae: 1y 10m GSL
Eunice H w/o Richard d 11 Oct 1844 ae: 37y F:14
Francis d 13 June 1867 ae: 92y GSL
Frances C d/o Charles d 20 Nov 1848 ae: 18m SD H:70
Fred s/o James d 1 Dec 1867 ae: 5d GSL
John s/o William d 11 July 1860 ae: 2y Strangers' Ground GSL
Joseph d 15 Oct 1860 ae: 22y GSL
Joseph d 10 Sept 1875 ae: 63y GSL
Levi I s/o Richard & Eunice H d 10 Aug 1843 ae: 4y SBE F:14
Richard b1812 d1845 F:14
Sarah E d/o Charles C d 8 Sept 1858 ae: 22y GSL
William F d 3 Oct 1857 ae: 7m 2d GSL
**COLLINS**, Bridget d 15 July 1853 ae: 20y Old Catholic Ground GSL
Celia d/o John d 7 Nov 1852 ae:

**COLLINS** (continued)
15m Catholic GSL
Edgar C s/o William d 7 Oct 1862 ae: 11m GSL
Eleanor w/o Timothy d 11 Nov 1846 ae: 30y Catholic GSL
William s/o William H d 2 Sept 1859 GSL
**COLON**, William s/o Barnard d 31 Aug 1850 ae: 2y Catholic GSL
**COLYER**, Thomas w/o William d 14 Aug 1864 ae: 13m Strangrs' Ground GSL
**CONKLEY**, Joanna w/o Timothy d 18 Aug 1852 ae: 40y Catholic GSL
**CONLEY**, ____ s/o Owen d 18 Sept 1856 ae: 26y Old Catholic Ground GSL
Bartholomew d 17 Jan 1857 ae: 35y Strangers' Ground GSL
Bridget d/o John d 15 Sept 1854 ae: 3y 6m Catholic GSL
Bridget d/o Patrick d 18 June 1855 ae: 16y Catholic Strangers' Ground GSL
Catherine d/o William d 7 Oct 1853 ae: 11m Old Catholic Ground GSL
Elizabeth d/o Arthur d 3 Oct 1857 ae: 15m GSL
Margaret d/o John d 10 Jan 1848 ae: 18m Catholic GSL
Margaret w/o John d 11 Apr 1855 ae: 30y Catholic GSL
Martin s/o Patrick d 5 Nov 1854 ae: 6y Catholic GSL
Mary d/o John d 6 Apr 1854 ae: 4y 10m Catholic GSL
Mary d/o Patrick d 5 Nov 1854 ae: 4y Catholic GSL
Mary Ellen d/o William d 9 July 1861 Boston, Maine ae: 8y GSL
Peter s/o Patrick d 17 Oct 1858 ae: 2y 2m 3d Catholic GSL
**CONNELL**, John s/o David d 6 June 1851 ae: 4y GSL
**CONNELLY**, Bridget d/o John d 16 Dec 1851 ae: 3y 6m Old Catholic Ground GSL

**Connelly,** Bridget d/o Patrick d 19 May 1855 ae: 13m Catholic GSL

Frances d/o John d 14 Mar 1854 ae: 14m Catholic GSL

**CONNING,** Joanna d/o Morris d 21 Apr 1850 ae: 7m Catholic GSL

**CONNOR,** Ann d/o Michael d 21 Dec 1857 ae: 3y Catholic GSL

Ella d/o Michael d 12 Oct 1857 ae: 11m Catholic GSL

Eliza Jane d/o Neal & Sarah O d 5 June 1853 ae: 7y SD I:3 (See Addendum)

John d 5 Aug 1858 ae: 7m Catholic Strangers' Ground GSL

John s/o Neal & Sarah O d 9 Mar 1841 ae: 7m SD I:3 (See Addendum)

Julia d/o Patrick d 6 June 1855 ae: 13m Catholic GSL

Mary Ellen d/o Michael d 15 Oct 1854 ae: 3y 6m Catholic GSL

Michael d 17 Dec 1857 ae: 57y Catholic GSL

Michael O d 21 Jan 1854 ae: 50y Native of Leck Parish, Co Tyrone, Ireland Catholic SD J:3 (See Addendum)

Thomas d 7 Mar 1868 ae: 63y Catholic GSL

Thomas s/o Martin d 7 Nov 1854 ae: 6y Old Catholic Ground GSL

Timothy s/o Daniel d 29 Oct 1860 ae: 6m Catholic GSL

**CONROY,** Emma w/o George E d 21 Oct 1877 ae: 26y SD C:20

Mary d/o James d 6 Sept 1857 ae: 2m GSL

**CONSTIBLE,** James F s/o William d 3 Sept 1860 ae: 14m GSL

Joseph s/o William d 1 Sept 1857 ae: 5m GSL

**CONWAY,** Ellen d/o Roger d 17 Oct 1856 ae: 2y 8m GSL

Rachel w/o Roger d 27 Dec 1856 ae: 35y GSL

**CONWICK,** Charles Pettes s/o

**CONWICK** (continued) Neal d 3 Dec 1849 ae: 6w Catholic GSL

**COOK,** Edward s/o Richard d 2 June 1856 ae: 2m 8d GSL

Eliza w/o E d 14 Oct 1849 ae: 42y GSL

Ellen w/o Philip d 8 May 1853 ae: 76y GSL

Emma Alicia d/o late William d 2 June 1862 ae: 7y SD H:28

James F s/o William & Julia d 15 Oct 1856 ae: 3y 3m 3d SD H:28

Mary d/o Matthew d 23 Aug 1851 ae: 1y Catholic GSL

Mary d/o Thomas d 18 Mar 1853 ae: 8m Catholic GSL

Mary w/o Thomas d 9 May 1851 ae: 32y Catholic GSL

Patrick s/o Richard d 3 Apr 1856 ae: 9d Catholic GSL

William d 12 Jan 1862 ae: 37y H:28

William s/o Michael d 19 Aug 1854 ae: 2y Catholic GSL

**COOKE,** Alice C d/o Hiram T d 8 Dec 1864 ae: 3y GSL

**COOLBROOTH,** Anna d/o LH & AM d 26 Sept 1859 ae: 3m 6d SD F:75

Betsy Merrill w/o Lemuel b1815 d1908 J:247

Cecelia A Nelson w/o Charles C b 13 Apr 1857 d 19 July 1907 J:247

Charles Augustus s/o Jonathan & Eunice d 19 Oct 1841 ae: 6m SD F:75

Charles C s/o Lemuel & Betsy M b 16 Sept 1852 d 31 Dec 1922 J:247

Edwin Francis s/o Jonathan & Eunice d 4 Oct 1849 ae: 19y 4m F:75

Eunice w/o Jonathan M d 23 Aug 1856 ae: 53y F:75

Hannah Ann d/o Lemuel & Betsy M b1842 d1857 J:247

Harriet M d/o Edwin d 29 Sept 1874 ae: 8w GSL

John L s/o George F d 29 Oct

**COOLBROOTH** (continued)
1866 ae: 1y 6m GSL
Lemuel b1813 d1892 J:247
Lemuel d 4 May 1900 ae: 36y 8m
J:247
Martha Burnham b1820 d1894
F:75
Mary Burnham b1817 d1892 F:75
Mehitable b 10 Dec 1814 Buxton,
Maine d 28 Oct 1904 Portland,
Maine F:75
**COOLIDGE**, Willie C s/o widow
d 5 Oct 1857 ae: 4m GSL
**COOMBS**, Andrew H s/o Charles
& Janeta d 22 Nov 1838 ae: 5y
SBE G:20
Charles H d 6 Jan 1845 ae: 49y
Lost at sea SBE G:20
James s/o Charles d 11 Mar
1844 ae: 18y SD G:20
James E s/o John d 5 June 1850
ae: 9m GSL
James H s/o Charles & Janeta d
12 Mar 1844 ae: 19y SBE G:20
Janeta wid/o Charles d 8 Oct
1861 ae: 62y GSL
Janeta M d/o Charles d 19 Oct
1850 ae: 11m G:20
Maria A w/o James no burial
record SD F:145
William H d 24 Mar 1851 ae: 28y
G:20
**COPNEY**, Jeremiah s/o Jeremiah
d 3 June 1857 ae: 5w GSL
**COPPS**, Betsy w/o William d 11
July 1843 ae: 42y GSL
**CORDIFF**, Ellen w/o John d 4
Aug 1854 ae: 40y GSL
Ellen Victoria d/o John d 4 Aug
1854 ae: 17y GSL
Julia d/o John d 4 Aug 1854 ae:
9y GSL
Margaret d/o John d 4 Aug 1854
ae: 19y GSL
Signora d/o John d 4 Aug 1854
ae: 1y GSL
**CORNISH**, William d 24 July
1848 ae: 49y Catholic GSL
**CORRIGAN**, Mary d/o James d 28
Apr 1854 ae: 3y GSL
Margaret d/o John d 14 Oct 1854
ae: 5y 3m GSL

**COORIGAN** (continued)
John d 11 Oct 1854 ae: 28y GSL
Lucy w/o John d 5 Oct 1854 ae:
26y GSL
John s/o John d 20 Nov 1854 ae:
15m GSL
Thomas d 18 Oct 1856 ae: 25y
GSL
**CORSER**, George H d 30 Aug 1850
ae: 19y GSL
**COSTELLO**, Catherine w/o John
d 16 Sept 1854 GSL
Eddie s/o Matthias d 11 Sept
1858 ae: 4y 2m GSL
Matthew d 13 Apr 1855 ae: 30y
GSL
Patrick d 30 July 1857 ae: 63y
Catholic SD I:11A
Patrick s/o Patrick & Hannah d
13 July 1847 ae: 5y Catholic
I:11A
Richard s/o Patrick & Hannah d
19 Dec 1840 ae: 5m Catholic
I:11A
**COTTON**, Kate d/o Edward d 8
Sept 1854 ae: 1y GSL
Mary Ann d/o Edward d 6 Sept
1854 ae: 4y GSL
**COUSINS**, James s/o James d 8
Nov 1858 ae: 1d GSL
**COVAN**, Ann d 14 Aug 1848 Saco,
Maine ae: 15y Catholic buried
Timothy Griffin lot GSL
**COVELL**, William E s/o Stanley
d 11 Nov 1851 ae: 14m GSL
**COWANK**, Catherine d/o James d
22 Sept 1850 ae: 8m Catholic
GSL
**COWLEY**, Timothy s/o late
Timothy d 10 Apr 1855 ae: 6m
Buried in father's grave GSL
**COX**, Alvin s/o Warren & Sally d
19 Dec 1853 ae: 9y 9m C:48
Hannah w/o Warren d 3 July
1845 ae: 37y Killed by lightn-
ing GSL
Hannah E d/o Warren d 27 Oct
1865 ae: 15y C:48
Hattie E d/o Warren & Sally d 27
Oct 1865 ae: 15y 5m C:48
Mark s/o Warren & Sally d 13
Feb 1857 ae: 15y 5m C:48

28

**COX** (continued)

Mary d/o Warren & Harriet d 5 Apr 1853 ae: 6m SBE C:48

Sally w/o Warren d 3 July 1845 ae: 38y C:48

Sally d/o Warren & Harriet d 8 Feb 1852 ae: 4y SD C:48

Sarah T d/o Josiah d 10 May 1871 ae: 6m GSL

Warren d 30 Nov 1857 ae: 53y. SD C:48

**COYLE**, Ann w/o John d 31 Aug 1854 ae: 42y Strangers' Ground GSL

**CRAFTS**, Thomas H B d 8 June 1887 ae: 49y 7m Daniels tomb A:19

**CRANE**, Frank B s/o William & Mary d 4 Sept 1849 ae: 11m H:65

Mary J d/o Guilford s/o Joseph & Mary d 21 Mar 1900 ae: 47y SD F:65

William d 22 July 1858 ae: 45y H:65

**CRAWFORD**, George d 3 Oct 1841 ae: 3y 3m GSL

George W s/o William d 24 July 1844 GSL

Sarah E d 3 Oct 1841 ae: 3y 3m. GSL

William d 19 June 1852 ae: 30y SD H:50

William H d 7 Nov 1841 ae: 5y 6m SD H:50

**CRESSEY**, Rev Noah d 15 Dec 1867 ae: 91y 8m F:130

Sophia s w/o Rev Noah d 25 Aug 1845 ae: 56y F:130

**CRINK**, James s/o James d 1 Apr 1858 ae: 16m GSL

**CRIPPS**, Amos C d 12 Oct 1884 ae: 49y Civ/War: 7th Reg Maine Inf Co F H:80

Susan A wid/o Amos C d 13 Mar 1899 ae: 56y 4m 15d SD H:80

**CROCKER**, Armena J B d/o John & Jane d 1 Aug 1856 ae: 15m F:101

Calvin s/o Ira d 7 Mar 1858 Washington, DC ae: 33y 6m 7d Longfellow tomb A:12

**CROCKER** (continued)

Charles J s/o John d 15 Aug 1867 ae: 8m 12d SD F:101

**CROCKETT**, Charles s/o John d 13 Sept 1859 ae: 10m GSL

Charles D d 20 Sept 1864 ae: 6w GSL

Joseph D s/o Richard d 28 Jan 1872 New York City ae: 36y GSL

Solomon d 1 Apr 1849 ae: 53y GSL

**CRONAN**, Henry s/o John d 18 Sept 1842 ae: 18m Catholic GSL

Patrick d 7 Sept 1848 ae: 23y Catholic I:16

**CROOKER**, Elizabeth d 28 Aug 1874 ae: 98y GSL

**CROSBY**, Thomas s/o Hugh d 7 Nov 1854 ae: 18m Catholic GSL

**CROSS**, Harriet E d/o Joseph d 3 Aug 1865 ae: 11m GSL

Harriet E w/o Joseph d 9 Apr 1904 ae: 64y GSL

Joseph d 31 July 1876 ae: 72y GSL

Joseph s/o Joseph d 18 Aug 1865 ae: 5y 3m GSL

Mary w/o Joseph d 25 Aug 1857 ae: 33y GSL

**CROSSMAN**, Ann A Hersey w/o George d 21 Aug 1854 ae: 29y B:46

Annie A d/o Charles B d 11 Sept 1872 ae: 2m GSL

Carolyn d/o Benjamin d 23 Aug 1868 ae: 14y 2m GSL

Charles C d 7 Oct 1873 ae: 46y Crossman tomb Location unknown

Levi G d 1 Nov 1858 ae: 48y GSL

Mehitable w/o James d 17 July 1871 ae: 58y GSL

**CROSSWELL**, David Allen d 20 May 1862 Haggett tomb A:18

Hannah w/o Joseph d 1 Nov 1854 GSL

Joseph d 16 Nov 1854 GSL

**CROUNEYN**, Timothy d 7 June 1853 ae: 20y Native Macroon,

CROUNEYN (continued)
Ireland Catholic SBE I:19A

CROWLEY, Cornelius d 12 May 1855 ae: 24y Strangers' Ground GSL

Ellen d/o Alphonso d 28 Jan 1847 ae: 10m Catholic GSL

Joseph s/o Patrick d 17 Sept 1856 ae: 15m Old Catholic Ground GSL

Julia d/o Cornelius d 4 Dec 1846 ae: 3y Catholic GSL

Michael d 27 July 1853 ae: 6y Old Catholic Ground GSL

Timothy s/o Timothy d 29 Jan 1857 ae: 9m Catholic GSL

CROWTHER, Eunice S w/o John W d 5 Sept 1837 ae: 33y 6m J:83

George T d 8 Sept 1850 ae: 6m 12d J:83

Capt John W b 17 June 1813 Liverpool, England d 9 Dec 1893 J:83

Sarah w/o Capt John W d 30 May 1859 aboard the *Sarah B Hale* ae: 46y 8m SB J:83

CUHUGION, Richard s/o James d 29 Jan 1849 ae: 6m Catholic GSL

CUMMING, Bridget inf d/o John d 23 Jan 1855 Catholic GSL

Bridget d/o Richard d 12 Mar 1855 ae: 2y 8m Catholic GSL

CUMMINGS, Benjamin d 18 Dec 1857 ae: 37y Hilborn tomb A:10

Charles Edward s/o Nathaniel G d 28 July 1854 ae: 7m GSL

Rev Cyrus d 9 Sept 1859 ae: 68y J:228

E L d 21 Jan 1859 ae: 31y 7m Hilborn tomb A:10

Edwin s/o Samuel B & Lucy AS d 7 Aug 1848 ae: 1y 8m 16d SBE H:90

Elizabeth w/o Rev Cyrus d 8 Feb 1868 ae: 78y J:228

Elizabeth Ellen d/o Rev Cyrus & Elizabeth d 11 July 1834 ae: 5y J:228

Ellen d/o Frank d 1 May 1857

CUMMINGS (continued)
ae: 18m GSL

Frances w/o Daniel d 13 Jan 1855 ae: 37y Cummings tomb A:58

Frank W d 11 Jan 1885 Philadelphia, Pennsylvania ae: 45y Cummings tomb A:13

Ida Gertrude d 7 Jan 1870 ae: 13y GSL

James B d 18 July 1888 New York City ae: 50y Cummings tomb A:13

John B d 13 May 1880 ae: 79y Cummings tomb A:13

Julia d/o Rev Cyrus & Elizabeth d 25 June 1832 ae: 2y 5m J:228

Lillian L d/o Nathaniel G d 4 Oct 1856 ae: 1y 5m 25d GSL

Margaret d/o Dr John M d 3 Aug 1853 ae: 13m GSL

Mary A S w/o John B d 16 Apr 1883 ae: 73y Cummings tomb A:13

Mary C d/o Silas A d 3 Feb 1853 ae: 8m GSL

Patrick s/o Jeremiah d 19 July 1855 ae: 18m GSL

Samuel A s/o Samuel B & Lucy AS d 1 Sept 1850 ae: 4y 10m 22d H:90

Samuel B d 7 Feb 1879 ae: 28y SD H:90

William G s/o Dorcas d 30 Aug 1852 ae: 15m GSL

William Harrison s/o Rev Cyrus & Elizabeth d 13 July 1832 ae: 7y J:228

CUNARD, Mary d/o Edward d 21 Apr 1858 ae: 5m GSL

CUNNINGHAM, Frank s/o Frank d 22 May 1854 ae: 11m Catholic GSL

Margaret d/o Francis d 4 Feb 1852 ae: 1y 7m Catholic GSL

Mary E d/o Frank d 28 Apr 1861 ae: 6w Catholic GSL

Thomas d 27 Sept 1853 ae: 18m Catholic GSL

CURRAN, Ann w/o Martin d 4 Sept 1854 ae:21y Buried beside

CURRAN (continued)
Martin Catholic Strangers' Ground GSL
Bridget d/o Miles d 10 July 1857 ae: 5m Catholic GSL
Ellen d/o Martin & Ann d 4 Sept 1854 ae: 1y 9m Buried with parents Catholic GSL
John s/o Martin d 12 Sept 1854 ae: 2m Buried in father's grave Catholic GSL
John J s/o Thomas d 12 Aug 1866 ae: 11d Catholic GSL
Martin d 3 Sept 1854 ae: 32y Catholic Strangers' Ground GSL
Thomas d 25 May 1857 ae: 13m Catholic GSL
CURREY, Timothy d 25 Mar 1851 ae: 46y GSL
CURRIER, George s/o Joseph d 29 Oct 1842 ae: 3y GSL
George E s/o GE & CA d 3 Jan 1881 ae: 3d SD F:61
John d 15 Mar 1848 ae: 31y GSL
CURRY, James d 9 Mar 1866 Alms House ae: 58y GSL
Maria A w/o James d 29 Feb 1856 ae: 29y SD F:145
Mary d 29 Aug 1849 ae: 58y Catholic GSL
CURTIS, Caroline F w/o William L d 2 July 1870 ae: 70y F:100
Eliza H d 26 Aug 1857 ae: 1y 5m Cummings tomb A:13
Eugene N s/o William d 24 Sept 1858 ae: 3m 11d Cummings tomb A:13
Mark d 28 Mar 1853 ae: 25y Catholic GSL
William L d 5 June 1870 ae: 71y F:100
CUSHMAN, Alvin d 5 Aug 1859 ae: 72y GSL
Nathaniel E s/o NP d 5 Mar 1856 ae: 21y Sawyer tomb A:14
Sarah d/o Alvin d 5 May 1852 ae: 22y GSL
CUSKBY, Eliza d/o Martin d 21 Nov 1857 ae: 9m 6d GSL
CUTTER, Asa H d 30 Oct 1850 ae: 39y J:107

CUTTER (continued)
George G d 20 Dec 1865 ae: 26y 8m J:107
Lucy d 19 Apr 1858 ae: 88y GSL
DACEY, Frederick d 7 Aug 1886 ae: 31y 11m GSL
DAGGETT, Alice M d/o Charles d 1 June 1866 ae: 4y 4m GSL
DAGIN, Susan d/o Charles d 23 June 1846 ae: 6m Catholic GSL
DAICY, Ammi d 5 Apr 1886 ae: 35y 10m GSL
Susan A w/o William d 30 Mar 1904 ae: 84y 4m GSL
William d 30 June 1888 ae: 71y 10m GSL
William W d 13 Jan 1886 ae: 35y 7m GSL
DAILEY, Catherine w/o Thomas d 28 Feb 1855 ae: 24y Strangers' Ground GSL
Edward s/o Edward d 11 Sept 1854 ae: 5y Strangers' Ground GSL
Hannah d/o Timothy d 4 Feb 1853 ae: 14y Catholic GSL
Patrick s/o Peter d 14 Jan 1853 ae: 1y 10m Catholic GSL
DAIN, John P d 19 Apr 1863 ae: 44y GSL
DALTON, James d 5 Sept 1847 ae: 60y Catholic GSL
DALY, Bridget w/o Matthew d 10 Mar 1844 ae: 39y Catholic I:21A
Catherine d/o Edward d 6 Nov 1859 ae: 14y 9m GSL
Edward d 9 May 1864 ae: 47y GSL
Grace d/o Richard L d 24 July 1855 ae: 2y GSL
Hannah d 30 Aug 1863 ae: 9y Strangers' Ground GSL
James d 22 Feb 1869 ae: 26y 6m GSL
Joanna d/o Timothy d 10 Jan 1849 ae: 3y Catholic GSL
John s/o Michael d 11 Aug 1846 ae: 1m Catholic GSL
John s/o Philip d 17 Aug 1854 ae: 3y GSL

DALY (continued)
Margaret d/o Timothy d 27 Aug 1849 ae: 9y Catholic GSL
Maria w/o Edward d 19 Mar 1852 ae: 32y Catholic GSL
Mary d 25 Apr 1850 ae: 47y Catholic GSL
Mathius d 13 Jan 1880 ae: 69y GSL
Patrick s/o Edward d 13 Jan 1852 ae: 2m Catholic GSL
Thomas s/o Benner d 1 Dec 1850 ae: 2y GSL
Thomas s/o H d 3 Sept 1848 ae: 1m Catholic buried O'Neal lot GSL
Timothy d 2 Apr 1849 ae: 50y Catholic GSL
DAM, Stillborn c/o Edward L & Kate L d 1 Dec 1905 SD G:15
Clara H L d/o Leader & Hannah d 1 Aug 1849 ae: 6m SD G:15
Elizabeth T d/o Leader d 24 Mar 1899 Greely Hosp ae: 41y SD G:15
Eugene W s/o Leader d 27 Aug 1852 ae: 2m SD G:15
Hannah Jane d/o Leader d 8 Feb 1862 ae: 1m SD G:15
Hannah L w/o Leader d 6 Dec 1888 ae: 67y 7m SD G:15
Leader b 1816 d 1881 G:15
Mary J w/o Leader d 25 Oct 1843 ae: 25y G:15
Thomas J d 24 Sept 1854 ae: 36y GSL
DAMERY, James d 30 Aug 1873 ae: 60y GSL
Mary wid/o James d 24 Aug 1893 ae: 60y GSL
William s/o John d 19 Mar 1864 ae: 12y Catholic GSL
Dennis s/o John d 7 Sept 1847 ae: 7m Catholic GSL
DANA, David d 28 May 1842 ae: 66y Daniels tomb A:19
Harriet M T d/o WS d 30 Aug 1850 Bath, Maine ae: 3y SD C:57
DANE, Ann d/o John d 21 Oct 1864 Charlestown, Massachusetts ae: 27y GSL

DANE (continued)
Marcia H d/o John P d 2 Apr 1855 ae: 19m GSL
DANIELS, Dexter s/o James & Rebecca d 5 Jan 1893 ae: 83y 7m 11d Daniels tomb A:19
Ebenezer d 26 July 1865 ae: 79y Daniels tomb A:19
Ella F d/o Dexter d 27 Dec 1857 ae: 6y Daniels tomb A:19
Ellen F d/o Charles d 20 Oct 1854 ae: 1y GSL
Lincoln s/o Ebenezer d 14 Aug 1843 ae: 17y 6m Daniels tomb A:19
Sarah b1811 d1893 H:105
DANLEY, Patrick d 27 Mar 1846 ae: 42y Catholic GSL
DARLING, Ann w/o Tobias d 10 May 1858 ae: 34y GSL
Annah widow d 11 Apr 1849 ae: 81y GSL
DARWIN, Patrick d 13 Oct 1857 ae: 22y 7m GSL
DAUGHERTY, Barney d 22 Oct 1841 ae: 7y Catholic GSL
Hugh d 19 July 1841 ae: 29y Foreigner GSL
DAVEIS, Anne Emery d/o John TG & Frances E Gilman b 29 July 1848 d 16 Apr 1900 E:2
Caroline Elizabeth youngest c/o Charles S & Elizabeth T no burial record no dates on stone E:2
Charles Stewart b 10 May 1788 d 29 Mar 1865 E:2
Edward Henry s/o Charles S & Elizabeth T Gilman b 3 Apr 1818 d 12 Dec 1909 E:2
Elizabeth Taylor Gilman w/o Charles Stewart b 11 Aug 1788 d 23 Apr 1860 E:2
Frances d/o John TG & Frances E Gordon b 25 Oct 1852 d 1 Aug 1853 E:2
Frances Ellen Gordon w/o John Taylor Gilman b 4 Dec 1822 d 8 Dec 1909 E:2
John Taylor Gilman b 21 Mar 1816 d 9 May 1873 E:2
Mabel Stewart d/o Edward H &

DAVIES(continued)
Susan WB b 3 May 1859 d 25 Feb 1946 E:2
Mary Gilman d/o Edward H & Susan WB b 13 Aug 1855 d 14 Mar 1942 E:2
Susan Williams Bridge w/o Edward Henry b 8 Nov 1830 d 27 July 1922 E:2

DAVID, Charles d 4 Oct 1850 ae: 30y Catholic GSL

DAVIDSON, Susan L w/o Robert d 9 May 1890 ae: 43y SD C:85

DAVIS, Burley H d 28 Nov 1872 ae: 74y GSL
Calem S s/o Samuel d 30 Nov 1848 ae: 14y GSL
Charles E s/o William G d 23 Aug 1863 ae: 1y 11m 20d GSL
Charles N d 1 Nov 1885 ae: 39y Civ/War: 1st Reg Maine Cav Co E B:66
Cynthia M w/o Amos d/o Charles Anderson of Windham, Maine d 15 Apr 1858 ae: 27y GSL
Eliza A w/o James N d 26 Sept 1896 ae: 73y 1m 19d I:142
Elizabeth F w/o Charles S d 3 Apr 1860 ae: 71y GSL
Ellen Eliza d/o Frederick d 14 June 1858 ae; 5y 6m SD H:84
Ellen Louise d/o Frederick E d 16 June 1876 SD H:84
Emma C d/o Amos d 1 Apr 1858 ae: 1y GSL
Francis G s/o Charles d 31 May 1852 ae: 11w GSL
George s/o Moses d 10 Mar 1852 ae: 33y J:55
George H s/o John d 19 July 1881 ae: 38y SD J:174
Harriet N d/o Asa & Ruby d 7 May 1919 ae: 84y 25d SD I:142
James N b1822 d1886 I:142
Jane M d/o George R d 18 Aug 1854 ae: 6m GSL
Lorene W w/o Walter S d 18 Oct 1901 ae: 21y 5m SD B:5
Louisa P w/o Capt Charles M d 5 Apr 1858 ae: 61y GSL

DAVIS (continued)
Maria w/o Moses d 13 May 1851 ae: 54y J:55
Mary A Burnham w/o William d 14 Dec 1902 ae: 84y 9m J:245
Max s/o Frederick E d 9 Aug 1880 ae: 3y GSL
Moses d 20 Oct 1858 ae: 72y SB J:55
Nellie M d/o Charles N d 3 Nov 1885 ae: 36y SD B:66
Samuel d 5 Jan 1878 ae: 77y SD H:79
Samuel s/o Samuel d 28 Dec 1854 ae: 23y SD H:79
Sarah E w/o Thomas G d 11 Aug 1887 ae: 64y SD B:66
Sumner s/o Samuel d 27 Dec 1854 ae: 18y SD H:79
Susan w/o Samuel d 7 May 1863 ae: 62y SD H:79
Susan Caroline d/o James N & Eliza A d 30 Nov 1848 ae: 1y 4m I:142
Tasman s/o Thomas G & Sarah E d 10 Dec 1848 ae: 2m SD B:66
Thomas G d 16 Apr 1850 ae: 35y SBE B:66
William M d 7 Feb 1881 ae: 62y J:245

DAY, Abraham d 7 Oct 1848 Saco, Maine ae: 52y GSL
George A s/o Moses W d 10 Oct 1849 ae: 2m SD J:115
John E s/o Abraham d 8 Oct 1845 ae: 9m GSL
Moses W d 20 Oct 1858 ae: 72y SB SBE J:115
Rebecca J w/o Sylvanus d 6 Mar 1847 ae: 20y B:54
Rheuly w/o Moses d 7 Apr 1852 ae: 23y SD J:115

DEAN, Charles H s/o Samuel d 28 Apr 1856 ae: 23y 4m GSL

DEANE, Charlotte A w/o George L d 30 Dec 1856 ae: 19y 4m GSL
Frederick A d 16 Mar 1867 at sea ae: 42y Civ/War: Sgt 30th Reg Maine Inf Co D B:8
John s/o John G & Rebecca D d

**DEANE** (continued)

19 Nov 1836 ae: 21y Lost at sea B:8

John G d 10 Nov 1839 ae: 54y B:8

Josephine d/o Samuel d 20 Aug 1854 ae: 3y 6m GSL

Mary d/o John G & Rebecca D d 14 May 1839 ae: 21y B:8

Melvin G d 21 Mar 1854 ae: 32y 4m B:8

Rebecca D w/o John G d 12 May 1872 ae: 80y B:8

Sarah A d/o Thomas d 9 Nov 1864 Charlestown, Massachusetts ae: 20d SBE B:8

William W b 2 Aug 1833 d 22 July 1870 Civ/War: Adj 12th Reg Maine Inf B:8

**DEEHAN**, Bridget d/o Patrick & Margaret d 25 June 1848 ae: 13m Catholic SBE J:183

Catherine d/o John d 19 Dec 1864 ae: 11m 19d Strangers' Ground GSL

Charles H d 4 Aug 1857 ae: 11y Old Catholic Ground GSL

Cornelius s/o Patrick & Nancy b 15 Oct 1843 d 18 Aug 1844 Catholic SBE I:32

James s/o Charles d 2 Aug 1854 ae: 10m GSL

John s/o Patrick & Margaret d 2 July 1851 ae: 1m Catholic SBE J:183

Margaret d/o Patrick & Nancy d 14 Sept 1841 Catholic SBE I:32

Margaret d/o John & Margaret d 18 May 1846 ae: 2y 10m I:53

Mary d/o Patrick d 29 Aug 1856 ae: 8m Old Catholic Ground GSL

Mary wid/o Michael d 25 Apr 1856 ae: 76y Old Catholic Ground GSL

Nancy w/o Patrick d 14 Oct 1853 ae: 45y Catholic SBE I:32

Patrick d 19 Oct 1857 ae: 95y GSL

Patrick d 15 Mar 1863 ae: 56y Native Cumber Parish, Co Deery, Ireland Catholic SBE

**DEEHAN** (continued)

I:32

Pierce s/o Michael d 28 Mar 1865 ae: 8m GSL

**DEEKIN**, James s/o Peter d 4 May 1846 ae: 2y 9m GSL

**DEERING**, Amos Harrod s/o Charles F d 5 Nov 1861 ae: 5y 10m GSL

Ann Tate w/o Charles d 20 Feb 1887 ae: 58y 8m Ingraham tomb A:16

Charles s/o C d 22 Sept 1857 ae: 1y 7m GSL

Charles H s/o Charles d 9 Jan 1879 ae: 24y Ingraham tomb A:16

Frank K s/o HW & ED d 14 Feb 1853 ae: 2y 8m SD D:17

George s/o John d 14 Aug 1848 ae: 1y GSL

Georgia T d 20 Apr 1880 ae: 23y Ingraham tomb A:16

Hannah wid/o Elliot d 4 May 1848 ae: 78y GSL

James J s/o Noah & Elizabeth d 24 Nov 1841 ae: 5y SD J:120

James N s/o Noah & Elizabeth d 17 Nov 1835 ae: 5y SD J:120

John d 2 Apr 1848 ae: 72y GSL

Joseph d/o Noah & Elizabeth d 28 Nov 1835 ae: 11m SD J:120

Margaret M d/o Alvin & Margaret d 21 Nov 1848 ae: 1y 7m SD D:17

Mary Ann w/o Elliot d 23 Jan 1872 ae: 82y 9m Sherwood tomb D:30

Mary E d/o Noah & Elizabeth d 2 Nov 1851 ae: 27y SBE J:120

Richie M s/o James & Kate d 27 Jan 1853 ae: 2y 8m SD D:17

**DEGURO**, Catherine W d/o John & Sophia d 4 Nov 1823 ae: 16m F:70

Galen J s/o John & Sophia d 7 July 1830 ae: 2y F:70

Harriet S d/o John & Sophia d 4 Jan 1830 ae: 4y F:70

John d 6 Oct 1844 ae: 47y 5m F:70

John w s/o John & Sophia d 17

DEGURO (continued)
Jan 1842 ae: 18y 5m F:70
Sophia w/o John d 16 June 1885
ae: 90y 9m F:70
DEHAN, John s/o Patrick d 30
June 1851 ae: 1m Catholic
GSL
DeHANEY, Mary d/o Eben d 20
Aug 1854 ae: 2y 6m GSL
DELA, Ann w/o Peter d 26 Sept
1853 ae: 45y Old Catholic
Ground GSL
Aria A d/o Matthew & Louisa H
d 10 Dec 1840 ae: 2y 2m G:91
Augustus H s/o Matthew &
Louisa H d 21 Jan 1842 ae: 2y
G:91
Augustus H s/o Matthew &
Louisa H d 30 June 1846 ae:
2y 5m SD G:91
Matthew L s/o Matthew &
Louisa H d 21 Jan 1842 ae: 1y
7m G:91
Matthew Lewis s/o Matthew &
Louisa H d 25 June 1849 ae:
33y G:91
Sarah L d/o Matthew & Louisa H
d 21 June 1848 ae: 9y 7m G:91
DELAND, Elizabeth Jane w/o
Frederick J b 1849 d 1898 D:20
Frederick d 15 Dec 1883 ae: 74y
6m G:53
Frederick J d 13 Feb 1884 ae:
45y 8m D:20
Frederick J Jr s/o Frederick &
Elizabeth Jane d 10 May 1871
ae: 19m D:20
Jane C w/o Daniel T d 3 Apr
1857 ae: 39y 2m GSL
Mary F w/o Frederick d 21 Aug
1881 ae: 60y 6m G:53
Phebe Mrs d 4 Feb 1851 ae: 67y
GSL
DELANO, Maria wid/o Joshua d
19 Oct 1867 Boston, Massa-
chusetts ae: 66y GSL
Martha d 14 June 1852 ae: 82y
GSL
DELANY, John d 20 Nov 1848 ae:
45y Catholic GSL
Julia w/o John d 21 Aug 1846 ae:
42y Catholic I:34

DELANY (continued)
William d 19 July 1856 ae: 30y
Catholic GSL
DENNING, Ruth B d/o Frederick
& Clarissa d 25 Jan 1848 ae:
22y SD D:64
DENNINGTON, Harriet d/o John d
20 July 1859 ae: 15m GSL
Joseph s/o John d 2 Apr 1857 ae:
4w GSL
DENNIS, Charles S d 24 Apr 1848
ae: 39y Death caused by fall-
ing from top gallant yard of
brig *Frances Ellen*, striking his
skull on the deck; he lived but
a few minutes SB H:103
DENNISON, Albert E b1833 d1868
B:4
Alberto s/o Albert & Esther No
burial record SD B:4
Brett Harris s/o George A & Jean
d 28 June 1857 Lewiston,
Maine ae: 10d NS B:4
Esther Hilborn w/o Albert E
b1832 d1866 B:4
George Albert Jr s/o Albert E &
Della b 24 Sept 1882 d 16 Oct
1965 B:4
John Joseph s/o John J d 15 Aug
1862 ae: 7m GSL
Mattie Louise w/o George A
b1889 d1975 B:4
DEPLES, Charles s/o Charles d
13 Sept 1860 ae: 1y 1m GSL
DERSEY, Ellen d 27 May 1858
ae: 22y GSL
DEVINE, Bridget d/o Henry &
Unity d 28 Mar 1849 ae: 2y 7m
Catholic J:163
Catherine d/o James d 9 Nov
1841 ae: 9m GSL
Elizabeth wid/o James d 2 Oct
1855 ae: 42y GSL
Ellen d/o James d 25 May 1853
ae: 10m GSL
Harriet Ellen d/o John & SR d 22
Mar 1846 ae: 1y Catholic SD
F:141
Henry d 10 Mar 1853 ae: 36y
Catholic SD J:163
Hugh d 3 Jan 1852 Boston, Mas-
sachusetts ae: 88y Catholic

**DEVINE** (continued)
GSL
Hugh s/o Patrick d 22 Jan 1850 ae: 5y Catholic GSL
James d 1 Nov 1854 ae: 45y Catholic GSL
James s/o Anthony d 17 Dec 1841 ae: 4y Catholic GSL
James s/o Henry & Unity d 20 Mar 1849 ae: 2y 7m Catholic J:163
James s/o James d 21 Jan 1858 ae: 1y 8m Catholic GSL
John d 4 Feb 1849 ae: 35y Catholic GSL
John d 26 Sept 1851 ae: 6y Catholic GSL
John s/o James d 17 July 1853 ae: 17m Catholic GSL
Mary d 2 Sept 1849 ae: 76y Catholic GSL
Mary w/o Miles d 21 Nov 1842 ae: 40y Catholic GSL
Mary E d/o James d 12 Oct 1861 ae: 11m Catholic GSL
Patrick d 25 May 1850 Lewiston, Maine ae: 32y Catholic GSL
Patrick s/o James d 7 Nov 1854 ae: 22y Catholic GSL
Rosa d/o Edward d 5 Sept 1856 ae: 18m Catholic GSL
Sarah d/o Miles d 16 Nov 1842 ae: 6m Catholic GSL
Violet d/o Henry d 27 Mar 1849 ae: 13m Catholic J:163
**DeWOLFE**, Arthur C s/o William d 6 Oct 1892 ae: 1y 1m SD G:18
Eliza d/o John d 4 Nov 1865 ae: 3y GSL
Eliza w/o Robert d/o Robert & Eliza Dean d 29 Sept 1910 ae: 88y G:18
Elizabeth Dean w/o James b1858 d1885 G:18
Elsie M d/o Benjamin & Louise d 6 Apr 1900 ae: 7m 16d NS G:18
Grace w/o John d 19 Oct 1865 ae: 33y GSL
John s/o Robert & Eliza b1850 d1853 G:18

**DeWOLFE** (continued)
Lizzie d/o Robert & Eliza b1856 d1858 G:18
Lydia A d/o JF d 27 July 1852 ae: 1y 8m GSL
Robert d 23 June 1884 ae: 66y G:18
Robert s/o Robert & Eliza b1854 d1861 G:18
Robert Benjamin s/o Robert d 29 Sept 1891 ae: 9m 15d NS G:18
Susan D d/o Robert & Eliza b1861 d1863 G:18
**DICKERSON**, George H s/o George H d 22 Sept 1854 ae: 11m GSL
**DICKEY**, Mary d/o Charles d 25 May 1843 ae: 20d First mention of "Catholic Ground" Catholic Ground GSL
Mary d/o Capt William C d 27 July 1853 ae: 3y 6m GSL
Robert N s/o William C & Susan S d 25 Sept 1848 ae: 18m SBE D:19
Susan S w/o William C d/o Lawrence & Mary Vanbuskirk d 26 Sept 1882 ae: 71y 9m D:19
William C d 20 Dec 1887 Rockland, Maine ae: 72y Civ/War: 25th Reg Maine Inf Co C SD D:19
**DICKING**, Margaret d/o Patrick d 13 Sept 1841 ae: 5m Catholic GSL
**DICKSON**, Thomas d 3 June 1862 ae: 65y Catholic GSL
William s/o Thomas d 12 June 1845 ae: 15m Catholic GSL
**DIEHAN**, Patrick d 5 Feb 1863 ae: 61y Catholic GSL
**DIGGIO**, Joseph H s/o Joseph d 3 Sept 1850 ae: 1y GSL
**DILLING**, John d 22 Dec 1885 Greely Hosp ae: 65y D:7
Sophia R w/o John b1821 d1894 D:7
**DINSMORE**, Eben R d 8 July 1875 ae: 39y Civ/War: Musician 2nd Reg Maine Inf Co H J:57

DIXEY, Zenas s/o Zenas d 23 Sept 1848 ae: 9m GSL
DIXON, Thomas d 3 June 1862 ae: 54y Native Co Mayo, Ireland Catholic SD J:285
DODGE, Annie E d/o Ruloff & Sarah b 10 Nov 1850 d 6 Aug 1923 D:53
Elizabeth Evans w/o Hartley G d 5 Oct 1905 ae: 85y B:68
Elizabeth J d/o Ruloff & Sarah d 11 Jan 1867 ae: 28y 11m SD D:53
Etta L d/o Ruloff & Sarah d 23 May 1889 ae: 35y 17m D:53
Hartley G b1823 d1890 B:68
James B s/o Joseph W & Sarah b 29 Aug 1844 d 3 Sept 1910 Boston, Massachusetts D:53
Joseph W s/o Ruloff & Sarah E b 15 July 1848 d 8 Mar 1911 D:53
Ruloff d 19 Feb 1879 ae: 64y D:53
Sarah A d/o Ruloff & Sarah d 27 Sept 1860 ae: 19y D:53
Sarah E w/o Ruloff d 6 Dec 1879 ae: 61y 9m D:53
Sarah M w/o Joseph W d 22 Aug 1877 ae: 24y 11m SD D:53
DOHERTY, Andrew d 27 Aug 1854 ae: 46y Old Catholic Ground GSL
Catherine d/o James d 15 Sept 1855 ae: 15m Catholic GSL
John s/o John d 4 Apr 1854 ae: 7w Catholic GSL
Margaret d/o Andrew d 16 Aug 1854 ae: 9y Catholic GSL
Mary J d/o John d 16 Sept 1854 ae: 4y Catholic GSL
DOLAN, Mary A d/o Thomas F d 1 June 1847 ae: 2d Catholic GSL
DOLLEY, John s/o Michael d 9 Mar 1848 Lewiston Falls, Maine ae: 9y Catholic GSL
DONAHUE, Ann w/o John d 2 May 1856 ae: 24y Catholic GSL
Bridget w/o Thomas d 8 Nov 1859 ae: 38y Catholic GSL

DONAHUE (continued)
Catherine w/o Jeremiah d 25 Sept 1857 ae: 37y Catholic GSL
Catherine d/o Thomas d 12 Oct 1859 ae: 7d Catholic GSL
D d/o Michael d 8 Nov 1857 ae: 15m Catholic GSL
Eliza J d/o Thomas d 17 Nov 1854 ae: 9m Catholic Strangers' Ground GSL
Hannah d/o Thomas d 22 July 1850 ae: 6m Catholic GSL
Horatio N s/o Timothy d 19 Aug 1858 ae: 8m 17d Catholic GSL
James s/o Michael d 6 July 1847 ae: 5d Catholic GSL
Jane d/o Michael d 9 Apr 1861 ae: 2y 9m Catholic GSL
Jeremiah s/o John d 3 Oct 1854 ae: 1y Catholic GSL
Joanna d/o Thomas d 3 Dec 1854 ae: 2y Catholic Strangers' Ground GSL
Margaret d/o James d 31 Aug 1854 ae: 18m Catholic GSL
Margaret d/o Patrick & Mary d 8 Feb 1845 ae: 21m Catholic SD I:27
Mary d/o Patrick d 4 Dec 1853 ae: 2w Catholic Stangers' Ground GSL
Mary d/o Thomas d 21 Oct 1852 ae: 9m Catholic GSL
Mary Ann d/o Thomas d 28 Sept 1859 ae: 16m Catholic GSL
Matilda d/o James d 10 Sept 1850 ae: 6m Catholic GSL
Michael d 4 May 1855 ae: 35y Catholic Strangers' Ground GSL
Michael s/o Michael d 8 Oct 1855 ae: 16m Catholic GSL
Thomas d 20 July 1848 Merchanic Falls, Maine ae: 22y Catholic GSL
Timothy d 3 Sept 1866 ae: 30y Catholic GSL
William H s/o Timothy d 8 Jan 1863 ae: 2m Catholic GSL
DONAN, Margaret d/o Patrick d 6 Aug 1855 ae: 2m 2w Catholic

DONAN (continued)
GSL
DONOVAN, Catherine d/o Richard
d 11 July 1848 ae: 6m Catholic
SD I:38
Daniel d 28 Feb 1851 ae: 37y
Catholic GSL
Daniel d 15 Aug 1857 ae: 58y
Catholic GSL
Dennis s/o John d 25 Sept 1855
ae: 11m Catholic GSL
Honora d/o Michael d 30 Jan
1857 ae: 3m Catholic GSL
James s/o Richard d 6 Mar 1846
ae: 9m Catholic GSL
John d 10 Jan 1859 ae: 69y
Catholic GSL
Margaret d/o Michael d 26 May
1855 ae: 16w Catholic GSL
Mary d/o James d 1 Feb 1856
ae: 3y 3m Catholic GSL
Mary d/o Thomas d 23 Feb 1850
ae: 11m Catholic GSL
Mary Ann d/o John d 12 Sept
1854 ae: 15y Catholic GSL
Patrick s/o John d 3 May 1848
ae: 22y Catholic GSL
Richard d 7 Aug 1856 ae: 21y Old
Catholic Ground I:38
Timothy d 7 Aug 1856 ae: 35y
Catholic Strangers' Ground
GSL
William d 29 Feb 1856 ae: 22y
Old Catholic Ground GSL
DOODY, James s/o Wagin d 25
Nov 1850 ae: 1y Catholic GSL
Margaret w/o Orin d 9 Mar 1848
ae: 28y Catholic GSL
Mary w/o Owen d 28 Aug 1854
ae: 30y Catholic GSL
Owen d 2 Sept 1854 ae: 35y
Catholic GSL
Thomas s/o Orin d 19 May 1849
ae: 2y Catholic GSL
Cornelius s/o Cornelius d 7 Sept
1856 ae: 9m Catholic GSL
DOOLY, Eliza d/o Andrew &
Sarah d 31 May 1846 ae: 4d
Catholic I:30
Emily d/o Andrew & Sarah d 3
June 1849 ae: 9d Catholic SD
I:30

DOOLY (continued)
Sarah A d/o Andrew & Sarah d 18
Nov 1858 ae: 10y 4m Old
Catholic Ground SD I:30
Timothy w/o Philip d 12 July
1857 ae: 2y Catholic GSL
William s/o Andrew & Sarah d
14 Oct 1856 ae: 22m 12d
Catholic SD I:30
William T s/o Andrew d 2 Nov
1856 ae: 9m Catholic GSL
DORR, Lucy d/o John d 6 Aug
1841 ae: 7w GSL
DORRANCE, Dr James d 28 Jan
1861 Kennebunk, Maine ae:
90y GSL
DORSETT, John d 31 May 1875
ae: 82y Hosack tomb A:17
DOUGHER, James s/o George d
20 Nov 1857 ae: 1y 10m
Catholic GSL
James s/o Patrick & Amelia d
21 Aug 1853 ae: 5w Catholic
SBE J:202
Mary d/o John d 12 June 1853
ae: 6m Old Catholic Ground
GSL
DOUGHERTY, John s/o Michael
d 25 May 1849 ae: 16y
Catholic GSL
Michael s/o Michael d 27 Nov
1846 ae: 22y Catholic GSL
Daniel s/o Michael d 11 Sept
1843 ae: 17y Catholic GSL
DOUGHTY, John w/o William d
10 May 1853 ae: 4y 9m
Drowned Old Catholic Ground
GSL
DOUGLASS, Abigail w/o William
d 22 Apr 1841 ae: 76y SB F:33
Abigail wid/o Ebenezer d 19 Aug
1841 ae: 90y B:7
Annie F d/o Robert & Frances
AC d 4 Sept 1858 ae: 5m SBE
B:7
Caroline C w/o Robert d 14 Oct
1854 ae: 23y J:72
Ebenezer d 3 Sept 1798 New
London, Connecticut ae: 52y
B:7
Elizabeth no burial record SBE
B:21

DOUGLASS (continued)
Frank no burial record SBE B:7
Joseph d 18 Oct 1850 ae: 43y
GSL
Lucy d/o Ebenezer & Abigail d 2
Mar 1838 ae: 60y SBE B:7
Mary d/o G d 8 Dec 1857 ae: 2y
GSL
Mary w/o Robert d 21 Jan 1836
ae: 57y J:72
Robert b1822 d1885 SD J:72
Robert d 3 Feb 1833 ae: 74y
Rev/War: veteran J:72
DOUTHER, Mary w/o John d 11
Sept 1856 ae: 45y Old Catholic
Ground GSL
Dow, Mrs E Smith d 11 Mar 1863
ae: 45y W Merritt tomb Loca-
tion unknown
Ella E d/o Luther B & Sarah A d
21 Sept 1849 ae: 1y 8m H:66
Ellen E d/o Luther B d 4 May
1871 ae: 19y SD H:66
Luther B d 4 Sept 1854 ae: 33y
H:66
Sarah A wid/o Luther b d 28 May
1866 ae: 43y 5m H:66
DOWNEY, Dennis d 10 Sept 1854
ae: 40y Catholic GSL
DOYLE, Abbie H d/o Capt Ran-
dall & Ann d 30 Aug 1883 ae:
29y B:5
Ann d 3 Dec 1897 Brunswick,
Maine ae: 81y 11m SD B:77
John d 3 Dec 1850 ae: 33y
Catholic GSL
John R s/o Capt Randall d 3 Mar
1880 ae: 23y 8m B:77
Mary L d/o Capt Randall d 7
May 1882 ae: 33y 3m B:77
Capt Randall d 13 Apr 1878 ae:
69y 3m 19d B:77
DRAKE, Alpheus b1782 d 15 Oct
1854 C:28
Edwin Standish s/o Levi F &
Hannah F d 30 May 1909 ae:
73y 10m 23d C:28
Ella w/o Edwin Standish d 19
Aug 1896 ae: 56y 3d C:28
Hannah Fobes w/o Levi Fair-
banks b1814 d 1 Mar 1848 C:28
Julia Angeline d/o Levi F &

DRAKE (continued)
Hannah F b1838 d1839 C:28
Julius Algernon s/o Levi F &
Hannah F b1839 d 27 July 1863
Baton Rouge, Louisiana
Civ/War: Sgt 12th Reg Maine
Inf C:28
Levi Fairbanks b1808 d1878 C:28
Sybil Fairbanks w/o Alpheus
b1788 d 15 Mar 1868 C:28
DRANSCOMB, Lucy w/o Solomon
d 2 Dec 1875 ae: 21y GSL
DRESSER, Elizabeth w/o Jona-
than d 13 May 1849 ae: 88y
F:31
Fred E s/o Daniel R d 22 May
1886 Somerville, Massachu-
setts ae: 24y GSL
Jonathan d 12 Nov 1800 Fryburg,
Maine Unusual granite stone
F:31
John d 28 Dec 1861 ae: 49y GSL
Mary A d 17 Dec 1864 ae: 59y
GSL
DREW, ____ wid/o Jeremiah d 17
Aug 1855 ae: 47y GSL
Daniel G d 3 Dec 1850 ae: 29y.
D:64
Ellen Matilda d/o Daniel G &
Matilda C d 5 July 1847 ae: 2y
8m D:64
James W s/o Ezra d 24 July
1854 ae: 6m GSL
Matilda C w/o Daniel G 1 Nov
1851 ae: 28y SB D:64
Sarah d 11 May 1872 ae: 80y GSL
DRISCOLL, Bridget w/o Patrick d
19 Nov 1853 ae: 35y Catholic
GSL
Catherine d/o Charles d 13 Nov
1859 ae: 4y Catholic GSL
Dennis d 25 Apr 1848 Brunswick,
Maine ae: 35y Old Catholic
Ground GSL
James d 10 Dec 1849 ae: 35y
Catholic GSL
John d 11 Nov 1863 Old Catholic
Ground GSL
John s/o John d 30 Nov 1864 ae:
11m Catholic GSL
John s/o Mary d 1 Aug 1857 ae:
9y Catholic GSL

**DRISCOLL** (continued)
Margaret A d 16 May 1864 ae:
19y 5m Catholic GSL
Mary A d/o Randolph d 27 July
1884 ae: 6w GSL
Mary Ellen d/o Daniel d 18 Dec
1861 ae: 11m GSL
**DRISCON**, Ellen d/o Timothy d
30Mar 1850 ae: 3y Catholic
GSL
**DROWNE**, Michael s/o Thomas d
5 July 1850 Saco, Maine ae: 2y
Catholic GSL
**DUDDY**, Henry s/o Richard d 7
July 1849 ae: 2y Catholic. GSL
Margaret w/o Francis d 3 Sept
1856 ae: 27y Native of Co
Derry, Ireland Catholic J:222
Thomas s/o Richard J d 27 Oct
1854 ae: 12y Catholic GSL
**DUFFIE**, Mary w/o Peter d 20
Aug 1854 Catholic GSL
Peter d 23 Aug 1854 ae: 58y
Catholic GSL
Rosanna w/o Peter d 28 Sept
1853 ae: 24y Catholic GSL
**DUKEY**, Margaret d/o William d
3 Apr 1848 ae: 3m Catholic
GSL
**DUNAGNY**, Michael d 12 May
1848 ae: 41y Catholic GSL
**DUNCAN**, Albert c s/o Charles C
d 6 Apr 1856 ae: 4y SD H:34
Charles C d 16 Mar 1877 ae: 68y
Civ/War: 17th Reg Maine Inf
Co E H:34
Charles L s/o Charles C d 22
Oct 1850 ae: 6m SD H:34
Edgar s/o Charles C d 24 Oct
1847 ae: 10d SD H:34
Susan S w/o Charles c d 2 Jan
1867 ae: 54y SD H:34
**DUNIVAR**, John d 9 Dec 1849 ae:
35y Catholic GSL
**DUNLAP**, Amelia d/o John S d 27
Feb 1859 Cleveland, Ohio ae:
9y Sawyer tomb A:14
Helen Louisa d/o John S d 7 Nov
1846 ae: 18m GSL
Capt John d 14 July 1842 ae: 66y
GSL
Susan P d/o John d 29 Jan 1860

**DUNLAP** (continued)
ae: 31y GSL
**DUNN**, inf c/o William H d 5 Aug
1853 ae: 9m GSL
Albert s/o Crockett & Adeline d
3 Apr 1929 ae: 70y 6m 28d NS
B:75
Allasandro s/o Crawford & Mary
A b 1852 d 1856 B:75
Crawford b 1826 d ---- no burial
record Civ/War: 5th Reg
Maine Inf Co H B:75
Cyrus Herbert s/o Cyrus d 27
Mar 1858 ae: 6m GSL
Daniel d 10 July 1869 ae: 33y
Dyer tomb A:15
Emma A d/o Samuel & Caroline
F d 20 Nov 1861 ae: 18y D:57
Joseph M b 6 June 1811 d 5 Mar
1852 F:92
Martha A w/o William H d 30
Mar 1854 ae: 30y SBE G:86
Mary A w/o Crawford d 10 Jan
1905 Augusta, Maine ae: 77y
B:75
Ronald Crawford d 15 Oct 1905
ae: 79y 3m 27d SD B:75
Susan M d/o Joseph & Mary d 15
Feb 1842 ae: 3y 2m F:92
Velma no burial record SD G:86
Willie C s/o Crawford & Mary A
b 1861 d 1865 B:75
Zebulon s/o Joseph & Mary d 19
July 1841 ae: 1y 4m SD F:92
**DUNPHY**, Thomas d 2 Jan 1858
of gun shot wound ae: 26y GSL
**DUNSCOMB**, Elizabeth w/o Solo-
mon d 3 Apr 1909 Somerville,
Massachusetts ae: 82y 2m 9d
SD J:236
Elizabeth w/o William d 30
June 1887 ae: 29y SD J:236
John S d 21 May 1895 Some-
rville, Massachusetts ae: 36y
SD J:236
Solomon G d 9 May 1880 ae: 63y
SD J:236
Thomas G d 30 Nov 1921 ae: 76y
3m 19d Civ/War: 3rd Reg US
Inf SD J:236
Wiliam s/o William J d 3 Aug
1880 ae: 11y SD J:236

DURAN, Josiah b 1812 d 1887 D:71
Julia A d/o Peter d 2 Jan 1853 ae: 11y GSL
Lilly Grace d/o Joel d 2 Aug 1860 GSL
Marietta d/o Benjamin d 8 Jan 1850 ae: 1y GSL
Miranda d/o Peter d 28 Feb 1853 ae: 9m GSL
Rebecca P w/o Josiah, d/o Samuel Edwards b 1825 d 1895 D:71
DURGIN, Ambrose d 10 June 1858 ae: 45y GSL
Diana d/o Joshua Keene d 16 Nov 1894 ae: 86y 6m 16d SD H:24
Elizabeth R d/o Walter d 25 Apr 1855 ae: 15y GSL
John s/o William d 1 Apr 1900 ae: 72y 10m 26d SD H:24
Mary Ann w/o Ambrose d 17 Apr 1849 ae: 23y GSL
DURHAM, Lena d 11 Jan 1880 ae: 5w GSL
DURKIN, Pete d 13 Dec 1848 ae: 36y Catholic GSL
DUROY, Eliza Ann w/o Marshall M d 27 July 1847 ae: 37y GSL
DUTTING, Ann w/o Tobias d 10 May 1858 ae: 32y Catholic SB I:79
DYER, inf d/o Alvin & Sarah G no dates on stone; no burial record B:74
Albert s/o Gardner & Mary d 5 Jan 1844 ae: 10m SD G:16
Albina d/o Gardner d 5 July 1873 ae: 30y SD G:16
Alvin S d 18 Oct 1874 ae: 66y Civ/War: 26th Reg Maine Inf Co C SD B:74
Alvin S Jr d 28 Mar 1872 ae: 29y Civ/War: 17th Reg Maine Inf Co E B:74
Annie L d/o Fred P d 31 Aug 1875 ae: 5m GSL
Charles d 18 Aug 1880 ae: 66y Civ/War: 6th Reg Maine Inf Co H Dyer tomb A:15
Charles E s/o Ebenezer & Mary

DYER (continued)
d 11 Sept 1894 ae: 70y Civ/War: 1st Reg Maine Inf Co D H:33
Charlie s/o Charles & Nancy no dates on stone; no burial record J:258
Christopher d 26 Jan 1892 ae: 83y D:78
Deborah J w/o Lemuel d 7 Sept 1876 ae: 72y GSL
Ebenezer L d 20 Jan 1850 ae: 48y SD D:78
Eddie F s/o E L d 9 Aug 1873 ae: 7m GSL
Edward E s/o Charles d 18 Aug 1848 ae: 8m GSL
Ellen S w/o Jabez d 5 Oct 1853 ae: 38y Jordan tomb D:28
Emmeline S d/o Ebenezer L & Mary b 1839 d 1926 D:78
Ethel M d/o Fred P d 27 Sept 1877 ae: 5w GSL
Etta L d/o Fred P d 27 Sept 1877 ae: 1y GSL
Eunice w/o Lemuel d 10 Jan 1871 ae: 65y Hilborn tomb A:10
Garafeilia M s/o Christopher & Lucy b 6 Oct 1840 d 2 Jan 1917 D:78
Gardner d 30 May 1873 ae: 72y SD G:16
Harriet w/o Charles d 29 June 1854 ae: 42y Dyer tomb A:15
Harry B s/o Edward L d 18 Sept 1876 ae: 11m GSL
Howard C s/o Christopher d 28 Aug 1856 ae: 1y 8m SD D:78
Jabez s/o Nathan d 10 Oct 1867 ae: 55y Dyer tomb A:15
James B s/o Nathaniel d 21 Apr 1844 ae: 2m GSL
James G s/o Ebenezer L d 14 Mar 1863 ae: 28y SD D:78
Jane wid/o Gardner d 13 July 1890 ae: 81y SD G:16
Josephine A b 28 June 1836 d 9 Dec 1928 D:78
Lucy Amelia w/o Christopher d 17 Mar 1848 ae: 34y SD D:78
Maria B w/o John d 12 May 1876

**DYER** (continued)
ae: 45y GSL
Mary A d/o Ebenezer L d 18 Oct 1847 ae: 6y SD D:78
Mary A d/o Gardner & Jane d 19 Mar 1908 ae: 65y G:16
Mary B d/o Edward L d 22 Nov 1879 ae: 1y GSL
Mary C w/o Ebenezer L d 13 Dec 1885 Natick, Massachusetts ae: 87y SD D:78
Mary G d/o Ebenezer & Mary d 19 Oct 1847 ae: 6y H:33
Mary Louise d/o Joseph H & Mary d 4 Sept 1850 ae: 3m D:78
Mercy H wid/o Nathan d 7 July 1900 ae: 89y 5m 23d Dyer tomb A:15
Nancy w/o Capt Samuel d 18 Sept 1852 ae: 61y J:258
Nathan d 28 Nov 1890 ae: 83y 5m Dyer tomb A:15
Oscar L s/o Stephen R 2nd d 23 Mar 1868 ae: 7m 23d Dyer tomb A:15
Reuben s/o Capt Robinson d 19 July 1855 ae: 19y 9m GSL
Samuel d 12 Sept 1861 ae: 55y GSL
Capt Samuel s/o Judah d 7 Nov 1868 ae: 74y 7m War/1812: veteran J:258
Sarah C Pickett w/o Alvin S d 28 June 1842 ae: 25y SD B:74
Sarah C d/o Alvin S & Sarah C d 19 July 1842 ae: 2m 14d B:74
Stephen K d 15 Aug 1890 Auburn, Maine ae: 69y Dyer tomb A:15
Theodore no burial record SD I:172
**EASTMAN**, Eliza B d/o Page d 29 July 1850 ae: 17y Native of Bartlett, New Hampshire Haggett tomb A:18
Mary d 2 Sept 1864 ae: 79y F:118
**EATON**, Annie L d/o Edmond A d 26 Aug 1873 ae: 16d Dyer tomb A:15
Emily L d/o E K d 21 Aug 1855 ae: 16m GSL
George d 11 Feb 1852 ae: 54y

**EATON** (continued)
GSL
Rev J S d 27 Sept 1856 ae: 46y GSL
Julia A wid/o Charles C d 5 July 1860 Chelsea, Massachusetts ae: 24y GSL
Mary E d/o George d 9 May 1868 ae: 27y 9m GSL
Mary J W Mrs d 16 Oct 1858 GSL
Olive d/o Nathaniel d 13 Sept 1854 ae: 21y Safford-Hall tomb A:20
Phebe d 12 Aug 1859 ae: 90y GSL
Wyman H s/o W H d 19 July 1848 ae: 2y 6m GSL
**EDGECOMB**, Annie L d/o Clement & Maria d 8 Aug 1862 ae: 14m SD D:18
Clement A d 26 Apr 1912 ae: 87y D:18
Ella A Huff w/o Clement A b 1839 d 1925 D:18
Maria C w/o Clement A d 12 July 1862 ae: 32y 6m 22d D:18
**EDMOND**, Abby C d/o John d 29 Dec 1847 ae: 28y SBE D:48
Abigail w/o John d 26 Aug 1839 ae: 57y D:48
Charles s/o John d 15 Apr 1854 ae: 37y SD D:48
Jane d 3 May 1849 ae: 39y SBE D:48
John d 18 Feb 1863 Chelsea, Massachusetts ae: 56y GSL
John d 21 Feb 1866 ae: 88y 5m SD D:48
John Jr d 20 May 1834 ae: 26y D:48
Margaret E w/o Alexander d 29 May 1848 ae: 37y SB D:48
Sarah A d 8 Jan 1887 ae: 74y 6m SD D:48
**EDMUNDS**, Capt John d 18 Feb 1863 ae: 57y 3m C:74
Laura B d 19 Jan 1852 ae: 10y 1m C:74
Martha Ellen d/o John & Sarah Ann d 24 Mar 1831 ae: 7m C:74

EDMUNDS (continued)
Martha W d 22 Feb 1838 ae: 7m
C:74
Sarah A Gooding w/o Capt John d
6 Jan 1887 ae: 74y C:74
EDWARDS, Albert H s/o Otis C
& Frances C d 16 Jan 1849 ae:
5m SD D:71
Angelina w d/o Nathaniel & Jo-
anna W d 8 Oct 1855 ae: 24y
I:69
Ann b w/o Samuel d 17 Mar 1869
ae: 56y GSL
Augusta d/o Nathaniel & Joanna
no date on stone; no burial
record I:69
Emma L s/o Samuel & Mary
Burr d 4 Aug 1838 ae: 13m
D:71
Frances C w/o Otis C d 4 Oct
1849 ae: 30y D:71
Henrietta G no date on stone; no
burial record I:69
Joanna W w/o Nathaniel d/o Hon
A Bradman of Minot, Maine d
18 Mar 1879 ae: 72y I:69
Laura d/o Nathaniel & Joanna W
no date on stone; no burial
record I:69
Lila M d/o Nelson d 19 Aug 1886
ae: 1y GSL
Loring H s/o Bela d 23 Jan 1868
ae: 15m GSL
Martha d/o Calvin d 15 Ma 1847
ae: 23y Merrill tomb D:35
Mary Ann B d/o Samuel & Mary
Burr d 17 Mar 1869 ae: 56y
D:71
Mary Burr w/o Samuel d 1 Mar
1859 ae: 65y D:71
Nathaniel no date on stone; no
burial record I:69
Philanda d/o Nathaniel & Joanna
W no date on stone; no burial
record I:69
Samuel d 13 Feb 1853 ae: 65y
D:71
Samuel C s/o Samuel & Mary
Burr d 12 Dec 1836 ae: 18m
D:71
Samuel O s/o Otis C & Frances
C d 2 Sept 1847 ae: 2y 3m SD

EDWARDS (continued)
D:71
Sarah a w/o Bela d 10 Aug 1868
ae: 41y I:69
Susan B d/o Samuel & Mary Burr
d 24 Mar 1839 ae: 21m D:71
Susan L w/o Calvin d 25 Nov
1851 ae: 58y GSL
ELDER, Edward F s/o Samuel d
8 Sept 1850 ae: 11m SD L:3
Samuel d 15 Oct 1856 ae: 51y SD
L:3
Samuel H s/o Samuel d 4 Dec
1864 ae: 18y 6m Civ/War:
29th Reg Maine Inf Co F SD
L:3
Sarah H w/o Samuel d 3 July
1852 ae: 44y SD L:3
ELDRIDGE, C Columbus s/o
Perez H & Dorothy d 16 Mar
1840 ae: 18y SD F:11
Charles L d 31 July 1878 Haver-
hill, Massachusetts ae: 8y
GSL
Dorothy H w/o Perez H d 27 Jan
1853 ae: 50y SD F:11
Perez H d 15 Apr 1845 ae: 45y
SD F:11
ELLIOTT, Ellen w/o Jedediah d
20 Aug 1871 ae: 39y GSL
Eunice w/o Moses d 26 Oct 1874
ae: 85y H:2
James S s/o J d 22 June 1857
ae: 18y GSL
Mary A d/o John B d 18 Aug
1880 ae: 17m GSL
Moses d 8 Dec 1853 ae: 62y SB
H:2
ELLSWORTH, Frances E w/o
George L, d/o Charles & Mary
Staples d 8 May 1858 ae: 26y
SD G:58
Nathaniel s/o George S d 5 Jan
1859 ae: 1y 3m SD G:58
ELWELL, Ella A d/o Edward H d
25 Oct 1853 ae: 4m 12d GSL
EMERSON, Charles A C s/o
Erasmus & Eunice d 15 Dec
1850 ae: 9y 6m SBE C:5
Erasmus d 11 May 1862 ae: 67y
SD C:5

**EMERSON** (continued)

Eunice w/o Erasmus d 9 Aug 1853 ae: 46y C:5

George G s/o Erasmus & Eunice d 25 Sept 1834 ae: 1m C:5

James L s/o Erasmus & Eunice d 29 Aug 1841 ae: 4y 9m SBE C:5

**EMERY,** Alfred H d 15 Mar 1853 ae: 31y 8m 15d SB & SBE D:16

Ann T w/o Nicholas d 29 Jan 1848 ae: 67y E:1

Charlotte d/o Nicholas & Ann T b 20 Oct 1853 d 20 Oct 1888 E:1

Charlotte B d/o Nicholas & Ann T d 8 Aug 1904 ae: 87y 5m 6d SD E:1

Deborah S wid/o John d 6 June 1861 ae: 83y GSL

Eunice E d 28 Apr 1848 ae: 15y Native of Poland Maine GSL

George s/o wid d 24 Sept 1841 ae: 4y GSL

Harrie S s/o Francis & Octavia d 7 Apr 1870 ae: 3m 9d C:73

Harriet B w/o Alfred H d 8 Dec 1848 ae: 28y 3m 8d SBE D:16

John H s/o Henry & Elizabeth d 23 Sept 1840 ae: 4y 1m 22d F:41

John W s/o J d 11 May 1852 Saco, Maine ae: 11m GSL

Mary Jane d/o Nicholas & Ann T d 8 Feb 1844 ae: 30y E:1

Nicholas b 1 Sept 1770 d 24 Aug 1861 E:1

Nicholas Jr s/o Nicholas & Ann T d 8 Mar 1842 ae: 20y. E:1

Pamelia d/o Henry & Elizabeth d 17 Aug 1849 ae: 16y 4m SBE F:41

Thomas S s/o Francis & Octavia d 8 May 1855 ae: 8d Stone on C:17 C:73

**EMORY,** William s/o William d 25 Feb 843 ae: 2w GSL

**ENGLISH,** Margaret d 11 Dec 1854 ae: 25y GSL

Mary Ellen d/o John d 12 May 1856 ae: 2y 5m GSL

William H s/o John d 17 Sept

**ENGLISH** (continued)
1857 ae: 10m GSL

**ENIS,** John s/o Manuel d 5 Sept 1852 ae: 1y 4m Catholic GSL

**ERSKINE,** Eunice Mrs d 12 Feb 1861 ae: 60y GSL

Betsy d 16 July 1857 ae: 57y GSL

**ESLER,** William s/o Joseph d 4 Aug 1880 ae: 2y GSL

**ESTERBROOK,** Horatio T s/o Horatio d 14 June 1850 ae: 1y GSL

James d 22 Sept 1849 ae: 40y Haggett tomb A:18

**ESTES,** Manuel H d 17 June 1868 ae: 26y GSL

**ETCHINGHAM,** Thomas F s/o Thomas & Adelia d 3 May 1856 ae: 14m SD J:216

**EUSTIS,** Willie H s/o L d 15 June 1869 ae: 2y 9m GSL

**EVANS,** George F s/o late Geroge C d 9 Oct 1847 ae: 23y GSL

Josephine P d/o Albert d 1 Sept 1857 ae: 9m GSL

William B s/o Daniel d 23 July 1849 ae: 14m GSL

**EVELETH,** Frank Edwin s/o Charles E & Sarah b 10 Sept 1876 d 7 July 1961 J:83

Sarah H w/o Charles E, d/o John W & Sarah Crowther b 28 Oct 1845 d 6 Apr 1932 J:83

**FABYAN,** Ezra C s/o John d 20 Apr 1865 ae: 26y. GSL

Julia w/o John d 14 May 1884 ae: 66y GSL

Julius d 8 Mar 1851 ae: 59y Haggett tomb A:18

Sarh H d/o Thomas d 24 Oct 1841 ae: 19m GSL

Silas d 10 July 1881 ae: 45y GSL

**FADEN,** Elizabeth wid/o William d 13 Apr 1855 ae: 67y Native of St Peters, Nova Scotia GSL

**FAGAN,** Charles s/o Thomas & Martha K d 18 Sept 1848 ae: 5y Catholic SD I:83

Harriet d/o Thomas & Martha K b 1831 d 1884 Catholic I:83

Isabella d/o William d 11 Sept

FAGAN (continued)
1880 ae: 3y Catholic GSL
John d 6 OCt 1856 ae: 31y Cath-
olic I:83
Julia d/o Thomas & Martin d 13
Feb 1842 ae: 4y Catholic SBE
I:83
Martha Knight w/o Thomas b
1803 d 1866 Catholic I:83
Thomas b 1780 d 1857 Catholic
I:83
FAHEY, Elizabeth d/o Martin P
d 16 Aug 1856 ae: 4y 2m 14d
Catholic GSL
Thomas s/o Peter & Ann d 30
Apr 1852 ae: 2y 7m Catholic
SD I:33
FAIRFIELD, Harriet R d/o Ed-
ward d 28 Aug 1852 ae: 13d
GSL
J Howard s/o Edward d 1 June
1852 ae: 5y GSL
Lucy d/o Edward d 30 May 1852
ae: 11y GSL
Mary E d/o Edward d 10 Sept
1852 ae: 17y GSL
FALBY, Charles d 19 Dec 1867
ae: 37y GSL
FARMER, Sarah Bridge no burial
record SD A:9
FARNHAM, Jessie H s/o George
H d 20 Apr 1874 ae: 2w GSL
Joseph D d 26 July 1854 ae: 40y
5m F:126
Lemuel R s/o Joseph D d 29
July 1854 ae: 4y SD F:126
Margaret wid/o Joseph D d 13
Oct 1898 ae: 90y 9m F:126
Ruth L d/o William d 17 June
1906 City Hospital NS J:232
Ellen E d/o George F d 31 OCt
1871 ae: 22y GSL
FARR, Alvah s/o George W d 16
May 1859 ae: 3y GSL
Martha w/o George W d 23 May
1859 South Paris, Maine ae:
37y GSL
Michael s/o Thomas d 22 Aug
1860 ae: 2w GSL
FARRA, Daniel s/o Samuel d 18
May 1860 ae: 18y SD G:35
Deborah H w/o Samuel d 10 Oct

FARRA (continued)
1853 ae: 47y G:35
Howard buried 2 June 1873 ae:
21y Drowned SD G:35
Mary d/o Samuel d 23 Nov 1844
ae: 4w SD G:35
Mary L Thoir d/o Samuel &
Deborah H d 20 Oct 1844 ae:
4w SB G:35
Samuel s/o Samuel & Deborah H
d 16 May 1860 ae: 18y G:35
Samuel d 25 May 1889 ae: 89y
1m SD G:35
FARRELL, Bridget d 12 Oct 1853
ae: 2d Catholic SD J:19
William d 21 Apr 1858 ae: 39y
Old Catholic Ground GSL
FARRINGTON, Amasa d 13 Nov
1846 ae: 79y Haggett tomb
A:18
Johanna d 20 May 1874 ae: 89y
GSL
FARROW, Wilber F s/o John P d
31 May 1860 ae: 1y 2m GSL
FARWELL, Absalom d 4 Mar
1854 ae: 71y Last name only
on granite Mmt niche for
daguerreotype empty J:254
Lydia P wid/o Absalom d 22 Nov
1855 ae: 60y Last name only
on granite Mmt J:254
FAUSBY, Fred C s/o George d 25
Sept 1862 ae: 4m GSL
FAVOR, Hazen C d 3 Nov 1846
ae: 32y H:12
Sarah A w/o Hazen C no burial
record SD H:12
Sarah B d/o Hazen C & Sarah A d
8 June 1851 ae: 13y H:12
FAY, Charles Edwin s/o Josiah &
Hannah no burial record SBE
G:74 (See Addendum)
FEENEY, Bartlett d 28 Dec 1854
ae: 55y Catholic GSL
Bridget w/o Daniel d 7 Sept 1854
ae: 40y Catholic Strangers'
Ground GSL
John s/o Matthew d 14 Feb 1855
ae: 3y Catholic GSL
Michael d 10 Oct 1854 ae: 22y
Catholic SBE L:13
Richard s/o Timothy d 25 Apr

FEENEY (continued)
1853 ae: 2y 6m Catholic Strangers' Ground GSL
FELLS, Harris s/o Joseph d 30 Sept 1856 ae: 5y 3m GSL
FELT, Mary W d/o Jesse d 26 Aug 1849 ae: 15m GSL
FENLEY, Grace L d/o William A d 19 May 1859 ae: 11m GSL
FENNEY, John d 3 Oct 1848 ae: 22y Catholic GSL
FERDINAND, Francis s/o Francis d 30 July 1846 ae: 8m GSL
FERGUSON, Matthew d 30 July 1851 ae: 23y Catholic GSL
FERNALD, inf d/o Samuel R & Laura L no burial record SBE F:35
Clara d/o Joseph C & Hope b 1842 d 1882 F:35
Ellen L d 2 Nov 1885 ae: 65y 6m GSL
Hope w/o Joseph C d 16 July 1864 ae: 89y F:35
James H s/o Samuel R & Laura L d 12 Sept 1840 ae: 2y 6m F:35
John M s/o James E d 23 Sept 1854 ae: 5m GSL
Joseph G s/o Samuel R & Laura L d 3 Mar 1849 ae: 79y F:35
L Ellen d/o Samuel R & Laura L d 24 Feb 1853 ae: 13y 4m SD F:35
Laura Little w/o Samuel no burial record SD F:35
Mad L d/o Samuel & Ellen d 10 Nov 1936 Boston, Massachusetts ae: 81y 6m 5d F:35
Samuel R b 14 Aug 1814 d 14 Oct 1859 F:35
FERRIS, Mary Shattuck w/o William H d 15 Oct 1857 ae: 38y GSL
FESSENDEN, Albert H s/o George & Marcia A d 19 July 1845 Boston, Massachusetts ae: 2y 1m G:12
Charlotte d/o George & Marcia A d 19 Sept 1850 ae: 10m G:12
Cragie d/o William & Nellie d ae: 3d no burial record; no

FESSENDEN (continued)
dates on stone G:12
Elizabeth w/o John d 11 Aug 1849 ae: 57y G:27
Emily S d/o Nathan & Mary P d 6 Oct 1853 ae: 5m GSL
Ezra T s/o George & Marcia A d 10 Oct 1843 ae: 5y G:12
Frances E d/o John & Elizabeth d ae: 10m no burial record; no dates on stone G:27
Frank H s/o John Jr & Thankful d 21 Apr 1854 ae: 19m SD G:27
George W d 5 Oct 1885 ae: 50y 11m Civ/War: 5th Reg Maine Inf Co I SD G:27
George W s/o George W d 27 Apr 1885 ae: 4y 10m SD G:27
Grace d/o William d 3 Apr 1869 ae: 3m GSL
John d 7 Aug 1849 ae: 65y War/1812: veteran G:27
John E s/o John d 4 Nov 1864 ae: 7y 8m G:27
Jonathan s/o Sylvanus D & Lucy d 28 Dec 1847 ae: 7y D:76
Louisa d/o John & Elizabeth d ae: 11y no burial record; no dates on stone G:27
Marcia A w/o George, d/o Capt William & Mercy Tobie d 17 Nov 1853 ae: 39y G:12
Rinaldo s/o Sylvanus D & Lucy d 7 Sept 1849 ae: 6y SD D:76
Sarah S A d 16 Aug 1851 D:76
Sylvanus D d 8 Nov 1853 ae: 40y SBE D:76
Sylvanus Rinaldo s/o Sylvanus D & Lucy d 7 Sept 1849 ae: 6y 6m D:76
Thomas E s/o Nathan & Mary P d 14 Dec 1841 ae: 7y GSL
FICKETT, inf d/o Henry & Lucy A no burial record SD C:27
Addie A d 15 Sept 1871 ae: 8w GSL
Asa d 28 Oct 1842 ae: 31y GSL
Benjamin d 5 Nov 1851 ae: 84y G:1
Eliza d/o Benjamin & Sarah d 8 Dec 1847 ae: 42y G:1

**FICKETT** (continued)

Frances d/o Asa d 14 Aug 1842 ae: 11m GSL

Henry d 21 Dec 1871 ae: 80y 4m 13d C:27

Lucy A w/o Henry d 8 July 1870 ae: 77y 9m C:27

Sarah w/o Benjamin d 3 June 1843 ae: 64y G:1

**FIELD**, Galen J d 12 Jan 1851 ae: 24y H:92

O E w/o Edwin d 19 Oct 1869 ae: 23y GSL

Olive d 27 Nov 1860 Danville, Maine ae: 54y 11m GSL

William s/o Moses d 7 Nov 1846 ae: 6m GSL

**FIELDING**, Charles S s/o Robert H d 21 Sept 1872 ae: 1y GSL

Emma A d/o Alfred S d 15 Aug 1876 ae: 2w GSL

Frederick s/o Caroline d 23 Oct 1872 ae: 3y GSL

Mary C w/o Robert H d 13 Sept 1907 ae: 56y SD J:255

Olive wid d 22 Dec 1847 ae: 70y GSL

**FIELDS**, Samuel C d 30 Oct 1844 ae: 23y GSL

Thursey E s/o Alonzo d 20 Apr 1849 GSL

**FILL**, John s/o Michael d 13 Sept 1857 ae: 6m Catholic GSL

**FILLMORE**, Jane B w/o Charles d 1 Apr 1858 ae: 40y GSL

John s/o Charles C d 2 Sept 1856 ae: 11y GSL

Ruth M d/o Charles C d 16 Oct 1856 ae: 1y GSL

**FINN**, John s/o Thomas d 3 Sept 1856 ae: 5m Strangers' Ground GSL

**FINNEY**, Timothy s/o Timothy d 4 Sept 1856 ae: 1y Strangers' Ground GSL

**FITZGERALD**, Edmond d 26 Mar 1855 ae: 28y Native of Yohel Parish, Co Cork, Ireland Catholic SD I:6

John d 16 Nov 1844 ae: 44y Catholic GSL

Margaret d 2 Sept 1856 Biddeford

**FITZGERALD** (continued)

Maine ae: 24y Old Catholic Ground GSL

Morris d 14 Feb 1842 ae: 38y Catholic GSL

Charlotte w/o James d 24 Dec 1851 ae: 40y Catholic GSL

James s/o James d 10 Dec 1847 ae: 2y Catholic GSL

**FITZPATRICK**, Edmund s/o John d 31 Aug 1854 ae: 5y GSL

Edwin d 24 Feb 1855 ae: 28y GSL

**FIVIN**, Michael d 16 Nov 1850 Westbrook, Maine ae: 26y GSL

**FLAGG**, Harriet C d/o John & Mary Ann d 11 July 1852 ae: 3y 6m SBE B:35

**FLAGGIN**, Samuel d 20 Feb 1850 ae: 22y Catholic GSL

**FLAHERTY**, inf c/o Matthew d 10 Apr 1854 ae: 2d Catholic GSL

Eunice d 29 Nov 1869 ae: 48y Catholic GSL

Hannah d 30 Mar 1858 ae: 21y Catholic GSL

James d/o Matthew d 16 Sept 1857 ae: 10m Catholic GSL

John s/o Michael d 17 June 1860 ae: 9m Catholic GSL

Margaret d/o Michael d 4 Apr 1856 ae: 16m Catholic Strangers' Ground GSL

Martin F s/o Patrick d 11 Sept 1853 ae: 1y Catholic GSL

Mary A d/o Patrick d 6 Nov 1852 ae: 1y 8m Catholic GSL

Wiliam s/o Michael d 5 May 1863 ae: 1y 9m Catholic GSL

Willie s/o Jeremiah d 19 Oct 1857 ae: 16d Catholic GSL

**FLANDERS**, Charlie s/o George & Mary N d 31 Dec 1874 ae: 5y 6m B:72

Mary N Saville w/o George d 26 Jan 1911 Boston, Massachusetts ae: 67y 7m 2d B:72

**FLANNAGAN**, inf c/o William d 30 Mar 1862 ae: 3m Catholic GSL

Elizabeth d/o Patrick d 22 July

47

FLANNAGAN (continued)
1856 ae: 4m Catholic GSL
James s/o Martin d 19 June 1856
ae: 2y 3m Catholic GSL
Joanna d 15 June 1851 ae: 12y
Catholic GSL
Margaret w/o James d 25 Sept
1850 ae: 60y Catholic GSL
Margaret d/o William d 13 Sept
1850 ae: 1y Catholic GSL
Maria d/o William d 19 Mar
1858 ae: 2m 13d Old Catholic
Ground GSL
Mary Ann d/o Jeremiah d 16 Sept
1851 ae: 19m Catholic GSL
Philip d 30 July 1847 ae: 10m
Catholic GSL
Philip s/o William d 3 Oct 1854
ae: 18m Catholic GSL
William s/o William d 16 Sept
1853 ae: 2y 8m Catholic GSL
William s/o William d 12 May
1859 ae: 3y Catholic GSL
FLEMMING, Elizabeth d 10 Jn
1879 ae: 62y GSL
Martin d 17 July 1855 ae: 23y
Strangers' Ground GSL
FLETCHER, Eugene s/o Rollin
C & Sarah B d 8 Apr 1844 ae:
4m SD F:1
Frank s/o Rollin C & Sarah B d
12 Dec 1843 ae: 2y SD F:1
Sarah B w/o Rollin C d 1 Mar
1845 ae: 29y SBE F:1
Sarah S d/o Rollin d 29 Aug 1850
ae: 8m SD F:1
FLEURY, John F s/o Michael d
11 Dec 1850 ae: 14d Catholic
GSL
FLOOD, Luther d 3 May 1855 ae:
64y GSL
FLOYD, Gardner s/o Joseph M no
burial record SD D:9
Hannah d/o Joseph M no burial
record SD D:9
Joseph M s/o Gardiner & Hannah
d 12 May 1863 ae: 5y 8m SBE
D:9
Josiah M s/o Gardiner d 12 May
1863 ae: 6y 8m SD D:9
Lizzie F w/o Joseph, d/o
Charles M Green d 22 Nov

FLOYD (continued)
1913 ae: 65y SD D:9
FLUTIN, James d 27 Dec 1849
ae: 35y Catholic GSL
FLYNN, Catherine d/o John d 11
May 1855 ae: 4y 7m Catholic
GSL
Louisa B d/o Philip d 6 Nov
1869 ae: 11m Catholic GSL
Mary d/o John d 24 Aug 1858 ae:
1y 8d Catholic GSL
Patrick d 31 Oct 1854 ae: 33y
Catholic GSL
Patrick s/o Patrick d 17 Oct
1855 ae: 9m Catholic GSL
FODEN, Ellen H w/o Thomas d 2
Oct 1868 ae: 34y SD F:103
Joseph H s/o Thomas d 15 Aug
1864 ae: 1y SD F:103
Thomas s/o Thomas & Ellen H d
18 Aug 1856 ae: 9m F:103
FOGG, Annette Augusta d/o
Simon & Hannah b 8 Aug 1835
d 19 July 1837 SSB C:26
Capt George W d 10 Mar 1855 ae
30y Lost at sea F:44
Harriet d 14 July 1842 ae: 19y
GSL
Harriet J d/o Orrin d 11 Apr 1857
ae: 2y 6m GSL
Harriet K w/o George W d 19
July 1906 ae: 78y 8m NS F:44
Capt Robert b 28 Mar 1822 d 7
Nov 1853 Curacao, West
Indies F:44
FOLEY, Ann w/o Peter d 8 Aug
1857 ae: 27y Catholic GSL
Ellen d/o Patrick d 18 Mar 1857
Gorham, Maine ae: 26y Cath-
olic GSL
John d 18 June 1850 ae: 19y
Catholic GSL
John s/o William d 7 Oct 1842
ae: 16m Catholic GSL
Julia w/o Patrick d 28 July 1854
ae: 49y Casualty of railroad
Catholic Strangers' Ground
GSL
Margaret w/o William d 16 Apr
1851 ae: 35y Catholic GSL
Martin d 17 July 1855 ae: 28y
Catholic Strangers' Ground

48

FOLEY (continued)
GSL
Mary d/o William d 14 Nov 1845
ae: 2y 3m Catholic GSL
Mary Ann d/o John d 7 Mar 1851
ae: 8m Catholic GSL
Michael d 23 July 1857 Island
Pond, Vermont ae: 25y Cath-
olic GSL
Michael d 16 Apr 1864 ae: 37y
Catholic GSL
Patrick d 30 Sept 1854 ae: 22y
Catholic GSL
Patrick s/o Michael d 15 Sept
1856 ae: 11d Catholic GSL
Peter A s/o John d 7 July 1857
ae: 18m Catholic GSL
Sarah d/o Bartlett d 16 Nov 1858
ae: 4m Catholic GSL
Thomas d 6 Apr 1850 South
Paris, Maine ae: 30y Catholic
GSL
Thomas s/o Thomas d 7 May
1858 ae: 2d Catholic GSL
FOLLANSBEE, Mary C d/o Ro-
bert d 27 Nov 1864 ae: 4y 11m
Wilson tomb D:33
FOLLETT, George W d 20 May
1860 ae: 45y SB J:272
Hiram d 7 Apr 1900 Philadelphia,
Pennsylvania ae: 65y SD H:47
Jane w/o James d 19 Sept 1852
ae: 28y GSL
FOLSOM, Ednah Ela wid/o
Thomas d 8 Apr 1851 ae: 75y
6m D:40
Louisa d/o Thomas H & Ednah b
1819 d 1841 SB D:40
Ruth Wyer b 30 May 1780 d 21
May 1854 E:1
FORD, Eunice wid/o Timothy d
23 Sept 1892 ae: 84y SD F:81
James F s/o Stephen d 27 May
1847 ae: 17y SD H:22
Patrick d 21 June 1848 ae: 37y
Death caused by fall of a tree
at Lewiston Falls, Maine
Catholic GSL
Stephen d 27 Dec 1848 ae: 55y
9m H:22
Timothy F d 10 Apr 1846 ae: 38y
SD F:81

FOREN, Ann M d/o James d 4
Mar 1846 ae: 5w Catholic SD
I:51
James d 28 Dec 1860 of lauda-
num ae: 50y. SD I:51
FORNAH, C E d/o J P d 20 Feb
1855 ae: 1y 6m Hilborn tomb
A:10
FORSAYTH, S F no burial record
SD B:29
Sarah wid/o Thomas d 20 May
1854 ae: 70y SD B:29
Thomas F d 21 Dec 1849 ae: 43y
SD B:29
FOSS, Abigail d 14 Aug 1884 ae:
87y GSL
David d 27 Sept 1899 ae: 75y 5m
26d Civ/War: 29th Reg Maine
Inf Co F SD J:136
Frances E d/o David & Mary d
27 Dec 1851 ae: 2y 6m SD
J:136
Freddie s/o Mosley d 13 Sept
1878 ae: 2m GSL
Mary A w/o David d 16 July 1898
ae: 75y SD J:136
Maud d/o Moses d 20 Aug 1880
ae: 8m GSL
William d 27 Oct 1854 ae: 55y
SD C:12
FOSTER, Andrew J s/o Andrew J
d 20 Jan 1863 ae: 15y GSL
Eliza w/o Ebenezer d 16 Oct
1853 ae: 44y GSL
Eugene E s/o Moses c d 26 Oct
1850 ae: 1y 11d J:51
Jackson s/o Jeremiah d 18 May
1854 ae: 19y GSL
Jeremiah B d 12 July 1866 ae:
71y 7m GSL
Nathan d 23 Mar 1857 ae: 39y
GSL
Rosina A d 20 Aug 1847 ae: 16m
Catholic GSL
Sarah w/o James d 2 Jan 1857
ae: 22y Hosack tomb A:17
Sarah H wid/o Jeremiah B d 13
Oct 1868 ae: 79y GSL
Timothy W s/o Jeremeiah B d 2
Sept 1850 ae: 27y GSL
FOUNTAIN, Anna d/o Joseph d 7
July 1863 ae: 6y GSL

FOWLER, Charles Shannon s/o R C S d 27 Oct 1856 ae: 4y 2m GSL
Josephine d/o R C S d 20 Sept 1856 ae: 20m GSL
FOX, Daniel Jr d 5 Sept 1863 ae: 46y 5m J:103
Flossie d/o Daniel W & E H b 4 Oct 1874 d 30 June 1876 SBE J:103
Mary wid/o John d 12 Feb 1853 ae: 55y GSL
Mary J d/o Thomas d 26 Dec 1850 ae: 1y Catholic GSL
Susan Whitney w/o Daniel d 11 July 1882 ae: 66y 8m J:103
FOYE, Edwin G s/o William H & J d 3 Mar 1853 ae: 2y 3m Foye tomb D:29
Henry d 25 Jan 1854 ae: 73y Foye tomb D:29
James Munroe d 12 June 1861 ae: 43y Foye tomb D:29
Julia A w/o William H d 31 Dec 1878 ae: 57y Foye tomb D:29
Mary L wid/o Henry d 10 Dec 1857 ae: 73y Foye tomb D:29
Monroe L B s/o William H d 3 Dec 1849 ae: 10m Foye tomb D:29
William H d 22 Apr 1878 ae: 63y Foye tomb D:29
FRANCIS, William H s/o Horatio d 22 Aug 1863 ae: 6m Trowbridge tomb Location unknown
FRANKLIN, Frederick b s/o Lt, Coast Survey d 27 Aug 1855 ae: 23y GSL
FRASIER, Jesse s/o John A d 11 Sept 1859 ae: 4y 4m GSL
FRATES, Almira A w/o Manuel d 15 Oct 1850 ae: 32y H:83
Franklin s/o Manuel & Almira d 17 Nov 1848 ae: 19m H:83
Mary w/o Antonio d 14 Dec 1838 ae: 81y GSL
William F s/o Manuel & Almira d 2 Sept 1903 ae: 52y 9m 23d SD H:83
William H s/o Manuel & Almira d 27 Nov 1848 ae: 7y 1m H:83

FRAZIER, John A d 27 May 1871 ae: 52y GSL
FREDERICKS, Elizabeth d/o John d 26 Sept 1856 ae: 6m GSL
John H s/o John d 20 Jan 1864 ae: 5y 5m GSL
FREEMAN, Ada L A inf d/o Col Hersey & Harriet d 29 June 1844 F:5
Alice d/o R T d 26 July 1854 ae: 3y GSL
Asenath w/o Ebenezer d 3 Apr 1852 ae: 48y GSL
Ella L R inf d/o Col Hersey & Harriet d 11 Feb 1850 F:5
Harriet N w/o Col Hersey d/o Samuel & Lydia D Bridge d 22 Apr 1857 ae: 37y 6m 21d F:5
Col Hersey d 5 July 1856 ae: 52y F:5
Jerry L s/o J R d 18 Jan 1859 ae: 6w GSL
Lydia A A d/o Col Hersey d 25 June 1844 ae: 15m SD F:5
FRENCH, Addie G d 14 Nov 1882 ae: 23y GSL
Angeline M w/o William d 15 Aug 1876 ae: 47y SD I:140
Charles H d 15 Apr 1911 ae: 64y Civ/War: Sgt 12th Reg Maine Inf Co G I:140
Charles M d 6 May 1886 ae: 39y SD D:20
Daniel s/o Daniel d 21 Jan 1844 ae: 8w GSL
Elizabeth d 11 Apr 1874 ae: 75y GSL
Franklin J s/o Joseph B d 15 July 1856 ae: 2m GSL
John A s/o William f d 7 Mar 1866 ae: 6m SD I:140
Joseph B d 22 June 1856 ae: 38y GSL
William d 2 Aug 1874 SD I:140
William s/o William F d 1 Sept 1866 ae: 10y SD I:140
William F Jr s/o William F d 10 Apr 1873 ae: 3y SD I:140
William M s/o William & Angeline d 17 Apr 1856 ae: 3y 24d I:140

50

FROST, Ella Frances d/o Charles d 1 Mar 1859 ae: 20m 18d Frost tomb D:31

Ellen M d 6 Dec 1883 Dover, New Hampshire ae: 61y Frost tomb D:31

Henrietta C d/o John T d 28 Feb 1850 ae: 3y Frost tomb D:31

John Lewis s/o Charles R d 23 July 1854 ae: 4m Frost tomb D:31

John T d 2 Feb 1851 ae: 36y Frost tomb D:31

FRY, Charles Edwin s/o Josiah & Hannah B d 15 May 1853 ae: 5m 8d SD G:73

Peter d 11 Apr 1857 ae: 40y GSL

FRYE, Benjamin d 9 Oct 1854 ae: 38y GSL

Charles E s/o Josiah d 15 May 1853 ae: 6m SD G:73

Daniel W d 22 Aug 1849 ae: 25y Stone "Erected by wife Mary Jane Frye." SB D:58

Hannah B w/o Josiah d 6 Oct 1859 ae: 36y SD G:73

Josiah d 11 May 1862 ae: 49y SD G:73

Josiah w s/o Josiah d 31 Oct 1856 ae: 1y 4m SD G:73

FULER, Susan w/o Isaiah d 5 Feb 1863 ae: 87y C:9

FULLER, Anna A d/o Benjamin d 12 Nov 1857 ae: 3y 10m GSL

Charles M s/o David B d 17 May 1869 ae: 8m GSL

George A d 10 May 1870 ae: 19y 4m SBE F:2

John d 18 Oct 1859 ae: 45y. Native of Bedford, England SBE F:2

Nancy d 18 June 1894 ae: 76y SD F:2

William Henry s/o John d 14 Aug 1854 ae: 4m SBE F:2

FULLERTON, Mary Ann w/o Capt James d 30 July 1853 ae: 30y GSL

Nathan W s/o James d 26 Apr 1849 ae: 3y GSL

Nathan Winslow s/o Capt James d 27 July 1853 Old Point Com-

FULLERTON (continued) fort, New York ae: 13m GSL

Patrick d 9 Dec 1854 GSL

FUNCE, Frances d 14 Nov 1843 ae: 41y Trowbridge tomb Location unknown

FURLONG, Abba d/o Thomas & Esther d 11 Sept 1851 ae: 8m SBE I:64

Abby w/o Thomas d 15 Mar 1849 ae: 21y GSL

Charles s/o Charles d 8 Apr 1864 ae: 10w GSL

Ellen Mira d/o Benjamin & Eliza d 23 Nov 189 ae: 10m SBE I:64

Esther A w/o Uriah H b 14 Jan 1805 d 12 Feb 1866 F:67

Henry F s/o F H & E S d 24 Nov 1852 ae: 16m F:67

Laura E d/o Charles H d 23 Feb 1867 ae: 4m GSL

Uriah H b 22 Nov 1807 d 15 Oct 1865 F:67

Winship R s/o John d 13 Apr 1851 ae: 2m GSL

GABETIS, Catherine d/o Thomas d 20 Feb 1853 ae: 21y GSL

GALLAGHER, Barney d 8 Dec 1857 ae: 4y 1m Catholic Strangers' Ground GSL

Margaret J d/o Peter d 29 Sept 1864 ae: 8m 16d Catholic GSL

GALLISON, Dennis d 28 July 1853 ae: 29y Catholic GSL

GAMMON, inf c/o E D d 25 July 1859 ae: 6d GSL

Alice d/o Albert d 18 Feb 1882 ae: 5d GSL

Charles N s/o Wiliam & Phebe d 14 Sept 1850 ae: 1y 5d SBE I:144

Charles T s/o Samuel d 9 May 1865 ae: 8m GSL

Constantine s/o Charles d 21 June 1857 ae: 6m GSL

Ephraim d 18 Apr 1872 ae: 63y SD J:69

Ephraim s/o Samuel H d 12 July 1862 ae: 14m GSL

Ezekiel D b 1807 d 1888 D:27

Hannah w/o Ezekiel D d 5 Dec 1844 ae: 36y D:27

51

GAMMON (continued)

Hannah J w/o Ezekiel D b 1815 d 1892 D:27

Helen Eliza d/o Ezekiel D & Hannah d 16 May 1835 ae: 4y 4m D:27

Howard s/o Charles d 29 Aug 1855 ae: 1y GSL

Julia M w/o Charles G d 28 June 1857 ae: 25y 3m GSL

Martha A d 22 Apr 1886 Everett MA ae: 62y 5m GSL

Mary A d/o Samuel H d 22 Oct 1880 ae: 21y GSL

Mary Ann d 25 Aug 1881 ae: 70y GSL

Mary Eliza d/o Ephraim & Mary d 2 Oct 1835 ae: 1y SBE J:69

Thaddeus P s/o Ezekiel & Hannah d 30 Aug 1848 ae: 19m D:27

Willard D s/o Daniel P & Martha A d 19 May 1851 ae: 8d SBE C:77

William E s/o Ephraim & Mary d 15 Mar 1851 ae: 10y SBE J:69

William H s/o John & Phebe d 8 Aug 1856 ae: 2y SBE I:144

William H s/o William d 18 Aug 1850 ae: 6y GSL

GARDNER, Abigail w/o John d 12 May 1860 ae: 53y SD C:84

Delia S w/o Joseph b d 15 Sept 1865 ae: 53y Tenbroeck tomb A:11

Helen W w/o Charles C d 20 Oct 1877 ae: 37y Tenbroeck tomb A:11

Henrietta M d/o John & Abigail d 7 Sept 1849 ae: 3y C:84

Henry M s/o John & Abigail d 15 Aug 1844 ae: 8y C:84

John B s/o Franklin A d 16 Apr 1868 ae: 8d GSL

GARDINER, Charles T s/o John a d 10 Sept 1886 ae: 5y 4m GSL

Elmer A s/o John A d 7 Dec 1889 ae: 6w GSL

William W d 12 Mar 1869 ae: 72y 11m GSL

GARLAND, Benjamin H s/o Daniel & Hannah d 22 Nov 1849 ae: 2y 6m SBE C:87

Daniel d 12 Dec 1882 ae: 72y C:87

Franklin H s/o Daniel d 13 Aug 1872 ae: 13y SD C:87

Hannah w/o Daniel d 7 Mar 1877 ae: 65y 6m C:87

James d 6 Oct 1879 ae: 88y 6m H:20

James Jr s/o James & Mary Ann d 15 Sept 1851 ae: 20y H:20

John E s/o William d 3 Sept 1856 ae: 2y SD F:3

John W s/o Daniel d 15 Feb 1870 ae: 38y SD C:87

Mary Ann d/o Daniel & Hannah d 22 June 1836 ae: 11m SBE C:87

Mary Ann w/o James d 11 Dec 1847 ae: 49y 10m SBE H:20

Mary W d/o Daniel & Hannah d 9 Feb 1887 ae: 46y 10m C:87

Sarah E d/o Daniel & Hannah d 31 May 1854 ae: 16y 8m SBE C:87

William N s/o William d 31 Aug 1857 ae: 6m 11d Buried James Ross Lot GSL

William M b 1835 d 1914 Civ/War: 30th Reg Maine Inf Co I B:39

GARRISON, Martha E d/o Robert D d 19 Aug 1849 ae: 9m GSL

GARVIN, Benjamin d 22 Oct 1854 ae: 57y GSL

Mary Jane d/o John d 28 Oct 1854 ae: 11m GSL

Mary M d/o Benjamin d 30 May 1866 ae: 38y GSL

GARY, Lorietta M d/o Daniel d 8 Mar 1850 ae: 7m GSL

GASH, Benjamin d 30 Sept 1857 ae: 36y Catholic GSL

John d 9 Mar 1853 ae: 22y Catholic GSL

GATELY, John d 3 Sept 1857 ae: 38y GSL

GATES, Charles S s/o Frederick J d 29 June 1846 ae: 10m SD G:89

**GATES** (continued)

Fredeick J d 16 Nov 1846 ae: 31y G:89

Isabella A wid/o Frederick J d 11 Jan 1892 ae: 72y 6m SD G:89

**GAY**, Benjamin s/o James d 12 Aug 1844 ae: 16m GSL

Edward s/o John H d 21 Feb 1865 ae: 3m 14d GSL

Eliza w/o James d 6 Oct 1859 ae: 55y Haggett tomb A:18

Martha Ann b 1808 d 1890 C:93

Mary C w/o Anthony d 9 Jan 1884 ae: 75y GSL

Mary Jane d/o James & Mary d 4 May 1898 ae: 83y 10m 24d C:93

Mary McLean wid/o James b 1771 d 1849 C:93

**GEEHAN**, Ann d/o Patrick d 23 Mar 1849 ae: 3y Catholic GSL

Elizabeth d/o Patrick d 25 Mar 1849 ae: 5y Catholic GSL

James s/o Patrick d 27 Mar 1849 ae: 1y Catholic GSL

**GEROULD**, Harriet M Proctor w/o Edward P d 17 May 1899 Saugus, Massachusetts ae: 54y G:84

**GERRETY**, Catherine d/o Andrew d 18 Aug 1850 ae: 20d Catholic GSL

**GERRISH**, Albert s/o Matthew & Phebe d 15 Sept 1841 ae: 23y SBE F:87

Franklin S s/o Leonard H & Mary E b 1851 d 1853 H:55

Isabella d/o Matthew & Phebe d 26 Oct 1837 ae: 2y SBE F:87

J S s/o Leonard d 15 July 1855 ae: 11m SD H:55

Joseph M d 29 Apr 1853 ae: 70y Gerrish tomb Location unknown

Leonard H b 1825 d 27 Mar 1854 H:55

Mary E Staples w/o Leonard b 1827 d 1893 H:55

Matthew s/o Matthew & Phebe d 2 Aug 1843 ae: 37y F:87

**GETCHELL**, Mary F d/o William W d 25 Nov 1858 ae: 1y GSL

**GIBBINS**, Hannah d/o Patrick d 4 Sept 1855 ae: 2y 4m Catholic GSL

John s/o Patrick d 8 Oct 1851 ae: 15m Catholic GSL

**GIBSON**, Catherine d/o David d 30 July 1856 ae: 18m GSL

Lilla F d/o Robert d 25 Apr 1872 ae: 11m GSL

Mary d/o David d 7 Nov 1865 ae: 14y 3m GSL

**GIDDINGS**, Ambrose d 14 June 1890 ae: 67y 9m SB B:52

Catherine A w/o Ambrose d 3 Apr 1891 ae: 70y 3m SB B:52

Elizabeth P w/o Jacob d 14 Apr 1848 ae: 55y SB B:52

Elizabeth H d/o Ambrose & Catherine A b 10 Oct 1850 d 31 May 1913 B:52

Jacob d 11 Mar 1873 ae: 81y SB B:52

Karl Ambrose s/o Ambrose & Catherine A d 27 Nov 1900 Seattle, Washington ae: 14y SB B:52

William F b 21 Aug 1855 d 7 Oct 1894 B:52

**GIFFORD**, Ellen d/o John d 20 May 1856 ae: 18m GSL

John d 6 Jan 1857 ae: 45y GSL

**GILBERT**, Etson d 11 May 1881 ae: 67y GSL

**GILDAY**, John s/o John d 19 Dec 1847 ae: 17m Catholic GSL

John s/o John d 26 May 1849 ae: 14m Catholic GSL

**GILL**, Henry s/o John d 4 May 1853 ae: 6m Catholic GSL

Joseph s/o Thomas d 21 Aug 1850 ae: 14m Catholic GSL

Margaret w/o John d 6 Nov 1854 ae: 27y GSL

Sarah w/o Ellis d 9 Apr 1852 ae: 47y Catholic GSL

William d 27 Sept 1856 ae: 17y Catholic GSL

**GILLAM**, Mary w/o William d 30 June 1843 ae: 67y Native of

**GILLAM** (continued)
Harpswell, Maine G:2

**GILLESPIE**, Julia w/o Edward H d 25 Oct 1857 ae: 45y GSL

William no dates on stone; no burial record Civ/War: 1st Lt 2nd Reg Maine Cav J:20

**GILLIGAN**, Ann d/o Michael d 6 Apr 1857 ae: 10y Catholic GSL

Catherine d/o Michael d 22 July 1856 ae: 20m Catholic GSL

John s/o John d 31 Oct 1851 ae: 5m Catholic GSL

**GILLIS**, Sophia M d/o Hugh d 25 Sept 1872 ae: 43y SD C:49

**GILMAN**, Isaiah s/o Isaiah d 11 Dec 1850 ae: 4y GSL

**GILMARTIN**, Edward s/o William d 2 July 1857 ae: 1y Catholic GSL

**GILPATRICK**, George E s/o Martin d 10 June 1862 ae: 3m Catholic GSL

**GILSON**, Calvin B d 19 June 1853 ae: 28y I:95

Calvin B d 29 Sept 1853 ae: 54y SD I:95

Lucinda A w/o Calvin B d 19 Feb 1844 ae: 16y I:95

Luther G s/o Calvin B & Lucinda A d 20 Nov 1862 ae: 17y 6m Stone on J:67 I:95

Rosanna T w/o James H, d/o George & Mary Strout d 17 Dec 1927 ae: 82y I:95

Rose A s/o James d 20 May 1870 ae: 2y 11m GSL

**GINNEY**, John s/o Patrick d 27 Sept 1850 ae: 1y Catholic GSL

Timothy s/o Patrick d 29 Sept 1856 Biddeford, Maine ae: 18m Catholic GSL

**GITHANLY**, Mary d/o Patrick d 29 Aug 1856 ae: 1y Old Catholic Ground GSL

**GLACKIN**, James d 17 June 1858 ae: 61y Catholic GSL

**GLAZIER**, Joseph d 19 Apr 1869 ae: 87y GSL

Phebe w/o Joseph d 17 July 1872 ae: 81y GSL

**GLEASON**, Anna d/o Thomas d 6

**GLEASON** (continued)
June 1856 ae: 3y GSL

Jeremiah s/o Thomas d 2 Feb 1855 ae: 5d GSL

John d 17 Jan 1852 ae: 19y GSL

William s/o Thomas d 9 May 1864 ae: 2d GSL

**GLINES**, Lewellyn s/o Francis d 26 Nov 1866 ae: 3w GSL

**GLOCKIN**, Ellen d/o Dennis d 20 Apr 1854 ae: 3y 4m Catholic GSL

Mary Ann d/o Dennis d 21 Apr 1854 ae: 1y 7m Catholic GSL

**GLYNN**, Hugh s/o John d 26 Sept 1858 ae: 2y Catholic GSL

**GODSOE**, James E d 25 Oct 1882 ae: 64y SD H:39

Rhoda E wid/o James E d 20 Apr 1889 ae: 69y 5m SD H:39

**GOLDING**, James d 11 Apr 1847 ae: 40y Catholic GSL

**GOODALL**, Joseph R d 3 Apr 1841 ae: 22y Strangers' Ground GSL

**GOODE**, Hugh s/o William d 8 Mar 1857 ae: 8m GSL

Margaret d/o William d 7 Jan 1850 ae: 1y Catholic GSL

**GOODHALE**, Joseph R d 2 Aug 1841 ae: 21y Native of Monson, Maine F:29

**GOODING**, Alphonzo Gilkey s/o James & Amanda d 30 Oct 1861 ae: 10m SBE F;76

Evelina A d/o James & Amanda d 20 Nov 1853 ae: 5y 3m F:76

Henry s/o John d 10 Aug 1852 ae: 4y GSL

**GOODWIN**, Esther d/o John d 14 Oct 1853 ae: 6m GSL

**GOOLD**, Abner Jr b 1812 d 1858 C:2

Ann d/o James G d 13 Sept 1844 ae: 5m GSL

Hannah d/o Abner d 21 Sept 1846 ae: 18y SD C:2

Lucy A Green w/o Abner Jr b 1813 d 1860 C:2

Thomas d 26 July 1849 ae: 17y Catholic GSL

GORDON, Capt Burt C d 5 June 1876 ae: 52y Drowned SD I:145

Burty s/o Capt Burt & Lydia d 9 Sept 1857 ae: 1y 6m SBE I:145

Geneva d/o James d 13 Aug 1869 ae: 4m GSL

Harriet w/o William d 12 Nov 1873 ae: 77y GSL

Mary B w/o Nathaniel d 22 Aug 1874 ae: 76y H:59

Mary C w/o Joseph C d 28 dec 1864 South Weymouth, Massachusetts ae: 30y GSL

Nathaniel b 24 Nov 1799 d 1849 SB H:59

GORHAM, Mary Abby d/o Joseph B d 18 May 1855 ae: 13m GSL

GORMLEY, Andrew s/o Patrick d 3 Nov 1857 ae: 2y 7m Catholic GSL

Bridget Ann w/o Patrick d 11 Jan 1858 ae: 33y Catholic GSL

John s/o William d 8 Sept 1856 ae: 10m Old Catholic Ground GSL

Mary Ann d/o James d 2 Jan 1855 ae: 3y Old Catholic Ground GSL

William s/o William d 13 Aug 1858 ae: 17m Old Catholic Ground GSL

GORTREE, Michael d 19 May 1853 Marine Hospital ae: 40y Catholic GSL

GOSS, Eli d 19 July 1888 ae: 73y Hilborn tomb A:10

Sarah w/o Eli d 30 June 1863 ae: 44y Hilborn tomb A:10

GOULD, Abner d 13 July 1863 ae: 74y GSL

Alice d/o Thomas d 4 May 1856 ae: 6m 12d GSL

Charlotte S d 12 Dec 1848 ae: 48y GSL

Elizabeth w/o Abner d 27 Mar 1855 ae: 63y GSL

Elizabeth T d/o Russell & Mary A b 31 Mar 1863 d 12 Nov 1912 H:47

Emeline G w/o Thomas d 27 Sept 1861 ae: 26y GSL

GOULD (continued)

Emma C d/o Russell & Mary Ann d 29 Jan 1945 ae: 71y 1m 12d NS H:47

Florence M d/o Russell & Mary d 13 May 1958 ae? 83y 11m 22d H:47

Frederick G s/o Abner d 18 Nov 1842 ae: 2m GSL

Hiram s/o Russell & Mary d 16 Feb 1854 ae: 2m 7d H:47

Josiah s/o Josiah G & Martha d 28 Dec 1868 ae: 33y Civ/War: 10th Reg Maine Inf Co E F:68

Josiah G d 19 Oct 1875 ae: 66y F:68

Louisa A d/o Russell d 28 Jan 1874 ae: 1y SD H:47

Martha w/o Josiah G d 29 Jan 1892 ae: 85y F:68

Mary d/o William d 27 July 1859 ae: 3y 6m GSL

Mary A Follett w/o Russell b Jan 1832 d Mar 1908 H:47

Mary V d/o James P d 12 Nov 1847 ae: 17m GSL

Rosanna d/o James d 16 Sept 1843 ae: 8m Catholic GSL

Russell s/o Abner d 11 Apr 1905 ae: 74y 6m 27d H:47

Samuel Carter s/o Russell & Mary A b 11 Apr 1857 d 19 Apr 1925 H:47

Sarah d 29 Jan 1844 ae: 50y GSL

William s/o John d 19 Feb 1844 ae: 15d GSL

William s/o Russell d 13 Apr 1856 ae: 9m GSL

William F s/o Russell d 17 Nov 1866 ae: 1y 9m SD H:47

GRACE, Franklin s/o Samuel d 2 Aug 1849 ae: 8m GSL

Hannah wid/o James d 11 Aug 1855 ae: 85y GSL

GRAFFAM, Adeline A w/o Jedediah d 21 May 1870 ae: 52y GSL

Augustus L s/o John W & Lucy d 8 Feb 1931 Camden, New Jersey ae: 52y 11d NS F:129

Charles F s/o Jedediah d 8 Mar 1857 ae: 1y GSL

GRAFFAM (continued)
Harry W s/o John W & Lucy A b
1883 d 1885 F:129
John W s/o Clement P & Eliz-
abeth d 24 Apr 1925 ae: 74y
F:129
Lucy A w/o John W b 1853 d
1887 F:129
Mary d/o Phineas d 9 Oct 1842
ae: 7m GSL
Mary J w/o Phineas d 24 May
1844 ae: 27y GSL
Walter L s/o John W & Lucy A
b 1873 d 1879 F:129
Winifred d/o John d 10 Jan 1885
ae: 2y SD F:129
GRAFTON, Mary J d/o S & T d 7
Nov 1843 ae: 2y 4m F:136
GRAHAM, Dr Asa d 1 Feb 1857
ae: 59y 6m H:26
Charles C C Mason s/o Dr Asa &
Nancy M d 28 Feb 1844 ae: 7m
H:26
Eliza Ann d/o Dr Asa & Nancy M
d 2 July 1847 ae: 4m H:26
Nancy M w/o Dr Asa d 5 Oct
1859 ae: 56y H:26
GRAIN, Mary A d/o John d 6 Sept
1856 ae: 9m Strangers' Ground
GSL
GRANT, Augustus B s/o Nath-
aniel d 16 May 1859 ae: 2y
GSL
Frances S w/o Nathaniel S d 28
June 1865 ae: 40y GSL
GRAVES, inf d/o William W d 4
Apr 1855 ae: 2d GSL
Alpheus M b 1843 d 1926 Civ
War: 19th Reg Maine Inf Co K
G:66
Edwin Willis s/o Alpheus M &
Henrietta J d 3 Apr 1908 Bos-
ton, Massachusetts ae: 31y
11m 22d G:66
Eliza W B w/o William W d 6
Feb 1889 ae: 70y 10m SD C:59
Hattie Eliza d/o William W d 3
Oct 1862 ae: 5y 6m SD C:59
Henrietta Jordan w/o Alpheus M,
d/o Seth & Elizabeth Jordan d
14 May 1932 ae: 86y 10m G:66
Lottie Howard d/o William W d

GRAVES (continued)
6 Sept 1861 ae: 8y SD G:59
Mary Chandler d/o William W d
12 Apr 1854 ae: 3y 2m SD
G:59
Mary E d/o Sylvester d 9 Sept
1849 ae: 2m GSL
Mary E w/o Sylvester d 19 July
1849 ae: 20y GSL
Maria Louisa d/o William W d
21 Apr 1849 ae: 3y Buried at
the foot of Mrs Burbank's
grave SD G:59
Sarah Ann w/o Horace P d 21
Feb 1853 MS ae: 24y C:59
Sidney Louis s/o Alpheus M &
Henrietta J d 24 July 1889 ae:
15y 1m SBE G:66
William W d 2 Jan 1903 ae: 85y
SD C:59
GRAY, Bridget d 26 Oct 1886
Cambridgeport, Massachusetts
ae: 51y GSL
Ebenezer F d 16 Feb 1846 ae:
30y H:3
Maxola J d/o Ebenezer F d 25
Aug 1866 ae: 11m SD H:3
Sarah A wid/o Ebenezer F d 7
Feb 1879 ae: 65y H:3
Susan E w/o William d 12 Jan
1899 ae: 70y 19m Ingraham
tomb A:16
William d 16 Mar 1893 ae: 69y
Ingraham tomb A:16
GREELY, Ann G wid/o Eleazer
d/o William Vaughan d 29 Oct
1851 ae: 72y E:1
Charles H s/o Eleazer & Ann d
14 May 1858 ae: 46y SBE E:1
Eleazer d 12 Dec 1835 ae: 64y
E:1
Myra Adams Smith w/o William
b 20 Sept 1812 d 1 Jan 1905
Arlington, Massachusetts E:1
William E d 24 Nov 1858 ae: 52y
E:1
GREEN, Abner G d 5 Feb 1879
ae: 68y 6m Civ/War: US Navy
I:62
Annie C w/o Wyer d 5 Nov 1868
ae: 25y 6m SBE D:45
Catherine S d/o Capt William &

**GREEN** (continued)

Hannah R d 15 Apr 1843 ae: 20y Two infant children in same grave F:123

Charles M s/o Capt William & Hannah R d 22 Aug 1876 ae: 60y F:123

Charles M s/o John d 29 Jan 1865 ae: 66y 9m SD G:9

Charles S s/o Stephen P d 22 Aug 1857 ae: 5m 18d GSL

Eben W s/o Charles H & Elizabeth d 29 Mar 1850 ae: 2y 2m G:9

Elizabeth w/o Charles M d 5 Aug 1847 ae: 34y G:9

Eunice E d/o Abner & Eunice L d 2 Mar 1849 ae: 11y SBE I:62

Eunice L w/o Abner G d 18 May 1890 ae: 78y SB I:62

George H b 20 Sept 1838 d 31 Dec 1898 C:38

Hannah R w/o Capt William d 16 Jan 1866 ae: 70y 5m SBE F:123

Hannah S d 12 June 1899 Otisfield, Maine ae: 65y 10m SD C:6

Henry d 17 Dec 1883 ae: 68y 8m Civ/War: 10th Reg Maine Inf Co B B:34

Henry H s/o Stephen P d 1 Sept 1857 ae: 6m GSL

Ida d/o George d 13 Aug 1855 ae: 8m GSL

John d 22 Feb 1853 ae: 79y F:69

John M s/o Wiliam & Margaret d 21 Jan 1880 ae: 15y 11m 23d A:3

Lucy d/o Abraham Daniel d 1 Nov 1843 ae: 9y GSL

Margaret w/o Samuel d 4 Mar 1858 ae: 52y SBE A:3

Martha D w/o Charles M d 16 Apr 1864 ae: 43y SD F:123

Mary d 24 Dec 1853 ae: 26y Native of Clifden, Co Galway, Ireland Catholic SD J:172

Mary wid/o John d 14 Jan 1857 ae: 81y F:69

Mary Paine d/o Edward d 11 Dec 1844 ae: 1y 8m GSL

**GREEN** (continued)

Nelly d 24 Aug 1863 ae: 1y 8m A:3

Samuel s/o William d 13 Apr 1862 ae: 2y SBE A:3

Samuel Jr s/o Samuel d 20 Nov 1856 ae: 17y 6m SD A:3

Sarah B d/o Charles M d 17 Nov 1856 ae: 14y GSL

Sarah B w/o Henry d 19 Jan 1892 B:34

Sarah C w/o Charles d 2 Jan 1896 ae: 80y 9m 22d SD B:48

Sarah E d/o Henry & Sarah B d 15 Oct 1868 ae: 28y SBE B:34

Stephen P d 19 Sept 1859 Alexandria, Virginia ae: 27y GSL

Walter s/o George d 24 July 1855 ae: 6m GSL

William s/o Samuel d 8 Jan 1865 ae: 37y 8m Strangers' Ground SBE A:3

William H s/o Abner & Eunice L d ae: 16y no burial record SBE I:62

William H s/o William & Margaret McM d 9 Sept 1933 ae: 78y A:3

Zylpha T w/o George H b 17 Oct 1833 no burial record SBE C:38

**GREENE,** Emma Ellen d/o A L d 8 Sept 1861 ae: 2y GSL

John d 10 Feb 1858 ae: 63y Hosack tomb A:17

Margaret w/o Samuel d 4 Mar 1858 ae: 52y GSL

Mary no burial record Catholic SBE J:175

**GREENOUGH,** Henry H s/o James d 18 Aug 1861 ae: 3m GSL

**GREGG,** Elisa d/o L D d 6 May 1848 ae: 1d GSL

**GREY,** Francis O s/o Samuel A d 29 Oct 1846 ae: 7m GSL

**GRIER,** John F s/o John d 31 Aug 1858 ae: 5m GSL

**GRIFFIN,** inf c/o Richard d 6 May 1858 ae: 9m GSL

Alfred S d 24 Feb 1855 ae: 27y Casualty of railroad SD I:92

GRIFFIN (continued)

Andrew s/o Michael d 6 Sept 1854 ae: 6y Catholic Strangers' Ground GSL

Bridget d/o Patrick d 16 Aug 1863 ae: 7d Catholic GSL

Charles H s/o Caleb d 14 Sept 1857 ae: 16m GSL

Cornelius s/o Dennis d 27 Aug 1849 ae: 6m Catholic GSL

Daniel s/o Eben d 22 July 1855 ae: 7w GSL

Eliza A d 8 Feb 1884 ae: 74y SD J:240

Ella S d/o Agustus F & H L b 29 Sept 1874 d 17 Dec 1884 SD F:15

Ellen w/o Hugh d 29 Apr 1854 ae: 40y Catholic Strangers' Ground GSL

Ellen d/o Patrick d 11 Feb 1852 ae: 3d Catholic GSL

Ellen A d/o Jeremiah d 24 Sept 1855 ae: 3y 6m GSL

Emma E s/o Caleb d 1 Jan 1875 ae: 6y Dyer tomb A:15

Frances Ellen d/o William & Eliza Ann d 22 Feb 1861 ae: 18y 9m J:240

Freeman s/o J F & E A d 16 Feb 1884 ae: 6y 4m SBE F:126

Georgianna d/o A S & C F d 26 Feb 1852 ae: 6m SBE I:92

Georgianna V w/o William d 14 May 1867 ae: 27y GSL

Hannah M d 7 Oct 1902 ae: 81y 4m SD J:9

James s/o Patrick d 9 July 1853 ae: 9m Catholic GSL

James s/o Patrick d 5 Jan 1858 ae: 11m 4d Catholic GSL

James H d 7 Apr 1889 Boston, Massachusetts ae: 57y GSL

Jeremiah b 4 May 1802 d 4 Oct 1879 SD F:15

John s/o Timothy d 9 Oct 1849 Saco, Maine ae: 6y GSL

Margaret d/o Michael d 21 Nov 1854 ae: 3y Catholic Strangers' Ground GSL

Martha E w/o Horace d 25 Apr 1855 ae: 33y GSL

GRIFFIN (continued)

Mary A d/o Patrick d 15 Sept 1856 ae: 15y Catholic GSL

Patrick s/o Patrick d 12 Mar 1867 ae: 9d Catholic GSL

Sarah w/o Jeremiah d 16 Mar 1898 ae: 85y 9m 20d SD F:15

GROGAN, James d 30 Aug 1854 ae: 51y Old Catholic Ground GSL

GROVER, Abel d 28 Apr 1880 ae: 72y SD F:86

Augustus s/o Abel d 18 Sept 1842 ae: 10w SD F:86

Georgianna T d/o Abel & Harriet A d 27 Nov 1861 ae: 18y Stone on F:8 F:86

Harriet A wid/o Abel d 29 Oct 1882 ae: 77y F:86

Samuel A s/o Abel & Harriet d 18 Sept 1841 ae: 7y SBE F:86

GUIHER, John s/o William d 6 Jan 1869 ae: 2m GSL

GUILFORD, Abigail w/o Elijah d 14 Sept 1859 ae: 68y G:63

Arminta Atkins w/o John d 19 Aug 1905 ae: 85y 9m 19d G:61

Bertha G d/o Elijah d 26 Aug 1863 ae: 11m SD I:118

Charles E s/o John & Arminta A d 27 May 1863 ae: 8m 20d G:61

Charlotte d/o Joseph d 27 Dec 1847 ae: 6m SD F:6

Edwin A s/o John & Arminta d 24 Sept 1859 ae: 9m SD G:61

Elijah d 14 June 1854 ae: 63y Casualty of railroad G:63

Ella R d/o John & Arminta d 23 Jan 1904 ae: 51y 11m 7d G:61

Eva inf d/o Elijah & Dorcas d 17 June 1855 SBE I:118

Frances M d/o Joseph d 17 Sept 1848 ae: 4m SD F:6

Frank E s/o John & Arminta b 10 May 1854 d 7 Feb 1883 New York City G:61

Hannah E d/o William d 27 June 1841 ae: 4y 11m GSL

Helen A d/o John & Arminta d 30 May 1847 ae: 18m 8d SBE G:61

58

**GUILFORD** (continued)
James s/o Joseph d 15 Apr 1852 ae: 8m SD F:6
John d 13 Sept 1866 ae: 46y 10m G:61
John M s/o John & Arminta d 19 May 1870 ae: 20y 7m G:61
Joseph d 23 June 1892 Greely Hosp ae: 59y SD F:6
Winfield S s/o Joseph d 12 Aug 1871 ae: 4m SD F:6
**GULD**, John d 31 Mar 1866 ae: 64y GSL
**GULLIVER**, Elizabeth d/o John d 24 May 1859 ae: 3y GSL
Ellen d/o John d 28 Oct 1854 ae: 2y GSL
Frank s/o Frank d 17 May 1857 ae: 5m 15d GSL
Joseph s/o Patrick d 15 OCt 1853 ae: 17m Catholic GSL
Margaret d/o John d 30 Mar 1857 ae: 8m GSL
Mary E d/o Charles d 10 Sept 1850 ae: 10y GSL
**GURNEY**, Anna L d/o George N d 28 Oct 1875 ae: 31y GSL
Emily Jane d/o Lemuel d 15 Sept 1859 ae: 15y Lewis tomb Location unknown
Frank d 7 Oct 1871 ae: 5w GSL
James s/o James & Judith d 1 Sept 1854 ae: 52y Catholic J:182
John s/o James & Judith d 23 Feb 1851 ae: 48y Catholic J:182
John s/o James & Judith d 1 Aug 1846 ae: 11m Catholic SD J:182
Mary S d 10 Sept 1871 ae: 30y 7m GSL
Robert s/o James & Judith no burial record Catholic SBE J:182
Thomas s/o James & Judith d 22 Feb 1854 ae: 18y Catholic J:182
**HACKETT**, Bridget d/o John d 9 Aug 1856 ae: 15m GSL
**HADEN**, Sarah d/o Morris O d 4 Dec 1853 ae: 9m GSL

**HAGEN**, Alvina P w/o Patrick d 29 Oct 1851 ae: 26y Catholic H:29
George O s/o James O d 15 Aug 1872 ae: 2w GSL
Mary d 20 Oct 1857 ae: 72y Strangers' Ground GSL
**HAGGERTY**, Eliza d 25 Apr 1858 ae: 23y Native of St Andrews, New Brunswick GSL
George E Morrell s/o Samuel F d 28 June 1846 ae: 6y 4m Daniels tomb A:19
Isabella d/o late John d 10 Feb 1848 ae: 9y Catholic SD I:44
James s/o late John d 21 Sept 1850 ae: 20y Catholic SD I:44
John d 23 Feb 1847 ae: 56y Native of Cumber Parish, Co Londonderry, Ireland Catholic SB I:44
John s/o late John d 17 June 1850 ae: 22y Catholic SD I:44
Mark s/o Roger d 2 Mar 1849 ae: 3y Catholic GSL
Susan wid/o John d 7 Dec 1854 ae: 60y Catholic SD I:44
**HAGGETT**, Benjamin S s/o Samuel d 28 Feb 1867 ae: 42y Haggett tomb A:18
Caroline M wid/o Samuel d 14 Mar 1865 ae: 64y Haggett tomb A:18
Eliza J F w/o William d 14 Jan 1868 ae: 41y Haggett tomb A:18
Samuel d 19 Oct 1861 ae: 70y Haggett tomb A:18
**HAGUE**, Albert s/o Israel & Martha d 13 May 1854 ae: 1y 8m Catholic SBE J:44
Elizabeth d/o Israel & Martha d 16 Oct 1850 ae: 11m Catholic SBE J:44
Israel s/o Israel & Martha d 6 June 1870 ae: 45y 5m Catholic J:44
Mary G d/o Israel d 6 Feb 1868 ae: 1y 4m Catholic SD J:44
Matilda A d/o Israel d 19 Aug 1865 ae: 3y Catholic SD J:44
**HALEY**, Charlotte A w/o Samuel

**HALEY** (continued)

W d 14 Mar 1887 ae: 73y SD B:10

Matthew d 24 Aug 1850 ae: 20y Catholic Strangers' Ground GSL

Rosilla N adopted d/o Samuel W & Charlotte A d 26 Apr 1849 ae: 21y 9m SD B:10

Samuel W d 25 Oct 1855 ae: 46y 10m B:10

**HALL**, Anna w/o Samuel M d 1 Oct 1865 ae: 34y SD G:92

Arthur F d 7 Aug 1950 Somerville, Massachusetts ae: 71y 9m 30d Safford-Hall tomb A:20

Charles H s/o Samuel M & Anna d 20 May 1853 ae: 1y 3d SD G:92

Clara d 24 June 1864 ae: 73y GSL

Daniel Jr d 16 May 1852 ae: 34y 9m J:131

Eleanor Neal d/o William Edward & Jane L d 15 Dec 1868 ae: 94y SD C:44

Franklin M s/o Samuel H d 22 July 1854 ae: 5w 2d GSL

Hamilton d 22 Dec 1860 ae: 27y Sawyer tomb A:14

Hannah E w/o Daniel Jr d 18 Apr 1855 ae: 31y SBE J:131

James Arthur d 16 June 1917 Cambridge, Massachusetts ae: 66y 11m 28d Safford-Hall tomb A:20

James L w/o William Edward d 13 Dec 1859 ae: 24y SD C:44

Joel b 4 Dec 1775 d 27 May 1851 C:44

John R d 5 Oct 1853 ae: 28y 4m J:131

Martha wid/o John d 28 Mar 1857 ae: 82y A:4

Mary wid/o Joel d 6 Dec 1874 ae: 88y 8m SD C:44

Mildred L d 12 July 1895 ae: 8m 14d Safford-Hall tomb A:20

Moses d 6 Nov 1848 Westbrook, Maine ae: 64y GSL

Sarah w/o Joel d 23 Oct 1806 ae:

**HALL** (continued)

23y SBE C:44

Sarah B w/o James A d/o Theophilus & Emeline Barbarick d 1 Jan 1930 Cambridge, Massachusetts ae: 73y 19d Safford-Hall tomb A:20

Sarah S w/o Stephen D d 6 Apr 1875 ae: 55y Safford-Hall tomb A:20

Stephen d 7 Dec 1874 ae: 48y Civ/War: 4th Reg Maine Inf; 19th Reg Maine Inf Safford-Hall tomb A:20

Stephen D s/o Samuel d 12 Nov 1905 ae: 82y 4m 21d Safford-Hall tomb A:20

Walter D s/o Charles C d 8 Apr 1861 ae: 11m Hilborn tomb A:10

Walter S d 22 Aug 1956 ae: 74y Safford-Hall tomb A:20

William Edward s/o Joel d 29 Jan 1865 ae: 41y SD C:44

**HALLAGAN**, Bridget d 10 Nov 1852 ae: 80y Catholic GSL

**HALLIN**, Denis s/o Patrick d 2 Mar 1854 ae: 4y Catholic GSL

**HAM**, James s/o James d 21 Sept 1843 ae: 2d Catholic GSL

**HAMBLEN**, Elizabeth B d/o Daniel d 17 Sept 1863 ae: 6y GSL

**HAMBLIN**, Sarah L d 28 Dec 1880 ae: 90y Hossack tomb A:17

**HAMILTON**, Amelia no burial record SBE B:44

Capt Charles B d 4 July 1848 ae: 42y B:44

Charles E s/o Charles B & Mary L Barbour d 7 June 1866 ae: 21y Civ/War: 1st Reg Maine Cav Co K; wounded Gettysurg, Pennsylvania B:44

Frances Ellen d/o Charles B & Mary L d 5 Oct 1848 ae: 11y B:44

Francis Edward s/o Charles B & Mary L d 11 Apr 1849 ae: 11m B:44

Mary L wid/o Charles B b 14

HAMILTON (continued)
Feb 1814 d 10 Oct 1895 B:44
Wiliam P d 23 July 1875 ae: 32y
Civ/War: 10th Reg Maine Inf
Co C; wounded Winchester,
Virginia & Cedar Mt, Virginia
SD B:44
HAMLEN, John s/o J d 22 Sept
1857 ae: 9m GSL
HAMLIN, Isabell d/o Daniel d 20
Aug 1859 ae: 10m GSL
HAMMOND, Arthur S s/o Wil-
liam d 14 Mar 1857 ae: 4m
Foye tomb D:29
Hattie T d/o Charles N d 29 July
1890 ae: 6m D:25
HANEY, David s/o Peter d 19
Aug 1854 ae: 5y GSL
HANLEY, Mary d 23 Dec 1854
ae: 25y Strangers' Ground GSL
Sarah d/o James d 23 Aug 1857
ae: 3y Strangers' Ground GSL
HANNA, Mary w/o Peter d 23
Aug 1855 Yarmouth, Maine ae:
34y GSL
Willam P s/o Capt Peter d 30
Dec 1848 ae: 17y Trowbridge
tomb Location unknown
HANNAFORD, John d 24 July
1857 ae: 27y Old Catholic
Ground GSL
Margaret J d/o Robert & Rosan-
nah d 25 Feb 1856 ae: 16y 9m
I:76
Mary w/o Samuel d 5 OCt 1863
GSL
Rosannah w/o Robert d 12 Sept
1865 ae: 57y 8m SD I:76
HANNAGAN, Ann d/o Thomas d
3 Sept 1853 ae: 2y 2m Old
Catholic Ground GSL
Margaret d/o Michael d 9 July
1856 ae: 9m Catholic GSL
Mary A d/o Thomas d 3 Oct 1857
ae: 1y 7m Catholic GSL
Patrick d 14 May 1852 ae: 50y
Catholic GSL
HANRY, William s/o William d
2 Oct 1853 ae: 1m GSL
HANSCOM, Emma P d/o Stephen
d 21 Feb 1847 ae: 15m SD E:1
HANSON, Clarence d 9 Aug 1874

HANSON (continued)
ae: 6m GSL
Eliza P w/o Amos d 8 Nov 1900
ae: 76y 6m 21d SD I:95
Nancy d 23 July 1864 ae: 81y 7m
McCobb tomb D:32
Olive J b 22 Oct 1851 d 1 Nov
1879 H:42
HARDENBROOK, Annie B d/o
Nelson d 22 Nov 1938 Everett,
Massachusetts ae: 66y 15d SD
I:67
Charles W d 4 Nov 1864 Confed-
erate prison Salisbury, South
Carolina ae: 21y Civ/War: 1st
Reg Maine Cav Co C GSL
Charles W s/o Nelson & Harriet
d 15 July 1909 ae: 57y Civ/
War: 5th Reg Maine Inf Co A
SBE I:67
Hannah w/o Nathaniel d 11 May
1857 ae: 52y GSL
Harriet w/o Nelson d 12 May
1857 ae: 52y I:67
Isabella w/o Nelson b 1827 d
1878 I:67
Nelson b 1806 d 1874 I:67
HARDY, Mary G d/o John d 15
Sept 1864 ae: 70y GSL
HARFORD, ---- s/o Ezra d
Cuba; buried 8 Sept 1854 GSL
HARGADON, Mark s/o Roger d
31 Oct 1852 ae: 11m Catholic
GSL
HARKIN, Margaret d/o William d
26 Mar 1852 ae: 1y Catholic
GSL
HARLOW, Charles d 7 Feb 1853
Louisville, Kentucky ae: 36y
Daniels tomb A:19
Louisa H w/o William d 15 May
1851 ae: 28y GSL
Mary L d/o William d 21 Sept
1849 ae: 1y Daniels tomb
A:19
HARMON, A A d 6 Dec 1889 ae:
61y D:2
Aaron F d 14 Feb 1866 ae: 42y
SD J:100
Abigail d 27 June 1858 ae: 37y
GSL
Adaline K w/o John H d 12 Apr

**HARMON** (continued)

1855 ae: 29y Native Boston, Massachusetts GSL

Albert F s/o Edward d 21 Jan 1864 ae: 22y GSL

Charles s/o Ebenezer d 13 May 1842 ae: 15y GSL

Charles s/o Ebenezer d 23 Feb 1843 ae: 15m GSL

Charlotte C d/o Sylvanus d 19 Aug 1865 ae: 1y 18d GSL

Ebenezer d 29 Feb 1864 ae: 61y GSL

Edward d 28 Feb 1858 ae: 47y SD D:2

Franklin s/o John d 1 Sept 1858 ae: 5m 16d GSL

Frances A d/o Benjamin d 2 Apr 1844 ae: 10y GSL

Fred F s/o A F & M E d 12 OCt 1857 ae: 2y 6m J:100

George S s/o Sylvanus d 9 Nov 1857 ae: 15y GSL

James O d 29 May 1869 ae: 40y GSL

John s/o John d 5 Aug 1863 ae: 6m 11d GSL

John F s/o John d 13 Aug 1866 ae: 4w GSL

John F s/o John Jr d 10 Sept 1859 Buxton, Maine ae: 6w GSL

Mehitable w/o Edward d 11 Jan 1854 ae: 39y D:2

Sarah d 20 Aug 1865 ae: 80y GSL

Sarah J Mann w/o Reuben d 10 Jan 1892 ae: 61y 10m I:95

Shannon F s/o Sylvanus d 15 Sept 1855 ae: 1y 1m GSL

**H A R P E R**, Catherine C d/o Thomas d 10 Oct 1857 ae: 27y GSL

Lucy E d/o Charles A S d 6 Aug 1864 ae: 5y 4m GSL

Olive A d/o Charles A S d 23 Mar 1865 ae: 4y GSL

Samuel d 20 Oct 1857 ae: 84y Buried beside wife GSL

Sarah Mary Ann d/o Charles & Nancy d 11 Aug 1856 ae: 2y 9m 6d SBE F:102

Sarah N d/o Charles E S d 11

**HARPER** (continued)

Aug 1856 ae: 2y 9m 6d GSL

**HARRIGAN**, James s/o Patrick d 8 Aug 1852 ae: 3y 6m Catholic GSL

Patrick d 16 Sept 1856 ae: 45y Catholic GSL

William d 7 Jan 1850 ae: 13m Catholic GSL

**HARRINGTON**, Abby M d/o John d 8 Oct 1857 ae: 14m Catholic GSL

Gerry d 4 May 1848 ae: 22y Catholic GSL

Margaret d/o John d 19 May 1851 ae: 5m Catholic GSL

Mary d 6 July 1849 ae: 45y Catholic GSL

Mary d/o John d 8 Apr 1852 ae: 4w Catholic GSL

Octavia A w/o Ervin P d 27 Oct 1892 ae: 35y 7m SD J:236

Sarmiah d/o Daniel d 28 Sept 1850 ae: 1y Catholic GSL

**HARRIS**, Elizabeth d/o William d 1 Apr 1894 Greely Hospital ae: 89y 3m SD C:60

Emma d/o James d 25 Apr 1854 ae: 4w GSL

Franklin s/o Joseph d 10 Sept 1856 ae: 19m GSL

Jenny T twin d/o James d 13 Sept 1857 ae: 9m GSL

L Elizabeth w/o James d 13 Nov 1851 ae: 29y GSL

Louisa B twin d/o James d 13 Sept 1857 ae: 9m GSL

Lucy Ellen d/o James d 6 Aug 1865 ae: 10y GSL

Margaret K d/o William d 22 Feb 1855 ae: 40y Dyer tomb A:15

Mary d 25 July 1862 ae: 78y 4m B:39

Sarah wid/o John d 6 Apr 1855 ae: 70y Native of Windsor, Nova Scotia GSL

Stephen d 2 Nov 1880 ae: 65y SD B:39

William s/o James d 25 Nov 1845 ae: 9m GSL

William s/o James L d 4 Sept

HARRIS (continued)
1849 ae: 18m GSL
HARRISON, Daniel d 12 May
1842 ae: 29y Smith & Brown
tomb Location unknown
Nancy A d/o Samuel & Jane d 11
Oct 1858 ae: 22y SD I:74
HART, Lydia J w/o William G,
d/o Capt Joseph & Elizabeth B
Manchester d 20 Oct 1861 ae:
18y 7m 24d SD J:109
Maria L d/o William & Sarah d
19 Nov 1857 ae: 27y 3m SD
B:56
Sarah w/o Wiliam d 16 May 1866
ae: 73y SD B:56
Capt William d 3 May 1860 ae:
67y SD B:56
HARTFORD, Catherine w/o Solo-
mon d 11 Sept 1858 ae: 17y
GSL
Mary C d/o Simon d 30 Sept 1858
ae: 3w GSL
HARTSHORN, Abby M d/o Jesse
M d 12 Apr 1856 ae: 5y 11m
GSL
Albert s/o Jesse M d 3 July 1859
ae: 22y 2m GSL
William T d 4 Oct 1848 ae: 65y
GSL
HARTSHORNE, Vesta H w/o
Washington d 17 Nov 1861 ae:
61y SBE I:117
HARVEY, Charles W s/o Charles
H d 30 Sept 1851 GSL
HASELTINE, Alice Louisa d/o
James E d 23 Dec 1862 ae: 2y
21d GSL
HASKELL, Alexander P d 29 Oct
1884 ae: 75y GSL
Almira d/o Moses H d 17 Sept
1873 ae: 17y SD F:19
Amos T s/o Alfred d 22 May
1851 ae: 4m 6d GSL
Augusta w/o Alford d 16 May
1842 ae: 23d GSL
Gideon d 13 Jan 1853 ae: 77y
F:19
Henry A s/o Alfred d 7 Jan 1856
ae: 1y Daniels tomb A:19
Henry H s/o Moses d 26 Dec
1865 Albany, New York ae: 4y

HASKELL (continued)
5m SD F:19
John M d 18 May 1873 ae: 71y
SD F:19
Lovina d/o M H & Margaret d 5
Mar 1850 ae: 5y 2m SBE F:19
Lovina A T d/o Moses M d 15
May 1876 ae: 22y SD F:19
Margaret d 5 Mar 1890 Greely
Hospital ae: 70y SD F:19
Mark s/o Joseph d 10 Apr 1854
ae: 21y SD F:19
Moses M s/o Gideon d 14 Dec
1866 ae: 59y SD F:19
HASKINS, Charles Stewart Daveis
s/o Rev David G & Mary C b
13 Dec 1843 d 19 Apr 1844 E:2
Rev David Greene d 11 May 1896
Cambridge, Massachusetts ae:
78y 10m SBE E:2
Mary Cogswell Daveis w/o Rev
David Greene b 27 Mar 1820 d
1 May 1909 Cambridge, Mas-
sachusetts E:2
HASSON, Behick s/o Behick d 18
Nov 1846 ae: 18m Catholic
GSL
HASTON, Susan d/o J d 24 Nov
1841 ae: 15y GSL
HASTY, Ann E d/o Capt John &
Mary C b 1846 d 1850 G:50
David d 17 Mar 1838 at sea ae:
27y H:73
Eleanora d/o Capt John & Mary
C d 26 Aug 1915 ae: 72y 6m
25d G:50
Eunice A d/o Nathaniel d 21 Aug
1865 ae: 33y 10m SD H:73
Capt John b 1805 d 1889 G:50
Mary wid/o Nathaniel d 30 Oct
1855 ae: 79y SD H:73
Mary C w/o Capt John b 1810 d
1878 G:50
Nathaniel d 22 Jan 1834 ae: 56y
H:73
Nathaniel d 23 Apr 1850 ae: 40y
SD H:73
Sarah d/o Nathaniel d 5 Feb 1855
ae: 48y SD H:73
Sarah J w/o Nathaniel d 25 Dec
1864 ae: 33y SD H:73
HATCH, Ann Mrs d 24 Feb 1861

HATCH (continued)
ae: 80y GSL
Caleb C d 12 Sept 1868 ae: 67y
B:45
Charles W s/o David & Sarah E
d 28 Aug 1848 ae: 1y SD B:46
Clara E d/o T S d 29 Oct 1861
ae: 15m GSL
David S d 16 Nov 1866 ae: 53y
GSL
Elizabeth J d/o Caleb C & Jane
B d 12 July 1816 ae: 16y SBE
B:45
Harry T d 15 Aug 1876 South
Boston, Massachusetts ae: 4m
GSL
Isabella d/o Walter d 10 May
186 ae: 9y GSL
Jane B w/o Caleb C d 1 Oct 1869
ae: 81y 11m B:45
John H s/o David S d 8 Jan 1870
ae: 30y Civ/War: 1st Reg
Maine Inf Co C SD B:45
Joseph H s/o William d 31 Dec
1849 ae: 21y GSL
Lemuel D s/o Anthony d 3 Oct
1850 ae: 5y GSL
Lucinda w/o Charles d 19 Mar
1866 ae: 40y GSL
Lucy M d/o David & Sarah E d 3
Sept 1847 ae: 3y SD B:46
Marietta d/o Walter d 20 Oct
1850 ae: 8y Catholic GSL
Sarah E w/o David S, d/o Joseph
A & Elizabeth Crossman d 9
Mar 1916 ae: 99y 11m 9d
"Real dau – D A R." B:46
HAWES, Louisa Jane d/o
Charles S & Louisa H d 31 Aug
1847 ae: 4m D:56
HAWKES, Ann w/o Dana H d 3
Feb 1846 ae: 47y F:140
Benjamin F s/o Solomon d 4 Mar
1842 ae: 13m SD F:65
Ellen R d/o Solomon & Martha R
d 6 Aug 1838 ae: 5m F:65
Franklin s/o Solomon & Martha
R d 18 June 1845 ae: 7m F:65
Franklin s/o Solomon & Martha
R d 2 Mar 1842 ae: 13m F:65
Hamilton s/o Solomon & Martha
R d 16 Feb 1900 ae: 60y F:65

HAWKES (continued)
James Edwin s/o Solomon &
Martha R d 12 July 1843 ae:
17m F:65
Maria F d/o Solomon & Martha R
d 24 Jan 1848 ae: 7m F:65
Martha R w/o Solomon d 4 Sept
1892 ae: 82y F:65
Sarah E d/o Daniel d 20 Aug
1853 ae: 2-1/2m GSL
Solomon d 22 Jan 1850 ae: 49y
F:65
HAY, Dr Charles b 1768 d 1831
I:117
Chloe Smith wid/o Dr Charles b
1774 d 1854 I:117
Josephine w/o Henry M d/o Cal-
vin Gilson d 1 May 1850 ae:
26y I:117
Sophia A d 12 Aug 1853 ae: 37y
GSL
HAYES, Ellen d/o John d 9 Sept
1854 ae: 1y 8m Strangers'
Ground GSL
Fanny w/o George d 14 Aug 1851
ae: 72y GSL
James E s/o James d 13 Apr
1862 ae: 6m GSL
Jane d/o Daniel d 9 June 1855
ae: 3w GSL
Jeremiah d 21 Apr 1851 ae: 38y
Murdered GSL
John s/o James d 10 Sept 1850
ae: 1y Catholic GSL
John s/o Hatthias d 4 Sept 1858
ae: 9d Buried Daniel Hayes lot
GSL
John s/o Timothy d 3 June 1858
ae: 2m GSL
Martin s/o Daniel d 1 Sept 1858
ae: 10m 10d GSL
Mary d/o Timothy d 16 Oct 1855
ae: 4m GSL
Patrick d 14 Apr 1848 ae: 22y
Old Catholic Ground GSL
HAZELTON, Amanda D w/o
Samuel b 1804 d 1882 F:76
George inf s/o Samuel & Amanda
no dates on stone; no burial
record F:76
John s/o Samuel & Amanda d 20
Oct 1841 ae: 3m F:76

HAZELTON (continued)
Mary E wid/o Daniel d 3 Sept 1852 ae: 50y GSL
Samuel d 6 May 1856 ae: 62y 9m SD F:76
Sarah d 13 Mar 1847 ae: 78y GSL
HEALD, Edwin s/o Dr J H & Irene d 26 Jan 1848 ae: 18m G:94
Eugene s/o Dr J H & Irene d 13 Nov 1846 ae: 17m G:94
Irene w/o Dr J H d 8 Oct 1846 ae: 24y G:94
HEALY, Julia d 16 May 1858 ae: 75y GSL
HEARNEY, Elizabeth d 6 Apr 1853 ae: 22y Strangers' Ground GSL
HEARD, Charles s/o Capt Luke W & Mary B d ae 20y 11m no burial record F:84
Edmund C s/o Capt Luke W & Mary B d ae 14y 5m no burial record F:84
Sgt Geroge H s/o Capt Luke W & Mary B d 9 Aug 1862 ae: 23y Killed in action - Cedar Mt, Virginia Civ/War F:84
Hannah A d/o Capt Luke W & Mary B d 4 July 1836 Bangor, Maine ae: 1y F:84
Jonas A s/o Capt Luke W & Mary B d 14 Apr 1842 Bangor, Maine ae: 10m F:84
Joshua F s/o Capt Luke W & Mary B d 21 Sept 1841 Bangor, Maine ae: 2y 7m F:84
Capt Luke W b 13 June 1808 d 17 Feb 1866 F:84
Mary B wid/o Capt Luke W b 7 Feb 1806 d 25 Jan 1891 F:84
William d 17 Feb 1866 ae: 57y 8m GSL
Ens William L s/o Capt Luke W & Mary B d 27 Apr 1864 ae: 30y "He was lost aboard the gunboat *Covington*, on the Red River, near Alexandria, Louisiana." F:84
HEDGE, Sarah wid d 16 Dec 1852 ae: 90y GSL

HEDMAN, Charles b 1793 Stockholm, Sweden d 23 July 1856 G:11
Eleanor C d/o Charles & Sarah d 11 Apr 1859 ae: 23y G:11
Martha F d/o Charles & Sarah d 14 Jan 1855 ae: 21y SB G:11
Mary B d/o Charles & Sarah d 25 May 1853 ae: 24y G:11
Sarah w/o Charles d 23 Mar 1865 ae: 68y G:11
HEFFONAN, Stephen s/o Richard d 9 Aug 1843 ae: 3m Old Catholic Ground GSL
Stephen s/o Stephen d 23 Sept 1842 ae: 3y Catholic GSL
HEFFORD, Thomas s/o Davis d 6 July 1855 ae: 18y GSL
HEMINGWAY, Harry Baker s/o C H & I S B b 1880 d 1884 J:108
HENDERSON, Joseph Lincoln s/o R S d 8 Aug 1862 ae: 8m 8d GSL
Margaret w/o John d 13 Dec 1857 ae: 32y 2m GSL
HENDLEY, John d 20 Jan 1836 ae: 68y F:4
HENIGAN, Mary E d/o Richard d 29 Sept 1856 ae: 11y GSL
HENLON, Patrick d 18 Sept 1854 ae: 27y Catholic GSL
Patrick s/o Patrick d 24 Sept 1855 ae: 11m Catholic GSL
HENNESSY, ---- c/o Francis d 6 June 1853 ae: 3y Old Catholic Ground GSL
Ellen d/o Patrick d 7 May 1854 ae: 2y Catholic GSL
Mary Eliza d 18 May 1855 ae: 2y Catholic GSL
HENRY, James E s/o John d 9 Oct 1853 ae: 2y 1m 10d GSL
Leroy E s/o Charles d 23 Aug 1866 ae: 23y GSL
Lyndon R inf s/o Ernest & Mabel d 25 Jan 1897 J:101
HERBERT, Bridget w/o Thomas d 10 Apr 1855 ae: 55y Old Catholic Ground GSL
Joanna d/o John d 2 Sept 1852 ae: 9m GSL

**HERBERT** (continued)
Margaret H d/o William d 22
Sept 1857 ae: 1y GSL
Patrick d 25 Oct 1850 ae: 21y
Catholic GSL
Susan d/o William d 13 Aug
1854 ae: 2y GSL
**HERN**, Patrick s/o John d 7 July
1859 ae: 3y 3m Catholic GSL
**HERNAGE**, William d 8 Feb
1852 ae: 45y Catholic GSL
**HERSEY**, Elizabeth P d/o T C d
17 Oct 1849 ae: 18m Smith &
Brown tomb Location unknown
Nancy d 14 Nov 1856 ae: 60y
GSL
**HICKEY**, Henry d 18 Jan 1858 ae:
38y Catholic GSL
Isabella d/o Henry d 23 Oct 1852
ae: 10m Catholic GSL
William s/o William d 18 July
1852 ae: 16m Catholic GSL
**HIGGINS**, Elizabeth B w/o
Simeon d 17 Jan 1878 ae: 79y
SD F:41
Francis d 10 Dec 1852 ae: 63y
Catholic GSL
George M s/o Capt d 15 June
1856 ae: 12y 9m GSL
Helen Maria d/o John d 19 Mar
1852 SD I:103
Lavina d/o John d 17 Feb 1866
ae: 10m GSL
Patrick d 12 Oct 1849 ae: 41y
Catholic GSL
Simeon 2nd d 4 Aug 1853 ae: 55y
SBE F:41
Stephen s/o Amos d 1 Mar 1873
ae: 40y GSL
**HILAND**, John s/o late Patrick d
10 Feb 1858 ae: 4y GSL
Mary d/o Thomas d 7 Aug 1854
ae: 6w GSL
Michael s/o Thomas d 30 Oct
1858 ae: 3y 1m GSL
**HILBORN**, Arthur G s/o Gilbert E
d 27 Dec 1886 ae: 7y 1m Hil-
born tomb A:10
Betsy w/o Seth d 27 Aug 1865
ae: 73y Hilborn tomb A:10
Edward s/o Gilbert d 30 Aug
1860 ae: 8m 13d Hilborn tomb

**HILBORN** (continued)
A:10
Elizabeth d/o Philip d 23 Apr
1855 ae: 1y 9m GSL
Erastus d 11 July 1858 ae: 45y
10m Hilborn tomb A:10
Mary H d 11 May 1889 ae: 75y
Hilborn tomb A:10
Seth d 6 June 1878 ae: 89y Hil-
born tomb A:10
**HILL**, Charles buried 20 May
1851 ae: 52y Drowned in Mar
1851 GSL
Ellen M d/o Stinson d 12 May
1856 ae: 22y Hosack tomb
A:17
Horatio d 12 Mar 1867 ae: 51y
5m Daniels tomb A:19
Josephine d/o Joseph d 27 June
1850 ae: 1y Jordan tomb D:28
Mary E d/o Joseph d 26 Nov
1849 ae: 2y Jordan tomb D:28
**HILLER**, Benjamin F b 1843 d
1865 Lost at sea C:88
Charles s/o George E d 13 Aug
1861 ae: 3m GSL
Edward d 27 Mar 1873 ae: 74y
3m C:88
Emily J d/o George E & Chris-
tiana M d 31 Oct 1849 ae: 9m
SD I:163
Henry C s/o Edward d 15 Mar
1862 ae: 3y 11m SD C:88
James R d 1 Mar 1903 ae: 66y
11m 14d Civ/War: 25th Reg
Maine Inf Co H C:88
Jane d/o Edward d 3 Oct 1856
ae: 3m GSL
Phebe J d/o Edward d 25 Oct
1856 ae: 3m GSL
Sally w/o Edward d 12 May 1874
ae: 70y 3m SD C:88
**HILLOND**, Mary d 26 Jan 1853
ae: 30y Catholic GSL
**HILTON**, Mary d/o John & Abi-
gail d 17 July 1840 ae: 4y F:26
**HINDS**, Janes E d/o Jane E d 24
Nov 1851 ae: 5y 11m GSL
Mary d/o Thomas d 3 Oct 1854
ae: 4m GSL
Michael s/o Patrick d 22 Nov
1854 ae: 6m Strangers' Ground

HINDS (continued)
GSL
Patrick d 2 Sept 1854 ae: 28y
Strangers' Ground GSL
HINMAN, Ellen d/o Franklin d 3
Oct 1864 ae: 4y GSL
HITCHENS, George C d 3 Aug
1889 ae: 39y GSL
HOBBS, Mary F d/o Joshua d
Providence, Rhode Island bur-
ied 24 Nov 1854 ae: 19y GSL
Oren d 2 Dec 1874 ae: 63y SD
G:12
Sarah A w/o Oren & wid Hazen C
d 26 Dec 1857 ae: 37y SD
G:12
HODGDON, Allen s/o Charles W
d 26 Sept 1851 ae: 1y 22d GSL
Charles W d 30 Sept 1873 ae:
10m GSL
Lucy Belle d/o G M & Georgia d
10 OCt 1887 ae: 4y 7m GSL
Oliver F s/o G M & Georgia d 10
Oct 1887 ae: 2y 5m GSL
HODGESON, Ada May d/o E W &
M S d 10 Aug 1863 ae: 6m
G:71
Mary S wid/o Edwin W d 16 Sept
1930 Boston, Massachusetts
ae: 89y 4m 20d G:71
HODGKINS, Elizabeth M w/o
William B, d/o Charles H &
Greta E Carruthers b 12 Apr
1859 d 31 Jan 1940 Gorham,
Maine SBE D:72
Nathaniel d 27 Nov 1865 ae: 58y
GSL
HOGAN, Alvina w/o Patrick d 29
Oct 1851 ae: 26y GSL
Ellen d/o John d 20 Oct 1843 ae:
7m Catholic GL
John s/o Patrick d 1 Oct 1842
ae: 4y Catholic GSL
Michael s/o Michael d 24 Feb
1852 ae: 2y 2m Catholic GSL
HOLBROOK, Edwin s/o I &
Rachel d 15 Apr 1855 ae: 4y
C:38
Elizabeth wid/o Samuel b 8 July
1790 d 8 Oct 1863 B:7
Rachel d 20 Oct 1856 ae: 47y
C:38

HOLDEN, Helen d/o Robert &
Mary d 23 Aug 1887 ae: 9m
GSL
Melvin A d 11 Apr 1854 ae: 14y
Cummings tomb A:13
HOLLAND, Mary A d/o Patrick d
8 Oct 1852 ae: 2m Catholic
GSL
Mary W d/o Charles H d 8 Sept
1861 ae: 6m GSL
HOLLY, Matthew d 24 Dec 1865
ae: 23y GSL
HOLMES, Ann b w/o Eleazer Jr
d 12 Nov 1857 ae: 49y H:88
Charles F s/o Daniel O d 8 May
1873 ae: 16y Hosack tomb
A:17
Eleazer d 28 Oct 1849 ae: 73y SB
H:88
Eleazer Jr b 1807 d 1882 H:88
Francis d 17 Sept 1894 ae: 72y
8m SD H:88
Lydia S d/o Eleazer Jr b 31 Jan
1812 d 22 Dec 1885 H:88
Phebe d 22 Dec 1852 ae: 72y
GSL
Ruth W d/o Eleazer Jr b 3 Aug
1806 d 23 Dec 1875 Boston,
Massachusetts H:88
Ruth Waterman w/o Eleazer d 30
June 1851 ae: 70y H:88
Sarah A w/o Eleazer Jr d 17 June
1909 ae: 93y 5m H:88
HOLT, Lottie d 13 May 1871 ae:
17d SD G:28
Nehemiah d 3 July 1844 ae: 44y
G:28
Sally b 31 Jan 1795 d 22 Mar
1861 G:28
HONYON, Oener s/o Thomas d
31 Jan 1849 ae: 4y Catholic
GSL
HOOPER, inf c/o Robert d 26
July 1856 ae: 8m GSL
Henry Abbott s/o J A & H L b 6
Dec 1844 d 8 Sept 1846 SD
B:61
Mary d/o James d 2 Apr 1855 ae:
6y SD B:61
Samuel Robinson no burial record
SD B:61
HORR, Almira B w/o John H d 12

HORR (continued)
Apr 1894 ae: 66y GSL
Calvin C s/o Calvin d 1 Sept 1849 ae: 4w GSL
Cora Ellen d/o John H & Almira B d 11 May 1870 ae: 3y 10m 25d GSL
William d 6 Nov 1865 ae: 64y GSL
HORTON, Amelia w/o Joshua d 22 Oct 1877 ae: 67y C:16
Joshua d 13 Sept 1864 ae: 56y Native of Wallace, Nova Scotia SBE C:16
Relief C w/o Robert d 23 May 1871 ae: 78y 2m G:2
Robert d 12 Nov 1860 ae: 95y "Run over by the cars back of Bramhall's Hill." G:2
HOSACK, Achsa d 9 Sept 1909 ae: 64y 3m Hosack bomb A:17
Albert Gerard d 28 Dec 1883 Boston, Massachusetts ae: 47y Civ/War: 5th Reg Maine Inf Co H Hosack tomb A:17
Betsy d 15 Aug 1890 ae: 92y 4m Hosack tomb A:17
Charles d 20 Jan 1872 ae: 77y Hosack tomb A:17
Elijah K d 29 May 1888 ae: 61y Hosack tomb A:17
John D s/o Charles d 18 OCt 1841 ae: 2y GSL
William C s/o Charles d 20 May 1856 ae: 31y Dyer tomb A:15
HOUGHTON, Albertine P Brackett w/o Harley O d 22 Mar 1925 ae: 59y 11m 16d C:56
HOULIHAN, William d 23 Aug 1857 ae: 65y GSL
HOTHAUSE, Eliza d/o Henry d 27 Oct 1848 ae: 18m Catholic GSL
HOWAGAN, Michael d 2 June 1851 ae: 36y Catholic GSL
HOWARD, Abby d 1 Nov 1879 ae: 75y GSL
Abigail w/o Ephraim d 26 Oct 1850 ae: 78y I:163
Anna d/o Ephraim & Abigail d 2 Sept 1856 ae: 66y I:163
D s/o John D L d 16 Aug 1856

HOWARD (continued)
ae: 9m Dyer tomb A:15
Ephraim d 26 Apr 1835 ae: 78y I:163
Frank s/o H D d 10 Nov 1859 ae: 9d GSL
Ida S d 15 Feb 1917 Cambridge, Massachusetts ae: 40y 8m 1d Safford-Hall tomb A:20
HOWE, inf s/o Calvin d 14 Aug 1854 GSL
Apollo d 12 June 1858 ae: 67y GSL
Caroline Dana d/o Apollo & Elizabeth b 21 Aug 1824 d 30 Oct 1907 D:62
Eben b 1827 d 1913 J:55
Elizabeth M w/o Eben d 18 Nov 1909 ae: 77y 6m 2d SD J:55
Elizabeth W wid/o Apollo d 5 Feb 1868 SD D:62
Eugene no dates on stone; no burial record D:62
Frank A d 7 Jan 1881 ae: 54y GSL
Frank L s/o Frank d 19 May 1906 ae: 48y Suicide - shot SD D:62
Louisa M d/o Calvin d 25 Oct 1857 ae: 5m GSL
Maria E Davis w/o Eben b 1832 d 1909 J:55
HOWELL, Abigail wid d 26 Oct 1849 ae: 78y GSL
Edwin H s/o Emory d 27 Nov 1852 ae: 14m GSL
Eleanor w/o John d 16 July 1858 ae: 65y J:72
Hannah wid/o Robert d 4 July 1859 ae: 74y GSL
Martha D d 14 Aug 1838 ae: 22y E:8
Robert d 19 Aug 1849 ae: 62y GSL
HOYT, Michael s/o Brown d 24 Sept 1849 ae: 1y GSL
HUBBARD, Eliza M w/o Stephen d 29 May 1885 ae: 59y 5m SD J:68
Elizabeth d/o George B d 13 July 1851 ae: 2y 7m SD B:68
George B d ae 70y no burial

**HUBBARD** (continued)
record Lost at sea B:68
Harriet d 4 Nov 1872 ae: 71y F:36
Mary E w/o George B d 19 Mar 1886 ae: 69y B:68
Sarah M w/o E M d 11 Nov 1839 ae: 20y C:59
**HUBERT**, James s/o Thomas d 8 Feb 1861 ae: 6w GSL
**HUCKINS**, Elizabeth w/o Freeman E d 15 June 1868 ae: 40y 7m 11d I:85
Freeman E d 5 Nov 1858 ae: 36y I:85
Lavina M w/o Capt J H d 16 Feb 1853 ae: 40y D:45
Mary E d/o Capt J H & Lavina M d 12 Aug 1836 ae: 3y 8m D:45
Selden M s/o Capt J H & Lavina M d 28 Dec 1848 ae: 6m D:45
**HUDSON**, Joseph E s/o James O d 30 Aug 1851 ae: 4m GSL
Mary d/o Robert d 19 Nov 1849 ae: 5y GSL
Mary Jane d/o Samuel d 20 Sept 1847 ae: 6m GSL
Robert d 12 Mar 1872 ae: 70y GSL
**HUFF**, Edwin A s/o Samuel Jr & Martha d 10 Oct 1857 ae: 2y 5m H:14
Martha inf d/o Samuel Jr & Martha d 17 Nov 1857 H:14
Martha w/o Samuel Jr d 14 Nov 1857 ae: 26y 6m H:14
Orpha w/o Samuel d 25 Feb 1872 ae: 65y SD H:14
Samuel Jr d 14 Oct 1864 Alexandria, Virginia of disease ae: 31y Civ/War: 17th Reg Maine Inf Co E H:14
William C no burial record. SD F:54 (See Addendum)
**HUGHES**, Catherine d/o P J & Elizabeth d 26 Jan 1854 ae: 2y 1m J:194
P J d 18 May 1857 ae: 31y GSL
**HUMPHREY**, Clara Hill s/o Henry S d 28 Nov 1870 ae: 3m SD H:38
Frederick B s/o Asa d 18 Oct

**HUMPHREY** (continued)
1858 ae: 8m GSL
Henry T s/o Henry d 1 Apr 1864 ae: 2y 5m SD H:38
Lucinda w/o M A d 14 Dec 1852 ae: 29y SD D:13
Maggie H d/o Henry C d 27 Mar 1876 ae: 1y SD H:38
Ralph David s/o H & ALice M d 26 Oct 1881 ae: 3m SD H:38
Ralph Vose s/o Harry d 9 Jan 1895 ae: 1y 1m 9d SD H:38
**HUNKAR**, James s/o William d 24 Aug 1849 ae: 3w Catholic GSL
**HUNKINS**, Margaret w/o William d 30 July 1866 ae: 43y GSL
**HUNNEWELL**, Richard d 14 May 1823 ae: 66y Rev/War: veteran GSL
**HUNT**, Eben s/o John d 12 Nov 1850 ae: 11m GSL
Eunice A Green w/o James d 2 June 1897 ae: 91y F:69
Hannah d/o John d 7 Dec 1841 ae: 10m Catholic GSL
James d 23 Jan 1851 ae: 45y GSL
John d 30 Nov 1847 ae: 37y Catholic GSL
John d 8 Nov 1874 ae: 42y Cause of death: "Rum did it." GSL
Mary d/o wid Eunice d 26 May 1842 ae: 4y 6m GSL
Nancy w/o Israel d 17 June 1856 ae: 70y F:106
Sarah R d/o James M & Eunice d 19 Jan 1929 ae: 89y F:69
**HUNTER**, Mary wid/o Thomas d 3 Feb 1854 ae: 72y Native of St John, New Brunswick H:32
**HUNTRESS**, Charles H w/o Edmund & Eunice C d 8 Aug 1844 ae: 7y G:25
Edmund d 1 Jan 1844 ae: 44y G:25
Eunice c w/o Edmund d 24 Aug 1847 ae: 47y G:25
Frances E d/o Edmund & Eunice C d 6 Apr 1844 ae: 4m 8d G:25
Cpl James d 20 Aug 1865 New Orleans, Louisiana ae: 41y

HUNTRESS (continued)
Civ/War: 1st Batt Maine Lt
Art G:25
HURD, James s/o James d 19
Sept 1851 ae: 13m GSL
Mary w/o James d 27 Oct 1855
ae: 33y GSL
HURLEY, Jeremiah s/o Michael
d 9 Oct 1859 ae: 1d Catholic
GSL
HUSSEY, Obed d 9 Aug 1854 ae:
58y "Died from being run over
by the cars in Exeter, New
Hampshire." Hosack tomb
A:17
Thomas s/o Patrick d 17 May
1853 ae: 12y Old Catholic
Ground GSL
HUSTON, Ada Faustina d/o Al-
bert d 9 Oct 1854 ae: 15m GSL
Eunice wid/o Robert d 3 Apr
1862 ae: 83y GSL
Frances E d/o Albert d 3 Sept
1847 ae: 18m GSL
John d 23 Apr 1864 ae: 62y 7m
GSL
John s/o John d 23 Aug 1849 ae:
3m GSL
Susan w/o John d 21 June 1846
ae: 46y GSL
Thomas s/o Robert d 10 Sept
1870 ae: 64y GSL
HUTCHINS, Ella F d 26 Nov
1856 ae: 17m GSL
Franklin s/o J R d 20 Aug 1854
ae: 21m GSL
HUTCHINSON, Eleanor d 23 May
1861 ae: 8m GSL
Frederick s/o Frederick A d 17
Aug 1859 ae: 7m GSL
Sarah w/o Jeremiah d 31 Dec
1902 ae: 73y 8m 11d SD J:258
Capt Stephen d 9 June 1837 Bos-
ton, Massachusetts ae: 43y
F:137
Susan d/o Stephen & Susan d 3
Nov 1844 ae: 22y SD F:137
Capt William B d 18 Aug 1860
New York City ae: 45y Struck
by lightning Cummings tomb
A:13

HYDE, two inf c/o William &
Julia d 1833 SBE C:33
Edward d 13 May 1858 ae: 25y
GSL
Harriet Clark d/o Gresham &
Sarah d 5 Mar 1832 ae: 3y 3m
C:33
Julia d/o William & Julia d 8
Apr 1826 ae: 4y 3m C:34
Marshall G s/o William A d 23
Nov 1856 ae: 5y 10m GSL
William s/o William d 17 Aug
1858 ae: 10m Trowbridge tomb
Location unknown
HYLAND, Patrick d 19 Nov 1857
ae: 31y GSL
HYMES, Austin d 2 May 1856 ae:
29y J:213
ILSLEY, Ann Maria w/o Capt
Stephen d 20 Feb 1861 ae: 57y
10m 5d GSL
Charles T s/o Stephen M & Mary
F d 24 Apr 1859 ae: 1y 9m
G:29
Charlotte d/o Theophilus d 29
Mar 1843 ae: 6w GSL
Clarence M s/o Stephen L d 9
Oct 1879 ae: 10m SD G:29
Helen J d 10 Sept 1863 ae: 25y
GSL
Joseph d 29 July 1851 ae: 75y SD
F:46
Lucy Ann d/o Joseph & Phebe d
31 Oct 1842 ae: 24y SD F:46
Parker d 3 Jan 1851 ae: 83y C:8
Phebe w/o Parker d 23 Dec 1837
ae: 72y C:8
Phebe J wid/o Joseph d 14 Nov
1860 ae: 85y SD F:46
Stephen d 17 Sept 1873 ae: 73y
SD G:29
Virginia E d/o Arthur L d 8 Aug
1860 ae: 17y Dyer tomb A:15
Washington s/o Theophilus d 25
Dec 1848 ae: 10m GSL
William D s/o Stephen M &
Mary F d 1 Aug 1862 ae: 1y
4m G:29
INGALLS, Betsy w/o Francis d
25 Apr 1872 ae: 86y D:43
Cad no dates on stone; no burial
record D:43

INGALLS (continued)
Clara Augusta d/o Isaiah & Sarah
Milliken d 24 Jan 1873 ae: 25y
D:43
Esther d/o Isaiah & Betsy b 3
Jan 1794 d 23 June 1879 D:43
Eva F s/o P d 26 Nov 1857 ae:
5y Hilborn tomb A:10
Florence Eva d/o Isaiah & Sarah
Milliken d 26 Nov 1857 ae: 5y
D:43
Isaiah b 4 Sept 1816 d 2 Apr 1906
D:43
Jennie Merrill d/o Isaiah & Sarah
d 5 Nov 1865 ae: 3y D:43
Sarah Milliken wid/o Isaiah b 7
Sept 1826 d 10 July 1907 D:43
INGERSOLL, Clinton R s/o Rich-
mond H d 10 Apr 1861 ae: 6w
GSL
Eva E d/o Daniel d 20 June 1857
ae: 18m GSL
INGRAHAM, Charles H s/o Holt
d 9 Jan 1866 Detroit, Michigan
ae: 33y Ingraham tomb A:16
Edward d 11 Aug 1874 ae: 89y
Ingraham tomb A:16
Holt d 2 Oct 1877 ae: 77y In-
graham tomb A:16
Mary S w/o Edward d 16 Apr
1876 ae: 91y Ingraham tomb
A:16
Sarah A w/o Edward d 12 Nov
1869 ae: 64y Ingraham tomb
A:16
INNES, inf s/o Charles G d 6 Sept
1855 ae: 16d Haggett tomb
A:18
John s/o Manuel & Bridget d 22
Sept 1852 ae 1y 6m SD I:50
Martha A Tarr w/o Charles G d
27 Oct 1855 ae: 29y C:17
INOS, John s/o Manuel & Bridget
no burial record SD I:50 (See
Addendum)
ISKIN, Charley H d 19 July 1851
ae: 3m J:209
JACKSON, Alden d 8 Nov 1855
ae: 57y I:75
Andrew J s/o Isaac d 21 Dec
1852 ae: 3y 8m GSL
Catherine S w/o Samuel H d 6

JACKSON (continued)
June 1870 ae: 42y Haggett tomb
A:18
Charles A s/o Isaac d 15 Mar
1846 ae: 22m GSL
Charles A H s/o Isaac d 8 July
1853 ae: 6y 6m GSL
Elizabeth d/o Valentine R d 28
Aug 1861 ae: 7m GSL
Elizabeth w/o Valentine d 9 Feb
1861 ae: 22y 6m GSL
Elizabeth Durgin w/o Henry b 3
Oct 1786 d 27 Aug 1857 SBE
J:86
Henry d 22 Aug 1860 ae: 67y J:86
James G s/o James d 3 Oct 1855
ae: 4w GSL
John s/o John d 10 July 1846 ae:
13m Catholic GSL
John B d 6 July 1872 ae: 38y
Civ/War: 1st Reg Maine Cav
Co F J:259
Maggie d/o John B d 5 Aug 1866
ae: 1y 1m GSL
Martha d/o John W d 6 July 1864
ae: 3w GSL
Mehitable O w/o Alden d 3 Apr
1839 ae: 39y SBE I:75
Samuel B s/o L H & Annie d 15
Dec 1880 ae: 7y D:6
Sarah L d/o Samuel H d 6 Dec
1871 ae: 18y Haggett tomb
A:18
William Swan s/o Alden & Me-
hitable A d 6 Aug 1839 ae:
11m I:75
JACOBS, Frank s/o Joshua B d
11 June 1858 on board bark
*Canada* ae: 2y 11m GSL
Philip H s/o Harry M d 26 Oct
1895 ae: 1d SD F:35
JAMES, Mary d/o William d 28
Aug 1843 ae: 2m GSL
JANICAN, Ellen d/o John d 2 Oct
1856 ae: 7m GSL
JANNE, John s/o James d 31
July 1848 ae: 11m Catholic
GSL
JEFFORD, Henry s/o Robert d 9
May 1856 ae: 17m GSL
JEFFORDS, Edward s/o William
& Julia d 2 Aug 1854 ae: 2y 8d

JEFFORDS (continued)
Catholic SD J:47
Elizabeth d/o William & Julia d
25 Aug 1854 ae: 19y SD J:47
Ellen d 16 Mar 1869 ae: 77y GSL
John s/o John d 2 Oct 1854 ae:
18m GSL
Julia w/o William d 22 Aug 1852
ae: 23y Native of Co Cork,
Ireland Catholic SD J:47
Thomas s/o John d 19 June 1858
ae: 2y 1m GSL
William d 13 Aug 1853 ae; 27y
Native of Co Cork, Ireland
Catholic SD J:47
JENNES, Agnes J d/o John d 31
Aug 1849 ae: 9m Catholic GSL
JENNY, Daniel s/o Matthew d 5
Apr 1857 ae: 4m GSL
JEWELL, Pilipianna d/o Thomas
d 23 Oct 1866 ae: 14y GSL
Sophia d 27 Feb 1860 ae: 34y
I:169
JEWETT, Frank s/o William d
31 May 1851 ae: 14m GSL
George s/o Annie d 21 June 1873
ae: 4w Jewett tomb Location
unknown
Joseph d 15 July 1796 ae: 47y
Remains moved from Andover,
Massachusetts GSL
Moses C d 25 Oct 1863 ae: 50y
Sawyer tomb A:14
Susan d 23 Feb 1890 ae: 64y
Sawyer tomb A:14
JOHNSON, Angela d/o Elbridge d
23 Feb 1851 ae: 11m SD F:22
Ann w/o Capt Ebenezer Jr d 31
Dec 1837 ae: 32y SD I:66
Karen S d/o William d 7 Apr
1874 ae: 3w GSL
Caroline S d/o Nathaniel & Mary
d 26 Oct 1919 ae: 76y I:121
Charles s/o Capt Elbridge &
Joanna d 3 Nov 1841 ae: 6y
F:22
Charles E s/o Thomas d 30 May
1856 ae: 18m GSL
Charles H s/o Daniel & Mary b
1845 d 1858 H:23
Charles W s/o Capt Elbridge &
Joanna d 16 July 1909 ae: 67y

JOHNSON (continued)
Civ/War: 5th Reg Maine Inf Co
A F:22
Daniel b 1815 d 1876 H:23
Capt Ebenezer d 1 Jan 1852 ae:
81y I:66
Capt Ebenezer Jr d 12 Feb 1870
ae: 71y 5m I:66
Elbridge s/o Capt Elbridge &
Joanna d 12 June 1844 ae: 6y
9m F:22
Eliza Jane d/o Ephraim & Eliza
d 28 Dec 1847 ae: 10y C:63
Ellen A d/o Capt Ebenezer Jr &
Mary A d 7 Apr 1849 ae: 1y
I:66
Ellen L d/o Ephraim & Eliza d 9
Sept 1853 ae: 18y 6m SD C:63
Eunice K d/o Capt Ebenezer Jr &
Mary A d 29 Jan 1853 ae: 12y
9-1/2m I:66
Freddie s/o George d 7 Dec 1881
ae: 5m GSL
George s/o Capt Elbridge &
Joanna d 22 Dec 1840 ae: 3m
SD F:22
George H s/o Joseph & Rebecca
S d 22 Sept 1851 ae: 2y 5m SB
B:56
Georgianna A Poole w/o Moses
P d 23 May 1911 ae: 61y B:35
Greely H d 6 Oct 1894 Boston,
Massachusetts ae: 63y 7m
D:82
Hannah d/o Eben d 5 Aug 1857
ae: 3y GSL
Joseph b 18 Nov 1815 d 12 Nov
1891 B:56
Joseph d 16 May 1859 ae: 55y
GSL
Joshua d 19 July 1834 ae: 44y SD
B:71
Leonard s/o Leonard & Irene d
15 Oct 1841 ae: 2y F:22
Lewis S s/o James T d 30 Sept
1861 ae: 1y 9m GSL
Louisa d/o Ephraim & ELiza d
28 Aug 1830 ae: 7m SD C:63
Louisa d/o Ephraim & Eliza d 9
Jan 1836 ae: 4y SD C:63
Mary d 23 May 1863 ae: 30y 8m
GSL

JOHNSON (continued)
Mary A w/o Capt Ebenezer Jr d
29 Sept 1877 ae: 67y I:66
Mary A d/o Joseph & Rebecca S
d 5 Aug 1856 ae: 5y 6m SD
B:56
Mary A K d 25 Sept 1871 ae: 28y
Dyer tomb A:15
Mary E d/o Capt Elbridge &
Joanna b 1845 d 1909 F:22
Mary E d/o Henry d 17 July 1859
ae: 2y 3m GSL
Mary Locke d 30 Dec 1889 ae:
85y 1m GSL
Mary Nason w/o Daniel b 1814 d
1891 H:23
Mary S w/o Greely H b 1818 d
1896 D:82
Mercy w/o Capt Ebenezer d 20
Jan 1828 ae: 36y I:66
Moses P b 1846 d 1920 B:35
Peter P d 5 Dec 1855 ae: 41y
Black GSL
Rebecca w/o Joseph b 4 Nov
1818 d 9 Nov 1907 B:56
Rosetta A w/o Edmund L d 27
June 1853 ae: 20y 5m F:19
Samuel S s/o Helen M d 25 Apr
1866 ae: 3d GSL
JONES, inf s/o Andrew & Char-
lotte d 15 Feb 1865 ae: 6m SD
B:6
Alice L d/o Sarah E d 27 Sept
1879 ae: 14y GSL
Bridget d/o Michael d 29 Mar
1843 ae: 9y Catholic GSL
Cordelia w/o Benjamin F d 31
July 1863 ae: 42y 2m Ingraham
tomb A:16
Edward inf s/o Enoch & Louisa
nodates on stone, no burial
record H:35
Emily Jane d/o John W d 7 Sept
1855 ae: 20m GSL
Emma d/o Lewellen d 30 Apr
1869 ae: 6w GSL
Emma F d/o John & Mary d 8
Sept 1855 ae: 1y 8m SD C:79
Enoch d 12 Mar 1870 ae: 44y
H:35
Ephraim R d 22 Sept 1883 ae:
72y SD B:6

JONES (continued)
Ephriam s/o Ephraim & Sarah d
13 Jan 1930 City Hospital ae:
81y 10m 15d NS B:6
Frederick s/o Andrew L T d 15
Feb 1864 ae: 6m GSL
Hannah d/o Michael d 30 Oct
1855 ae: 9y Catholic GSL
Hannah L d 4 Sept 1878 ae: 56y
H:35
James s/o Michael d 25 Oct
1855 ae: 5y Catholic GSL
Joanna w/o Michael d 13 Feb
1845 ae: 26y Catholic GSL
John s/o Michael d 22 June 1851
ae: 1w Catholic GSL
Julia w/o Michael d 15 Apr 1844
ae: 35y Catholic GSL
Julia w/o Michael d 12 Sept 1846
ae: 34y Catholic GSL
Louisa w/o Enoch d 24 Apr 1852
ae: 27y SB H:35
Margaret d/o Michael d 9 June
1846 ae: 12y Catholic GSL
Margaret wid d 25 Mar 1849 ae:
61y GSL
Maria w/o William d 7 Feb 1848
ae: 30y Catholic GSL
Mary D w/o Enoch d 1 Mar 1860
ae: 33y H:35
Mary H d/o Enoch & Louisa d 6
Sept 1849 ae: 1y H:35
Michael s/o Michael d 30 July
1847 ae: 5y Catholic GSL
Orville B s/o William H & Ever-
lina d 3 Jan 1851 ae: 3d SD
J:61
Robert d 12 Apr 1854 ae: 38y Old
Catholic Ground GSL
Robert s/o Bridget d 15 Apr 1856
ae: 3y Old Catholic Ground
GSL
Robert s/o Robert d 13 Apr 1846
ae: 2y Catholic GSL
Roxanna L w/o Thomas K d 19
June 1859 ae: 22y GSL
Ruth E d/o Osgood d 30 Jan 1869
ae: 1y 3m Dyer tomb A:15
Sarah A w/o Ephraim d 25 Oct
1896 ae: 77y 4m 12d SD B:26
Sarah Ellen wid/o Enoch, d/o
Ebenezer & Eleanor Dyer d 2

JONES (continued)
Nov 1930 ae: 88y 2m 19d H:35
Capt Thaddeus d 14 Feb 1844 ae:
26y GSL
William s/o Michael d 22 Aug
1842 ae: 3y Catholic GSL
JORDAN, inf s/o James d 3 Sept
1857 ae: 3w GSL
Albert C s/o Capt Seth & Eliz-
abeth Ann b 28 Apr 1842 d 7
Sept 1846 G:65
Albert F d 31 July 1875 ae: 2y
GSL
Alfred s/o Daniel & Rebecca d
31 July 1875 ae: 2y 8m F:10
Alvin Jr b & d 1856 C:75
Anna H Mrs d 16 Apr 1860 ae:
19y 6m Haggett tomb A:18
Calvin d 20 Dec 1859 ae: 73y
GSL
Calvin s/o Daniel & Rebecca d
18 Jan 1875 ae: 21y 1m 29d
F:10
Charles A s/o R L d 6 Nov 1857
ae: 4y 2m GSL
Charlotte E d/o I d 18 Aug 1857
ae: 19m 8d GSL
Daniel d Carrollton, Virginia no
burial record Civ/War: 15th
Reg US Inf Co A SD F:10
Edward H s/o Albus R d 10 Oct
1860 ae: 22m 16d J:106
Elizabeth d/o James d 22 Oct
1863 ae: 2y 9m 19d GSL
Elizabeth Ann w/o Capt Seth d 2
Jan 1850 ae: 34y G:65
Elizabeth Horton d/o W & Eliz-
abeth d 16 Dec 1835 ae: 6y
10m J:106
Fitz Henry s/o late Hiram d 4
Apr 1861 ae: 21y GSL
Frank A b & d 1853 C:75
George s/o Daniel d 6 Sept 1849
ae: 3y GSL
Gilman s/o James d 12 Aug 1846
ae: 1y GSL
Hiram d 6 Sept 1849 ae: 36y
Daniels tomb A:19
Lizzie G d 23 Aug 1888 ae: 31y
SD B:1
Luther d 12 Dec 1845 ae: 32y
Daniels tomb A:19

JORDAN (continued)
Mercy wid/o Charles d 14 July
1861 ae: 74y SD D:28
Rebecca w/o Daniel d/o Daniel
& Sarah Hunt b 15 Sept 1815 d
24 Nov 1896 F:10
Ruth d 23 Feb 1867 ae: 79y GSL
Sarah Maria Akers w/o Hiram C
d 14 Apr 1854 ae: 20y 4m C:8
Seth s/o Capt Seth d 2 Apr 1858
ae: 17y 10m G:65
Capt Seth b 19 Aug 1811 d 2 June
1852 G:65
Susan S d/o James d 10 Sept
1862 ae: 3y 7m GSL
William H s/o late Capt Charles
d 8 July 1860 ae: 49y SD D:28
Woodbury s/o Hiram d 28 Aug
1847 ae: 10m GSL
JOY, Charlie R s/o Samuel W &
Mary H b 8 Mar 1872 d 8 Feb
1876 C:42
Frank Woodbury s/o Samuel W
& Mary H b 26 Aug 1868 d 3
Feb 1927 C:42
Fred Sumner s/o Samuel W &
Mary H b 22 Sept 1873 d 22
Dec 1898 C:42
Jennie F d/o Samuel W & Mary
H b 28 Aug 1863 d 2 Oct 1863
C:42
Lillie Belle d/o Samuel W &
Mary H b 2 Mar 1867 d 22 Aug
1867 C:42
Mary H Thompson w/o Samuel
W b 4 July 1842 d 9 Feb 1882
C:42
Minnie Ellen d/o Samuel W &
Mary H b 29 Oct 1869 d 28
Sept 1961 C:42
Rosie May d/o Samuel W &
Mary H b 6 June 1864 d 13 OCt
1867 C:42
Samuel W s/o John & Julia Ann
b 20 Sept 1837 d 11 Aug 1929
C:42
JOYCE, Mary d 15 May 1855 ae:
56y H:91
KALOW, Mary d/o Daniel d 11
Nov 1857 ae: 14m GSL
KANE, Mildred L d/o Edward &
Annie d 12 Sept 1900 ae 2m

KANE (continued)
10d SD C:67
KARNAN, James s/o John H &
Sarah H d 11 Sept 1850 ae: 14d
SBE J:73
Sarah H w/o John H d 13 Oct
1850 ae: 27y SB J:73
KARWIN, Mary w/o Daniel d 25
Aug 1852 ae: 47y Catholic GSL
KEEFE, John s/o James d 4 Aug
1859 ae: 2y 4m GSL
Johnea d/o Timothy & Catherine
d 1 Jan 1844 ae: 2y Catholic
SB L:8
Timothy d 9 Oct 1856 ae: 50y
Catholic Strangers' Ground SB
L:8
KEENE, John d 15 Aug 1847 ae:
24y Strangers' Ground GSL
KEEHAN, Matthew d 5 June 1854
ae: 58y Old Catholic Ground
GSL
KEESE, James d 28 June 1851
ae: 50y GSL
KEITH, Harris J s/o Judson J d 4
Apr 1867 ae: 7m GSL
KELLEN, Abby E w/o Rev Robert
d 3 Nov 1859 Boston, Mas-
sachusetts ae: 30y SD D:75
KELLOGG, Caroline d/o Rev Eli-
jah & Eunice no dates on
stone; no burial record J:108
Dorothy d/o Rev Elijah & Eunice
no dates on stone; no burial
record J:108
Edward Payson inf s/o Rev Eli-
jah & Hannah P no dates on
stone; no burial record J:108
Rev Elijah d 9 Mar 1842 ae: 80y
Rev/War: veteran War/1812:
veteran SBE J:108
Rev Elijah b 20 May 1813 d 17
Mar 1901 J:108
Eunice McLellan w/o Rev Elijah
d 17 Oct 1850 Harpswell,
Maine ae: 80y 9m J:108
Eunice M d/o Rev Elijah &
Eunice d 13 May 1828 So
Harpswell, Maine ae: 27y
J:108
Frank Gilman s/o Rev Elijah &
Hannah d 7 Sept 1927 ae: 70y

KELLOGG (continued)
10m 21d J:108
Grace H b 1859 d 1923 J:108
Hannah Pearson Pomeroy w/o
Rev Elijah b 1821 d 1891 J:108
John s/o Rev Elijah & Eunice no
dates on stone; no burial
record J:108
Joseph H s/o Joseph M & Sophia
B d 21 Apr 1887 ae: 61y J:108
Joseph M s/o Rev Elijah &
Eunice d 8 Apr 1870 ae: 81y
J:108
Mary McLellan d/o Rev Elijah &
Eunice d 26 Dec 1816 ae: 22y
J:108
Sophia Brazier w/o Joseph M d
27 Mar 1878 ae: 77y J:108
KELLY, ---- w/o Jeremiah d 4
Dec 1851 ae: 35y Catholic GSL
Almira C d/o Ralph & Eliza C b
25 Apr 1849 d 9 Dec 1931 H:38
Andrew J s/o Edward d 23 June
1856 ae: 3y 10m GSL
Ann E d/o Patrick d 5 Sept 1859
ae: 8m Catholic GSL
Anna d 7 May 1858 ae: 25y 8m
GSL
Anne d/o Edward & Mary d 7 Jan
1842 ae: 2d Catholic SBE I:52
Bridget d/o Edward & Mary no
burial record Catholic SBE
I:52
Bridget d/o William d 22 Aug
1853 ae: 8w GSL
Eleanor d 11 Aug 1844 ae: 63y
Catholic GSL
Eliza w/o Ralph b 16 Mar 1808 d
8 Sept 1889 H:38
Ellen d/o Edward & Mary d 7 Jan
1842 ae: 2d SBE I:52
Emma J d/o William M d 28
Aug 1864 ae: 7m GSL
Frances E d/o William M d 11
Jan 1857 ae: 16m GSL
Rev George William b 3 Nov
1844 d 10 Jan 1934 H:38
Jeremiah d 21 July 1851 ae: 43y
Catholic GSL
Jeremiah s/o Jeremiah d 21 Aug
1852 ae: 9m Catholic GSL
John s/o John d 27 May 1863 ae:

KELLY (continued)
7y 18d GSL
John J s/o William M d 5 Sept
1855 ae: 18m GSL
Leonora d/o Jeremiah d 20 Aug
1849 ae: 8m Catholic GSL
Levi Morris C s/o Ralph & Eliza
C d 27 Jan 1849 ae: 7y 10m
SBE H:38
Lucy d 24 Apr 1850 ae: 30y GSL
Mary d/o Patrick d 31 July 1854
ae: 2y Catholic GSL
Mary D d/o William M d 27 Dec
1856 ae: 5y 4m GSL
Mary Eliza d/o Ralph & Eliza C
d 16 Apr 1848 ae: 8y 6m H:38
Mary J d/o Edward & Mary d 26
Nov 1850 ae: 3y 4m Catholic
I:52
Matilda w/o John d 4 Feb 1858
ae: 27y Old Catholic Ground
GSL
Michael d 17 Oct 1847 ae: 26y
GSL
Ralph s/o John & Sarah d 6 June
1897 ae: 91y H:38
Rosanna d/o Edward & Mary d 1
July 1848 ae: 8y Catholic I:52
Rosanna d/o Patrick d 9 July
1855 ae: 9m Catholic GSL
Sarah Jane d/o Ralph & Eliza C
d 2 Jan 1849 ae: 2y 5m SBE
H:38
Thomas d 14 Apr 1859 ae: 35y
GSL
Thomas s/o Patrick d 30 July
1854 ae: 1y Catholic GSL
William d 29 May 1860 ae: 55y
GSL
KELSEY, Ellen T d/o James &
Julia A d 6 June 1853 ae: 8y
SD H:8
James b 1821 d 1894 H:8
James W s/o James & Julia A d
7 June 1853 ae: 6y H:8
John M s/o James & Julia A d
28 June 1853 ae: 10m H:8
Julia A Elwell w/o James d 3
Apr 1896 ae: 77y 2m 22d H:8
Julia E d/o James & Julia A d 6
June 1853 ae: 8y H:8
Julia F d/o James & Julia A d

KELSEY (continued)
20 Sept 1857 ae: 1y 3m H:8
Mary I d/o James & Julia A d 11
June 1854 H:8
Martha E d/o James & Julia A b
1851 d 1919 H:8
Samuel E s/o James & Julia A d
7 June 1853 ae: 4y H:8
KENNARD, Catherine d/o Dixon d
17 July 1856 ae: 26y GSL
Henry s/o Cyrus B d 8 Apr 1845
ae: 18m GSL
Herbert R s/o Richard W d 14
Oct 1851 ae: 5m GSL
KENNEDY, Catherine G d/o Mar-
tin d 19 Sept 1854 ae: 14m
GSL
Daniel s/o Daniel d 23 May 1858
ae: 2y GSL
Daniel F s/o Thomas d 26 Oct
1854 ae: 1y 6m GSL
Edward s/o Michael d 20 July
1852 ae: 2y Catholic GSL
Ellen d/o Michael d 27 July 1859
ae: 11m Catholic GSL
Honora w/o Patrick d 27 Aug
1849 ae: 31y Catholic GSL
James s/o Edward d 7 June 1852
ae: 17y Catholic GSL
John s/o Michael d 30 June 1857
ae: 2y 6m Catholic GSL
Margaret d/o Stephen d 17 Nov
1857 ae: 1y 4m GSL
Margaret H d 10 Apr 1854 ae: 42y
GSL
Mary d/o Francis d 4 Aug 1853
ae: 3y GSL
Michael d 7 Apr 1855 ae: 66y
Catholic GSL
Michael d 30 July 1858 ae: 65y
Old Catholic Ground GSL
Sarah J w/o Thomas d 15 July
1858 ae: 22y 3m GSL
Thomas d 30 Sept 1853 ae: 17y
Old Catholic Ground GSL
KENNELLY, Hattie d 1 Oct 1899
ae: 54y 9d SD C:87
KENNEY, Bridget d 29 Sept 1857
ae: 66y GSL
Mary d/o Michael d 11 July 1864
ae: 10m GSL

KENSEY, Florence M d 10 Sept 1869 ae: 4m GSL

KENT, Charles b 1796 d 1880 SBE F:25

Elizabeth P w/o Charles b 1797 d 1855 Stone on F:19 F:25

Sophia J C d 4 Dec 1888 ae: 59y SBE F:25

William L d 23 Oct 1880 Cohasset MA ae: 84y SD F:25

KERAN, Edward s/o Edward d 28 July 1855 ae: 13m Strangers' Ground GSL

KERR, Robert W s/o Robert C d 15 Aug 1850 ae: 1y GSL

KILBORN, Caroline d/o Seth d 2 Aug 184 ae: 9y GSL

Hannah w/o Isaac d 27 Oct 1845 ae: 36y F:135

Isaac d 17 Apr 1861 Worcester, Massachusetts ae: 47y SD F:135

Mary H d/o Seth B d 17 Apr 1845 ae: 14y GSL

William s/o Isaac d 10 July 1846 ae: 6y SD F:135

KILBY, Thomas s/o Thomas d 4 July 1860 ae: 2w Strangers' Ground GSL

KILDAY, Catherine d/o John d 26 Aug 1855 ae: 9m GSL

William s/o William d 25 Apr 1857 ae: 8y "Run over by the Boston cars." Old Catholic Ground GSL

KILGORE, Amelia P F d/o Moses d 3 June 1849 ae: 15y GSL

Margaret Jane d/o William & Sarah d 22 Aug 1843 ae: 9m SBE G:7

William s/o William & Sarah d 1 May 1845 ae: 9m G:7

John Newton s/o James d 28 June 1853 ae: 10m GSL

KIMBALL, Albion Augustus s/o John & Nancy d 29 Sept 1845 ae: 22y B:65

Caroline d/o Annis d 8 Jan 1853 ae: 7m Hilborn tomb A:10

Charles O B d 15 Aug 1876 ae: 42y 8m 7d F:62

KIMBALL (continued)

Fannie E wid/o Frank C d 24 Jan 1937 ae: 86y 8m 21d H:78

Frederick T s/o William G d 27 Feb 1857 Westbrook, Maine ae: 2y 6m Hilborn tomb A:10

George P w/o William C d 21 Aug 1862 ae: 10m GSL

Huldah Besse w/o Jacob d 1 Apr 1896 ae: 84y F:62

Jacob b 1805 d 30 July 1852 F:62

Lizzie M d/o A M d 2 Oct 1866 ae: 6w GSL

Mary J w/o Jacob d 31 Jan 1882 ae: 66y GSL

KING, Annie H d/o William A & Nancy D d 3 Oct 1879 ae: 6m SBE F:76

Bartholomew d 29 May 1854 ae: 40y Old Catholic Ground GSL

Charles N d 18 Mar 1912 Boston, Massachusetts ae: 38y 4m SD F:76

Charles W s/o William A & Nancy D b 1870 d 1911 F:76

Flora P d/o J R d 19 Apr 1864 ae: 7y GSL

Jane S w/o Jarius R d 7 Sept 1851 ae: 33y GSL

Margaret d/o Peter d 16 Oct 1855 ae: 10m GSL

Mary d/o Michael d 3 Aug 1854 ae: 8m GSL

Mary d/o Thomas d 7 Mar 1847 ae: 2y GSL

Nancy D w/o William A, d/o Samuel & Amanda Hazeltine d 18 Dec 1929 ae: 90y 7d F:76

Patrick d 22 May 1856 ae: 28y "Casualty by Rail Road." Native of Clifden, Co Galway Ireland, Catholic SBE SB J:175

Sarah Adaline d/o Franklin & Nancy d 23 May 1847 ae: 2y SD F:129

Sarah G w/o J R d 24 may 1858 ae; 30y 11m GSL

William s/o William b 1864 d 1873 SBE F:76

William A d 18 Mar 1905 Boston, Massachusetts ae: 67y

KING (continued)
13m Civ/War: 4th Reg Maine
Inf Co H F:76

KINSMAN, Angela d 3 Jan 1891
Washington DC ae: 87y 10m
18d SD D:52

Edgar s/o William H d 27 July
1862 ae: 16y Kinsman tomb
A:17

Eleanor d/o Nathan & Eliza d 14
Mar 1879 Washington DC ae:
66y SD D:52

Eliza w/o Nathan d 29 June 1841
ae: 58y SD D:52

Eliza C d/o William H d 19 Sept
1854 ae: 17m Kinsman tomb
A:17

Elizabeth Ann w/o William H d
22 Apr 1862 ae: 39y Kinsman
tomb A:17

Elizabeth D d/o Nathan & Eliza
d 18 Dec 1832 ae: 1y SD D:52

Frank E s/o Capt William H d 6
Oct 1855 ae: 5m 12d Kinsman
tomb A:17

John D s/o Nathan & Eliza d 27
May 1850 Belfast, Maine ae:
44y SD D:52

John Dafforne s/o John D & Angela d 16 Mar 1842 ae: 11y SD
D:52

Joseph d 2 Jan 1857 ae: 75y
Kinsman tomb A:17

Capt Joseph d 24 Apr 1862 ae:
43y Kinsman tomb A:17

Martha d/o Nathan & Eliza d 27
June 1841 ae: 52y SD D:52

Mary Ella d/o John & Regina d
25 Feb 1859 ae: 2y 5m G:11

Nathan d 26 Feb 1825 ae: 51y SD
D:52

Regina w/o John d/o Charles
Hedman d 21 July 1858 ae: 27y
G:11

Rhoda w/o Joseph d 23 Dec 1866
ae: 76y 9m Kinsman tomb
A:17

William C d 7 Oct 1897 ae: 48y
2m GSL

KINLEY, Elizabeth d/o Paul d 14
Nov 1861 ae: 1y GSL

KINNEY, James s/o Alfred d 31

KINNEY (continued)
Aug 1856 ae: 24y Old Catholic
Ground GSL

Mary d/o Micah d 12 Sept 1857
ae: 1y GSL

Michael d 10 Oct 1851 ae: 30y
Catholic GSL

KIRBY, Edward d 4 May 1855 ae:
35y GSL

Joanna d/o James MD d 26 Sept
1856 ae: 18m GSL

KIRWIN, John s/o Michael d 29
Nov 1854 ae: 5y GSL

KNAPP, Eliza O d 9 Jan 1857 ae:
54y Walker tomb D:36

KNIGHT, "Mother" unknown F:40

Ada K buried 15 Dec 1936 no
burial record NS G:38

Albert E s/o Albert L & Sarah L
d 20 Dec 1917 ae: 62y 1m 22d
C:38

Albert L s/o Albert E & Ida G d
24 July 1900 ae: 68y 8m C:38

Ann d/o R H B d 18 July 1843
ae: 10m Knight tomb Location
unknown

Ann C w/o Robert H d 19 Mar
1843 ae: 24y F:40

Ann Christina d/o Robert H &
Ann C d 19 July 1843 ae: 10m
F:40

Ann Maria d/o William L & A D
d 10 Dec 1848 ae: 10y SD
F:12

Aphia D w/o William L d 7 Aug
1868 ae: 49y SD F:12

Charlena d/o Samuel A & Elizabeth d 1 Sept 1854 ae: 8m
G:82

Charles B s/o Robert d 21 Oct
1841 ae: 20y SD F:40

Charles B s/o Robert W d 31
Aug 1864 ae: 35y 11m GSL

Charles M s/o Stephen & Sarah E
d 20 Oct 1841 ae: 16y F:8

Charlotte w/o Robert d 8 Apr
1855 ae: 58y SBE F:40

Dorcas R w/o Thomas d 24 May
1896 ae: 73y 3m 10d I:124

Eliza d/o Stephen & Sarah E d 19
Sept 1840 ae: 2y F:8

Emma L wid/o Herbert d 23 Oct

KNIGHT (continued)

1889 ae: 35y GSL

Fanny P w/o Charles A d 30 July 1863 ae: 18y 5m GSL

Freeman L d 19 Sept 1890 ae: 67y 4m SD F:8

George s/o George d 12 Apr 1843 ae: 17m GSL

George H d 23 Dec 1852 ae: 41y F:120

George W s/o Robert & Charlotte d 28 Apr 1841 ae: 20y F:40

Georget C d/o J W C & Julia d 20 Apr 1850 ae: 8y 1m I:98

Harriet F w/o Robert H d 26 Dec 1849 ae: 22y F:40

Ida K w/o Albert E d/o Lewis & Mary Allen d 13 Dec 1936 ae: 78y 7m 15d C:38

Isabella H d 21 Feb 1894 Somerville, Massachusetts ae: 85y 5m 7d GSL

James A D d 14 Mar 182 ae: 32y GSL

John W C d 6 Dec 1895 ae: 72y SD I:98

Julia A w/o John W C d 12 Jan 1890 ae: 65y 3m I:98

Margaret w/o Freeman L d 12 Feb 1855 ae: 21y SD F:8

Mary w/o Stephen d 18 Apr 1829 ae: 33y F:8

Mary A d 8 Nov 1881 ae: 95y GSL

Mary A w/o Charles B d 13 June 1911 ae: 86y 1m 8d SD I:124

Mary S d/o Jabez d 2 Oct 1846 ae: 17m GSL

Rachel A w/o Robert W d 13 Apr 1868 ae: 64y 7m F:40

Robert H d 4 Feb 1845 ae: 25y F:40

Sarah E w/o Stephen d 2 Oct 1839 ae: 28y F:8

Sarah R Holbrook w/o Albert L b 1838 d 1904 C:38

Sophia Ann d/o Barker & Mary d 12 Aug 1831 ae: 18y F:2

Stephen d 8 Sept 1862 ae: 62y F:8

Stephen C d 3 Dec 1880 ae: 36y GSL

KNIGHT (continued)

Susan Ann d/o Robert & Charlotte d 22 Jan 1843 ae: 17y F:40

Thomas E b 3 July 1817 d 28 July 1868 I:124

Thomas E Jr s/o Thomas E & Dorcas R d 18 Jan 1850 ae: 2y SBE I:124

Weslyn s/o Ezra d 6 Sept 1849 ae: 16m GSL

KNIGHTS, Helen Marr d/o Jacob & Harriet d 9 Mar 1836 ae: 14m C:31

George F s/o James d 20 Apr 1850 ae: 8y Plummer tomb Location unknown

Sarah A w/o George H d 11 July 1854 ae: 34y F:120

KNOWLES, Mary E d/o Charles & Eliza d 11 Aug 1851 ae: 14y 6m J:140

Sarah R d/o Charles & Eliza d 26 Aug 1851 ae: 17y J:140

KNOWLTON, Sarah E w/o C T d 3 Apr 1866 ae: 28y GSL

KYNE, Sarah d/o Michael d 7 Aug 1857 ae: 14m GSL

LABOY, Almazada s/o late Rudolph d 11 Mar 1887 ae: 18y GSL

Almoora A d/o Rudolph d 22 Nov 1868 ae: 14y 6m GSL

Caroline d/o Rudolph d 2 Aug 1863 ae: 7m 13d GSL

Frank D s/o Rudolph d 8 Aug 1868 ae: 2m 12d GSL

Thomas s/o Rudolph d 16 May 1872 ae: 1y GSL

LADD, Edith d/o Noah M d 26 Oct 1852 ae: 17m GSL

LADDY, James s/o Thomas d 29 Apr 1855 ae: 3m Catholic GSL

William s/o Thomas d 24 Apr 1852 ae: 6m Catholic GSL

LAHEFF, Mary d 9 Sept 1857 ae: 47y Old Catholic Ground GSL

LAMSON, Alice Marion d/o Rufus & Ella d 15 May 1880 ae: 3m Stone on I:129 J:72

LANCASTER, Elizabeth w/o Zelotes d 17 Aug 1861 ae: 46y

**LANCASTER** (continued)
SB G:45

William s/o Zelotes & Elizabeth d 19 Apr 1845 ae: 3y 10m SB G:45

Zelotes d 16 Sept 1853 ae: 49y SB G:45

**LANDERS,** Christopher s/o Richard d 19 Sept 1847 ae: 7y Catholic GSL

**LANE,** Charles E s/o Nathaniel d 13 Dec 1857 ae: 30y SD F:133

**LANG,** Charles R s/o Samuel d 17 May 1858 ae: 34y GSL

Lydia A w/o Capt William b 28 Apr 1817 d 17 Sept 1875 C:85

Capt William d 18 Mar 1863 ae: 46y 9m C:85

**LAREY,** Dennis d 25 Nov 1851 ae: 45y Catholic GSL

**LARKIN,** Bridget w/o Francis d 27 Nov 1839 ae: 28y Native of Co Tyrone, Ireland Catholic I:1A

Daniel d 20 Nov 1853 ae: 25y Old Catholic Ground GSL

James H d 15 June 1884 Biddeford, Maine ae: 32y Catholic GSL

Martha w/o Felix d 14 Apr 1865 ae: 67y GSL

Mary d 8 Dec 1846 ae: 18y Catholic GSL

Mary Ellen d/o Andrew & Sarah d 22 Sept 1845 ae: 1y Catholic I:20A

Patrick d 12 Jan 1857 ae: 41y Catholic GSL

Philip d 14 Sept 1860 ae: 38y GSL

William H s/o Andrew d 13 June 1849 ae: 2y Catholic GSL

**LEACH,** Charles d 29 Apr 1859 ae: 33y Sawyer tomb A:14

Ella Jane d/o Charles A d 15 Sept 1851 ae: 16m Jordan tomb D:28

Susan d/o Amory d 2 Jan 1846 ae: 25y GSL

Zilpha d/o Edmund C Delano d 18 Sept 1893 ae: 86y 4m Jordan tomb D:28

**LEAVITT,** Amy M G d/o James d 1 June 1847 ae: 18m Haggett tomb A:18

Ellen d/o John d 22 Sept 1843 ae: 1y 9m H:56

Elizabeth d/o Charles d 22 Aug 1860 ae: 11m Strangers' Ground GSL

James Folger s/o Joseph d 28 Dec 1857 ae: 7y 3m GSL

Jemima wid/o John d 20 July 1851 ae: 75y SD H:56

John d 16 Feb 1830 ae: 58y SD H:56

John B s/o William & Mary d 25 Aug 1837 Havana, Cuba ae: 15y H:56

Joseph s/o John & Jemima d 13 Dec 1798 ae: 4y H:56

Julia A d/o Charles d 24 Aug 1854 ae: 2y 10m Strangers' Ground GSL

Lydia d/o John & Jemima d 8 May 1812 ae: 2y H:56

Lydia d/o John & Jemima d 9 Oct 1813 ae: 5m H:56

Melorah W d 9 Feb 1853 Boston, Massachusetts ae: 4y GSL

Sarah G d/o Joseph & Eliza d 28 Dec 1841 ae: 5y 6m SD H:56

Susan W d/o Joseph & Eliza d 20 Dec 1842 ae: 2y 3m SD H:56

Capt William s/o John & Jemima d 16 Aug 1821 Havana, Cuba ae: 28y SB H:56

**LEE,** Ann d/o John d 31 Aug 1852 ae: 9m GSL

Ann w/o Gill d 16 Apr 1849 ae: 24y Catholic GSL

John s/o Gill d 6 Mar 1850 ae: 11m Catholic GSL

Patrick s/o Gill d 12 Aug 1849 ae: 3m Catholic GSL

**LEFAVOR,** Elizabeth Mrs d 23 May 1846 ae: 75y GSL

**LEGGETT,** Mary B d 20 July 1851 ae: 55y SB I:98

Mary B d 25 Aug 1877 ae: 78y SD I:98

William d 27 June 1860 ae: 66y 7m I:98

**LEIGHTON**, Clarissa D w/o Joseph d/o Joseph & Mary Keazer d 29 Aug 1853 ae: 21y 8m H:39

Nancy Preble Skillings w/o J Wilson d 13 Mar 1901 ae: 73y 1m SD J:68

Willard s/o Joseph d 15 Apr 1843 ae: 5y GSL

**LEMON**, John s/o Charles d 1 Nov 1861 ae: 8d Catholic GSL

Mary Ann d/o Charles d 1 Nov 1854 ae: 5m Old Catholic Ground GSL

**LENFESTEY**, Hannah d/o Peter d 10 Sept 1847 ae: 14m H:4

Jennie L d/o Peter d 4 Sept 1858 ae: 10y SD H:4

**LEONARD**, Thomas s/o Patrick d 18 June 1857 ae: 1y 10m GSL

**LESLIE**, Gertrude M d/o Walter d 27 Sept 1882 ae: 4w SD J:236

**LEWIS**, Charles A s/o Charles d 5 May 1846 ae: 3m SD F:72

Francis A w/o James A d 24 July 1919 ae: 66y Sawyer tomb A:14

Hezekiah B d 22 Aug 1846 ae: 28y Buried "near the center of the yard." GSL

Katherine Eloise d/o James F & Fannie A d 16 Apr 1917 ae: 45y SD J:240

Lillian Mary d/o James F d 28 Oct 1874 ae: 8d GSL

**LIBBY**, Abner H twin s/o Alvah d 27 Sept 1841 ae: 17m Trowbridge tomb Location unknown

Alvah A twin s/o Alvah d 27 Sept 1841 ae: 17m Trowbridge tomb

Andrew b 1792 d 11 Sept 1864 B:51

Calvin d 11 Apr 1865 ae: 3y 5m GSL

Charles H s/o Andrew & Elizabeth b 1837 d 1865 Civ/War: 12th Reg Maine Inf Co C B:51

Charles H s/o John & Eliza d 27 Sept 1837 ae: 17d G:83

Deborah Pinson w/o William H b 1820 d 1887 B:51

Earl Jr s/o Earl & Lillian d 3

**LIBBY** (continued)
1906 ae: 3m GSL

Eliza w/o John S d 27 June 1884 ae: 80y SD G:83

Elizabeth Lakeman w/o Andrew b 1793 d 5 June 1883 B:51

Ellen w/o Lorenzo Dow d ae: 64y no dates on stone; no burial record H:52

Frances E d/o Phineas d 16 Dec 1845 ae: 4m GSL

George W s/o Andrew & Elizabeth b 1821 d 23 June 1838 B:51

George W s/o William H & Deborah P b 1840 d 1910 B:51

Hannah W d/o Alpheus d 31 Mar 1848 ae: 4y GSL

Hosea J d 26 Nov 1894 Chelsea, Massachusetts ae: 63y SD G:83

Jane w/o Rev Elias d 17 Dec 1852 ae: 63y Hilborn tomb A:10

John d 11 Aug 1846 ae: 24y GSL

John E s/o John & Eliza d 27 May 1862 ae: 26y 6m Civ/War: 1st Reg Maine Inf Co B SBE SB G:83

John S d 13 Jan 1878 Wakefield, Massachusetts ae: 70y SD G:83

Joshua d 8 Apr 1870 ae: 32y Hosack tomb A:17

Lorenzo Dow b 7 Feb 1816 d 4 Oct 1884 H:52

Lucy E S d/o Storer & Rebecca S d 8 Aug 1857 ae: 14m A:7

Luella A d/o William H & Deborah P b 1852 d 7 Apr 1877 B:51

Martha W w/o Lorenzo Dow d 29 July 1898 ae: 64y 1m 11d SD H:52

Mary E w/o Edward G d 26 Feb 1862 ae: 26y 1m 2d H:78

Mary Frances d/o John & Eliza d 27 May 1849 ae: 8y SB G:83

Matthias d 5 Aug 1859 ae: 57y Hilborn tomb A:10

Richard H s/o Thomas d 1 Sept 1851 ae: 2y 9m GSL

**LIBBY** (continued)

Sarah w/o Daniel b 25 July 1822 d 17 Aug 1853 D:25

Sarah Ann d 23 Aug 1853 ae: 30y GSL

Storer b 30 June 1824 d 28 May 1871 A:7

William s/o Enoch d 15 Aug 1851 ae: 4m GSL

William H s/o Andrew d 15 Mar 1911 ae: 92y 6m 6d B:51

**LIGHTFORD**, Henrietta d/o John & C d 3 Oct 1852 ae: 14m Catholic GSL

**LINCOLN**, John W d 5 Jan 1864 ae: 48y GSL

Lydia w/o Nathaniel d 10 May 1851 ae: 60y SD C:85

**LINES**, Margaret d/o George & Alice d 9 Nov 1854 ae: 3y 8m Native of Caloctee Parish, Co Donagal, Ireland SD H:19

**LING**, Amanda M w/o L DeM d 10 Mar 1851 ae: 22y GSL

Ella w/o Edward E d 9 Oct 1885 ae: 28y GSL

Sylvanus d 23 Sept 1864 ae: 55y GSL

Sylvanus s/o Sylvanus d 29 Jan 1851 ae: 2y GSL

Walter M s/o M J d 18 Sept 1858 ae: 14m GSL

**LINNEHAN**, Abby d/o Gerret d 22 Aug 1857 ae: 4y GSL

**LIPTILL**, Susan d 7 May 1853 Work House ae: 50y GSL

**LITTLE**, Eddie no burial record SD B:40

Frederick Freeman d 23 Mar 1870 GSL

Julia Adelaide Augusta d/o Eugene d 10 July 1851 ae: 5y 6m GSL

Willie no burial record SD B:40

**LITTLEFIELD**, Marrabee d 20 June 1864 ae: 70y SD J:66

**LOCKHART**, Charles W s/o James d 24 Oct 1852 ae: 4y GSL

Lydia wid/o Daniel d 1 May 1852 ae: 84y GSL

**LOCKPORT**, James L d 4 Apr 1862 ae: 57y GSL

**LOGAN**, Frances May d/o Theodore d 2 Oct 1884 ae: 5d GSL

**LOMBARD**, Charles s/o R M & O T d 11 Dec 1853 ae: 2m F:116

Frances E w/o C F d/o Lemuel & Betsy Coolbroth b 1847 d 1871 J:247

Frank A d 29 Nov 1888 ae: 35y 5m GSL

Frederick E s/o Frank A d 25 Mar 1878 ae: 5m GSL

**LONEY**, Daniel d 14 Sept 1851 Catholic GSL

**LONG**, Henry d 2 Jan 1853 ae: 37y Catholic GSL

John s/o Daniel d 4 Mar 1855 ae: 18m GSL

John s/o Walter d 17 Nov 1854 ae: 3y GSL

Kate d/o Walter d 27 May 1857 ae: 3w GSL

Lydia J w/o Thomas J d 23 Mar 1866 ae: 18y 3m GSL

Reuben A s/o Thomas J d 17 Oct 1864 ae: 4m GSL

Thomas s/o Walter d 24 July 1854 ae: 1y 6m GSL

**LONGFELLOW**, Nellie P d/o Henry W d 4 Mar 1867 ae: 4m Longfellow tomb A:12

Rev Samuel s/o Stephen & Zilpha d 3 Oct 1892 ae: 73y Longfellow tomb A:12

Stephen d 3 Aug 1849 ae: 73y Longfellow tomb A:12

Stephen Jr s/o Stephen & Zilpha d 19 Sept 1850 ae: 45y Longfellow tomb A:12

Zilpha wid/o Stephen d 12 Mar 1851 ae: 73y Longfellow tomb A:12

**LONGWORTH**, Deborah w/o John d 31 Mar 1856 ae: 55y J:54

John d 23 Mar 1851 ae: 61y J:54

Nancy w/o George d 26 Dec 1858 ae: 29y GSL

**LOONEY**, Bartholomew s/o Jane d 4 Dec 1848 ae: 12d Catholic GSL

Ellen w/o Michael d 2 Aug 1854

LOONEY (continued)
ae: 20y Native of St John, New
Brunswick Catholic GSL
John G s/o Patrick d 7 Sept 1849
ae: 2y Catholic GSL
Michael s/o Bartholomew d 19
Nov 1853 ae: 2y 10m Catholic
GSL
Timothy d 3 July 1852 ae: 53y
Catholic GSL
LORD, Almira w/o George d 18
May 1858 ae: 39y 11m GSL
Caleb d 24 May 1837 ae: 64y
C:69
Emma F d/o George d 16 Apr
1858 ae: 2w GSL
Fannie d 5 June 1886 Greely
Hospital ae: 35y GSL
George d 7 Nov 1860 ae: 49y GSL
George W s/o William H d 19
Sept 1872 ae: 8m GSL
Josephine A d/o George d 23 Aug
1846 ae: 2y 6m GSL
Mary A d/o Samuel d 5 Sept 1853
ae: 11y 2m GSL
Pamela C w/o William H d 18
May 1872 ae: 21y GSL
LOTSON, Mary w/o David d 20
Jan 1848 ae: 45y Catholic GSL
LOVE, James d 13 Jan 1866 ae:
42y C:4
Susan w/o James d 29 Sept 1859
ae: 32y C:4
LOVEJOY, Ellen S d/o William
H & Martha Q d 25 May 1872
ae: 21y 10m F:34
Georgiana w/o Charles d 9 Dec
1852 ae: 25y GSL
Lydia A w/o Aaron d 5 Aug 1864
ae: 33y GSL
Martha Q Green wid/o William H
d 13 Jan 1908 Norway, Maine
ae: 79y F:34
William H d 5 May 1871 ae: 48y
F:34
William Henry s/o William H &
Martha Q d 18 Sept 1849 ae: 2y
5m SBE F:34
LOW, Mary w/o Edward d 14 Sept
1850 ae: 35y Catholic GSL
LOWE, Elmira w/o William d 22
Mar 1853 ae: 62y GSL

LOWE (continued)
Theodore s/o John W d 7 Sept
1863 ae: 6m GSL
LOWELL, Aaron D d 7 Oct 1846
ae: 35y C:41
Jane w/o Joseph H d 25 Dec
1854 ae: 54y GSL
Judith wid d 16 Jan 1847 ae: 71y
GSL
LOWLEY, Timothy c d 8 June
1853 ae: 25y GSL
LOWN, Ada M d/o George d 20
Jan 1861 ae: 7y 1m Dyer tomb
A:15
George Clinton s/o George d 25
Jan 1861 ae: 5y 2m Dyer tomb
A:15
LOWRY, Nancy S wid d 10 Aug
1849 ae: 48y GSL
William J s/o William d 1 Oct
1860 ae: 10m GSL
LOWTON, Bridget d/o Bart d 1
Feb 1849 ae: 1y Catholic SD
J:9
LUCAS, George M w/o William d
13 Oct 1854 ae: 6w SD F:128
John W s/o William & Mary d 4
Apr 1853 ae: 7m SBE F:128
LUCE, Gertrude R wid/o Frank S
d/o, Jacob W & Martha A
Robinson b 12 Oct 1869 d 9
Aug 1946 North Orange, Mass-
achusetts H:40
LUDY, Thomas s/o Thomas d 30
July 1853 ae: 3y 2m Strangers'
Ground GSL
LUFKIN, Joseph R d 8 Mar 1854
ae: 35y Cummings tomb A:13
LUKINE, Frances d/o Henry d 13
July 1849 ae: 5m GSL
LUNT, Alice D d/o George F d 19
Oct 1856 GSL
Edith d/o John & Phebe R
Chamberlain no dates on
stone; no burial record I:143
Edwin M s/o Noah d 30 Aug 1863
ae: 10m GSL
Margaret d/o George & Mary no
burial record SBE H:19
LYMAN, Seward d 3 May 1860
ae: 56y I:166 (See Addendum)
LYNCH, Hannah d/o Michael d

**LYNCH** (continued)
29 July 1859 ae: 11d Catholic GSL
M J s/o John d 5 May 1855 ae: 1y GSL
Margaret d/o Patrick d 7 Oct 1853 ae: 6w Catholic GSL
Patrick d 29 Jan 1859 ae: 37y Catholic SD J:178
Thomas s/o Patrick & Sarah d 6 Oct 1852 ae: 1y 5m SBE J:178
**LYONS**, Margaret d/o George d 16 Sept 1854 ae: 3y 7m Native of Toronto, Canada GSL
**MacDONRUESS**, John d 3 Dec 1848 ae: 20y Catholic GSL
**MACHINE**, John d 20 May 1842 ae: 27y Catholic GSL
**MACK**, Patrick s/o Ann d 13 July 1848 ae: 8y Catholic GSL
William B d 14 Apr 1862 ae: 32y Catholic GSL
**MACKIN**, Annie C d/o James H d 5 Mar 1857 ae: 1y 5d Catholic GSL
James H d 9 May 1858 ae: 25y 4m 5d Catholic GSL
Joseph A s/o Patrick d 29 Apr 1846 ae: 2d Catholic GSL
Luke d 9 Feb 1838 ae: 30y Native of Clogher, Co Meath, Ireland Catholic I:40
**MADDIN**, M d 1 May 1856 ae: 21y Old Catholic Ground GSL
Micah Sampson s/o Patrick d 15 Dec 1857 ae: 3w Catholic GSL
**MAGNER**, Thomas d 24 May 1857 ae: 70y GSL
**MAHAN**, Julia d/o Martin d 16 Mar 1857 ae: 5w Catholic Strangers' Ground GSL
**MAHANEY**, Catherine d/o Maurice d 22 Aug 1855 ae: 11m Catholic GSL
James s/o Patrick d 9 Feb 1857 ae: 7y Catholic GSL
**MAHON**, Margaret d 17 Aug 1855 ae: 25y Catholic Strangers' Ground GSL
Margaret d/o Patrick d 19 Sept 1854 ae: 5y Catholic GSL
**MAHONEY**, Barney d 1 Jan 1853

**MAHONEY** (continued)
ae: 21y Catholic GSL
Catherine w/o Patrick d 7 Mar 1855 ae: 34y Catholic GSL
David s/o Patrick d 7 Aug 1859 ae: 11m Catholic GSL
John s/o Patrick d 9 Dec 1849 ae: 2y Catholic GSL
Julia B w/o Michael d 25 June 1851 ae: 26y Catholic GSL
Patrick s/o Cornelius d 9 Sept 1847 ae: 30m Catholic GSL
Thomas s/o Matthew d 15 Dec 1851 ae: 2y 6m Catholic GSL
William T s/o Michael d 10 Nov 1852 ae: 5m Catholic GSL
**MALLADA**, Michael d 20 May 1853 ae: 32y GSL
**MALONEY**, Betsy w/o Patrick d 26 May 1849 ae: 32y Catholic GSL
John s/o Michael d 29 Jan 1860 ae: 4m Catholic GSL
Margaret E d/o James d 5 Jan 1863 ae: 2y Catholic Strangers' Ground GSL
**MAMY**, Thomas s/o Dennis d 24 Jan 1849 ae: 5m Catholic GSL
**MANCHESTER**, Elizabeth B Sawyer w/o Capt Joseph d 6 Aug 1896 ae: 86y 10m J:109
Frederick H s/o Henry & Ruth d 11 Dec 1941 ae: 68y 1m 4d J:83
Capt Joseph b 1802 d 1855 J:109
Sarah E w/o Frederick H d/o Charles E & Sarah Eveleth d 1 Apr 1941 ae: 70y 9m 2d J:83
**MANELUS**, Harry d 25 Aug 1848 ae: 35y "Death by a fall." Catholic GSL
**MANGUS**, George H s/o George d 3 Oct 1851 ae: 4y 1m SD C:75
Hugh s/o George & Abigail no burial record SD C:75
Jennie d/o E A & H L d 14 Aug 1861 ae: 2w SD C:75
**MANN**, Grace d 17 Mar 1858 ae: 20y Native of Fredericton, New Brunswick Catholic GSL
William s/o Larke d 2 Feb 1849 ae: 3y Catholic GSL

MANNELOW, Mary buried 2 June 1850 no death record GSL
MANNING, Daniel d 9 Aug 1854 ae: 32y Catholic GSL
John s/o James d 13 May 1861 ae: 8m Catholic GSL
Patrick s/o Patrick d 9 Mar 1858 ae: 6d Catholic GSL
MANSFIELD, Eugene Williams s/o Joseph W d 29 June 1847 ae: 7m GSL
John L s/o Stephen d 11 Sept 1846 ae: 17m GSL
Stephen P d 19 Apr 1847 ae: 26y GSL
MARCUS, George William s/o John d 25 Aug 1858 ae: 9m GSL
MAREEN, Esther M N w/o Josiah d 28 Mar 1865 ae: 57y Haggett tomb A:18
MAREHALL, Ann d/o Thomas d 22 Sept 1849 ae: 19m Catholic GSL
MARRINER, Anthony d 8 Aug 1832 ae: 21m F:125
Anthony b 30 Nov 1832 d 3 Feb 1863 F:125
Anthony d 23 Nov 1832 ae: 82y F:125
Edward d/o James d 28 Sept 1843 ae: 17m GSL
John d 18 July 1821 ae: 41y G:68
John D d 7 Jan 1876 ae: 56y GSL
Margaret d/o John B & Rachel M d 2 Feb 1856 ae: 2m F:112
Mary wid/o John d 16 Aug 1847 ae: 62y G:68
Mary A w/o John B d 30 Apr 1866 ae: 33y 7m GSL
Rachel M w/o John B d 2 Nov 1861 ae: 38y 6m F:112
Sally w/o James d 13 Feb 1859 ae: 70y GSL
Stephen d 17 Aug 1865 Bath ME ae: 63y GSL
MARRS, John d 10 Aug 1858 ae: 80y GSL
MARSH, Geroge H d 23 May 1861 GSL
MARSHALL, Addie F s/o William d 8 Feb 1871 ae: 6m GSL

MARSHALL (continued)
William H d 2 Aug 1874 ae: 44y SD J:72
MARSTON, Patrick d 11 Feb 1847 ae: 27y Catholic GSL
MARTIN, Frederick s/o Robert H d 7 Jan 1884 ae: 22y GSL
George F s/o Patrick d 14 Oct 1856 ae: 1y 10d GSL
Hannah d/o Michael d 15 Oct 1850 ae: 8m GSL
Lucy A w/o Robert d 2 Mar 1871 ae: 48y SD J:56
Robert d 22 Oct 1889 ae: 78y SD J:56
Samuel D s/o Robert d 5 Aug 1855 ae: 6m SD J:56
Willie R d 5 Sept 1874 Somerville, Massachusetts ae: 19y SD J:56
MARWICK, Abigail w/o George d 19 Apr 1872 ae: 82y C:75
Charlie no dates on stone; no burial record C:75
Hugh s/o George & Abigail d 12 Oct 1818 ae: 13m C:75
Sarah Jane d/o George & Abigail d 13 May 1843 ae: 22y C:75
MASON, Abby d/o late L D d 23 Sept 1862 ae: 19y G:39
Amanda Melissa d/o Lorenzo D d 17 Nov 1835 ae: 4y 9m G:39
Charles R s/o Lorenzo D & Charlotte W d 13 May 1854 ae: 19y 9m G:39
Charlotte W w/o Lorenzo D d 30 Oct 1865 ae: 57y 6m SD G:39
Daniel W d 12 Aug 1863 ae: 22y Civ/War: Musician 5th Reg Maine Inf Co G G:39
Frederick A d 15 Jan 1887 ae: 37y SD G:39
George Henry s/o Lorenzo D & Charlotte W d 28 Feb 1853 ae: 14y 5m G:39
Lorenzo D d 20 July 1853 ae: 45y SB G:39
MATTHEWS, Andrew s/o William d 21 Dec 1859 ae: 3y 10m GSL
Frank E s/o Abigail & Elizabeth d 23 Nov 1853 ae: 1y 6m J:261

**MATTHEWS** (continued)

George Ripley s/o Thomas & Mary d 5 Sept 1852 ae: 15m 2d SBE F:66

George W s/o Abel d 12 May 1858 Charlestown, Massachusetts ae: 3y 4m GSL

James s/o William & Eliza J d 16 Apr 1856 ae: 2y 6m J:140

Michael d 22 Sept 1849 ae: 26y Native of Co Meutha, Ireland Catholic J:3

Robert s/o William d 2 May 1864 ae: 1y 8m GSL

William d 22 Aug 1870 ae: 1y 4m GSL

William s/o William d 2 Nov 1859 ae: 13m GSL

**MAXWELL,** Margaret Ann d/o William d 6 Apr 1865 ae: 15m Strangers' Ground GSL

**MAY,** William Henry s/o Jeremiah d 23 June 1848 ae: 4y GSL

**MAYBERRY,** D w/o Daniel M d 25 Sept 1880 Chelmsford, Massachusetts ae: 60y GSL

Julia H w/o William H d 18 Feb 1860 ae: 30y GSL

**McANNELLY,** Susan Jane d/o Thomas d 26 May 1855 ae: 1m Catholic GSL

**McANTER,** James s/o William d 18 Aug 1856 ae: 6m Catholic Strangers' Ground GSL

**McCANN,** Charles M s/o Edward & Sophronia d 18 Mar 1863 Washington DC ae: 24y SBE H:48

Ellen w/o Cornelius d 10 Aug 1851 ae: 28y Catholic GSL

Edward d 6 June 1847 ae: 40y SBE H:48

James s/o William d 9 Aug 1856 ae: 1y 9m GSL

Mary w/o Barney d 14 Sept 1856 ae: 25y Murdered by husband Catholic GSL

Peter s/o Rose d 10 Aug 1854 ae: 20y 11m Native of Bellmount, Co Louth, Ireland Catholic J:190

**McCANN** (continued)

Rose d 20 Aug 1854 ae: 58y 4m Native of Bellmount, Co Louth, Ireland Catholic J:190

Samuel T s/o Edward & Sophronia d 11 Mar 1851 ae: 17y H:48

Sophronia w/o Edward d 26 May 1854 ae: 52y H:48

William H s/o Danield 1 Apr 1856 ae: 16d GSL

**McCARTHY,** Hannah d/o Patrick d 8 Oct 1863 ae: 4y Catholic GSL

John d 6 May 1856 ae: 21y Old Catholic Ground GSL

John s/o Dennis & Margaret d 2 May 1851 ae: 2y Catholic I:60

John s/o Moses d 8 May 1867 ae: 4m Catholic GSL

**McCARTY,** Bridget d/o Patrick d 14 June 1856 ae: 16y Catholic GSL

Catherine d 12 Apr 1851 ae: 1y Catholic GSL

Catherine d/o Dennis & Mary d 18 Aug 1832 ae: 18m Catholic J:30

Catherine d/o Henry d 11 Oct 1843 ae: 13m Catholic GSL

Charles d 19 Oct 1855 ae: 37y Catholic Strangers' Ground GSL

Charles s/o Charles d 1 Sept 1856 ae: 8m Catholic Strangers' Ground GSL

Daniel s/o Daniel d 15 Mar 1851 ae: 16y Catholic GSL

Dennis d 13 Sept 1849 ae: 29y Catholic GSL

Dennis s/o Dennis d 17 Sept 1854 Catholic GSL

Edmund s/o Colman d 25 July 1859 ae: 1d Catholic GSL

Edward s/o Dennis & Mary d 21 May 1850 ae: 22y Catholic J:30

Edward s/o Moses d 14 Apr 1859 ae: 21m Catholic GSL

Ella d 16 Aug 1858 ae: 7m Catholic Strangers' Ground GSL

Ellen w/o Dennis d 7 Sept 1849

McCARTY (continued)
ae: 23y Catholic GSL
James s/o Dennis & Mary d 10
Aug 1828 ae: 9m Catholic J:30
Jane w/o Charles d 27 Jan 1856
ae: 28y Catholic Strangers'
Ground GSL
Jane d/o Theophilus d 19 Sept
1851 ae: 4y Catholic GSL
Jeremiah d 5 Feb 1848 Freeport,
Maine ae: 24y Catholic GSL
Jeremiah s/o Jeremiah d 18 Aug
1856 ae: 9m Catholic GSL
Moses Lewis s/o Dennis & Mary
d 19 June 1826 ae: 4y Catholic
J:30
Johanna d/o T d 28 July 1857 ae:
13y Catholic GSL
John d 9 Sept 1856 ae: 35y Cath-
olic GSL
John s/o Coleman d 26 Aug 1859
ae: 2d Catholic GSL
Margaret d/o Thomas d 2 Oct
1852 ae: 7m Catholic GSL
Mary d/o Dennis d 30 July 1850
ae: 1y Catholic GSL
Mary d/o Patrick d 16 Sept 1860
ae: 1y Catholic GSL
Mary A d/o J d 14 Oct 1857 ae:
13m Catholic GSL
Mary Ann d/o Charles d 25 Nov
1856 ae: 2y Catholic GSL
Patrick d 16 Jan 1856 Alms
House ae: 21y Catholic Stran-
gers' Ground GSL
Sarah d 23 Nov 1851 ae: 47y
Catholic GSL
Timothy s/o John d 1 Sept 1852
ae: 1y Catholic GSL
William s/o Dennis & Mary no
dates on stone; no burial re-
cord Catholic J:30
McCASEY, Daniel d 2 Sept 1857
ae: 22y Catholic GSL
McCAULEY, Mary w/o John E d
29 Apr 1889 ae: 70y Catholic
GSL
Rachael d/o John & Jane d 26
July 1837 ae: 3y 7m Unusually
large slate stone Catholic I:35
Timothy s/o Thomas d 24 Apr
1853 ae: 1y Old Catholic

McCAULEY (continued)
Ground GSL
McCLARY, Peter d 31 Aug 1848
ae: 41y Catholic GSL
McCLINSEY, John s/o Andrew d
9 May 1848 ae: 14m Catholic
GSL
McCOBB, Henry B d 21 May 1855
ae: 43y McCobb tomb D:32
Parker d 27 Jan 1847 ae: 62y
McCobb tomb D:32
Rebecca wid/o Parker d 30 Nov
1851 ae: 61y McCobb tomb
D:32
Thomas d 1817 ae: 37y Moved
from Phippsburg, Maine Aug
1897 McCobb tomb D:32
McCOLLEY, Jane d 28 Aug 1851
ae: 75y Catholic GSL
McCOME, Charles d 18 Mar 1863
Washington DC ae: 24y Cath-
olic GSL
McCONTEN, Bridge d/o Patrick
d 20 Dec 1849 ae: 2y Catholic
GSL
McCORMICK, John d 12 July
1867 ae: 32y GSL
Ronald s/o Neil d 22 Oct 1854
ae: 17y Native of New Bruns-
wick, Canada GSL
McCRACKIN, Ann J d/o Samuel
d 23 Sept 1856 ae: 1y 4m GSL
John s/o Samuel d 19 Mar 1859
ae: 2w GSL
Robert s/o Samuel d 22 Mar 1866
ae: 2d GSL
Thomas s/o Samuel d 20 July
1863 ae: 9m GSL
McCRUM, James G s/o James d
22 June 1853 ae: 1y GSL
McCUMMIN, Patrick s/o John d
25 Aug 1855 ae: 1y Catholic
GSL
McCURDY, Sophronia d 2 Aug
1850 ae: 28y GSL
McDONALD, Catherine d 3 May
1873 Newton, Massachusetts
ae: 83y SD F:59
Frederick S s/o Maj S d 18 Nov
1865 ae: 3y 3m GSL
George E s/o Edward Major d 2
May 1856 ae: 4m GSL

**McDONALD** (continued)

Harriet M d/o John Colley d 15 May 1870 ae: 34y GSL

Thomas s/o Thomas d 12 Nov 1857 ae: 1y 13d GSL

**McDONNELL,** Jeremiah s/o Felix d 9 Apr 1851 ae: 13y 4m Catholic GSL

Margaret d/o John d 22 Apr 1856 ae: 3d Catholic GSL

Michael s/o John d 27 Nov 1855 ae: 9m Catholic GSL

**McDONOUGH,** Catherine d 2 Nov 1853 ae: 20y Catholic GSL

Joseph d 19 Apr 1853 ae: 17y Catholic GSL

**McDOWELL,** Rachel d/o James d 24 Oct 1854 ae: 18y 8m GSL

**McDOWNY,** Edward s/o James d 14 Oct 1857 ae: 4y Strangers' Ground GSL

**McDUFF,** William C s/o William C & Abby d 8 June 1848 ae: 4y SD F:54

**McFARLAN,** George s/o G d 9 Apr 1856 ae: 3y GSL

**McGAHEY,** Michael d 19 Nov 1857 ae: 55y Catholic GSL

**McGILL,** Benjamin Franklin s/o Benjamin & Mary d 18 July 1855 ae: 23y Catholic SD F:29

Charles s/o Benjamin d 26 Oct 1855 ae: 23y Catholic SD F:29

Mary E w/o Benjamin d 14 Sept 1857 ae: 62y Catholic SD F:29

**McGINTY,** Edward s/o Michael d 14 July 1858 ae: 11w Catholic GSL

**McGLAUGHLIN,** Mary d/o James M d 1 July 1858 ae: 6y 7m Catholic GSL

**McGLENNIHUE,** Martha d/o Andrew d 4 Aug 1846 ae: 13m Catholic GSL

**McGLINCHY,** Andrew d 24 Sept 1856 ae: 42y 24d Old Catholic Ground GSL

Bridget d 28 Apr 1845 ae: 36y Catholic GSL

Bridget d/o Andrew d 1 Oct 1843 ae: 17m Catholic GSL

Catherine w/o James d 7 May

**McGLINCHY** (continued)

1852 ae: 20y Catholic SBE J:177

Charles s/o Andrew d 1 May 1855 ae: 2d Catholic GSL

Ellen w/o James d 14 Sept 1849 ae: 26y Catholic GSL

James s/o James d 4 Aug 1857 ae: 10y 5m 23d GSL

John s/o James d 18 Nov 1848 ae: 2y Catholic GSL

John s/o John d 22 Sept 1853 ae: 14y 9m Old Catholic Ground GSL

John H s/o Patrick d 12 Aug 1848 ae: 1y Catholic GSL

Margaret d/o James d 4 July 1858 ae: 2m 15d Catholic GSL

Margaret d/o Patrick d 14 Mar 1851 ae: 1y Catholic GSL

Mary w/o John d 27 Sept 1856 ae: 45y Catholic GSL

Matthew s/o Patrick d 15 Mar 1851 ae: 10y Catholic GSL

Patrick d 9 Mar 1851 ae: 7y Catholic GSL

Patrick s/o Andrew d 15 Sept 1857 ae: 5y Catholic GSL

Patrick s/o Timothy d 9 Sept 1858 ae: 15m Catholic GSL

Sarah G d/o James d 9 Oct 1849 ae: 1m Catholic GSL

Thomas s/o Patrick d 4 Oct 1852 ae: 17m Catholic GSL

**McGLOTHLIN,** John S s/o Daniel d 26 June 1851 ae: 10m Catholic GSL

**McGLYNN,** Catherine d/o Hugh d 26 Sept 1856 ae: 16m Catholic GSL

**McGEON,** Betsy d/o Terrance d 20 Sept 1855 ae: 33y Catholic GSL

**McGOWEN,** Hannah d 28 June 1858 ae: 42y Old Catholic Ground GSL

Margaret d/o Terrance d 18 Aug 1847 ae: 4y Catholic GSL

Michael s/o Terrance d 8 Sept 1858 ae: 3y 10d Catholic GSL

Terrance d 18 Oct 1849 ae: 23y Catholic GSL

McGRATH, Catherine d/o James d 19 Nov 1856 ae: 2y Catholic GSL

Ellen d 21 Mar 1849 ae: 22y Catholic GSL

Ellen d/o Daniel d 17 Nov 1859 ae: 6w Catholic GSL

McGREGOR, Laura A d/o Capt Stephen d 7 July 1858 ae: 3w GSL

McGUIRE, Charles d 18 May 1864 of wounds received at Spottsylvania, Virginia ae: 37y Civ/War: 32nd Reg Maine Inf Co C J:96 (See Addendum)

Mary d/o Ross d 11 Sept 1855 ae: 1y 10m GSL

McGURK, Ellen w/o Arthur d 1 Oct 1847 ae: 26y Catholic GSL

McHOWE, Thomas s/o Martin d 21 Aug 1856 ae: 9m Strangers' Ground GSL

McHUGH, Michael d 27 Aug 1850 ae: 19y Catholic GSL

McINTIRE, Fanny L w/o John L d/o William H & Eliza A Adams d 25 Dec 1887 ae: 28y 6m B:3

Mary Ann d 15 Jan 1856 ae: 20y GSL

McKELLEY, Margaret d/o Tueley d 19 Apr 1848 ae: 8y Old Catholic Ground GSL

McKEDSEY, Rosey d/o James d 3 Feb 1850 ae: 7y Catholic GSL

McKENNAN, Donald d 27 May 1854 ae: 35y "Fell from ship at Westbrook." Strangers' Ground GSL

McKENNEY, Alvin L s/o Eleazer d 10 Aug 1849 ae: 3y GSL

Cyrus d 10 Oct 1859 ae: 48y GSL

Edward M d 19 Sept 1889 ae: 41y GSL

Hannah wid/o Thomas d 18 Feb 1855 ae: 79y G:42

Helen V w/o Orin d 4 Aug 1893 ae: 35y 3m SD C:67

Mary C d 2 Apr 1870 ae: 19y 7m GSL

Mary E d/o William & Mary M d

McKENNEY (continued) 23 Apr 1870 ae: 19y 7m G:42

Mary Mange w/o William b 1813 d 1892 G:42

Orin s/o William & Mary M d 10 May 1864 ae: 20y 4m Killed in action – Battle of the Wilderness, Virginia Civ/War: 5th Reg Maine Inf Co F G:42

Patrick s/o Charles d 26 July 1857 ae: 9m Old Catholic Ground GSL

Patrick s/o Patrick d 7 Feb 1868 ae: 10m Catholic GSL

Patrick J E s/o Patrick d 19 Sept 1861 ae: 8m Catholic GSL

Thomas d 7 Mar 1853 ae: 73y G:42

Walter E s/o Orin d 27 July 1892 ae: 3m SD C:67

William s/o Thomas & Hannah b 1804 d 23 Apr 1869 G:42

William H s/o William & Mary M d 18 Nov 1890 ae: 55y Civ/War: 1st Reg Maine Cav Co E G:42

McKENNON, Margaret d/o A d 10 Oct 1857 ae: 1y 5d GSL

McKESEY, Thomas s/o Thomas d 9 Sept 1849 ae: 1y Catholic GSL

McKINNEY, Edward M s/o William d 3 Mar 1845 ae: 2y 3m GSL

Thomas s/o Thomas d 26 Jan 1865 ae: 65y GSL

McKOVEN, Mary Ann d/o Dennis d 27 Apr 1851 ae: 3y Catholic GSL

McLANEY, Sophia d 18 Dec 1852 ae: 50y Catholic GSL

McLAHIN, Rose d 6 Nov 1849 ae: 64y Catholic GSL

McLAUGHLIN, James E s/o J d 21 OCt 1857 ae: 14m GSL

Patrick d 6 Feb 1851 ae: 50y Catholic J:148

Rose d 7 Nov 1849 ae: 63y Catholic J:5

William d 24 Mar 1857 ae: 42y GSL

McLESLIE, Michael s/o Thomas d 31 Oct 1843 ae: 5m Catholic GSL

McMAGAN, Henry s/o James d 26 Sept 1849 ae: 3y Catholic GSL

McMAHAN, John s/o Thomas d 15 Sept 1853 ae: 13m Strangers' Ground GSL

McMAHONE, Mary A d/o Martin d 9 Aug 1856 ae: 2y Old Catholic Ground GSL

Thomas s/o Martin d 21 Aug 1856 ae: 9m Strangers' Ground GSL

McMAIN, John s/o Edward d 2 Sept 1849 ae: 7y Catholic GSL

Martha w/o Edward d 25 Oct 1843 ae: 36y Catholic GSL

McMANNY, James s/o Michael d 3 Oct 1852 ae: 2y Catholic GSL

McMARSO, Michael s/o Michael d 31 Aug 1850 ae: 6m Catholic GSL

McMASTER, Ellen d/o William d 20 Aug 1859 ae: 2y 1m SD J:259

Ellen w/o William d 26 Sept 1896 Whitman, Massachusetts ae: 78y 8m 1d J:259

John s/o William & Ellen d 25 Mar 1863 New York City ae: 18y J:259

Nelly d/o William & Ellen d 20 Aug 1859 ae: 2y J:259

William b Liverpool, England d 25 Sept 1858 ae: 58y J:259

William d 18 Dec 1884 ae: 42y "Erected by his wife Elizabeth." Civ/War: 17th Reg Maine Inf Co D J:259

McMEHAN, Mary w/o John d 14 Jan 1864 ae: 27y Catholic GSL

McMORE, Thomas s/o Peter d 30 Dec 1856 ae: 16m GSL

McMORROW, Patrick d 3 Sept 1850 ae: 25y Catholic GSL

McMURRAY, Catherine d/o Patrick d 23 Aug 1857 ae: 1y Catholic GSL

Jane d/o Patrick d 20 Aug 1857

McMURRAY (continued) ae: 5y Catholic GSL

McNABNY, John d 21 July 1858 ae: 23y "Drowned in Gilead, Maine." GSL

McNAIR, Judith w/o Peter d 4 Nov 1848 ae: 28y Catholic GSL

McNAMARA, Ellen d/o John d 19 July 1864 ae: 6m 19d Catholic GSL

Mary Ann d/o Patrick d 8 Sept 1855 ae: 5w Catholic GSL

Patrick s/o Michael d 27 Mar 1853 ae: 1y Catholic Strangers' Ground GSL

McNARY, James s/o Michael d 21 Oct 1857 ae: 1y 11m Catholic GSL

McNELLIS, Hugh d 20 Nov 1856 ae: 46y Old Catholic Ground GSL

Mary d 13 Oct 1863 ae: 45y Catholic GSL

Nancy d 29 Nov 1856 ae: 76y Catholic GSL

Sarah d/o Thomas d 4 Apr 1860 ae: 10m Catholic GSL

McNERNEY, Thomas s/o Thomas & Catherine d 8 Feb 1852 ae: 16m SD L:14 (See Addendum)

McNULTY, James s/o John d 12 June 1853 ae: 7m Old Catholic Ground GSL

McPHERSON, Fanny d 18 Dec 1874 ae: 22y Catholic GSL

Jennie d 22 Apr 1874 Boston Highlands, Massachusetts ae: 17y Catholic GSL

John d 13 Apr 1857 ae: 39y Old Catholic Ground GSL

Pamelia K d/o Charles Staples d 15 Feb 1872 ae: 43y Staples tomb Location Unknown

McQUADE, Michael s/o Patrick d 8 June 1857 ae: 8m Catholic GSL

Thomas s/o Patrick d 15 Nov 1853 ae: 7m Catholic GSL

McSHAFFREY, Edward d 9 Sept 1846 ae: 39y Catholic GSL

McSHEA, Sarah d/o Miles d 29

McSHEA (continued)
Dec 1857 ae: 10d Catholic GSL
McSORELY, Francis s/o Francis
& Catherine d 24 Dec 1840 ae:
30y Native of Co Tyrone,
Ireland Catholic SB I:12A
Mary Ann d/o Francis & Cath-
erine no burial record Catholic
SD I:12A
Robert s/o Francis & Catherine d
2 June 1846 ae: 6y Catholic SD
I:12A
McVARNEY, Thomas s/o Thom-
as & Catherine no burial record
SD L:14
MEAGHERS, Helen F d/o Joshua
d 22 May 1857 ae: 9y 8m GSL
MEAGITT, Sarah d/o Francis d
23 Mar 1850 ae: 5y Catholic
GSL
MEALY, George d 18 Apr 1850
ae: 34y Catholic GSL
MEANS, Sarah A d 6 Oct 1879 ae:
86y Cummings tomb A:13
Sarah A d/o Anthony d 10 Nov
1868 ae: 3y 8m Cummings
tomb A:13
Thomas d 7 June 1866 ae: 81y
5m Cummings tomb A:13
MEARS, John d 10 Aug 1858 ae:
80y A:5
Mary A wid/o John d 28 Aug
1866 ae: 84y SD A:5
MEEHAN, inf c/o Martin d 21
June 1853 Catholic Strangers'
Ground GSL
Daniel s/o Martin d 8 Oct 1855
ae: 2y 6m Catholic Strangers'
Ground GSL
MEGGUIER, "Mother" w/o Ben-
jamin b 18 Feb 1767 d 27 Jan
1860 J:96
Frances M d 13 Dec 1857 ae: 70y
GSL
MEGGUIRE, Charles Eugene s/o
Benjamin & Charlotte d 15
Sept 1850 ae: 14m 16d SD
J:96
MELLEN, Bernard s/o Lawrence
& Catherine d ae: 2y 2m no
burial record Catholic SD I:13
(See Addendum)

MELLEN (continued)
Caroline M d/o Prentiss & Sarah
H b 26 Mar 1801 d 10 Nov 1876
F:9
Grenville s/o Prentiss & Sarah H
b 19 June 1799 d 5 Sept 1841
New York City F:9
Patrick s/o Lawrence & Cath-
erine d 9 June 1851 ae: 4y 7m
Catholic SD I:13 (see Adden-
dum)
Prentiss b 11 Oct 1764 d 31 Dec
1840 1st Chief Justice: Maine
Supreme Court F:9
Sarah Hudson w/o Prentiss b 22
Jan 1767 d 10 Sept 1838 F:9
MERRILL, Aaron d 16 Mar 1861
ae: 42y GSL
Abigail w/o Phineas d 25 Sept
1848 Scarboro, Maine ae: 58y
GSL
Alice Franklin d/o James M d 18
Aug 1858 ae: 20m GSL
Amelia d/o Edmund C d 12 July
1846 ae: 4y 4m GSL
Frances E d/o Edmund C d 19
May 1849 ae: 1y GSL
Franklin s/o Edmund d 15 Aug
1849 ae: 14m GSL
Jane d 27 Oct 1863 ae: 79y 9m
SD F:9
Leonard W s/o Leonard W d 19
Aug 1848 ae: 5m Merrill tomb
D:35
Lorenzo b 1841 no burial or death
record Civ/War: 13th Reg
Maine Inf Co G G:37
Lorenzo G s/o Lorenzo & Mary L
d 21 Mar 1857 ae: 8y 6m G:37
Lucy A d/o Lorenzo & Mary L d
4 Aug 1853 ae: 20m SD G:37
Mary L w/o Lorenzo G d 10 Oct
1859 ae: 49y SB G:37
Seward Henry s/o James d 9 Dec
1857 ae: 6y 3m GSL
Sophia N d/o Isaac D d 14 Aug
1849 ae: 10m GSL
William buried 4 Mar 1855
"Remains brought from the
South." Merrill tomb D:35
MERRITT, William O d 23 July
1869 ae: 11m GSL

MERROW, Elizabeth E w/o John d 3 Sept 1921 ae: 90y SD I:159
Etta B d 14 Dec 1892 Boston, Massachusetts ae: 40y I:159
MERRY, John d 25 Aug 1847 ae: 38y Strangers' Ground GSL
MESERVE, Alice d/o Jonathan d 3 Dec 1857 ae: 3y GSL
Amos b 1835 d 1890 Civ/War: 10th Reg Maine Inf Co B H:87
Anna w/o Amos b 1839 d 1886 Women's State Relief Corps - G A R H:87
Isaac W s/o Jonathan d 12 May 1850 ae: 9y GSL
MIDDLETON, Allison Allan w/o Robert d 7 Feb 1857 ae: 45y Native of Scotland SBE F:3
MILLER, Ella E d/o Charles C d 16 Jan 1850 ae: 5w GSL
Etta M w/o Milo C d/o Nathaniel & Sarah M Stimson d 4 Nov 1935 ae: 75y I:69
Maud d/o Edward K d 7 Oct 1876 ae: 22m GSL
MILLETT, Carrie d/o E P d 19 Sept 1855 ae: 17m 17d Dyer tomb A:15
Mary d/o Edward d 18 Dec 1827 ae: 3w GSL
Mary J d/o Charles d 15 Oct 1856 ae: 3w GSL
MILLIGAN, John s/o Patrick d 15 Sept 1849 ae: 1y Catholic GSL
MILLIKEN, inf c/o Earl & Hannah S d ae: 6m no burial record SD C:6
Alexander Jr d 9 Apr 1832 E:6
Amanda Winslow w/o Alexander d 15 Sept 1836 ae: 41y SB E:6
Ann d/o Thomas d 14 Apr 1856 ae: 4y GSL
Ann Maria d/o Alexander & Anna C d 28 Aug 1828 ae: 1y E:6
Charles H s/o Alexander & Anna C d 23 Oct 1835 SBE E:6
Earl d 14 Feb 1872 ae: 42y C:6
Earl Jr s/o Earl & Hannah S d 22 Oct 1861 ae: 8m SD C:6
George s/o John F d 21 Aug 1849 ae: 4m GSL

MILLIKEN (continued)
George H s/o Earl & Hannah S d 24 June 1857 ae: 5y 9m SD C:6
George S s/o James & Ursula d 3 May 1863 ae: 22y 4m Killed in action - Battle of Chancellorsville, Virginia Civ/War: 17th Reg Maine Inf Co B SD J:128
Hannah S w/o Earl d 12 June 1899 ae: 68y C:6
John F d 18 Dec 1858 ae: 53y 11m Trowbridge tomb Location unknown
Joseph d Aug 1826 ae: 4m no burial record SBE E:6
Mahalia w/o John F d 20 July 1869 ae: 60y 8m GSL
Mary d/o Frank d 23 July 1874 ae: 6m GSL
Mary A w/o Charles d 30 Sept 1864 ae: 22y GSL
Mary Ann d/o James & Ursula d 25 Oct 1851 ae: 18y 9m SD J:128
Sarah w/o Michael d 20 Feb 1855 ae: 35y Strangers' Ground GSL
Sarah w/o Michael d 16 June 1885 ae: 89y 10m GSL
Ursula S d 30 Dec 1884 ae: 73y SD J:128
MILLS, Annie M d 11 Aug 1875 ae: 27y GSL
Betsy d 21 Feb 1886 ae: 74y 8m GSL
Bridget d 27 Apr 1851 ae: 72y Catholic GSL
Deborah w/o Dea Jacob d 15 Dec 1842 ae: 41y SD F:30
Elon s/o Jacob d 25 Aug 1847 ae: 2y SD F:30
Frederick w/o William d 15 Aug 1856 ae: 13y 3m GSL
George s/o Samuel d 18 Aug 1843 ae: 13m GSL
George s/o Samuel d 27 Aug 1846 ae: 10m GSL
Harriet w/o Jacob d 18 May 1872 ae: 62y SD F:30
Horace s/o Jacob d 22 Oct 1842 ae: 16m SD F:30

**MILLS** (continued)

Horace L d 24 Aug 1886 Boston, Massachusetts ae: 43y GSL

Jacob d 14 Apr 1843 ae: 80y SD F:30

Jacob d 25 Sept 1878 ae: 71y SD F:30

James s/o Lawrence d 27 July 1856 ae: 1y GSL

Samuel d 31 Jan 1888 Boston, Massachusetts ae: 83y 6m GSL

Samuel s/o Samuel d 13 July 1841 ae: 8y GSL

Sarah w/o Dea Jacob d 14 Dec 1832 ae: 67y F:30

**MINNARD**, Rebecca d 17 Sept 1850 ae: 60y I:81

**MINOT**, Edward M s/o Edward & Harriet d 27 July 1853 ae: 6y 9m I:137

**MITCHELL**, Ann Maria d/o Rev D M & M C d 24 Sept 1847 ae: 20y SB J:235

Bridgett d 13 May 1863 GSL

Charles D s/o Bela d 30 July 1844 ae: 4m GSL

Ellen d/o Patrick d 19 Sept 1856 ae: 11m GSL

Ellen M d/o Patrick d 28 Mar 1860 ae: 3y 1m GSL

George O s/o N J & H A d 27 May 1843 ae: 8y 6m F:115

Jeremiah d 19 Dec 1858 ae: 63y GSL

Mary A d/o Peter d 15 Aug 1862 ae: 3y GSL

Mary Ann w/o Bela d 20 Mar 1849 ae: 23y GSL

Tristram G s/o A R & P C d 15 Nov 1861 ae: 62y J:235

Wiliam Dodge s/o W K d 24 Feb 1852 ae: 3m GSL

**MOLLERS**, William H s/o Robert d 23 Sept 1855 ae: 2w GSL

**MONAGAN**, Catherine d 7 Nov 1856 ae: 80y GSL

**MONAHUE**, James d 5 May 1853 ae: 35y "Run over by train in Westbrook." GSL

**MONAN**, Dennis s/o Dennis d 10 Aug 1852 ae: 7m Catholic GSL

**MONAN** (continued)

Patrick d 9 Sept 1852 ae: 22y Catholic J:193

**MOODY**, Charles 3rd d 22 Mar 1852 ae: 33y GSL

Mary d/o George d 14 Sept 1864 ae: 65y GSL

**MOORE**, James d 7 Mar 1855 ae: 44y GSL

**MORAN**, Charlotte d/o John d 16 Nov 1854 ae: 2y Catholic GSL

George M s/o John d 1 June 1852 ae: 2y 5m Catholic GSL

John s/o John d 18 Nov 1854 ae: 1y 3m Catholic GSL

**MORGAN**, Alice d/o Eben d 8 Aug 1855 ae: 15m GSL

Annie Louise w/o Clarence, d/o Charles W & Sarah E Bartlett d 19 May 1933 ae: 50y 9m 27d NS I:84

Nellie A w/o William, d/o Lorenzo Dow & Ellen Libby d 25 Feb 1927 ae: 64y 2m 16d NS H:52

**MORIN**, Edward s/o Edward d 27 July 1855 ae: 13m Strangers' Ground GSL

**MORING**, Daniel s/o James d 15 Sept 1857 ae: 6m GSL

**MORRILL**, Carrie Clifford d/o George H & Hattie A b 31 Jan 1883 d 7 Nov 1887 F:8

Chloe E d/o Levi d 3 May 1848 ae: 9y Trowbridge tomb Location unknown

Hattie A d 13 June 1912 Saco, Maine ae: 58y 5m SD F:8

Herbert Knight s/o George H & Hattie A b 22 Sept 1877 d 20 Mar 1896 F:8

Warren C s/o Edward d 23 Aug 1849 ae: 7m GSL

**MORRIS**, Cordelia E w/o George P d 28 May 1862 ae: 20y 3m GSL

Francis E s/o George T d 12 Apr 1862 ae: 2m 19d GSL

John s/o John P d 1 Oct 1855 ae: 13m GSL

Mary d 27 Mar 1848 ae: 80y Catholic GSL

MORRISON, Ellen w/o William d 17 Sept 1852 ae: 52y Catholic GSL

Henry Francis d 5 Feb 1855 ae: 1y 9m GSL

Martha J d/o David d 27 Aug 1867 ae: 18y GSL

MORSE, Alfred G s/o James d 3 Mar 1867 ae: 13m GSL

Alfred L d 25 Sept 1863 ae: 26y GSL

Florence E d/o William & Hannah d 6 Apr 1862 ae: 9m 27d SBE I:91

Frank s/o Lorenzo d 24 July 1859 ae: 2y GSL

George H s/o Henry T d 11 Jan 1857 ae: 12w SD B:50

Hannah H w/o William T d 16 Nov 1895 ae: 61y SD I:91

Henrietta d/o John d 28 Nov 1864 ae:15y Hosack tomb A:17

Joseph s/o Joseph d 27 Mar 1844 ae: 5m GSL

Lois M w/o Henry P d 29 Sept 1870 ae: 31y 9m GSL

Marcia Albertine d/o Charles A B d 3 Dec 1853 ae: 4y 2m GSL

Mary A w/o Asa A d/o Herbert Nichols d 6 Apr 1915 ae: 89y G:48

Willard s/o James d 21 Nov 1843 ae: 6m GSL

William s/o Seth & Abigail d 3 Sept 1905 ae: 74y 11m 12d SD I:91

MORTLEIGH, Mary E d/o Rachel d 8 May 1854 ae: 16y 5m Hilborn tomb A:10

MORTON, Mary Elizabeth w/o Van R b 1845 d 1881 H:102

MOSES, Alfred L s/o Rufus & Margaret d 25 Sept 1863 ae: 26y Civ/War: 1st Reg Maine Inf Co B SBE C:24

Henry O s/o Rufus & Margaret d 30 Dec 1853 ae: 14y SBE C:24

Margaret F d/o Rufus & Margaret d 7 Oct 1840 ae: 12y SB C:24

Margaret W wid/o Rufus d 6 May 1896 ae: 93y 8m 1w C:24

Rufus d 8 Feb 1893 ae: 97y 7m

MOSES (continued) 11d C:24

Rufus W d 26 Apr 1895 ae: 48y 6m SD C:24

MOTLEY, Leonard d 14 Jan 1857 ae: 26y Hilborn tomb A:10

MOULTON, Alonzo H s/o Enoch & Elizabeth d 11 June 1852 ae: 10m GSL

Harriet F w/o Morris M d 8 Nov 1885 Greely Hosp ae: 52y 4m GSL

John W C d 23 Apr 1855 ae: 22m GSL

Sarah C d/o William d 11 Nov 1849 ae: 14y GSL

MOWEN, Thomas d 3 July 1849 ae: 32y Catholic GSL

MUGFORD, Ezra d 3 Dec 1873 ae: 80y I:165

Samauel T s/o Ezra & Sarah d 19 May 1852 ae: 7m 8d SBE I:165

Sarah w/o Ezra d 5 Apr 1837 ae: 39y SBE I:165

MULBERRY, Hugh d 7 Aug 1844 ae: 61y Catholic GSL

MULLEN, Bernard s/o Lawrence & Catherine d 6 July 1851 ae: 2y 2m Catholic I:14

Catherine d/o Charles d 16 Nov 1856 ae: 2m Catholic GSL

Catherine w/o Edward d 23 Feb 1851 ae: 29y Catholic GSL

Edward d 28 Sept 1857 ae: 8y 5m Catholic GSL

Francis s/o Thomas d 26 Aug 1857 ae: 17m Catholic GSL

Mary Ann d/o Patrick d 29 Aug 1852 ae: 2y Catholic GSL

Patrick s/o Lawrence & Catherine d 6 July 1851 ae: 4y 7m Catholic I:14A

MULLIGAN, Ann d/o Thomas d 13 Apr 1856 ae: 4y Catholic GSL

Cornelius s/o Thomas d 23 May 1856 ae: 1y Catholic GSL

MULLINS, Mary A d/o Daniel d 17 Jan 1853 ae: 12y Catholic GSL

MULLOY, Bridget d/o John d 18 Oct 1852 ae: 22m Catholic

MULLOY (continued)
GSL
Catherine Foy w/o John d 20 Dec
1852 ae: 21y Catholic J:23
Edward d 2 Sept 1854 ae: 30y
Catholic GSL
James s/o John d 11 Jan 1853
ae: 2m Catholic GSL
MULNIX, Alice M d 28 Aug 1857
ae: 1y 11m G:47
Elizabeth d 12 Sept 1859 ae: 85y
SD G:47
Helen T d/o Andrew & Mary A d
29 Jan 1866 ae: 5y 7m G:47
MULVEY, Hugh d 8 Aug 1844 ae:
62y Native of Ireland Catholic
I:20A
MUNDY, James d 11 Feb 1858
ae: 49y Old Catholic Ground
GSL
MUNGER, Edward H s/o J W d
26 Mar 1858 ae: 2y 5m Trow-
bridge tomb Location unknown
Clara E d/o John W d 10 Aug
1849 ae: 19m GSL
Emma Louisa d/o John W d 26
Aug 1844 ae: 15m GSL
John Philip s/o John W d 25 Feb
1858 ae: 5y 9m Trowbridge
tomb Location unknown
MURCH, Charles A d/o John R &
Eleanor b 1881 d 1885 C:82
Charles Henry s/o John & Eunice
d 27 Feb 1838 SBE C:82
Clara A d/o John R & Eleanor E
b 1864 d 1887 C:82
Eleanor E w/o John R b 1837 d
1887 Chelsea, Massachusetts
C:82
Ella d/o John d 23 Mar 1858 ae:
6y 8m SD C:82
Frank H s/o John R & Eleanor E
b 1854 d 1886 C:82
George A s/o J J & S J d 27 Aug
1852 ae: 14m GSL
Helen d/o John 2nd & Eunice d
10 Apr 1845 ae: 5y 8m SBE
C:82
John R s/o John 2nd & Eunice d
1 Nov 1902 ae: 69y 10m C:82
Mary d 12 June 1864 ae: 72y GSL
MURPHY, Abigail w/o John d 24

MURPHY (continued)
Oct 1856 ae: 63y Catholic SBE
J:159
Benjamin B d 2 Oct 1851 ae: 16y
Catholic GSL
Caroline d/o Peter & Mary b
1845 d 1846 Catholic I:36
Catherine d/o Edward d 2 Sept
1857 ae: 8y Catholic GSL
Daniel s/o Daniel d 8 May 1854
ae: 8m 4d Catholic GSL
David s/o Martin d 10 May 1851
ae: 11y Catholic GSL
Deborah w/o Thomas d 22 Oct
1842 ae: 36y Catholic GSL
Edward b 1835 no burial record
Civ/War: 3rd Reg Maine Inf
Co I SD J:185
Edward s/o Edward d 7 Aug 1862
ae: 13m Catholic GSL
Elizabeth d/o Patrick d 12 Dec
1849 ae: 3m Catholic GSL
Ellen M d/o Peter & Mary J d 22
Jan 1906 ae: 70y Catholic I:36
Jeremiah d 12 Sept 1918 Med-
ford, Massachusetts ae: 61y
Catholic NS H:98
Jeremiah s/o Jeremiah d 7 Nov
1846 ae: 9d Catholic GSL
Joanna w/o Michael d 3 July
1847 ae: 25y Catholic Stran-
gers' Ground GSL
John d 5 Mar 1859 ae: 78y Cath-
olic SBE H:21
John d 26 Mar 1847 ae: 11m
Catholic GSL
John s/o Martin d 1 Jan 1847 ae:
6d Catholic GSL
John s/o Timothy d 23 Aug 1849
ae: 15m Catholic GSL
Julia Ann d/o Timothy d 10 July
1851 ae: 14m Catholic GSL
Margaret w/o Patrick d 21 Sept
1842 ae: 24y Catholic GSL
Margaret Ann d/o John W d 4
Jan 1858 ae: 2y 5m Catholic
Strangers' Ground GSL
Martin s/o Martin d 7 Jan 1845
ae: 14m Catholic GSL
Mary d/o Michael d 23 Feb 1847
ae: 1m Catholic GSL
Mary J Donley w/o Peter b 1811

MURPHY (continued)
d 1893 Catholic I:36
Michael d 21 Dec 1849 ae: 30y
Catholic GSL
Michael s/o J d 21 Sept 1857 ae:
19m Catholic GSL
Patrick s/o John d 9 Nov 1847
ae: 8m Catholic GSL
Peter Jr s/o Peter & Mary J d 18
Aug 1921 ae: 75y Civ/War: US
Navy Catholic I:36
Samuel b 1851 d 1892 Catholic
I:36
Susan E d/o Patrick d 7 Aug
1857 ae: 13y 11m Catholic
GSL
Thomas d 7 Feb 1850 Denmark,
Maine ae: 47y Catholic GSL
Timothy d 30 May 1856 ae: 35y
Catholic GSL
William s/o Edward d 3 Sept
1860 ae: 10m Catholic GSL
MURRAY, Andrew s/o Michael d
16 Oct 1848 ae: 5y Catholic
GSL
Berdelia d/o Michael d 28 Nov
1857 ae: 3y 6m Catholic GSL
Catherine d/o Dennis d 17 Oct
1859 ae: 3d Catholic Strangers'
Ground GSL
Edward d 19 Aug 1865 ae: 45y
Civ/War: US Navy Catholic SD
H:2
Edward s/o Michael d 12 July
1854 ae: 5y Catholic Strangers'
Ground GSL
James s/o Dennis d 16 July 1855
ae: 3y 6m Catholic GSL
Joan w/o Michael d 9 July 1855
ae: 25y Catholic GSL
Joanna w/o Dennis d 29 June
1858 ae: 30y Old Catholic
Ground GSL
John d 18 May 1847 ae: 68y Na-
tive of Aberdeen, Scotland SD
H:21
Mary w/o John d 11 Feb 1851 ae:
21y Catholic GSL
Mary L d/o Michael d 18 July
1856 ae: 2y Catholic GSL
Susan w/o Michael d 4 Sept 1852
ae: 38y Catholic GSL

NAMARA, Bridget d/o Patrick d
15 Sept 1856 ae: 6y Catholic
GSL
NASH, Charles E s/o Charles B d
14 Dec 1865 ae: 5y 8m GSL
Elizabeth w/o Charles B d 16
Nov 1856 ae: 20y GSL
Julia M d/o Charles B d 25 May
1872 ae: 29y GSL
Samuel T s/o Thomas d 25 July
1877 ae: 9y GSL
Walter s/o Thomas d 27 Aug
1874 ae: 5m GSL
Willie H s/o Thomas d 14 Aug
1883 ae: 4y GSL
NASON, Abigail Brown w/o John
b 1811 d 19 July 1853 J:50
Elizabeth J d 24 May 1898 ae:
48y 2m 9d SD D:20
Elisha no burial record SD J:50
James s/o James d 7 Aug 1856
ae: 1y 9m GSL
John d 12 Oct 1898 Greely Hosp
ae: 94y 1m Civ/War: 8th Reg
Maine Inf Co F J:50
John Jr s/o John & Abigail d 16
Apr 1852 ae: 23y SD J:50
Lydia w/o James d 30 Nov 1855
ae: 29y 3m GSL
Martha A F d 5 Apr 1852 ae: 21y.
SBE F:19
Sarah M d/o John d 27 Sept 1850
ae: 2y SD J:50
Wiliam H d 7 Dec 1860 ae: 28y
SD B:40
NAVARRO, Joseph G s/o Joseph
B F d 20 Nov 1865 ae: 5w GSL
NEAL, Caleb d 13 May 1853 ae:
70y GSL
Eleanor d/o John & Eleanor b
1844 d 17 Sept 1845 C:46
Eleanor w/o John b 1808 d 1877
C:46
James no dates on Mmt; no
burial record C:46
James b 1768 d 30 Jan 1832 C:46
James s/o John & Eleanor b
1831 d 21 Aug 1856 C:46
John no dates on Mmt, no burial
record C:46
John b 1793 d 21 June 1876 C:46
Capt John d 13 May 1852 ae: 78y

NEAL (continued)
H:54
John s/o Edward O d 14 Aug 1851 ae: 1y 7m GSL
John s/o J O d 25 Apr 1857 ae: 5y 10m GSL
John Pierrepont d 23 Apr 1915 Wernersville, Pennsylvania ae: 68y C:46
Lottie K wid/o John A d 7 June 1945 ae: 90y 10m 18d NS C:38
Margaret Eleanor b 1834 d 1927 C:46
Mary b 1829 d 1914 C:46
Mary d/o James d 15 Sept 1852 Boston, Massachusetts ae: 5m Catholic GSL
Rachel W d/o John & Rachel W b 1793 d 18 May 1858 C:46
Rachel W wid/o John b 18 July 1769 d 11 Dec 1849 C:46
Ruth d 10 Aug 1854 ae: 88y GSL
NEARLY, Bridget d/o Richard d 29 Aug 1860 ae: 9m Catholic GSL
NEE, John d 5 Oct 1853 ae: 20y "Killed on the Rail Road. Interred in the night." GSL
NEIL, John A d 13 Oct 1874 ae: 21y GSL
NELLY, Richard s/o Michael d 28 Aug 1863 ae: 1y GSL
NELSON, Caroline B d/o Alexander d 8 Aug 1859 ae: 1y GSL
Elmira E d/o Aaron B Holden d 30 Mar 1875 ae: 23y GSL
James E s/o William d 28 Sept 1855 ae: 8m GSL
John d 30 Jan 1881 ae: 21y GSL
NEVINS, Marion d 12 May 1833 ae: 62y SD E:4
NEWBEGIN, Nancy d/o Francis d 31 Mar 1856 ae: 5w GSL
NEWBOLD, Richard d 12 June 1845 ae: 21y 7m G:47
Josiah s/o Richard d 3 May 1851 ae: 7y G:47
NEWCOMB, Abram d 14 Nov 1863 ae: 22y Civ/War: 1st Reg Maine Inf Co D, Sgt 17th Reg Maine Inf Co C F:124
Jane C w/o Abram d 18 Nov 1858

NEWCOMB (continued)
ae: 18y 6m SB F:124
NEWELL, John W s/o Isaac d 24 June 1850 ae: 5y Catholic GSL
NEWMAN, Charles s/o Thomas d 27 Sept 1850 ae: 16y GSL
John N s/o Thomas d 21 July 1863 ae: 3y 2m GSL
NICHOLS, Amos d 9 Mar 1848 ae: 54y F:9
Augusta M w/o Amos d 27 Oct 1859 ae: 62y 10m F:9
Charles G d 30 Mar 1867 aboard USS *Vermont*, receiving ship, Brooklyn Navy Yard, New York ae: 38y Civ/War: 5th Reg Maine Inf Co G SD F:9
Dorothea N w/o Rev Ichabod d 17 Apr 1841 Body in 1st Parish tomb, Eastern Cemetery? SBE E:1
Frederick W s/o Herbert & Mary A d 24 Aug 1911 ae: 76y SD G:48
Ichabod s/o Dr Henry d 11 Oct 1842 ae: 3y E:1
Rev Ichabod b 5 July 1784 d 1 Jan 1859 Cambridge, Massachusetts E:1
Jane d 20 June 1817 ae: 15y Body moved from Phippsburg, Maine Aug 1897 McCobb tomb D:32
Josephine d/o Christopher d 21 Nov 1851 ae: 8m GSL
Mary Ann w/o Danforth D d 29 May 1865 ae: 44y SD D:67
Mary H d/o John Taylor Gilman & Caroline d 5 Feb 1868 ae: 6y 5m SBE E:1
May E wid/o John H d 1 Apr 1892 H:3
NICHERSON, Clara A d/o Phineas d 8 July 1850 ae: 7m GSL
NOBLE, Catherine M d 4 Feb 1849 ae: 41y GSL
E N no burial record SD I:15A
Henrietta d/o Rufus W d 10 Jan 1849 ae: 3m GSL
Isaac b 1793 d 1877 C:16
Mary Mrs d 15 Feb 1859 ae: 86y Trowbridge tomb Location un-

**NOBLE** (continued)
known
May w/o Isaac d 12 Mar 1868 ae: 72y SBE C:16
**NOLAN**, Patrick s/o Bartholomew d 6 Sept 1852 ae: 8m Catholic GSL
**NOLAND**, John d 4 May 1864 ae: 45y GSL
**NOON**, inf c/o John d 30 Apr 1853 ae: 6m 23d Old Catholic Ground GSL
Bridget d/o Stephen d 30 Aug 1854 ae: 7y Catholic GSL
Margaret d/o Stephen d 31 Aug 1854 ae: 2y Catholic GSL
Maria w/o Stephen d 25 Apr 1854 ae: 30y Catholic GSL
**NOONAN**, Ann w/o Thomas d 10 May 1866 ae: 42y SBE J:189
Catherine d/o Thomas & Ann d 20 Sept 1855 ae: 11m J:189
Dennis s/o Thomas & Ann d 26 May 1879 ae: 20y Fabyan, New Hampshire Catholic J:189
John E s/o Thomas & Ann d 21 July 1863 ae: 3y Catholic SBE J:189
Margaret d/o Thomas & Ann d 14 May 1858 ae: 15m Catholic SD J:189
Mary d/o Thomas & Ann d 27 Aug 1851 ae: 12d Catholic SBE J:189
Thomas d 24 Dec 1882 ae: 62y Native of Limerick, Ireland Catholic J:189
Wiliam s/o Thomas d 5 Apr 1871 ae: 18y 4m Catholic SD J:189
William T s/o Thomas & Ann d 5 Apr 1841 ae: 18y Catholic SBE J:189
**NORRIS**, Bertha M d/o W G d 26 Nov 1876 ae: 2y GSL
Betsy d/o Ezekiel & Eunice d 25 Feb 1846 ae: 22m SBE J:70
Betsy A d/o Ezekiel & Eunice d 15 Mar 1852 ae: 3m SBE J:70
Betsy K w/o Benjamin P d 29 Mar 1847 ae: 33y GSL
Eunice B w/o Ezekiel G d 20 Oct

**NORRIS** (continued)
1890 ae: 74y 6m SD J:70
Eunice E d/o E G d 28 Sept 1881 ae: 28y SD J:70
Ezekiel G d 1 Oct 1875 ae: 66y SD J:70
Lizzie E w/o Woodin G d 3 Oct 1877 ae: 35y GSL
**NORTON**, Caroline A d/o Benjamin d 29 May 1859 ae: 2y GSL
Joanna w/o William d 4 Oct 1844 ae: 50y GSL
Martin d 27 Dec 1865 ae: 40y GSL
Mary d/o Peter d 24 Dec 1856 ae: 4m GSL
Peter d 10 june 1857 ae: 22y GSL
**NORWOOD**, Lydia wid/o Joshua d 6 Sept 1847 ae: 65y D:59
**NOWLAND**, John s/o James d 23 Apr 1851 ae: 11m Catholic GSL
Sarah w/o Thomas d 12 Aug 1856 ae: 18y Strangers' Ground GSL
Susan w/o James d 7 May 1857 ae: 45y Catholic GSL
**NOWLEYN**, Joanna d/o William d 8 Oct 1844 ae: 14y Catholic GSL
John s/o James & Julia d 27 Oct 1851 ae: 11m Catholic SBE J:9
**NOWLYN**, Ellen d/o Bartholomew d 10 Aug 1864 ae: 7m Catholic GSL
**NOYES**, Anna F d/o John H d 15 Oct 1865 ae: 11y GSL
Arthur C s/o Ward d 21 Aug 1860 ae: 2m SD G:40
Clara A d/o Ward & Mary d 9 Jan 1851 ae: 19y G:40
Clarence W s/o Ward & Louisa d 17 Sept 1864 Andersonville Prison, Georgia ae: 18y 8m Civ/War: 1st Reg DC Cav Co B, 1st Reg Maine Cav Co L G:40
Henry N s/o Smith W d 17 Sept 1848 ae: 1y GSL
Lincoln s/o Ward d 10 Sept 1860 ae: 1m SD G:40

NOYES (continued)
Louisa F w/o Ward d/o Joel
Frost d 29 Aug 1852 ae: 40y
SD G:40
Mary w/o Ward d/o John Horr d
9 Jan 1845 ae: 39y G:40
Rosetta d/o John H d 13 Aug
1858 ae: 1y 10m GSL
Ward d 8 Aug 1869 ae: 65y SBE
G:40
William H s/o Ward & Mary d
12 Jan 1871 ae: 34y 1m 28d SD
G:40
NUTTER, inf d/o Nathan & Mary
C b & d 12 Apr 1817 B:21
Albert H S s/o Nathan & Mary C
d 22 Mar 1827 ae: 2y B:21
Alice M d/o Nathan & Mary C d
4 July 1896 Medfield, Mas-
sachusetts ae: 56y SBE B:21
Edward d 13 Feb 1904 Danvers,
Massachusetts ae: 72y B:21
Elizabeth d/o Nathan & Mary C d
30 Oct 1825 ae: 8y B:21
Francis Douglas s/o Nathan &
Mary C d 14 Jan 1852 Boston,
Massachusetts ae: 29y B:21
Joseph H no burial record SD
B:21
Mary Clapham w/o Nathan d 31
Aug 1852 ae: 56y B:21
Nathan d 31 Dec 1862 ae: 75y
SBE B:21
William s/o Nathan & Mary d 3
Apr 1833 ae: 6y B:21
NUTTING, Frances Ellen d/o
George S & Emma A d 27 May
1851 ae: 11m 10d SD C:80
Mighel d 12 Aug 1863 ae: 62y
GSL
O'BRIEN, Bridget d/o Thomas d
3 Jan 1857 ae: 4y Catholic
GSL
Daniel s/o Dennis d 15 Aug 1850
ae: 2y Catholic GSL
Elizabeth d/o John d 25 Sept
1857 ae: 14m Catholic GSL
Frances d 24 Apr 1861 ae: 15y
Catholic GSL
Jeremiah d 24 Aug 1850 ae: 35y
Catholic Strangers' Ground
GSL

O'BRIEN (continued)
Joanna d/o Lawrence d 11 Feb
1858 ae: 1d Catholic Strangers'
Ground GSL
John s/o John d 6 July 1858 ae:
3y Catholic GSL
John s/o Timothy d 25 Dec 1854
ae: 14m Catholic GSL
Lucy E d/o Michael d 4 Sept
1856 ae: 1y 9m Old Catholic
Ground GSL
Mary d 26 May 1849 ae: 70y
Catholic GSL
Nancy d/o Thomas d 16 Sept
1843 ae: 4y 8m Catholic GSL
William s/o Patrick d 6 Apr
1856 ae: 14m Catholic GSL
O'BRION, Benjamin F d Alms
House no burial record Cath-
olic GSL
Ellen d/o Thomas d 28 Mar 1857
ae: 5y Catholic GSL
Hannah d/o Charles d 24 June
1851 ae: 6m Catholic GSL
Jeremiah s/o John d 25 Aug 1848
ae: 11m Catholic GSL
Jeremiah s/o Timothy d 28 June
1857 ae: 5y Catholic GSL
Margaret w/o John d 21 Jan 1851
ae: 25y Catholic GSL
Moses d 27 Aug 1863 ae: 48y
Catholic GSL
Percy s/o Moses d 17 June 1863
ae: 1y Catholic GSL
Thomas d 28 Mar 1852 ae: 28y
Catholic GSL
O'CONNELL, ---- w/o Morris d
10 Sept 1854 ae: 40y Buried
beside husband Catholic Stran-
gers' Ground GSL
Elizabth d/o Manuel d 7 Sept
1853 ae: 1y 6m Catholic Stran-
gers' Ground GSL
Mary w/o Daniel d 8 Nov 1851
ae: 18y Catholic GSL
Mary Ann d/o David d 10 Oct
1855 ae: 22m Catholic GSL
Morris d 10 Sept 1854 ae: 42y
Catholic Strangers' Ground
GSL
Patrick d 5 Jan 1858 ae: 66y
Catholic GSL

O'CONNOR, Eliza Jane d/o Neal & Sarah d 5 June 1853 ae: 7y Catholic I:3A

George E s/o David d 23 Aug 1859 ae: 7m Catholic GSL

John s/o Neal & Sarah d 9 Mar 1841 ae: 7m Catholic I:3A

Michael s/o Neal & Sarah d 21 Jan 1854 ae: 50y Catholic SB I:3A

Thomas s/o David d 20 Sept 1860 ae: 7d Catholic GSL

ODION, Frederick D s/o Charles E d 4 May 1852 ae: 22m GSL

O'DONNELL, Dennis O d 23 Dec 1856 ae: 55y Buried "side of the bank." Catholic GSL

Hannah d/o Michael d 22 Sept 1855 ae: 4d Catholic GSL

Lizzie d/o Michael d 6 Mar 1860 ae: 2y Catholic GSL

Mary A d/o John d 4 Sept 1856 ae: 18m Catholic GSL

O'FLAHERTY, William s/o Michael d 10 Oct 1857 ae: 20m Catholic GSL

O'HERN, William s/o John d 10 Mar 1860 ae: 17m Catholic GSL

O'HERRO, Mary d 9 July 1856 ae: 13y Catholic GSL

OHION, David s/o David d 16 Aug 1846 ae: 14m Catholic GSL

OLESON, Anne Sewall d/o John & Matilda P b 17 Feb 1841 d 20 Apr 1841 SBE F:7

Edwin W s/o John & Matilda P d 11 Apr 1846 ae: 2y SBE F:7

Harriet Prince d/o John b 8 June 1853 d 4 Nov 1860 F:7

John b 14 Sept 1813 d 29 May 1882 F:7

Matilda Prince w/o John d 6 Jan 1891 ae: 74y 6m F:7

OLIVER, Uriah s/o Samuel d 23 Oct 1847 ae: 3m Catholic GSL

O'NEAL, Catherine d/o Patrick d 29 July 1859 ae: 2y Catholic GSL

Cornelius s/o Cornelius d 5 Apr 1845 ae: 3m Catholic GSL

O'NEAL (continued)

Cornelius s/o John d 31 Oct 1858 ae: 6w Catholic GSL

Ellen w/o Patrick d 12 Sept 1842 ae: 26y Catholic GSL

James d 15 May 1849 ae: 9m Catholic GSL

James d 6 Nov 1853 ae: 2m Catholic GSL

James s/o John d 13 Aug 1860 ae: 4m Catholic GSL

James s/o Susan d 7 Aug 1858 ae: 6m Catholic GSL

John s/o Cornelius d 25 Sept 1852 ae: 4m Catholic GSL

John s/o John d 5 Jan 1847 ae: 4m Catholic GSL

John s/o John d 9 June 1848 ae: 6m Catholic GSL

Margaret d 7 Apr 1849 ae: 8m Catholic GSL

Michael d 27 Jan 1858 ae: 8y Catholic GSL

Michael s/o Hugh d 5 Mar 1852 ae: 4y 11m Catholic GSL

Mary d/o James d 8 Oct 1855 ae: 1y Catholic GSL

Mary Ann d/o Michael & Mary J Deehan b 1856 d 1857 Catholic J:7

Mary E d/o James d 1 Oct 1862 ae: 5y Catholic GSL

Michael s/o Michael & Mary J Deehan b 1849 d 1858 Catholic J:7

Michael s/o John d 18 Nov 1852 ae: 7m Catholic GSL

Patrick s/o William d 29 Oct 1847 ae: 4y Catholic GSL

Simeon s/o Patrick d 15 Aug 1843 ae: 8m Catholic GSL

OSGOOD, Caroline A w/o John d 17 Feb 1856 ae: 46y SBE F:119

Henry s/o Henry B d 6 Oct 1841 ae: 7m GSL

George H s/o John & Caroline d 22 May 1865 Arlington Heights, Virginia ae: 21y Civ/War: 20th Reg Maine Inf Co E F:119

**OSGOOD** (continued)

John d 18 Dec 1844 ae: 38y F:119

John d 24 Dec 1844 ae: 29y GSL

Josiah D s/o John & Caroline d 7 July 1857 ae: 18y SBE F:119

Mary C d/o John & Caroline d 3 May 1843 ae: 4y 7m F:119

Sarah S d/o John & Caroline d 11 Feb 1837 ae: 4m SBE F:119

**O'SULLIVAN**, Hannah w/o Patrick d 15 Dec 1848 ae: 34y Catholic GSL

Henry s/o Timothy & Maria C b 1851 d 1853 Catholic I:170

Henry s/o Timothy & Maria C b & d 1860 Catholic I:170

Maria Connor w/o Timothy b 1829 d 1864 Catholic I:170

Timothy b 1821 d 1863 Civ/War: 47th Reg Massachusetts Inf, "Putnam Blues." Catholic I:170

William s/o Timothy & Maria b & d 1850 Catholic I:170

**O'ROAN**, Susan d/o John d 17 Aug 1855 ae: 1y 7m Catholic GSL

**O'SHEA**, Michael d 11 Mar 1855 Catholic GSL

**OTIS**, George d 11 Sept 1842 ae: 36y GSL

**OWEN**, Ella d/o George d 16 June 1862 ae: 8y GSL

Lydia wid/o John d 17 Aug 1854 ae: 62y GSL

Sarah E w/o E C d 30 Sept 1861 ae: 28y GSL

Thomas d 21 Apr 1848 ae: 48y Old Catholic Ground GSL

Thomas d 4 Sept 1855 ae: 78y GSL

**OWENS**, Bridget w/o Thomas d 6 June 1855 ae: 44y Native of Co Tyrone, Ireland SB J:155

Judith wid/o John d 20 Nov 1857 ae: 80y GSL

Susan w/o Thomas d 11 May 1864 ae: 31y Strangers' Ground GSL

**OXNARD**, Charles O s/o Edward P d 12 Apr 1865 ae: 7y B:27

**OXNARD** (continued)

Edward b 13 July 1791 d 21 Jne 1873 B:27

Martha w/o Edward b 17 Apr 1785 d 30 Jan 1860 B:27

Osborne d 17 Aug 1894 New York City ae: 70y B:27

**PADDOCK**, Mary wid/o Dr Thomas d/o Arthur McLellan d 8 Feb 1858 ae: 48y 10m Native of St John, New Brunswick GSL

**PADDY**, Patrick s/o Patrick d 25 Oct 1855 ae: 4y 8m Catholic GSL

**PAGE**, Caroline A d 4 Jan 1899 ae: 71y 8m 23d SD J:225

Elizabeth d/o Richard d 10 Apr 1856 ae: 4w SD J:255

Edward D d 12 Jan 1842 ae: 3y GSL

George W s/o Richard d 17 Aug 1867 ae: 5m SD J:255

Henry F d 19 Sept 1868 ae: 62y GSL

Henry R F d 4 Dec 1891 ae: 29y 7m J:255

Mary Emily d/o Addison d 30 Sept 1861 ae: 1y GSL

William H s/o Richard d 22 Aug 1854 ae: 4m SD J:255

Richard D d 11 Feb 1883 ae: 57y. "Erected by/The Relief Association/of the Portland Fire Department." J:255

**PAINE**, Ada d/o J S d 8 Aug 1856 ae: 8y SD F:143

Ann d/o William W d 18 Aug 1862 ae: 6m GSL

Bell d/o Alvin & Isabel no burial record SD B:76

Catherine D w/o Michael d 25 Mar 1850 ae: 40y "Found dead in Cape Elizabeth." Catholic GSL

Dorinda d/o Isaac & Hannah d 11 Aug 1857 ae: 36y 9m I:65

Isabel A McLenney w/o Alvin R d 13 Jan 1853 ae: 25y B:76

Jacob S d 26 Sept 1856 ae: 45y F:143

Rebecca B w/o Jacob S d 21 Oct

PAINE (continued)
1860 ae: 52y F:143
Thomas d 9 Dec 1857 ae: 35y
GSL
PALMER, John Gould s/o S G d
28 Aug 1853 ae: 7m 13d GSL
William d 28 Apr 1850 ae: 6d SD
B:40
PARIAN, Patrick d 26 Feb 1851
ae: 28y Catholic GSL
PARK, James d 10 OCt 1857 ae:
41y GSL
PARKER, Antena s/o Michael d
18 July 1849 ae: 10m Catholic
GSL
Charles s/o William & Abigail C
d 28 July 1846 ae: 5m G:26
Charles H s/o William & Abigail
C d 1 June 1845 ae: 4w G:26
Charles Pomeroy b 12 Apr 1852 d
2 Dec 1916 E:2
Edward s/o Thomas d 8 Feb
1858 ae: 3m GSL
Ellen A d/o William W d 16 Dec
1849 ae: 1y GSL
Frances Green w/o Charles P,
d/o David & Mary A Haskins b
25 Dec 1854 d 4 May 1939
Medford, Massachusetts E:2
Francis H s/o William d 6 Sept
1855 ae: 8m GSL
Harriet d/o William G d 17 Sept
1874 ae: 4m GSL
Kingsbury s/o Capt Kingsbury E
& Rezilva E d 9 Sept 1856 ae:
17m H:42
Capt Kingsbury E b 6 Apr 1824 d
5 Nov 1884 H:42
Plinney s/o Life & Hannah d 29
Mar 1849 ae: 3y 12d I:65
Rezilva E w/o Capt Kingsbury E
d 17 Dec 1866 ae: 38y H:42
Rosie d/o Capt Kingsbury E &
Rezilva E no dates on stone;
no burial record H:42
Snow d 28 Apr 1850 ae: 37y I:156
Thomas s/o Thomas d 3 June
1849 ae: 8m Catholic GSL
William S s/o William d 2 Apr
1850 ae: 9y GSL
PARKES, Bridget d 9 Apr 1855
ae: 60y Catholic GSL

PARKES (continued)
William d 16 Apr 1855 ae: 63y
GSL
PARKS, Catherine d/o William d
26 July 1856 ae: 20m 20d
Catholic GSL
James s/o William d 7 Feb 1853
ae: 9m Catholic GSL
Susan w/o Asa d 24 Feb 1852 ae:
38y G:90
PARLIN, George J d 7 Jan 1847
ae: 37y F:3
PARSLEY, Joseph d 28 Mar 1859
ae: 40y Buried Nathan Fessen-
den lot GSL
PARSONS, Emily w/o Samuel d 7
Aug 1883 ae: 76y SD H:75
Henrietta S d/o Joseph & Eliza d
29 Aug 1849 ae: 9m SB I:122
Joseph B d 8 Apr 1863 ae: 31y
Civ/War: 25th Reg Maine Inf
Co H H:75
Josephine K d/o Joseph & Eliza
d 25 Sept 1848 ae: 2y 7m I:122
Mary E d/o Samuel & Emily d 20
Sept 1852 ae: 18y H:75
Samuel N s/o Joseph B d 12
June 1868 ae: 2y GSL
Samuel N d 14 Apr 1877 ae: 67y
SD H:75
PARTRIDGE, Benjamin d 5 Apr
1869 ae: 56y GSL
Claude e s/o Samuel O d 14 Nov
1855 ae: 13m GSL
Emma G d/o Samuel & Thankful
H d 11 Aug 1912 ae: 91y G:81
George Conant s/o Joseph G d 25
July 1846 ae: 11m GSL
Joseph G d 11 Sept 1893 ae: 77y
9m GSL
Mary I w/o Joseph G d 14 Mar
1865 ae: 40y GSL
Mary T d/o Joseph d 29 Mar
1862 ae: 4y 7m GSL
Samuel b 1784 d 1849 G:81
Thankful H Baker w/o Samuel b
1795 d 1865 G:81
Warren H s/o Joseph G d 12 Sept
1848 ae: 22y GSL
PASTERLOW, Sarah d 22 Apr
1856 ae: 25y Old Catholic
Ground GSL

PATCH, Eugene M s/o Henry C & Frances E d 12 July 1875 Yarmouth, Nova Scotia ae: 13y C:38

Frances E w/o Henry C b 17 Apr 1835 d 21 Feb 1910 Chelsea, Massachusetts C:38

Henry C b 8 Apr 1831 d 8 July 1884 C:38

Lucy s d 28 Oct 1852 ae: 27y GSL

PATRICK, Charles A s/o William M d 18 Nov 1853 ae: 13m SD I:76

Elizabeth L d/o J W d 2 Sept 1858 ae: 2y 5m GSL

Stephen d 15 May 1866 ae: 79y GSL

William M d 25 Oct 1853 ae: 30y SD I:76

PATTEN, Eliza d 2 Mar 1882 Greely Hospital ae: 30y GSL

John s/o Margaret d 15 Nov 1857 ae: 20m GSL

Lucena E d/o Richard d 26 Oct 1856 ae: 17y GSL

PATTERSON, Albertina E d/o Henry A d 2 Sept 1864 ae: 8m 16d GSL

Arthur G s/o William G d 11 Dec 1875 ae: 17d GSL

Clara d 29 Apr 1850 ae: 2y 4m SD I:153

Clara F d/o Wiliam B d 11 Nov 1870 ae: 16y SD I:153

Elizabeth w/o William d 19 Sept 1867 ae: 83y C:49

Hannah d Apr 1898 Boston, Massachusetts of old age No death record SD F:127

James F twin s/o James d 29 Mar 1846 ae: 18w GSL

James G d 5 Oct 1864 ae: 74y F:127

Lydia Jane w/o James d 10 Jan 1846 ae: 28y C:50

Nancy Luella d/o William B & Sophia d 21 Feb 1860 ae: 7y SD I:153

Nancy W wid/o William Jr d 10 Nov 1845 ae: 34y C:50

Samuel G d 18 Oct 1844 ae: 34y

PATTERSON (continued) C:55

Simon d 18 Apr 1837 ae: 27y SD C:50

Capt Thomas d 18 June 1830 Ae; 31y C:55

Thomas H d 6 May 1857 ae: 28y C:55

William d 25 Jan 1854 ae: 83y SBE C:49

William J d 16 Aug 1845 ae: 40y C:50

PEABODY, Edward B s/o H B d 17 Aug 1863 GSL

Jane no burial record SD J:94

Phebe Ann d 27 Jan 1860 ae: 93y GSL

PEACHEY, Rozella R Small w/o Thomas d 254 May 1855 ae: 39y SBE F:91

PEARSON, Susan wid/o Samuel d 11 Dec 1855 ae: 78y GSL

PEASE, David d 18 Aug 1857 ae: 86y SBE C:45

Hannah w/o David d 16 Oct 1838 ae: 67y SBE C:45

Harriet d/o David & Hannah d 10 Mar 1844 ae: 46y SBE C:45

Jane M d/o David & Hannah d 23 Nov 1830 ae: 16y SBE C:45

John Curtis s/o Richard & Rebecca b 3 Apr 1832 d 12 Sept 1833 I:137

Maria d/o David & Hannah no burial record SBE C:45

Rebecca w/o Richard d 30 Dec 1857 ae: 59y SB I:137

Richard d 30 Apr 1860 ae: 84y I:137

PEEBLES, John d 28 June 1875 ae: 73y GSL

PENDERGAST, John d 9 May 1855 ae: 33y Catholic GSL

Michael s/o John d 11 Feb 1853 ae: 1y Catholic GSL

PENNELL, Alice I d/o Francis d 27 May 1913 ae: 61y 9m 7d SD I:172

Ann L d/o Clement Jr d 8 Jan 1850 ae: 3y Sawyer tomb A:14

Augustus H s/o Matthew L d 28 June 1846 GSL

103

PENNELL (continued)

Bertha L b 13 June 1882 d 21 Apr 1898 I:172

Charles H s/o Thomas & Elizabeth d 28 May 1852 ae: 6y 9m SD C:20

Celia Ashland d/o late Matthew L d 20 Dec 1849 Boston, Massachusetts ae: 2y GSL

Clement Jr d 13 Sept 1851 ae: 30y Sawyer tomb A:14

Eddy Chilton s/o Capt Thomas & Lucretia F d 7 Aug 1857 ae: 1y 11m SBE J:240

Edward s/o Thomas & Elizabeth d 26 May 1857 ae: 5y 7m SD C:20

Eliza Jane d/o Horace W d 7 Feb 1845 GSL

Francis s/o Walter S b 1816 d 1860 I:172

Fred O b 6 Oct 1876 d 4 May 1877 I:172

Frederick A s/o Clement d 26 Apr 1906 ae: 55y Sawyer tomb A:14

Harriet L d/o Thomas M & Lucretia F d 5 Dec 1902 ae: 43y 6m 21d SD J:240

Lemira w/o Walter S b 1821 d 1893 I:172

Levi d 17 Mar 1828 ae: 82y 16d Sawyer tomb A:14

Lucretia F w/o Capt Thomas d 8 July 1888 ae: 56y 3m J:240

Matthew L d 26 June 1849 Boston, Massachusetts ae: 33y GSL

May A d/o Thomas & Elizabeth d 24 Jan 1857 ae: 9m SBE C:20

Minnie d/o Capt Thomas & Lucretia F d 25 Dec 1849 SBE J:240

Minnie A d/o Walter S b 31 May 1875 d 8 Dec 1888 I:172

Sarah Elizabeth w/o Clement Jr d 9 June 1851 ae: 28y Sawyer tomb A:14

Sarah Louisa d/o Matthew d 21 June 1848 Boston, Massachusetts ae: 9y GSL

PENNELL (continued)

Susan B d/o Samuel F Ballard d 19 Mar 1933 Sawyer tomb A:14

Theodore R s/o Francis d 24 Sept 1849 ae: 4y GSL

Thomas Mancella s/o Capt Thomas & Lucretia F d 4 Jan 1831 Montevideo, Uruguay ae: 6w J:240

Walter S b 1 Jan 1848 d 4 Feb 1893 I:172

Willie Thomas s/o Capt Thomas & Lucretia F d 23 Aug 1843 SBE J:240

PERKINS, Eliza Sherburn Titcomb w/o George W d 25 Mar 1895 ae: 70y 7m G:23

Mary w/o Benjamin d 22 July 1853 ae: 45y GSL

PERRY, Aaron F d 16 July 1879 ae: 31y GSL

Apollo s/o Enoch L & Elizabeth E d 20 May 1847 ae: 13y 6m Buried in "white coffin, no plate." H:101

Elizabeth d/o Mary E d 13 Sept 1856 ae: 6m GSL

Elizabeth E w/o Enoch L b 29 Jan 1810 d 10 June 1878 H:101

Enoch L b 21 Dec 1801 d 27 Sept 1873 H:101

George H s/o Enoch d 15 May 1850 ae: 4y SD H:101

Harriette Stetson d/o Enoch L & Elizabeth E d 14 Sept 1856 ae: 5m H:101

Henry Boynton s/o Enoch L & Elizabeth E d 16 May 1850 ae: 4y H:101

Lois wid/o Moses E d 9 Mar 1866 ae: 75y I:158

Moses E d 15 Apr 1850 ae: 62y SBE I:158

PETTE, Maria d/o John d 10 Oct 1854 ae: 16m Old Catholic Ground GSL

PETERSON, Inez buried 8 Feb 1962 No burial record Safford-Hall tomb A:20

PETTES, James d 12 July 1855 ae: 65y Strangers' Ground GSL

John s/o John d 24 July 1856 ae:

PETTES (continued)
4m Strangers' Ground GSL
PETTIGREW, Mary A d 21 Feb
1870 ae: 43y GSL
PETTINGILL, Alonzo L s/o Capt
William & Mary T d 15 Nov
1856 ae: 21y F:85
Arthur P s/o Leonard A d 21 July
1872 ae: 4m GSL
George A s/o Capt William &
Mary d 3 July 1863 ae: 28y
Killed in action - Gettysburg,
Pennsylvania Ci/War F:85
Horace J s/o Capt William &
Mary T d 2 Sept 1849 ae: 21y
10m F:85
Lucretia d/o John d 22 Mar 1855
ae: 47y GSL
Martha A d/o Capt William &
Mary T d 23 Aug 1844 ae: 11m
F:85
Mary d/o James d 26 Mar 1842
ae: 6m GSL
Mary J d/o Capt William & Mary
T d 8 Nov 1848 ae: 23y 3m
F:85
Mary T w/o Capt William d 13
May 1880 ae: 76y SB F:85
Sarah wid/o True W d 19 Aug
1866 ae: 64y GSL
True W d 14 Dec 1859 ae: 54y
GSL
Capt William d 29 July 1863 ae:
70y F:85
PETTINGREW, Charles H s/o J
H & Eliza Newall d 29 Aug
1847 ae: 24y F:44
Eliza Newall w/o John H d 27
Feb 1884 ae: 79y 10m F:44
John H d 21 Jan 1869 ae: 65y
F:44
PETTY, Catherine w/o James d
30 Aug 1854 ae: 67y Catholic
Strangers' Ground GSL
Frederick d 8 Sept 1856 ae: 27y
Catholic GSL
Martha A d/o late Patrick d 22
Oct 1857 ae: 8m Catholic GSL
PHILBROOK, Daniel M d 2 June
1882 ae: 55y Civ/War: 3rd Reg
Maine Inf Co K C:88
Sarah J w/o Daniel M d/o Ed-

PHILBROOK (continued)
ward Hiller d 31 May 1915 ae:
86y 10m SD C:88
PHILLIPS, Eliza Jane d/o John d
18 Nov 1854 ae: 2y 1m 10d
GSL
Hannah d 13 Aug 1866 ae: 69y
GSL
John s/o William H d 2 Aug
1860 ae: 4y SD F:74
Sabina I wid/o William H d 25
Sept 1908 ae: 78y SD F:74
William H d 5 Sept 1889 ae: 59y
SBE F:74
PHINNEY, Alice M d/o Edward H
d 4 Mar 1863 ae: 2y 1m Hil-
born tomb A:10
Angelina B d/o Edward d 14 Aug
1862 ae: 3m Hilborn tomb
A:10
Anna d/o Daniel d 8 Sept 1862
ae: 1y 4m GSL
Catherine w/o Richard d 9 Nov
1853 ae: 33y Catholic Stran-
gers' Ground GSL
Charles K s/o Stephen d 20 Feb
1864 ae: 11m GSL
Elder Clement d 2 Mar 1855 ae:
74y GSL
Daniel s/o Bartlett d 17 Oct 1854
ae: 4y GSL
Helen d/o Elizabeth d 10 Dec
1842 ae: 5m GSL
Jesse d 3 Dec 1842 ae: 45y
Catholic GSL
Mary A d/o Hugh d 26 July 1857
ae: 9m GSL
Patrick s/o Richard d 24 Nov
1856 ae: 6w Catholic Stran-
gers' Ground GSL
Timothy s/o Timothy d 4 Nov
1854 ae: 6m Catholic Stran-
gers' Ground GSL
PHOENIX, Eunice w/o Richard d
24 Aug 1847 ae: 46y GSL
Francis E d/o Richard d 8 Aug
1846 ae: 4m GSL
Richard d 27 Aug 1847 ae: 47y
GSL
PIERCE, Alden d 1841 ae: 34y
J:273
Andrew J s/o Alden & Eliza Ann

PIERCE (continued)
d Aug 1852 ae: 24y J:273
Benjamin d 26 Nov 1851 ae: 38y
GSL
Charles E s/o Edward F & Har-
riet G d 5 July 1853 ae: 1y 2m
F:70
Eliza P w/o Alden d 2 May 1853
ae: 45y J:273
Franklin A s/o Charles F d 30
July 1880 ae: 4m F:70
Harriet G w/o Edward F d/o John
& Sophia Deguro d 28 Feb 1869
ae: 36y F:70
Melisa d/o Alden & Eliza Ann d
16 May 1853 ae: 18y J:273
PIERSON, George d 16 July 1837
F:93
PIMSEY, James W d 6 Nov 1849
ae: 29y GSL
PINGREE, Alice May d/o Aaron
W d 28 Nov 1865 ae: 2y 5m
GSL
Consuelo Imogeen d/o L F & S
M D d 18 July 1851 ae: 3y SD
H:29
PLACE, Clara E d/o Edward R d
23 Feb 1853 ae: 8m GSL .
Lovira w/o George O d 18 Aug
1871 ae: 32y 4m GSL
Perry s/o Jonathan & P d 10 Dec
1839 ae: 16y SD E:3
Sarah E w/o Edward R, d/o
Charles & Sarah Hedman d 14
Sept 1855 ae: 28y SD F:16
PLUMMER, Abbie W w/o
George H b 1839 d 1882 F:79
Ann Louise Virginia w/o Charles
F, d/o John & Elizabeth K
Garland d 2 Sept 1911 ae: 74y
B:35
Ann M d 22 June 1896 ae: 70y
9m SD B:36
Arthur d 21 Jan 1864 ae: 73y
Plummer tomb Location un-
known
Charles s/o Arthur d 31 Aug 1864
ae: 42y Plummer tomb Loca-
tion unknown
Charles F d 3 Apr 1867 ae: 2y
GSL
Charles F s/o Moses I & Mary d

PLUMMER (continued)
8 Sept 1905 ae: 75y 7m B:39
Edwin d 29 May 1858 ae: 33y
GSL
Emma L d/o George H & Abbie
W d 12 Nov 1879 ae: 5y SD
F:79
Lemuel Dyer d 21 Apr 1854 ae:
75y SB J:88
Louisa B d/o George H d 23 Jan
1869 ae: 11w GSL
Mary Ann d 20 July 1874 ae: 30y
GSL
Samuel M d 21 Apr 1854 ae: 75y
SD J:88
Sarah D wid/o Lemuel D d 2 Oct
1871 ae: 87y 16d SD J:88
Sophia w/o Arthur d 14 Apr 1857
ae: 65y Plummer tomb Loca-
tion unknown
William H s/o Charles d 22 Oct
1851 ae: 4m GSL
POLAND, Laura d/o William d
17 Dec 1855 ae: 1y GSL
POLK, Franklin H s/o A H & M E
d 11 Sept 1886 ae: 3w 2d GSL
POLLIES, William d 8 Apr 1852
ae: 62y GSL
POOLE, Ann w/o Asa S b 1825 d
1896 B:35
Asa S d 8 May 1855 ae: 33y SD
B:35
Georgianna A d/o Asa S & Ann d
31 Aug 1849 ae: 13m SD B:35
POOR, Charlotte C d/o Frederick
d 28 Dec 1847 ae: 3y SD F:40
Edwin B s/o Joseph & Elizabeth
· A H d 11 July 1889 ae: 50y
B:31
Elizabeth A H w/o Joseph d 25
Apr 1855 ae: 48y B:31
Joseph d 18 Oct 1849 ae: 42y
B:31
Joseph H s/o Joseph & Elizabeth
A H d 17 May 1889 ae: 57y
B:31
Thomas H s/o Joseph & Eliz-
abeth A H d 22 Jan 1864 ae:
26y Civ/War: 1st Reg Maine
Inf Co D B:31
PORTER, Annie Stover w/o
Samuel d 10 July 1833 ae: 50y

PORTER (continued)
B:55
Caroline d/o Samuel & Annie S d
15 Sept 1852 ae: 36y B:55
Charles H s/o Samuel & Annie S
d 7 Sept 1841 ae: 28y B:55
Delia A d/o Samuel & Annie S d
10 Aug 1829 ae: 25y B:55
Eliza w/o Stephen d 23 OCt 1847
ae: 53y GSL
Eliza F d/o Samuel & Annie S d
1 Nov 1828 ae: 19y B:55
Eunice w/o Henry d 5 Aug 1858
ae: 51y GSL
James s/o John d 8 Nov 1845 ae:
12y "Run over by a cab." GSL
John d 10 Nov 1864 in Con-
federate prison ae: 20y.
Civ/War: 1st Reg Maine Cav
Co A SD B:75
John H d 24 Feb 1886 ae: 47y 6m
GSL
Samuel d 20 Dec 1847 ae: 69y
B:55
Stephen d 3 Nov 1851 ae: 63y
GSL
POWELL, James s/o John d 12
Aug 1856 ae: 1y GSL
POWERS, Ann d/o Richard d 24
Mar 1853 ae: 11m Catholic
Strangers' Ground GSL
James s/o John d 28 Oct 1859
ae: 6w GSL
PRATT, Alexander b 1899 d 1971
no burial record B:24
Benjamin F d 1 Nov 1863 ae: 54y
GSL
Edgar s/o Thomas c & Grace C
no burial record SD H:46
Ellen w/o Franklin d 23 Sept
1852 ae: 39y GSL
George G s/o Benjamin d 19 Jan
1847 ae: 23m GSL
Grace C d 11 July 1922 East
Providence, Rhode Island ae:
76y SD H:46
Grace C w/o Thomas C d 8 Mar
1847 H:46
Helene Stetson b 1893 d 1980 no
burial record B:24
Thomas C b 19 May 1843 d 1 Jan
1879 Boston, Massachusetts

PRATT (continued)
Civ/War: 25th Reg Maine Inf
Co G SBE H:46
PRAY, John d 15 Dec 1854 ae:
42y GSL
PREBLE, Sarah A d 17 Apr 1904
Brookline, Massachusetts ae:
89y SD B:29
PRENTISS, Abigail F d 11 Oct
1874 ae: 69y GSL
Mary Ellen d/o Mary Ellen d 16
Jan 1864 ae: 3m GSL
PRESCOTT, Charles P d 26 Sept
1854 Roxbury, Massachusetts
GSL
Harriet E d/o John C d 28 Feb
1857 ae: 8y 7m GSL
Jane M d 28 Apr 1857 Roxbury,
Massachusetts ae: 51y GSL
Capt Lewis b 7 Aug 1783 d 25
Sept 1834 Norfolk, Virginia
G:29
Mary A d 29 Jan 1859 ae: 35y
GSL
Susan w/o Capt Lewis b 22 Jan
1795 d 10 Aug 1837 G:29
PRESLY, James s/o Patrick d 20
Aug 1855 ae: 1y 5m Catholic
GSL
PRESSY, Emily Jane w/o James
W d 4 Sept 1851 ae: 26y GSL
PRIME, George s/o George &
Jane d 22 Mar 1841 ae: 2y F:6
Georgiana d/o George W & Jane
d 9 Oct 1843 ae: 11m F:6
Julia Ann d/o George W & Jane
d 9 Mar 1841 ae: 10y 3m F:6
PRINCE, Blanche Horsley d/o
Charles M & Catherine M b 25
Aug 1850 d 18 Dec 1852 F:7
Catherine M w/o Charles M d 28
Mar 1902 Kittery, Maine ae:
78y 10m 27d SBE F:7
Charles L s/o Charles M d 25
Oct 1864 ae: 18y 3m Killed in
Baltimore, Maryland, gun-shot
wound SD F:7
Charles M b 9 Mar 1825 d 9 May
1891 Civ/War: 3rd Reg Maine
Inf Co A, 30th Reg Maine Inf
F:7
Clara Ella no burial record SBE

**PRINCE** (continued)
F:16

Gertrude Blumar d/o Charles M & Catherine M b 29 June 1849 d 22 Dec 1852 F:7

Henry L s/o Charles M & Catherine M b 5 July 1846 d 25 Oct 1864 of wounds received at Cedar Creek, Virginia Civ/ War: 1st Reg Maine Vet Vols Co F F:7

Mary D w/o Daniel d 22 May 1875 ae: 76y SD F:7

Mary S wid/o Sewall b 1798 d 1875 F:7

Sarah E d/o Tristram G & Hannah S d 22 June 1826 SD F:16

**PRINDLEY**, Mary d/o Morris d 22 Sept 1860 ae: 1y GSL

**PRIOR**, Rienzi W s/o William M & Rosamond C d 4 Mar 1837 ae: 7m B:70

**PRISCALL**, Jane w/o Dennis d 16 Jan 1848 Freeport, Maine ae: 35y Catholic GSL

**PROCTOR**, Charles Jenkins s/o Jeremiah & Jane H d 28 Feb 1842 ae: 5y G:84

Daniel W s/o John C d 13 Aug 1852 ae: 13m GSL

Edwin A s/o John C & L P d 18 Apr 1852 ae: 5y GSL

Jane Dow d/o Jeremiah & Jane H d 10 Aug 1910 ae: 68y G:84

Jane H w/o Jeremiah d 14 Jan 1855 ae: 45y SBE G:84

Jeremiah d 22 June 1872 ae: 72y G:84

Mary Jane d/o Jeremiah & Jane H d 23 Feb 1848 ae: 3y 5m G:84

**PUTNEY**, William d 23 Nov 1848 ae: 40y GSL

**QUARRIE**, Angus M d/o Angus d 20 Sept 1858 ae: 5m 16d GSL

**QUILL**, Hannah M d/o James & Hannah d 2 Sept 1847 ae: 1y 5m Native of Therle, Co Kerry, Ireland Catholic J:8

William s/o Thomas d 16 Jan 1857 ae: 5y GSL

**QUIMBY**, Charles H d 10 Dec 1851 ae: 21y GSL

George H s/o late James d 15 Nov 1850 ae: 22y GSL

Henry A s/o James d 29 Jan 1860 ae: 22y GSL

James d 17 June 1842 ae: 41y GSL

Martha wid/o James d 24 Apr 1855 ae: 54y GSL

**QUINAY**, John d 25 May 1850 ae: 61y Catholic GSL

**QUINBY**, Gertrude A d/o H M d 30 May 1882 Worcester, Massachusetts ae: 15m GSL

James d 29 Dec 1848 ae: 63y Catholic GSL

**QUINCY**, Harriet A P d/o Albert d 12 June 1847 ae: 9m GSL

Judith wid/o James d 28 Jan 1865 ae: 55y GSL

**QUINN**, Catherine w/o John d 1 Nov 1853 ae: 28y Catholic GSL

Edward s/o James d 29 Oct 1849 ae: 3m Catholic SD J:5

James s/o Charles d 17 Dec 1849 ae: 18m Catholic GSL

James Edward s/o James & Ellen McLaughlin d 30 Oct 1849 ae: 3m Catholic J:5

Mary Ann d/o James & Ellen d 2 Jan 1846 ae: 10m Catholic J:5

Mary Elizabeth d/o James & Ellen d 6 Sept 1848 ae: 1y Catholic J:5

Michael s/o James d 20 Sept 1855 ae: 10m 19d Catholic SD J:5

Rosanna w/o Francis d 27 Nov 1852 ae: 31y Catholic GSL

Rose Ellen d/o James & Ellen d 13 Oct 1853 ae: 2y 7m Catholic J:5

William s/o Francis d 26 Jan 1852 ae: 2y Catholic GSL

**RACKLEFF**, Charles s/o George E d 3 June 1856 ae: 20m GSL

**RADCLIFFE**, Arthur s/o Edward d 8 Mar 1857 ae: 7w Jordan tomb D:28

**RADFORD**, Betsy w/o William d 30 Sept 1854 ae: 66y G:74

RADFORD (continued)
Harriet w/o William Jr d 1 July
1854 ae: 29y G:74
William d 19 Feb 1870 ae: 90y
SD G:74
RAFTER, William T s/o Daniel
d 28 Feb 1857 ae: 2y 3m GSL
RAGAN, James s/o James d 1
Mar 1857 ae: 8w Catholic GSL
Margaret d/o James d 6 Aug
1849 ae: 1y Catholic GSL
RAIN, Winney w/o Martin d 9
Dec 1856 ae: 28y GSL
RAMSDELL, Albert s/o William
d 16 Feb 1865 ae: 6m Haggett
tomb A:18
Ida C d/o William d 26 Sept
1857 ae: 1y 7m 13d GSL
Linora V d/o William d 20 Mar
1866 ae: 2m Haggett tomb
A:18
RAMSEY, Edward B d 9 Feb 1897
Cambridgeport, Massachusetts
ae 81y SD C:21
Ferdinand d 29 Nov 1883 Cam-
bridge, Massachusetts ae: 32y
GSL
Ferdinand s/o Ferdinand d 16
July 1880 ae: 3m GSL
Frances E d 12 Feb 1897 ae: 72y
SD C:21
George S d 13 Aug 1907 Togus,
Maine SD C:21
Georgia A w/o George S d 17 Nov
1904 Lynn, Massachusetts ae:
47y SD C:21
Horatio M s/o Alonzo d 24 Feb
1850 ae: 6y GSL
Martha d 1 Nov 1882 ae: 4m GSL
Mary d/o Alonzo d 9 Apr 1850
ae: 8y GSL
Mary E w/o Alonzo d 24 Dec
1849 ae: 40y GSL
Susan Jane d/o E B d 8 May
1846 ae: 14m GSL
RAND, Almira w/o Joseph M d 11
June 1852 ae: 26y J:117
Anna d/o John W & H A d ae: 9d
no burial record SD H:99
Clara W d/o Watson C d 17 Dec
1866 ae: 1y 2m GSL
Clarence Allen s/o John W d 4

RAND (continued)
May 1858 ae: 4y H:99
Frank W s/o Joseph d 28 Aug
1857 ae: 5m GSL
Frederick Lewis s/o John W & H
A d 6 May 1858 ae: 2y SD H:99
Hannah A w/o John W b 15 Sept
1814 d 31 July 1907 H:99
John W b 5 Apr 1811 d 26 Nov
1875 H:99
John W s/o John W d 8 Oct 1849
ae: 18m SD H:99
Joseph M d 15 Nov 1868 ae: 45y
J:117
William E s/o J W d 7 July
1852 ae: 2y SD H:99
William Herbert s/o Watson d
24 Dec 1858 ae: 9m GSL
RANDALL, B P F s/o Paoli &
Rebecca d 29 Aug 1855 Bos-
ton, Massachusetts ae: 36y
Native of Horton, Nova Scotia
H:1
Charles W d 23 June 1859 ae:
38y GSL
Ella wid/o Nathaniel d 22 June
1867 ae: 87y GSL
Helen J d/o J F d 5 Sept 1852
ae: 5w GSL
J H P no burial record SD H:1
Lovina w/o Reuben d 1 June
1836 ae: 22y SBE D:9
Maria R A d/o Paoli & Theresa d
30 Mar 1856 ae: 6y 2m H:1
Mary D Mrs d 5 Feb 1861 ae: 43y
GSL
Mary R d/o Thomas d 7 May
1852 ae: 4y 9m GSL
Nathaniel d 21 June 1858 ae: 75y
GSL
Paoli b 11 July 1791 d 12 Apr
1864 H:1
Rebecca w/o Paoli b 10 Sept
1797 d 18 Aug 1843 Native of
Horton, Nova Scotia H:1
Thomas D s/o Thomas d 19 July
1856 ae: 1y GSL
Thomas N s/o Thomas d 30 Mar
1846 ae: 3w GSL
RANSON, John d 26 Mar 1857 ae:
35y GSL
RASFORD, Abigail d 12 Sept 1818

RASFORD (continued)
ae: 62y SD F:88
RAYMOND, Elizabeth d/o B d 22
Oct 1857 ae: 5y 11m GSL
READ, Joseph d 15 July 1880 ae:
75y GSL
REAMEY, Barney d 8 Dec 1862
ae: 55y Catholic GSL
REARDON, Fanny d 28 Oct 1856
ae: 67y Native of Ballin Hill
Parish, Co Galway, Ireland
Catholic SBE I:20
Mary w/o Patrick d 17 Oct 1852
ae: 22m Catholic GSL
REDLON, Adrianna M V d/o Cor-
nelius & Mary no burial record
SD F:26
Albert s/o Nathaniel & Janet d
16 Feb 1870 ae: 28y SBE F:20
Cornelius d 22 Nov 1862 ae: 75y
SD F:26
Edward s/o Nathaniel d 26 Sept
1848 ae: 6m SD F:20
Emily J d/o Nathaniel & Janet d
11 June 1846 ae: 10y SBE F:20
Lena F R d/o N R d 4 Oct 1857
ae: 13m GSL
Lucretia d/o Nathaniel & Janet H
d 18 Sept 1839 ae: 3m SD F:20
Phebe A w/o Thomas d 3 Apr
1855 ae: 45y GSL
Roscoe s/o Nathaniel d 9 Ssept
1846 ae: 7w SD F:20
REED, Ann Marie w/o Philemon
P d 1 Sept 1894 ae: 76y H:45
Anna H d/o Philemon P & Ann
Marie d ae: 10y no burial
record; no dates on stone H:45
Catherine J w/o Joseph Jr d 24
Feb 1862 ae: 38y 2m SD B:58
Charles G s/o Gilman & Elmira
A d 31 Aug 1860 ae: 2y 6m
D:81
Charles M s/o Gilman L d 16
Sept 1861 ae: 1y SD D:81
Eliza E d/o Gilman L & Elmira
A d 18 Dec 1858 ae: 5y 7m
SBE D:81
Eliza S w/o Joseph d 7 Apr 1877
ae: 70y SD B:58
Elmira A w/o Gilman L b 1828 d
1888 D:81

REED (continued)
F Elzader d/o Gilman L d 18
Dec 1857 ae: 2y 10m SD D:81
George C s/o Philemon P & Ann
Marie d 12 July 1886 ae: 34y
H:45
George Henry s/o Philemon P &
Ann Marie d 24 Oct 1844 H:45
Gilman L b 1823 d 1914 D:81
Hannah S w/o Joseph Jr d 12 Aug
1846 ae: 27y B:58
Isaac d 2 June 1864 ae: 67y D:81
Joann K w/o Capt John B d 8
Dec 1840 ae: 42y F:2
Capt John B d 20 Nov 1847 ae:
49y F:2
Joseph s/o Capt John B & Joann
K d 15 Apr 1836 ae: 2m F:2
Joseph d 15 July 1880 ae: 75y SD
B:58
Loamy E d/o Gilman L & Elmira
A d 18 Dec 1857 ae: 2y 10m
21d SBE D:81
Lorenzo D s/o James d 1 July
1847 ae: 12y GSL
Melvin G s/o Gilman L & Elmira
A d 16 Sept 1869 ae: 1y SD
D:81
Philemon P d 25 Feb 1869 ae:
56y H:45
Sarah d/o Thomas d 21 July 1842
ae: 1y Trowbridge tomb Loca-
tion unknown
William C s/o Joseph & Cath-
erine J d 23 Nov 1854 ae: 15m
SD B:58
William E s/o Gilman L & El-
mira A b 1867 d 1892 D:81
REGAN, Catherine d/o Richard &
Bridget d 24 May 1852 Cath-
olic SBE I:49
REID, Lucy M d/o J d 4 Mar 1874
ae: 18y SD G:71
REMICK, Anna M d/o John C d
17 July 1849 ae: 1y GSL
RENNARD, Frank S s/o A A d 26
Sept 1875 Chelsea, Massachu-
setts ae: 35y GSL
REYNOLDS, Zophar d 23 Mar
1848 ae: 50y GSL
RHODES, John H d 22 Sept 1849
ae: 44y H:7

RICE, Almira d/o Luther Jr d 28 Dec 1849 ae: 2m GSL
Daniel R d 12 July 1878 ae: 54y 4m J:36
Elizabeth d 28 Feb 1864 ae: 85y SD F:122
Isabella d/o Thomas d 13 Aug 1842 ae: 4y Catholic GSL
Joseph d 24 Aug 1858 Augusta, Maine ae: 78y GSL
Luther d 18 Aug 1853 ae: 83y 10m J:36
Luther d 19 Apr 1861 ae: 41y GSL
Mary w/o Luther d 10 Feb 1828 ae: 48y J:36
Nicholas d 20 Nov 1847 ae: 41y SBE F:122
Phebe H d 17 Dec 1881 ae: 35y GSL
Rudolphus d 7 Jan 1842 SBE F:122
RICH, inf d/o Samuel S d 4 Apr 1853 ae: 3d GSL
Albus Rea s/o Samuel S d 3 May 1853 ae: 21y 23d GSL
Dorcas Ann d/o Stephen d 18 June 1853 ae: 22y GSL
Ellen d/o Stephen d 13 Sept 1858 ae: 17y GSL
Frederick O s/o C H & S H d 13 Dec 1856 ae: 9m 16d SD B:47
Gerge W s/o Stephen d 29 Oct 1854 ae: 27y GSL
Hannah d 17 Aug 1866 ae: 68y 8m GSL
Helen F d/o John d 23 Dec 1841 ae: 3y GSL
Ida Louisa d/o Charles d 3 Oct 1869 ae: 5y GSL
Julia M d/o Samuel S d 18 Nov 1846 ae: 14m GSL
Lodiska d/o John S d 24 Aug 1849 ae: 2y GSL
Lydia M d/o Stephen d 23 Jan 1850 ae: 17y GSL
Mary E d/o Stephen d 23 Oct 1854 ae: 16y GSL
Samuel R s/o Samuel S d 2 Aug 1847 ae: 17y GSL
Sarah Jane d/o Stephen d 12 May 1850 ae: 27y GSL

RICH (continued)
Sarah M w/o Samuel d 19 Apr 1850 ae: 40y GSL
Stephen d 26 Mar 1860 ae: 67y GSL
Warren Lincoln s/o Samuel S d 16 Aug 1854 ae: 6y 7m GSL
RICHARDS, Adelaide d/o Joshua F d 12 Jan 1847 SD J:251
Albert Nelson s/o Joshua F d 16 July 1851 ae: 16m SD J:251
Benjamin F d 7 June 1919 ae: 65y 11m 6d SD H:77
Ann S w/o Horace B, d/o Seth B Hilborn d 18 Apr 1857 Hilborn tomb A:10
Benjamin C d 1 July 1894 Boston, Massachusetts ae: 80y 1m 24d SD H:77
Betsy E d/o Horace B d 27 Apr 1859 Hilborn tomb A:10
Caroline W d/o Horace B d 15 Aug 1847 ae: 18m Hilborn tomb A:10
Clinton M s/o Benjamin F d 24 Aug 1874 ae: 4m SD H:77
Ella no burial record SBE J:251
Emily Jane d 3 Oct 1854 ae: 1y Hilborn tomb A:10
Eunice w/o Benjamin F d 4 June 1871 ae: 54y 4m H:77
Horace B d 29 Oct 1866 ae: 48y Hilborn tomb A:10
John Franklin s/o Horace B d 5 Feb 1849 ae: 5y Hilborn tomb A:10
Joshua F d 15 Feb 1852 ae: 38y SD J:251
Lewis C s/o Horace B d 21 Mar 1865 ae: 16y Hilborn tomb A:10
Lizzie A d/o Benjamin C d 13 Aug 1860 ae: 8m GSL
Lizzie L d/o Benjamin E d 23 Aug 1866 ae: 8m GSL
Mary E d/o Thomas B d 9 Nov 1866 ae: 1y 4m Hilborn tomb A:10
Mary L d/o Joshua F d 28 Dec 184 ae: 10m SBE J:251
Mehitable F d/o Benjamin C d 20 May 1856 ae: 14m 12d GSL

**RICHARDS** (continued)

William s/o Horace B d 6 July 1863 ae: 1m 10d Hilborn tomb A:10

**RICHARDSON,** Elizabeth A d/o Joseph A d 22 Nov 1854 ae: 2y 3m GSL

Erma d 9 Mar 1899 ae: 79y Sawyer tomb A:14

Esther w/o Henry d 24 Feb 1865 ae: 33y 9m SBE C:27

George M s/o Roswell & A H d 25 Oct 1856 ae: 2y 5m GSL

Henry d 19 Feb 1882 ae: 87y 2m C:27

John A s/o John d 21 Aug 1856 ae: 5y Hilborn tomb A:10

John S d 11 Dec 1861 ae: 39y Civ/War: 9th Batt Massachusetts Lt Art Hilborn tomb A:10

**RICKER,** David B d 26 Jan 1892 ae: 63y 26d Cummings tomb A:13

Sarah M w/o David B d 27 Feb 1909 ae: 73y 2m 19d Cummings tomb A:13

Viletta w/o B F d 9 Feb 1860 ae: 25y GSL

**RIDER,** Abigail wid/o Samuel d 24 July 1865 ae: 81y SD F:132

Mark M d 8 May 1855 ae: 32y GSL

Polly d/o Samuel d 15 Nov 1865 ae: 65y SD F:132

Samuel d 3 Oct 1845 ae: 72y F:132

Thomas d 3 Dec 1873 ae: 61y GSL

**RIGGS,** inf c/o George d 14 Aug 1853 ae: 6w GSL

Ann d 2 Feb 1874 ae: 78y H:81

George s/o George d 18 Feb 1850 ae: 3m GSL

James d 20 Feb 1864 ae: 73y SD H:81

Josiah M s/o James d 17 Feb 1868 ae: 45y SD H:81

**RILEY,** Anna d/o John G d 6 Apr 1866 ae: 13y Catholic GSL

Betsy w/o Patrick d 23 Dec 1850 ae: 32y Catholic GSL

**RILEY** (continued)

Bridget d/o John d 6 Sept 1856 ae: 1y Catholic GSL

Hugh s/o Thomas d 8 Sept 1850 ae: 17m Catholic GSL

Isaac no burial record SD E:1

John s/o Michael d 20 Sept 1863 ae: 11m Catholic GSL

John Lawrence d 24 Dept 1863 ae: 11m Catholic SD J:166

Joseph W s/o John C d 23 Feb 1868 ae: 5m Catholic GSL

Julia d/o Patrick d 27 June 1859 ae: 12m Catholic GSL

Margarette J d/o William d 13 Dec 1865 ae: 3d GSL

Mary d/o Michael d 25 July 1865 ae: 11m Catholic GSL

Peter s/o James d 10 Dec 1873 ae: 1y Catholic GSL

**RINES,** Bridget d/o John d 12 Dec 1857 ae: 8m Catholic GSL

John s/o John d 23 Aug 1853 ae: 3m Old Catholic Ground GSL

Winney d/o John d 3 Apr 1857 ae: 18m Catholic GSL

**RING,** John E d 23 Aug 1854 ae: 23y GSL

Sarah A d/o Franklin & Nancy d 25 Dec 1851 ae: 67y SBE F:129

**RINGNEY,** Robert M s/o James d 3 Apr 1850 ae: 13m Catholic GSL

**RIPLEY,** Sarah B w/o William d 22 July 1854 ae: 25y GSL

**RITTER,** Almira w/o William H d 3 July 1851 ae: 25y SBE J:59

**ROACH,** John d 1 May 1851 ae: 28y Native of Clifden, Co Galway, Ireland Catholic J:174

John s/o John & Mary D d 9 June 1850 ae: 11y Catholic J:193

Mary D w/o John d 20 Aug 1843 ae: 33y Catholic J:193

**ROANYANE,** Catherine d/o Bartholomew d 17 Sept 1850 ae: 17d Catholic SD J:41

Ellen w/o Bartholomew d 29 Jan 1884 ae: 67y Native of Middleton, Co Cork, Ireland Cath-

ROANYANE (continued)
olic SD J:41
ROBBINS, Cora d/o Phillips,
William H & Sabina I d 10 Nov
1913 ae: 55y SD F:74
George H d 23 Apr 1880 ae: 57y
GSL
Lydia E d/o Ebenezer & Mercy d
11 Apr 1876 ae: 71y SB H:69
Mercy B w/o Ebenezer d 20 Mar
1857 ae: 74y H:69
ROBERSON, Almira d 10 Aug
1887 ae: 60y GSL
ROBERTS, Aaron b 22 Sept 1790
d 24 May 1850 SD D:79
Aaron Jr s/o Aaron & Rachel S b
24 Dec 1826 d 6 Apr 1857 SD
D:79
Acsach wid/o Joseph d 20 Oct
1845 ae: 62y C:31
Adeline S w/o Thomas F d 6 Aug
1850 ae: 32y C:30
Benjamin Stuart s/o John R d 25
Sept 1855 ae: 16m GSL
Charles E s/o John R d 11 Dec
1857 ae: 15y 7m Tenbroeck
tomb A:11
Charles F s/o William H d 7
June 1850 ae: 3m GSL
Clarissa E d/o Moses d 26 Sept
1847 ae: 14m SD C:58
Edward s/o Thomas A d 8 Jan
1849 ae: 22m GSL
Eliza d 1 Mar 1892 ae: 75y 9m
GSL
Elizabeth E d/o Thomas F &
Adeline S d 11 Ag 1863 ae: 18y
9m C:30
Elizabeth E d/o Aaron & Rachel
S b 27 Aug 1832 d 13 Apr 1881
Bosworth Relief Corps - G A R
D:79
Ella E d 25 Apr 1889 ae: 40y
GSL
Ellen Maria d/o Moses d 2 Dec
1855 ae: 4y SD C:58
Emma C d/o Thomas A d 31 Aug
1849 ae: 10m GSL
Ernest F s/o Henry B d 4 Sept
1858 ae: 10m 15d Native of
Roxbury, Massachusetts GSL
Evelyn L d/o Moses d 24 May

ROBERTS (continued)
1850 ae: 1y SD C:58
Frederick A s/o Thomas A d 11
Aug 1848 ae: 4m GSL
George F s/o Thomas F & Ade-
line S d 6 May 1854 ae: 18y
7m SD C:30
Harriet Maria d/o Moses d ae: 2y
4m no burial record SD C:58
Hezekiah b 23 Sept 1814 d 12
Mar 1882 F:73
James s/o Thomas d 5 Feb 1848
ae: 2y Catholic C:30
John R d 23 Jan 1859 ae: 50y
Tenbroeck tomb A:11
Joseph d 13 Sept 1835 ae: 52y
C:31
Joseph S s/o Joseph & Acsach b
1808 d 1892 C:31
Juliet M w/o Hezekiah b 14 Aug
1817 d 24 Apr 1854 F:73
Maria L wid/o John R d 26 Feb
1859 ae: 38y Tenbroeck tomb
A:11
Mary Caroline d/o Moses &
Susan M d 18 Mar 1845 ae: 4y
5m C:58
Mary Ellen d 1 May 1848 Boston,
Massachusetts ae: 3y SD C:58
Mary Frothingham d/o Aaron &
Rachel S b 26 Dec 1821 d 11
Aug 1862 D:79
Miriam w/o Nathaniel d 23 July
1840 ae: 44y SBE F:27
Moses d 4 Oct 1872 ae: 50y SD
C:58
Moses s/o Moses d 3 May 1848
Boston, Massachusetts ae: 5y
6m SD C:58
Nathaniel b 3 Apr 1793 d 17 Aug
1863 F:27
Rachel Swanton w/o Aaron b 21
June 1791 d 28 Apr 1860 SD
D:79
Sarah Cleaves w/o Joseph S b
1814 d 1883 C:31
Susan E w/o Nathaniel d 23 Dec
1846 ae: 44y F:27
Sarah E w/o Thomas F d 23 Nov
1855 ae: 29y C:30
Susan M w/o Moses d 25 Dec
1851 ae: 35y SD C:58

ROBERTS (continued)
Thomas F b 1813 d 1892 C:30

ROBERTSON, Frances L w/o Alfred, d/o Samuel S Stover d 16
Dec 1858 ae: 23y 8m 5d GSL

James S s/o Alfred d 13 Sept
1851 ae: 3m GSL

ROBINSON, Ann E d/o Capt Robert J & Patience d 31 Oct
1850 ae: 3m 23d J:101

Anna d/o Samuel d 15 Aug 1862
ae: 2y 4m GSL

Annis Willard w/o George d 30
May 1866 ae: 77y 6m H:40

Arlie How no burial record SD
B:21

Betsy C d/o Capt Samuel d 19
Apr 1853 ae: 38y Cummings
tomb A:13

Charles P d 9 Aug 1883 ae: 81y
SD H:13

Charles W s/o Richard L d 21
Aug 1848 ae: 14m GSL

Charles W s/o William d 26 Oct
1849 ae: 10w GSL

David Jr no burial record SD
B:21

Edna P no burial record SD I:99

Edward s/o John d 9 Mar 1870
GSL

Edward Douglass d 30 Nov 1853
ae: 2y SD B:21

Eliza D d/o Capt Robert J &
Patience d 6 Aug 1846 ae: 3m
6d J:101

Emeline A d/o Charles P &
Lydia d 5 Oct 1853 ae: 17y 3m
SD H:13

Emily C w/o Charles d 29 Jan
1882 ae: 75y GSL

George d 13 Jan 1862 ae: 75y
11m H:40

George H F s/o Charles P &
Lydia d 26 June 1854 ae: 20y
SD H:13

Gertrude A d/o Jacob W & Martha A b 23 Apr 1850 d 28 Sept
1865 H:40

Harriet d 27 May 1845 ae: 20y
F:8

Harriet Annis d/o Jacob W &
Martha A d 26 Mar 1895 ae:

ROBINSON (continued)
43y 7m H:40

Harriette d/o George W d 30 Sept
1891 ae: 6m 4d SD H:40

Jacob W s/o George & Annis
Willard b 1824 d 1914 H:40

John s/o Samuel d 10 May 1859
ae: 1y 8m GSL

John S d 3 Feb 1883 ae: 45y SD
I:99

Lydia G w/o Charles P d 22 Aug
1879 ae: 81y SD H:13

Martha d/o Samuel d 3 May 1859
ae: 6y 1m GSL

Martha A d/o George W d 28 Aug
1886 ae: 10m 7d SD H:40

Martha Allen w/o Jacob W d 5
Mar 1902 ae: 72y H:40

Mary A Nutter w/o David Jr no
burial record SD B:21

Mary C York w/o Capt Robert J b
1834 d 1892 J:101

Mary G d/o Alfred d 29 July 1853
ae: 3d GSL

Mary O w/o Robert J, d/o
Charles York d 1 Jan 1914 ae:
79y 8m 29d SD J:101

Patience w/o Robert J d 22 June
1859 ae: 40y 2m J:101

Capt Robert J b 1813 d 1892
J:101

Robert J s/o Capt Robert J &
Patience d 25 May 1841 ae:
4m 22d J:101

Capt Samuel d 27 Nov 1852 ae:
68y Cummings tomb A:13

Sarah Knight d 3 Mar 1880 ae:
83y F:8

ROBISON, Ann E d/o Robert d 30
Oct 1850 ae: 4m GSL

ROCK, Thomas s/o Barney d 9
Sept 1850 ae: 2y Catholic GSL

ROFF, Michael B d 27 Feb 1894
Essex, Massachusetts ae: 65y
SD H:87

ROGAN, Margaret d/o John d 26
Apr 1853 ae: 18m Buried Jere-
miah Spellman lot Catholic
GSL

May A d/o James d 28 Sept 1862
Catholic GSL

ROGERS, Charles s/o Daniel d 14

**ROGERS** (continued)
June 1859 ae: 13m GSL
Charles F s/o J d 13 July 1857 ae: 5y 9m GSL
Ellen d 14 Aug 1857 Biddeford, Maine ae: 56y GSL
Mary Ann d/o John d 2 June 1855 ae: 3m GSL
Zilpah w/o John d 21 Nov 1857 ae: 19y 11m Native of St Stevens, New Brunswick GSL
**ROLF**, Catherine C d/o Benjamin & Catherine d 23 Oct 1843 ae: 9d D:44
Charles H s/o Nathaniel & Polly d 20 June 1851 ae: 24y SB C:88
Cora Corilla d/o Jacob & Margaret G d 31 Dec 1851 ae: 2y 10d D:44
Jacob Sumner s/o Jacob & Margaret G d 12 Oct 1837 ae: 3y 3m D:44
Jacob Sumner s/o Jacob & Margaret G d 17 Feb 1845 ae: 21m D:44
Marion d/o Nathaniel & Polly d 15 Mar 1849 ae: 26y SB C:88
Nathaniel d 20 Oct 1854 ae: 64y C:88
Polly w/o Nathaniel d 6 May 1851 ae: 58y C:88
**ROLFE**, Charles E s/o Samuel J d 12 Sept 1847 ae: 3y Wilson tomb D:33
Sarah G w/o Joseph M d 20 Sept 1866 ae: 33y 4m GSL
**RONAN**, Hannah d/o Bartholomew d 31 Aug 1853 ae: 2m Old Catholic Ground GSL
**ROOD**, Marshall d 12 Apr 1854 ae: 34y Killed while working of P S & P R R J:93
**ROONEY**, James d 22 Sept 1839 ae: 67y Native of Co Meath, Ireland Catholic I:4
Mary w/o James d 7 Jan 1834 in Ireland ae: 60y Catholic I:4
Mary Jane d/o Bartholomew d 20 July 1855 ae: 15m Catholic GSL
Patrick d 13 Aug 1854 ae: 30y

**ROONEY** (continued)
Catholic Strangers' Ground GSL
Patrick s/o Patrick d 24 Oct 1842 ae: 6y Catholic GSL
**ROSE**, Clara G buried 21 Apr 1942 (Cremated) no burial record NS I:17
Elizabeth w/o John d 21 Apr 1871 ae: 63y SB I:144
John d 13 Sept 1881 Greely Hospital ae: 73y SD I:144
Richard d 9 July 1865 ae: 42y Black GSL
**ROSS**, Ann F wid/o Walter d 28 Apr 1855 ae: 73y GSL
Ann P w/o John M d 27 Mar 1883 ae: 63y SD C:89
Charlotte W w/o Duncan M d 10 Feb 1899 ae: 69y C:91
Clara Alice d/o George d 30 Apr 1850 ae: 2y 4m GSL
David w/o Walter d 8 Sept 1864 ae: 58y GSL
Duncan M b 1810 d 1886 C:91
Edward H s/o William d 23 Sept 1854 ae: 1y 2m 7d GSL
Elizabeth Jane w/o John E d 22 Aug 1868 ae: 37y 7m 25d SB I:145
Ella d/o William C d 19 July 1862 ae: 6y 6m GSL
Ellen M C d/o Duncan M d 15 Sept 1849 ae: 2m SD C:91
George F s/o William d 14 July 1870 ae: 9y GSL
George H s/o William & Elizabeth d 21 Sept 1853 ae: 2y 8m I:146
Hattie J d/o William d 18 Feb 1871 ae: 4y 5m GSL
Henry C s/o Robert & Jane d 22 Apr 1851 ae: 12y 3m H:29
James d 8 June 1856 ae: 48y SBE F:3
James w/o Walter d 14 Sept 1852 ae: 2y GSL
James M s/o James M & Lucinda Field d 12 Mar 1855 ae: 1y 5m SBE C:89
James M d 15 Dec 1895 Augusta State Hosp ae: 74y 9m 7d C:89

ROSS (continued)

Jane wid/o John d 9 Aug 1863 ae: 62y GSL

Jane w/o Robert d 19 Sept 1854 ae: 58y Native of Aberdeen, Scotland H:29

Jane M d/o Walter d 10 Jan 1849 ae: 40y GSL

John d 27 Mar 1851 ae: 55y GSL

John E d 20 Jan 1863 ae: 32y 11m SD I:145

John M s/o John d 16 Dec 1892 Greely Hospital ae: 74y SD I:144

Lucinda F w/o James M, d/o Elias Field d 12 Apr 1915 ae: 88y 11m C:89

Margaret E d 24 Aug 1886 ae: 76y GSL

Mary D d/o Duncan M d 15 Sept 1849 ae: 2y SD C:91

Mary E d/o William & Elizabeth d 18 Aug 1850 ae: 1y 11d SBE I:146

Mary G w/o Duncan d 23 Nov 1857 ae: 42y SD C:91

Melville Augustus s/o John d 5 Mar 1852 ae: 3y GSL

Olive w/o Daniel d 24 OCt 1862 ae: 52y GSL

Patty w/o Nathaniel d 6 Nov 1851 ae: 58y GSL

Robert d 22 Apr 1851 ae: 12y GSL

Robert d 9 Nov 1863 ae: 70y 8m H:29

Walter d 21 Feb 1855 Minot, Maine ae: 41y GSL

Capt William d 3 June 1873 ae: 52y SD I:146

William H s/o William C d 5 Sept 1859 ae: 15m GSL

ROUGH, Daniel s/o Daniel d 5 July 1856 ae: 6m Old Catholic Ground GSL

ROUNDS, Charles d 9 Apr 1857 ae: 50y SB C:83

Eddie M d 8 Mar 1877 Chelsea, Massachusetts ae: 8y SBE C:83

Lucy Ellen d 18 June 1890 ae: 54y 2m 21d C:83

ROUNDS (continued)

Sarah w/o Charles d 20 Nov 1869 ae: 66y SD C:83

ROWE, Almira Shurtleff d/o E W d 7 Nov 1860 ae: 13m 1d Trowbridge tomb Location unknown

ROWELL, Sarah d/o William d 13 June 1841 ae: 5y 6m GSL

ROYAL, B T s/o Bailey T d 5 Oct 1857 ae: 4m GSL

Mary C w/o Bailey T d 10 Oct 1857 ae: 38y GSL

RUBY, Thomas s/o Peter & Ann d 20 Apr 1852 ae: 2y 7m GSL

RUFUS, George A s/o John d 16 Nov 1848 ae: 1y GSL

RUSSELL, C F no dates on stone; no burial record Civ/War: 10th Reg Maine Inf Co C I:141 (See Addendum)

Charles Henry s/o G W & M J no burial record SBE I:141 (See Addendum)

Eliza Jane d/o G W & M J no burial record SBE I:141 (See Addendum)

Nancy w/o Moses d 5 Nov 1851 ae: 33y GSL

RUTERIAN, Dennis d 6 Sept 1848 Saco, Maine ae: 18y Buried Timothy Griffin lot Catholic GSL

RYAN, Catherine d/o Michael & Bridget d 24 May 1852 ae: 3y 11m Catholic SD I:50

James Martin s/o Bridget d 30 Aug 1847 ae: 16m Catholic GSL

John s/o John d 2 Aug 1858 Gorham, Maine ae: 3m Catholic GSL

Patrick d 21 Dec 1852 ae: 23y Catholic GSL

RYERSON, James s/o Andrea d 26 Aug 1856 ae: 4m GSL

Mary w/o Samuel d 17 May 1843 ae: 22y GSL

Mary F d/o Samuel d 3 Oct 1853 ae: 8y GSL

Nehemiah d 21 Nov 1846 ae: 48y GSL

RYERSON (continued)
Sarah H wid/o Nehemiah d 23 Apr 1868 ae: 73y GSL
SAFFORD, Almire w/o William F d 6 Nov 1887 ae: 74y Safford-Hall tomb A:20
Ann d/o John d 14 July 1850 ae: 2d GSL
Inez C d/o William F d 6 July 1887 ae: 41y 7m Safford-Hall tomb A:20
James M s/o William d 19 Mar 1900 ae: 57y 11m 20d Civ/War: 17th Reg Maine Inf Co C Safford-Hall tomb A:20
Matilda A d/o William F & Almira d 9 Feb 1920 ae: 66y 10m 5d Safford-Hall tomb A:20
Roland J s/o William H d 28 Aug 1861 ae: 2m GSL
Samuel D d 27 Oct 1882 ae: 38y Civ/War: 25th Reg Maine Inf Co A Safford-Hall tomb A:20
Seward Porter s/o Capt Joshua F d 25 Mar 1852 ae: 6y Safford-Hall tomb A:20
William d 3 Feb 1885 ae: 73y Safford-Hall tomb A:20
William Edwin Stodder s/o William F d 24 July 1851 ae: 13y Safford-Hall tomb A:20
SAMPSON, ---- w/o Micah d 3 Nov 1854 GSL
Esther d 6 May 1861 ae: 96y GSL
Frederick s/o Micah d 1 July 1851 ae: 9m GSL
John s/o Thomas d 23 July 1854 ae: 2y Old Catholic Ground GSL
Julia A d/o Micah d 28 June 1849 ae: 10w GSL
Micah d 23 June 1854 ae: 57y GSL
SANBORN, Charles Edward s/o Oliver L d 2 Sept 1851 ae: 3m GSL
SANDS, Louisa E d/o Charles B d 8 Oct 1849 ae: 15m GSL
SANFORD, Anne L d/o William d 10 Sept 1849 ae: 17m GSL
SARGENT, Albert A s/o Joseph A

SARGENT (continued)
& Maria d 25 Aug 1848 ae: 1y H:89
Josephine d/o JA d 31 Dec 1850 ae: 9m H:89
SARSTROFF, Francis d 22 May 1874 ae: 69y GSL
SATEINS, Peter d 12 Jan 1850 Leeds, Maine ae: 30y GSL
SAVILLE, George H b 17 July 1814 d 14 Sept 1890 B:72
Hannah w/o George H b 10 May 1821 d 25 Dec 1891 Neponset, Maine B:72
Harriet E d/o George H & Hannah H d 1 Oct 1929 Dorchester, Maine ae: 85y NS B:72
SAWYER, Abel Hargrove no burial record; no dates on stone Civ/War: 28th Reg Maine Inf Co I I:99
Adelaide Christianna d/o Andrew S & Mary A d 6 Mar 1849 ae: 19y 8m SBE F:1
Ann d/o Eben d 2 Apr 1853 ae: 9y 10m Old Catholic Ground GSL
Capt Charles no burial record SD I:71
Clement S s/o Capt Abel d 22 Aug 1845 ae: 15m Buried at the upper end of the walk GSL
Edward s/o William d 16 Oct 1848 ae: 16m GSL
Elizabeth H w/o Myrick d 26 Dec 1858 ae: 50y GSL
Esther A d 27 Nov 1861 ae: 60y GSL
George s/o Alvin d 26 Nov 1850 ae: 6m GSL
George A s/o George A d 15 Aug 1866 ae: 10m GSL
Henry W s/o Edward d 31 Aug 1848 ae: 4m Sawyer tomb A:14
John Erving s/o Andrew & Adelaide C d 8 Dec 1841 ae: 19m SD F:1
John H d 9 Feb 1842 ae: 38y GSL
John H s/o late John d 29 May 1844 ae: 1y 9m GSL
John W s/o Greenleaf d 30 Oct 1854 ae: 2y 6m SD I:71

117

SAWYER (continued)

Joseph s/o JL d 2 Oct 1857 ae: 15m 11d GSL

Joseph Eugene s/o Joshua L & Rebecca S d 3 Oct 1857 ae: 15m 11d SD F:24

John W s/o Capt Charles & Sarah d 5 Dec 1848 ae: 3y I:71

Levi d 25 Nov 1855 ae: 70y Sawyer tomb A:14

Levi s/o Levi d 2 Nov 1846 ae: 20y Sawyer tomb A:14

Lydia B d 2 June 1889 ae: 70y 3m GSL

Capt Mark d 9 Mar 1853 ae: 41y Sawyer tomb A:14

Martha Ellen d/o John G d 5 Aug 1847 ae: 2y GSL

Mary A d/o William d 31 Oct 1877 ae:12y SD G:19

Mary E d/o William H & Lydia d 30 Sept 1848 ae: 13m SD G:19

Mary E d/o William H & Lydia d 28 Feb 1865 ae: 3y 7m SBE G:19

Rufus H d 23 June 1848 ae: 26y GSL

Sarah w/o Levi d 21 Apr 1858 ae: 73y 7m Sawyer tomb A:14

Samuel Waite s/o Andrew S & Mary A d 28 Sept 1837 ae: 10y 8m Stone on F:7 F:1

Sophia d/o Joshua d 27 Nov 1846 ae: 18m GSL

Thomas L d 27 Oct 1902 ae: 82y 4m C:81

William A s/o Isaac d 18 Sept 1848 ae: 24y SBE F:80

William H d 20 Oct 1883 ae: 66y Civ/War: 1st Bat Maine Inf Co D F:80

William Hayden s/o Capt Albert d 6 Aug 1854 ae: 3m GSL

SCAGGELL, Elijah d 25 Sept 1857 ae: 33y GSL

SCAMMON, Anne C d/o Richard S d 28 Aug 1855 ae: 18m GSL

Frederick J s/o Richard d 3 Sept 1856 ae: 1y GSL

Georgianna H d/o Ezra d 10 Nov 1845 ae: 5m GSL

James F s/o Thomas & Eliza-

SCAMMON(continued)

beth d 3 Apr 1848 ae: 10m 5d SD H:37

John P s/o Richard S d 7 Feb 1865 ae: 3y 5m GSL

Julia d/o Ezra d 14 Nov 1845 ae: 6y 6m GSL

Mary C w/o Richard d/o Thomas Cobb d 10 May 1850 ae: 22y GSL

SCOTT, Caroline A w/o Wililam S d/o Charles P & Lydia G Robinson d 4 Aug 1914 ae: 73y 4m 5d I:161

Caroline H d/o William S d 16 Dec 1865 ae: 3w SD I:161

Charlie s/o William S d 9 July 1882 ae: 12y SD I:161

Chesley E s/o William S & Caroline A d 15 Mar 1942 ae: 66y 1m 15d I:161

Georgianna d/o William S & Caroline d 1 Nov 1950 ae: 86y 4m 23d I:161

Lydia G d/o William S d 20 Aug 1862 ae: 2m SD I:161

Mabel d 17 Sept 1872 ae: 1m GSL

William Stuart d 12 Nov 1903 ae: 79y I:161

SEARS, Francis B s/o James L d 29 June 1861 ae: 1y GSL

Herbert s/o James L d 16 May 1872 ae: 5y GSL

SEAVER, Elizabeth wid/o Henry d 12 Feb 1857 ae: 66y GSL

Henry d 5 Sept 1856 ae: 66y GSL

Sarah E d 19 June 1862 ae: 3y 7m GSL

SEWELL, Bell d/o William & Mira d 30 Sept 1857 ae: 1y SD B:76

Isabella P d/o William W d 28 Sept 1857 ae: 13m GSL

Mary Agnes d/o Isaac d 13 July 1854 ae: 11m Old Catholic Ground GSL

SEXTON, Bridget d/o Patrick d 28 Oct 1854 ae: 11y Catholic GSL

George s/o Peter d 6 Sept 1860 ae: 1y Catholic GSL

SEXTON (continued)
Michael s/o Peter d 7 Nov 1862
ae: 6y Catholic Strangers'
Ground GSL
SHACKFORD, ---- w/o Jesse d
28 Nov 1851 ae: 38y GSL
Benjamin Franklin d 26 Mar 1854
ae: 3y 2m J:230
Dixey S d 6 Sept 1852 ae: 31y
J:230
Francis A d 20 Sept 1848 ae: 20d
SD J:230
Franklin s/o Dixey S d 30 Mar
1854 ae: 3y 2m SD J:230
Georgia C d/o JS d 14 Sept 1857
ae: 7m GSL
Jesse s/o Jesse d 18 Aug 1854
GSL
Joseph s/o Jesse d 10 Oct 1848
ae: 4m GSL
Luella M d/o James H d 29 July
1859 Boston, Maine ae: 5m
GSL
Mary E d/o Jesse d 25 Sept 1855
ae: 25d GSL
SHACKLEY, Albert H s/o Henry
R & Eliza A d 9 Sept 1846 ae:
11m G:70
Henry R d 4 June 1856 Matanzas,
Cuba ae: 39y 4m G:70
Lillian M d 6 Oct 1881 ae: 5m
GSL
Percy L s/o Frank N d 25 Jan
1882 ae: 9m GSL
SHANAHAN, Jeremiah s/o
Jeremiah d 8 Mar 1860 ae: 9m
GSL
SHANKS, Julia B w/o James d 2
Aug 1869 ae: 18y GSL
SHANNON, Hannah w/o John d 4
Sept 1856 ae: 24y Catholic
GSL
John d 4 Apr 1860 ae: 24y
Catholic GSL
Mary E d/o Patrick d 21 Sept
1857 ae: 15y Catholic GSL
SHAUGHNESY, Catherine d/o
John & Hannah d 31 Aug 1855
ae: 1d Catholic SD L:6
Thomas s/o John & Hannah d 27
Sept 1853 ae: 2y 7m Catholic
SBE L:6

SHAW, Inf c/o Luther H d 12
June 1860 ae: 9m J:265
Abby L d/o Luther H & Sarah E d
5 Sept 1848 ae: 3m J:265
Abigail d 8 Apr 1887 ae: 76y GSL
Charles P s/o George W d 31
Apr 1850 ae: 9y 4m GSL
Eleazer F s/o Eleazer F d 16
Aug 1850 ae: 16y GSL
Emma D w/o Neal d 12 Sept
1851 ae: 50y GSL
Fanny wid/o Asa d 6 May 1856
ae: 77y GSL
Hannah d/o Thomas d 20 June
1863 ae: 8y 7m GSL
Harry Russell s/o Samuel P d 26
June 1857 ae: 16m 6d Cum-
mings tomb A:13
John s/o Thomas d 31 Jan 1858
ae: 14m Old Catholic Ground
GSL
Mary d/o John d 10 Nov 1843 ae:
3m GSL
Mary C d/o Samuel P d 17 June
1857 ae: 4y Cummings tomb
A:13
Mary L w/o Philip d 17 Aug 1848
ae: 46y MmtB D:85
Myra d/o James & Nancy M no
burial record SBE J:119
Nancy M w/o James d 29 July
1855 ae: 62y J:119
Nancy M d/o James & Nancy M
d 29 July 1855 ae: 62y J:119
Nellie d/o James d 9 Feb 1885
ae: 5w GSL
Philip no burial record MmtB
D:85
Quincy A s/o Samuel P d 18 Feb
1857 ae: 2y 7m Cummings
tomb A:13
Sarah E w/o Luther H d 6 Sept
1848 ae: 30y J:265
Thomas s/o Thomas d 30 July
1868 ae: 7y 9m GSL
Walter s/o Luther d 16 Aug 1853
ae: 18m GSL
SHEA, Patrick d 4 Sept 1855 ae:
22y Catholic GSL
SHEAN, Mary Ellen d/o Thomas
d 4 June 1861 ae: 1y Catholic
GSL

SHED, Charles F s/o Henry D & Elizabeth d 2 Aug 1847 ae: 15y Stone on C:17 D:67

Charles H s/o Henry D Jr & Martha C d 12 Dec 1865 ae: 2y 2m D:67

Elizabeth w/o Henry D d 30 Mar 1874 ae: 62y D:67

Henrietta M d/o Henry D Jr & Martha C d 25 Feb 1890 ae: 21y 7m SD D:67

Henry D d 6 June 1877 ae: 70y SD D:67

Henry D Jr d 28 Apr 1868 ae: 33y 6m SD D:67

John d 22 Jan 1827 ae: 44y SD D:67

John E s/o Henry D & Elizabeth d 14 Sept 1843 ae: 8m Stone on C:17 D:67

Martha C w/o Henry D Jr d 15 Jan 1872 ae: 33y SD D:67

Mary Elizabeth d/o Henry D & Elizabeth d 31 July 1851 ae: 20y 7m SD D:67

Olive D d/o Henry D & Elizabeth d 12 Nov 1856 ae: 22y 5m SD D:67

Olive D d/o Henry D Jr & Martha C d 28 Dec 1862 ae: 1y 4m D:67

Olive D w/o John d 16 June 1851 ae: 63y SD D:67

William s/o William d 8 July 1857 ae: 2y 10m GSL

SHEFFIELD, Mary LC w/o Ward d 13 Feb 1860 ae: 20y SD H:12

SHEEHAN, Daniel d 6 Mar 1860 ae: 55y Catholic GSL

John s/o Thomas d 18 Jan 1868 ae: 12y Catholic GSL

Margaret d/o Thomas d 7 Nov 1854 ae: 3y 6m Catholic GSL

Mary d/o Thomas d 27 July 1856 ae: 18m Catholic GSL

SHELDON, Ann d 10 Jan 1859 Stoddard, New Hampshire SD B:7

Cora D w/o Rev Nathan W d 4 Jan 1859 ae: 60y SD B:7

SHEPARD, Inf s/o OP d 2 Apr 1853 GSL

SHEPARD (continued)
Francis d 2 Sept 1862 ae: 72y Cummings tomb A:13

SHERIDAN, Hugh d 18 Jan 1853 ae: 47y Native of Co Donegal, Ireland Catholic J:217

James d 18 Jan 1853 ae: 50y Catholic GSL

James s/o Martin d 22 July 1858 ae: 27y 9m Catholic GSL

Patrick d 4 Aug 1855 ae: 46y Buried "on the Protestant Ground" Catholic GSL

SHERMAN, Mabelle Scott d/o Tanner, William H & Sarah d 31 Jan 1957 Bangor, Maine ae: 73y I:161

SHERWOOD, Dorcas wid/o Joseph T d 27 Dec 1861 ae: 8y Sherwood tomb D:30

Edward P d 12 Sept 1892 ae: 66y 10m Sherwood tomb D:30

George P d 21 May 1904 ae: 76y 19d Civ/War Capt 5th Reg Maine Inf Co F Sherwood tomb D:30

Helen d/o Joseph & Dorcas d 4 July 1871 ae: 52y Sherwood tomb D:30

Joseph T d 5 July 1849 ae: 59y Sherwood tomb D:30

Kate S C w/o George P d/o Randolph AL Codman d 2 Mar 1858 ae: 27y Sherwood tomb D:30

Thomas A D s/o Josepeh T d 20 Aug 1852 ae: 22y Sherwood tomb D:30

SHIELD, Catherine d 18 Jan 1850 Catholic SD I:13A

SHOREY, Ann E d/o William B d 15 Jan 1851 ae: 3y SD J:110

Elizabeth w/o William B b 28 Nov 1823 d 18 Oct 1906 Somerville, Massachusetts J:110

Henry s/o William B & Elizabeth b 20 Feb 1853 d 7 Nov 1881 J:110

Lillie d/o William B & Elizabeth no burial record SBE J:110

William B d 22 Feb 1823 d 25

SHOREY (continued)
Apr 1878 SBE J:110
William P s/o William B & Elizabeth d 11 Feb 1913 ae: 65y 3m 8d J:110
SHUL, Catherine d 17 May 1850 ae: 41y Catholic GSL
SHUMWAY, E widow d 1 July 1843 ae: 90y GSL
SHURTLEFF, Charles N s/o Andrew C d 2 Jan 1858 ae: 6y GSL
Helen M d/o Aurtas d 21 Aug 1848 ae: 1y GSL
SILBER, Joseph s/o Joseph & Mary d 17 July 1859 ae:11m 4d J:6
SILSBY, Eben B s/o Capt Samuel A & Elizabeth b1847 d1848 F:77
Elizabeth W w/o Capt Samuel A b1818 d1900 F:77
Capt Samuel A b1816 d1855 F:77
SILVA, James s/o Antonio d 19 Sept 1864 ae: 2y Catholic GSL
Joseph s/o Antonio d 14 May 1865 ae: 11m Catholic GSL
SILVER, Joseph s/o Joseph d 17 July 1859 ae: 11m GSL
SIMMONS, Samuel d 26 Mar 1853 ae: 69y GSL
SIMOND, James W S no burial record SD B:2
SIMONTON, George B s/o John M d 19 July 1872 ae: 8m GSL
John d 7 Nov 1851 ae: 56y GSL
Mary C d/o John d 10 Sept 1873 ae: 11w GSL
SIMPSON, Albert D s/o Gardner L d 21 Aug 1883 ae: 9y SD C:55
Eunice d 3 Feb 1846 ae: 55y Wilson tomb D:33
Capt John A d 23 Sept 1886 ae: 67y GSL
SINCLAIR, Dr Samuel d 21 May 1848 ae: 21y SB G:78
Willie F s/o John d 12 Aug 1857 ae: 2y 1m GSL
SKENCK, Julia B d 2 Aug 1869 ae: 18y B:48
SKILLIN, Annie E d/o Sumner W

SKILLIN (continued)
d 15 Feb 1872 ae: 13y GSL
Charles O s/o Walter H d 16 Dec 1879 ae: 3y GSL
Henry E s/o Walter A d 25 Sept 1874 ae: 5d GSL
Sarah D w/o Zebulon d 6 June 1877 Dover, New Hampshire ae: 81y GSL
SKILLINGS, Amanda no burial record SD G:30
Angelina d/o CP & Mary Ann d 8 Mar 1849 ae: 7y 3m 21d SD H:84
Bradley s/o Simeon d 7 Sept 1850 ae: 23y SD J:95
Carrie C w/o George H d 22 June 1887 ae: 27y GSL
Charles Edward d 23 Sept 1862 ae: 18y GSL
Cyrus d 9 Aug 1839 ae: 29y 7m SD H:77
Elizabeth C d/o Edward P d 5 Aug 1853 ae: 3m 20d SD G:30
Ellen A d/o David d 10 Sept 1846 ae: 16m GSL
Franklin s/o CP & Mary Ann d 6 May 1864 ae: 19y 24d Mortally wounded Battle of the Wilderness, Virginia Civ/War 17th Reg Maine Inf Co A SD H:94
George H s/o Edward P & Hannah d 16 Sept 1942 ae: 86y 3m 13d NS G:30
George W s/o Gideon d 2 Oct 1847 ae: 1y SD J:68
George W s/o Simeon & Nancy d 8 Nov 1865 ae: 58y J:68
H O no burial record SD F:52
Hannah H w/o Simeon b1806 d1866 J:95
Howard P s/o George H d 7 Feb 1888 ae: 9w GSL
John d 13 Feb 1849 ae: 64y SBE F:73
Joseph F d 13 Oct 1851 ae: 21y SBE J:95
Louisa d/o Zebulon d 18 Oct 1842 ae: 18y GSL
Martin s/o Cyrus d 30 May 1854 ae: 17y GSL
Mary w/o John d 31 Oct 1860 ae:

SKILLINGS (continued)
71y 6m F:73
Mary Ann w/o CP d 23 Feb 1848
ae: 31 6m 6d SD H:94
Mary E d/o Joseph F d 23 Nov
1854 ae: 3y 3m GSL
Mary R d/o George H d 2 Aug
1885 ae: 1y 6m GSL
Nancy w/o Simeon d 10 July
1869 ae: 79y 11m J:68
Oliver P s/o Simeon & Nancy d 9
June 1852 ae: 28y J:68
Otis B s/o John & Mary d 18 Oct
1831 ae: 26y SBE F:73
Silas B no burial record Mmt
face down J:68
Simeon b1793 d1863 J:95
Simeon d 17 Sept 1865 ae: 78y
3m J:68
Simeon B s/o Simeon & Hannah
H d 6 Sept 1850 ae: 23y SBE
J:95
Warren s/o CP & Mary Ann d 12
Mar 1852 ae: 5y 6m 5d SD
H:94
Albert s/o Gibson d 4 Aug 1843
ae: 2y GSL
SKINNER, Emily Augusta d/o
Joseph b d 2 June 1863 ae: 1y
10m GSL
SLINAY, James d/o James d 12
Sept 1855 ae: 5w Catholic
Strangers' Ground GSL
Michael d 16 Mar 1853 ae: 34y
Catholic GSL
SMALL, Almena S w/o John A d
22 Oct 1884 ae: 33y SD C:27
Annie M d/o Hiram & Susan d 10
Dec 1903 ae: 38y SD C:27
Charles S s/o MS d 5 Oct 1883
ae: 2m GSL
Clement P d 17 Aug 1878 ae: 60y
Civ/War 1st Reg Maine Cav
Co B F:91
Clementine d/o CP d 16 Nov
1861 ae: 57y GSL
Dorcas w/o Moses d 25 July
1841 ae: 56y GSL
Eben H s/o Moses & Dorcas d 22
Apr 1896 ae: 75y Stone on C:19
D:20
Eddie s/o Moses d 18 May 1881

SMALL (continued)
ae: 3m Sawyer tomb A:14
Edward Gardner s/o Arthur M &
Hannah d 7 May 1829 ae: 2y
8m H:71
Edward H s/o Oliver d 9 Feb
1852 ae: 9y GSL
Elizabeth w/o David d 3 July
1909 ae: 80y SD G:25
Elizabeth w/o Eben H d/o Wil-
liam & Elizabeth French d 18
Mar 1918 ae: 84y 10m 25d SD
D:20
Elizabeth w/o Dr Moses W d 23
June 1848 Woonsockett, Rhode
Island ae: 23y SB H:96
Elizabeth P w/o Samuel Jr d 1
Apr 1849 ae: 33y GSL
Emily d/o Jacob d 8 Sept 1860
ae: 1y 3m GSL
Frances A d/o Thomas & Sarah
b1829 d1848 C:75
Francis A d 6 Sept 1848 ae: 31y
3m GSL
Francis A s/o Eben & Elizabeth
d 1 Oct 1851 ae: 2y 9m J:126
Frank W s/o John S d 11 Dec
1863 ae: 10m GSL
Fred E s/o Oscar W d 2 May
1892 ae: 7d SD H:83
Frederick A s/o John M d 23 Feb
1842 ae: 4w GSL
Capt George W d 25 July 1850
Santiago, Cuba ae: 42y 10m
I:63
Harry G s/o John A d 19 Nov
1891 ae: 16y 4m 13d SD C:27
Helen V d/o Oscar W d 1 Sept
1893 ae: 3w SD C:67
Jane C w/o Capt George W d 29
Oct 1858 ae: 43y 10m I:63
John A s/o William B d 6 Apr
1898 ae: 49y 4m 4d SD C:27
John U s/o Capt George W &
Jane C d 11 Jan 1868 Hiogo,
Japan ae: 19y 7m I:63
Joseph d 27 July 1893 ae: 84y
1m 7d GSL
Leonard A no burial record
Civ/War 2nd Reg US Sharp-
shooters Co D SD C:27
Lily D d/o Capt Henry d 12 June

SMALL (continued)
1857 ae: 3m GSL
Margaret E w/o Oscar W d/o
William B & Annie Ewing d 11
Nov 1910 ae: 56y 18d SD C:67
Mary G w/o Samuel Jr d 6 Oct
1855 ae: 30y GSL
Morris no burial record SD F:105
Moses R d 20 Nov 1856 ae: 72y
GSL
Oscar W d 8 Apr 1893 ae: 46y
Civ/War 12th Reg Maine Inf
Co G C:67
John A d 6 Apr 1898 ae: 49y
Civ/War 12th Reg Maine Inf
Co G SBE C:27
Rebecca wid/o James d 25 Nov
1832 ae: 82y SD D:68
Rebecca M w/o William B d 29
Oct 1902 ae: 76y 10m 16d H:84
Samuel d 31 Oct 1863 ae: 72y
GSL
Sarah wid/o Alexander d 30 Aug
1854 ae: 75y SD H:71
Sarah wid/o Thomas d 7 Jan
1861 ae: 65y C:75
Sewall E s/o Moses S d 29 Sept
1879 ae: 1m GSL
Susan d w/o Artemus C d 20 Dec
1878 ae: 59y GSL
Susan W w/o Clement P d 29
Aug 1874 ae: 55y SD F:91
William B b1824 d 20 Feb 1870
Civ/War 17th Reg Maine Inf
Co D H:84
SMARDEN, Adam s/o Samuel d
12 June 1842 ae: 2y GSL
SMITH, Alfred A s/o James W d
26 Mar 1857 ae: 3m GSL
Ambrose Colby s/o late Henry L
d 22 Nov 1860 ae: 15m 12d
GSL
Aurilla w/o William H b 26 Jan
1844 d 7 Apr 1879 J:85
Bella D ae: 4y no dates on stone;
no burial record H:86
Bertha A d/o Anna d 16 Sept
1879 ae: 9m GSL
Betsy Gay w/o Charles Barstow
b1795 d1875 C:93
Charles Barstow b1790 d1862
C:93

SMITH (continued)
Charles N d 11 Apr 1846 ae: 22y
GSL
Charley D ae: 2y no dates on
stone; no burial record H:86
Clara T d 20 Aug 1882 ae: 40y
GSL
Rev David d 19 May 1837 ae: 76y
SD C:57
Drusila A d/o William H &
Aurilla b 10 July 1848 d 26
Aug 1850 J:85
Drusila R d/o William H &
Aurilla d 27 Sept 1864 ae: 12y
6m SBE J:85
Edward s/o William d 14 Sept
1851 ae: 3m GSL
Edward W s/o J D d 18 Aug 1863
ae: 1y Hilborn tomb A:10
Edwin Isaac d 27 Apr 1861 Cali-
fornia ae: 32y C:57
Elizabeth E w/o James d 1 Apr
1866 ae: 46y Plummer tomb
Location unknown
Elizabeth S d/o Joseph & Louisa
b 1831 d 1901 G:31
Ella M d/o J W & Sarah E d 29
Apr 1855 ae: 1y 6m SD D:82
Emily A w/o Frank A d 10 Apr
1903 ae: 65y 8m 10d Hilborn
tomb A:10
Frances A d/o William H &
Sarah G d 16 July 1836 ae: 2y
SBE J:85
Francis s/o John d 15 Nov 1842
ae: 15m Catholic GSL
Frances E w/o Levi A, d/o
James W & Julia Knight d 12
Mar 1934 ae: 73y 8m 8d NS
I:98
Frances L d/o Joseph d 26 Sept
1844 ae: 2y GSL
Frank Amos d 27 June 1904 ae:
75y 3m 27d Civ/War: 1st Reg
Maine Inf Co C Hilborn tomb
A:10
Frank L s/o Lewis B d 12 June
1859 ae: 1y 10m GSL
Franklin M s/o William H &
Sarah G d 20 Mar 1841 ae: 1y
SBE J:85
Frederick E s/o C M d 17 Jan

SMITH (continued)

1890 ae: 22y 5m GSL

George s/o Michael d 7 Sept 1850 ae: 7m Catholic GSL

George A d 23 Aug 1858 ae: 30y 5m GSL

George W s/o J S & M E d 19 Aug 1851 ae: 2y 1m SBE H:86

Georgianna Barstow d/o Charles Barstow & Betsy Gay b 1838 d 1894 C:93

Gilman R s/o Jotham S & M E d 27 Aug 1848 ae: 2m 17d SBE H:86

Harriet d/o Susan wid d 12 Oct 1843 ae: 13y GSL

Helena V d/o L B d 20 Sept 1849 ae: 14m GSL

Henry B s/o Marriner L d 9 Aug 1872 ae: 5m Hilborn tomb A:10

Isaac d 12 Sept 1846 ae: 64y Killed by a fall from a wagon SD C:57

James d 13 July 1849 ae: 76y . Native of Nova Scotia I:72

James s/o Michael d 7 Feb 1849 ae: 1y 3m Cathollic GSL

James E s/o James d 1 May 1861 ae: 3m GSL

John s/o Michael d 5 Nov 1854 ae: 3m GSL

John S s/o James d 16 Nov 1858 ae: 6y 6m GSL

Joseph b 1797 d 10 Nov 1881 G:31

Joseph Jr s/o Joseph d 28 Sept 1845 ae: 19y GSL

Jotham S s/o Jotham S & M E d 21 Mar 1895 SB H:86

Louisa w/o Joseph b 1805 d 1887 G:31

Lucy d/o William T d 22 July 1848 ae: 6y Drowned in Portland Harbor, mother & children buried in same grave GSL

Lydia d/o A d 6 Jan 1843 ae: 6y GSL

Margaret d 1 Aug 1848 ae: 3y Catholic GSL

Maria w/o James d 8 Nov 1856 ae: 69y SBE I:72

SMITH (continued)

Mary d/o John d 21 Sept 1849 ae: 1y Catholic GSL

Mary w/o John d 5 Apr 1847 ae: 26y Catholic GSL

Mary w/o John d 9 Mar 1848 ae: 50y Catholic GSL

Mary Ann Lyons w/o John d 9 Mar 1848 ae: 50y SD J:19

Mary E d/o William H & Aurilla no burial record SD J:85

Mary E d/o William H & Sarah G b 17 Mar 1844 d 21 Sept 1848 J:85

Mary Ellen d/o Michael d 25 Sept 1858 ae: 8m GSL

Mary J d/o James A d 8 Feb 1856 ae: 11m Plummer tomb Location unknown

Mary M d 8 Nov 1876 ae: 69y GSL

Mary Susan d/o James d 31 May 1860 ae: 1y GSL

Mercy Mrs d 28 June 1852 ae: 77y GSL

Monroe s/o William H & Aurilla b 3 Feb 1854 d 7 Mar 1861 J:85

Moses B d 6 Sept 1853 ae: 48y GSL

Myra Brackett w/o J Henry, d/o Isaac & Sarah M Brackett b 26 Feb 1867 d 31 July 1926 D:13

Oscar P s/o James P d 10 Apr 1858 ae: 9w 5d GSL

Priscilla w/o Isaac d 10 May 1877 ae: 83y SD C:57

Rebecca S d 13 May 1881 ae: 59y GSL

Robin H d 6 Sept 1854 ae: 20y SD C:93

Rolvin Hall s/o Abial & Mary Ann d 6 Sept 1854 ae: 20y SBE C:92

Sarah G w/o William H d 6 Apr 1847 ae: 36y J:85

Sarah J d/o John d 6 Sept 1841 ae: 15m Catholic GSL

Sarah M d 5 Aug 1889 Providence, Rhode Island ae: 45y GSL

Susan wid d 4 Mar 1844 ae: 74y

SMITH (continued)
GSL
Susan C wid/o Sidney d 4 Nov 1854 ae: 51y 11m 7d SD J:61
Susannah w/o Samuel d 4 Mar 1844 ae: 74y G:24
Thomas E s/o James E d 3 Sept 1871 ae: 4m GSL
Thomas W s/o Charles d 1 Oct 1857 ae: 17m GSL
Thomas W s/o James d 28 Aug 1858 ae: 5m GSL
William d 3 July 1846 ae: 63y GSL
William H d 15 May 1885 ae: 76y J:85
William H s/o William H & Aurilla d 4 Aug 1836 ae: 4y J:85
William H s/o William H & Sarah G d 4 Jan 1851 ae: 9m SBE J:85
William T s/o William T d 22 July 1848 ae: 8m Drowned in Portland Harbor, mother & children buried in same grave GSL
Willie s/o Frank M d 12 Sept 1880 ae: 3m GSL
Zena d ae: 9m no dates on stone; no burial record H:86
SNOW, Martha White w/o William A b 15 May 1830 d 15 Apr 1850 D:84
Mary A d 19 June 1875 ae: 59y GSL
Nancy M w/o James d 29 July 1855 ae: 62y GSL
Sarah wid/o Nathaniel d 11 Mar 1862 ae: 72y 5m SB I:126
SNOWMAN, Mary A d/o Thomas d 6 July 1857 ae: 7m 16d GSL
Sarah L d 6 Sept 1873 ae: 34y SD J:127
SOMERBY, Rebecca wid/o Abiel d 15 Aug 1858 ae: 86y 8m GSL
SOMERS, Barbara Abbie wid/o Michael, d/o Michael & Sarah Burke d 13 May 1945 ae: 95y Catholic NS D:83
Catherine Bannon w/o Michael d 15 May 1867 ae: 31y Catholic D:83

SOMERS (continued)
Elizabeth d/o Michael & Catherine B d 30 Sept 1864 ae: 2y 11m Catholic D:83
James M s/o Michael & Abbie d 1 Jan 1924 Richmond, Maine ae 42y 9m 7d Catholic SD D:83
Marcia d/o Michael & Catherine B d 8 Oct 1879 ae: 8y Catholic SBE D:83
Mary A d/o Michael & Catherine B d 25 Aug 1859 ae: 6m Catholic D:83
Michael d 29 Dec 1899 ae: 72y Native of Co Kerry, Ireland Catholic D:83
Samuel s/o Michael & Catherine B d 5 Aug 1860 ae: 5m Catholic D:83
SOULE, Alpheus G s/o Alpheus G & Mary d 18 Dec 1848 ae: 3m SD F:83
Elizabeth d 31 July 1848 Boston, Massachusetts ae: 73y GSL
Fostina d/o George & Mary d 5 Oct 1849 ae: 6m SBE I:82
Henry s/o Henry d 7 Oct 1849 ae: 6m GSL
Mary A w/o Alfred d 26 Feb 1853 ae: 23y GSL
SOUTHER, Deborah wid/o Lendall d 21 Sept 1868 ae: 83y H:44
Lendall S s/o Edward B d 17 Dec 1864 ae: 51y 5m SBE H:44
Mary G d/o Edward & Dolly T d 26 Nov 1901 ae: 97y 3m H:44
SPARROW, Clara d/o William d 11 Sept 1853 ae: 2m 15d GSL
SPEAR, John d 14 Nov 1883 New York City ae: 50y SD I:98
SPELLMAN, Joanna d 30 Mar 1850 ae: 56y Catholic GSL
SPENCER, Daniel s/o Daniel d 13 Sept 1856 ae: 3d Old Catholic Ground GSL
SPOFFORD, Frances E d/o Josiah d 12 Aug 1849 ae: 3y SD F:134
Josiah H d 17 Feb 1868 ae: 56y 4m F:134
Nancy w/o Josiah H d 3 Jan 1850

**SPOFFORD** (continued)
ae: 33y SBE  F:134
**SPOOR,** Charlotte Catherine d/o
Frederick & Rachel M d 27
Dec 1847 ae: 2y 9m I:123
Charlotte Frances d/o Frederick
& Rachel M d 27 Sept 1850 ae:
16m I:123
P L T no burial record SD  I:123
Rachel M w/o Frederick, d/o
Capt Thomas & Esther Mann d
19 June 1850 ae: 40y I:123
**SPRAGUE,** Ezra d 2 Aug 1848 ae:
49y GSL
Julia W d 21 Mar 1883 ae: 67y
J:250
**SPRING,** Grace d/o E C d 14 Aug
1854 ae: 2y 6m GSL
**SPRINGER,** Elizabeth Mrs d 12
July 1865 ae: 85y GSL
Henrietta Day d/o Capt Joseph F
d 13 Aug 1854 ae: 2y 5m Died
at sea of yellow fever SD  I:75
Jeanette Jackson wid/o Capt
Joseph F d 18 Oct 1883 ae:
61y I:75
Capt Joseph Foster b 8 Feb 1816
d 16 June 1876 Havana, Cuba
I:75
Moses d 21 Dec 1865 Winchen-
don, Massachusetts ae: 69y
10m GSL
**STACKPOLE,** Addison s/o Capt
David b 21 Oct 1817 d 4 Sept
1819 C:37
Charles H d 28 Jan 1864 Augusta
Hospital GSL
Capt David d 2 June 1855 ae: 74y
SBE  C:37
Judith H w/o David d 17 Jan
1879 Lisbon, Maine ae: 90y SD
C:37
Mary Blanchard d/o Capt David d
14 Apr 1844 ae: 19y SBE  C:37
Susan W d 30 Aug 1890 Lewis-
ton, Maine ae: 69y SD  C:37
**STANTON,** inf c/o Paul d 26 Sept
1856 ae: 4d GSL
**STANWOOD,** Elizabeth H w/o
Capt Gideon L b 10 June 1813
d 17 Mar 1889 SB  I:103
Franklin b 16 Mar 1852 d 20 June

**STANWOOD** (continued)
1888 "Marine Artist." I:103
Capt Gideon L b 20 Sept 1811 d
17 Jan 1885 I:103
Mary E d/o Capt Gideon L &
Elizabeth d 6 Feb 1850 ae: 13y
6m SBE  I:103
Mary G w/o Capt Samuel C d 29
May 1878 ae: 77y I:103
Capt Samuel C d 13 Mar 1857 ae:
61y I:103
**STAPLES,** Ada Louise d/o Leo-
nard C & Emily Louise d 16
Jan 1925 ae: 41y 9m 18d B:38
Albert s/o Capt Charles b 13 Oct
1828 d 2 Mar 1849 G:58
Alice B d/o Charles Jr d 24 July
1860 ae: 6m GSL
Ann L d/o Alfred d 14 May 1842
GSL
Anna Waterhouse d/o Charles d
24 Mar 1858 ae: 5y GSL
Blanche Lillian d/o Leonard C &
Emily L d 7 Feb 1957 ae: 66y
3m 24d B:38
Capt Charles d 2 Nov 1874 ae:
77y SD  G:58
Charles A s/o Charles Jr d 17
Oct 1856 ae: 21m GSL
Charlotte d/o Charles d 21 Feb
1848 ae: 6y SD  H:55
Cynthia B w/o Charles F d 9 Feb
1855 ae: 28y H:55
Cyrus d 17 July 1874 ae: 71y
H:55
Cyrus s/o Cyrus & Eliza b 15
Aug 1825 d 4 Sept 1825 H:55
Cyrus E s/o Cyrus & Eliza b 10
Dec 1830 d 11 Sept 1833 H:55
Edward A s/o Alfred d 1 Sept
1841 ae: 6y GSL
Edward Frost s/o Charles &
Mary b 30 Sept 1830 d 24 Aug
1831 G:58
Edwin s/o Cyrus & Eliza b 16
Nov 1833 d 13 June 1834 H:55
Eliza w/o Cyrus, d/o Thomas &
Mary Simonton d 24 Apr 1871
ae: 69y H:55
Ella d/o Edward F d 20 July
1861 ae: 1y GSL
Ellen Maria d/o Alfred d 10 Aug

STAPLES (continued)
1851 ae: 18m GSL
Emily G wid/o Capt James d 3
Sept 1853 ae: 30y GSL
Emily L w/o Leonard C b 1856 d
1925 B:38
Eugenia D d/o Charles & Cynthia
d 27 June 1859 ae: 8y H:55
Frances Burns w/o James b 1814
d 1891 Chicago, Illinois B:38
Frances E d/o Charles & Cynthia
d 3 Aug 1865 ae: 9m H:55
Frances E d/o George & Eliz-
abeth d 20 Aug 1849 ae: 6w
SBE G:58
Francis W s/o Alfred d 17 Mar
1850 ae: 2y GSL
Franklin s/o Cyrus & Eliza b 18
Oct 1840 d 16 Feb 1847 H:55
Frederick S s/o Edward F d 27
Aug 1866 ae: 1y 5m GSL
Granville E s/o James L &
Frances B d 13 Nov 1899 SD
B:38
Horace B s/o Cyrus & Eliza b 6
Oct 1837 d 16 Oct 1838 H:55
James b 1810 d 1883 Civ/War:
Lt Maine Coast Guards Co B
Heavy Art Ft Scammel B:38
Leonard C s/o James & Frances
d 30 May 1911 ae: 68y 5m 17d
Civ/War: Maine Coast Guards
Co B Heavy Art B:38
Mary w/o Charles, d/o Isaac
Pickett d 29 Mar 1871 ae: 71y
SBE G:58
Mary Elizabeth d/o Charles &
Mary b 28 Feb 1826 d 5 Mar
1833 G:58
Nathaniel s/o George & Eliza-
beth no burial record SBE
G:58
STAPLETON, Ann w/o William d
22 Feb 1849 ae: 20y Catholic
GSL
STARBIRD, Susan W w/o Thom-
as d 9 Sept 1856 ae: 41y 4m
C:73
Thomas d 10 Dec 1857 ae: 49y
1m C:73
Thomas E s/o Thomas &
Frances A d 23 Jan 1859 ae:

STARBIRD (continued)
5m 9d SD C:73
STEARNS, Lucy A H w/o Edward
P d 27 June 1881 Providence,
Rhode Island ae: 40y GSL
STEBBINS, Ethel May d/o Ella M
d 22 Feb 1893 ae: 8m 23d SD
F:17
George R s/o George & Faustina
d 8 July 1912 New York City
ae: 34y 6m SD F:17
George W d 12 Apr 1887 Greely
Hospital ae: 40y GSL
STEELE, Alexanger G s/o Wil-
liam & Mary J d 15 Feb 1854
ae: 15y J:252
Almira D w/o Eben d 13 Mar
1848 ae: 44y SBE F:33
Annie d/o William d 12 June
1856 ae: 28y SBE J:252
Benjamin H d 28 Sept 1862 ae:
26y SBE J:252
Eben d 8 Aug 1871 ae: 69y SBE
F:33
Edward Preble s/o William H d
25 Aug 1858 ae: 6w SD J:252
Eliza d/o William d 30 July
1864 ae: 23y SBE J:252
"Father" Unknown SBE J:252
Harriet D d/o Eben & Almira d d
15 June 1852 ae: 16y SBE F:33
Hattie w/o William H d 10 Apr
1859 ae: 30y J:252
John H s/o William & Mary d 4
Nov 1852 ae: 20y J:252
Judith w/o Capt Joseph d 28 Dec
1851 ae: 89y. F:33
Julia d/o Capt Joseph & Judith b
8 May 1799 d 16 July 1886 SD
F:33
William d 12 Apr 1865 ae: 59y
7m SD J:252
William Henry d 19 Dec 1861 ae:
36y J:252
STEER, John d 12 Oct 1883 New
York City, native of Cam-
bridge, Massachusetts I:98
STEPHENS, Emily w/o Leonard
no burial record GSL
Sophia d/o Peter d 6 Mar 1853
ae: 3m GSL
STEPHENSON, Almira w/o Henry

STEPHENSON (continued)
d 15 Sept 1850 ae: 53y SD J:94
Henry d 23 Sept 1880 ae: 85y 5m J:94
Henry s/o Henry & Almira d 23 Aug 1821 ae: 16m SBE J:94
Jane d/o Henry & Almira d 3 Dec 1832 ae: 10y 11m J:94
STETSON, Charles T s/o Thomas d 12 Aug 1852 ae: 14m GSL
Elizabeth w/o Lewis, d/o James & Sarah Walker d 18 Apr 1860 ae: 65y SBE B:50
Elizabeth T d/o Washington d 3 Dec 1845 ae: 4y GSL
Frank E s/o Albus R & Frances d 26 Feb 1854 ae: 5m 6d SBE J:266
Henrietta d 14 Sept 1856 ae: 5m SD H:99
Lewis d 9 May 1855 ae: 78y SB B:50
Ruth Briggs w/o Josiah d 2 Aug 1871 ae: 42y 4m B:24
Sarah Ella d/o Josiah & Ruth d 31 May 1855 ae: 13m SD B:24
STEVENS, Benjamin F s/o Benjamin Jr d 10 Mar 1853 ae: 4y 6m GSL
Eunice d w/o Charles d 16 Jan 1849 ae: 43y G:67
Jane Freeman w/o Nathaniel d 4 Jan 1891 ae: 78y 8m I:110
Joseph F s/o Nathaniel & Jane F b 26 Sept 1828 d 2 Dec 1856 I:110
Nathaniel d 10 Mar 1870 ae: 66y 2m 10d I:110
Sylvina w/o Benjamin Jr d 7 Aug 1851 ae: 27y GSL
T C w/o Jonathan d 3 Nov 1869 ae: 72y GSL
STICKNEY, Amy Chick d/o Amos & Elizabeth H Chick b 2 Apr 1843 d 8 Aug 1874 D:61
Lucy w/o Nicholas d 3 Dec 1858 ae: 73y SB I:171
Nicholas d 17 Feb 1864 ae: 79y 7m I:171
STILLINGS, Amos s/o David d 21 Feb 1850 ae: 3m GSL
David d 19 July 1844 ae: 2m GSL

STILLINGS (continued)
Ellen d/o David d 30 May 1843 ae: 5m GSL
Mahala F d/o David d 16 Apr 1852 ae: 3y GSL
STILSON, Clara Ella d/o Charles H d 24 Nov 1864 ae: 6w GSL
STINSON, Caroline A w/o William B d 5 July 1868 ae: 37y J:226
Joseph s/o Alexander d 10 Aug 1858 ae: 1y 6m GSL
Sarah A w/o Nathaniel d 2 Dec 1906 ae: 57y 2m 12d SD I:69
Willie H s/o William B & Caroline A d 12 Sept 1857 ae: 8w SBE J:226
STOCKMAN, Rev Lewis d 25 June 1844 ae: 31y GSL
STODDER, Turner d 10 May 1872 ae: 84y Safford-Hall tomb A:20
STONE, Susan B w/o John d 7 Apr 1887 Greely Hospital ae: 41y GSL
STORER, Fannie B d/o Horace P d 4 Sept 1851 ae: 15m GSL
Mary O d/o H P d 16 Aug 1849 ae: 18m GSL
Nellie d/o P d 25 Aug 1859 ae: 2y 7m GSL
STOVER, Charles R s/o Samuel & Martha d 9 Oct 1888 Boston, Massachusetts ae: 35y G:71
Harriet A C d/o Samuel & Martha d 8 Nov 1855 ae: 19y G:71
Martha A d/o Smith, William d 29 Nov 1894 Greely Hospital ae: 80y SD G:71
Samuel S d 29 Mar 1861 Boston, Massachusetts ae: 48y GSL
STRATTON, Daniel s/o William d 9 Dec 1856 ae: 6m GSL
STROUT, Charles S s/o Samuel & Susan S b 24 Aug 1858 d 31 Aug 1859 F:67
Edwin d 24 Dec 1869 ae: 47y GSL
Hannah w/o Capt William, d/o Samuel Waterhouse d 24 Nov 1845 ae: 34y F:138
Harry A M d 6 June 1886 ae: 27y

**STROUT** (continued)
5m GSL
Henry M s/o Edwin d 18 Aug 1857 ae: 2y 11m GSL
James W S s/o Edwin & Lydia B d 16 Sept 1849 ae: 1y 8m SD B:2
Joseph H s/o Sewall C d 12 Sept 1859 ae: 6w GSL
Nellie M d/o Stewart d 27 Oct 1865 ae: 3w GSL
Winfield S s/o Edwin S d 8 Sept 1866 ae: 7m GSL
**STUBBS**, Caroline L d/o Charles & Nancy b 1823 d 1891 J:49
Capt Charles d 3 Feb 1858 ae: 70y J:49
Edward K s/o Charles R d 28 Nov 1851 ae: 3y GSL
George R s/o Charles & Nancy b 1848 d 1851 J:49
Mary E d/o Edward & Sophronia d 1 Feb 1867 ae: 36y SBE H:49
Nancy w/o Charles d 25 Jan 1874 ae: 84y J:49
Octavia A d/o Charles & Nancy d 1 Jan 1896 ae: 85y 9m J:49
Olive A d/o Charles & Almira b 1846 d 1850 J:49
Olive A d/o Capt Charles & Nancy d 17 Sept 1836 ae: 9y J:49
**STURDIVANT**, George L s/o Henry W d 26 Aug 1875 ae: 5m GSL
**STYLES**, Willie H s/o Edward d 26 Sept 1869 ae: 6y 9m GSL
**SULLIVAN**, Dennis s/o John d 18 May 1862 ae: 3y 6m Catholic GSL
Dennis O s/o Michael d 14 Dec 1848 ae: 2y Catholic GSL
Gehanna s/o Gehanna d 16 July 1857 ae: 1y Catholic GSL
Henry s/o Timothy & Maria d 30 June 1853 ae: 1y 8m 8d Catholic SD I:170
James s/o James d 11 Mar 1853 ae: 1y Catholic GSL
James s/o John d 20 Mar 1863 ae: 10m Catholic GSL
Joanna d/o John d 4 Sept 1857

**SULLIVAN** (continued)
ae: 13m Catholic GSL
John s/o F d 3 Nov 1862 ae: 3y 3m Catholic GSL
John s/o John d 12 Aug 1860 ae: 1y 5m Catholic GSL
Joseph s/o Anthony d 21 Sept 1858 ae: 13m Catholic GSL
Julia S d/o Jeremiah d 6 May 1850 ae: 18m Catholic GSL
Lawrence s/o Jeremiah d 10 Aug 1842 ae: 9m Catholic GSL
Lucy E d/o John d 24 Oct 1852 ae: 4m Catholic GSL
Maria w/o Timothy d 18 Apr 1864 ae: 36y Catholic GSL
Martha d/o William d 10 Apr 1851 ae: 11m Catholic GSL
Mary d 17 Aug 1852 ae: 21y Catholic GSL
Mary A d/o John d 24 Oct 1852 ae: 7y Catholic GSL
Mary Ann d/o Patrick d 24 Nov 1851 ae: 13m Catholic GSL
Mary J d/o Patrick d 30 Oct 1849 ae: 4y Catholic GSL
Mary O d 16 Dec 1857 ae: 55y Catholic GSL
Michael s/o Daniel d 28 Apr 1849 ae: 1y Catholic GSL
Michael s/o J d 21 Dec 1857 Catholic Strangers' Ground GSL
Patrick d 7 Mar 1853 ae: 25y Catholic GSL
Patrick d 4 Aug 1851 ae: 1y Catholic GSL
Richard s/o Robert d 3 Oct 1851 ae: 2y Catholic GSL
Sarah E d/o Charles d 6 Jan 1862 ae: 4y Catholic Strangers' Ground GSL
Thomas s/o James d 1 Nov 1856 ae: 6m Catholic GSL
William s/o Dennis d 24 July 1856 ae: 8y Catholic GSL
William s/o Timothy & Maria d 25 Dec 1850 ae: 10m Catholic SD I:170
**SUTTON**, Wiliam s/o John d 19 Sept 1856 ae: 11m GSL
**SWEENEY**, Ellen w/o Daniel d

SWEENEY (continued)
16 Oct 1856 ae: 26y Catholic
GSL
John s/o Daniel d 21 Mar 1857
ae: 11m Catholic GSL
William s/o Daniel d 2 Oct 1855
ae: 11m 20d Catholic GSL
SWEETMAN, Catherine d/o Patrick d 13 Oct 1856 ae: 3y 2m
Catholic GSL
John F s/o Patrick d 15 July
1857 ae: 1y 9m Catholic GSL
SWEETSER, Frances A d/o John
d 12 July 1841 ae: 15y GSL
Georgianna d/o John d 11 July
1860 Cape Elizabeth, Maine
ae: 20y GSL
Hannah C w/o John d 6 July 1858
Scarboro, Maine ae: 62y GSL
Jane d/o Thomas d 25 May 1843
ae: 17m GSL
Samuel s/o Simeon & Sarah S d
22 Oct 1840 ae: 19y 4m SB
F:37
Sarah Smith w/o Simeon d 23 Oct
1880 ae: 87y SBE F:37
Simeon d 19 June 1854 ae: 67y
SBE F:37
SWETT, Albion s/o Benjamin d
29 May 1863 ae: 41y SD I:77
Charles O s/o Charles & Sarah A
d 23 Aug 1849 ae: 1y SBE I:77
Daniel B s/o Adam d 21 Feb
1894 ae: 71y Jordan tomb D:28
Dorothy w/o Benjamin b 12 Aug
1794 d 22 Apr 1875 I:77
Emily J d/o Benjamin & Dorothy
d 18 Feb 1856 ae: 20y I:77
Frances d/o William Hatch d 16
Jan 1861 ae: 29y 7m I:77
Sarah A w/o Charles d 12 June
1853 ae: 30y SB I:77
Susan H d/o Benjamin & Dorothy
d 27 Feb 1856 ae: 22y 6m SB
I:77
SWIFT, Charles E s/o Joseph &
Delia d 9 June 1883 ae: 65y
SBE I:125
Delia w/o Joseph d 15 Oct 1850
Augusta State Hospital ae: 67y
I:125
Frederick K s/o Joseph & Delia

SWIFT (continued)
d 30 Aug 1866 Minnesota ae:
43y SBE I:125
Joseph d 27 May 1850 ae: 77y
I:125
Joseph Jr s/o Joseph & Delia d 2
Aug 1834 ae: 17y I:125
Maria S d/o Joseph & Delia d 18
Apr 1845 ae: 29y I:125
William S s/o Joseph & Delia d
18 Aug 1850 ae: 23y SBE
I:125
SYLVESTER, Angela M d/o Isaac
& Phebe d 3 Nov 1850 ae: 3y
J:71
Caroline Dyer w/o Isaac no
burial record SD J:71
Deborah W w/o William d 31
Aug 1874 ae: 82y SD J:71
Edward H s/o Isaac & Caroline d
28 Apr 1945 ae: 83y J:71
Ella J w/o Edward H, d/o Henry
& Jane N Fling d 17 Feb 1929
ae: 68y 8m J:71
Fannie d/o Isaac & Caroline d 25
Mar 1881 ae: 21y SD J:71
Frank A d 25 Nov 1872 ae: 12y
SD J:71
Henry Edward b 1897 d 1978
WWI: veteran J:71
Isaac Jr no burial record SD J:71
Isaac N d 4 Nov 1892 Cambridge,
Massachusetts ae: 67y SD
J:71
Louisa P d/o Isaac N d 24 Jan
1864 ae: 10m SD J:71
Pink no burial record SD J:71
Ruth Sargent wid/o Henry Edward
b 1900 d 13 Oct 1986 J:71
Sarah D d/o Isaac N d 23 Apr
1879 ae: 27y SD J:71
William d 29 Dec 1855 ae: 65y
GSL
TALBOT, David d 12 Feb 1843
ae: 75y SD J:250
Electra d/o David & Hannah d 3
Feb 1853 ae: 56y 5m SBE
J:250
Hannah w/o David d 13 Dec 1852
ae: 80y J:250
TALCOTT, David d 10 June 1848
ae: 36y Native of Bolton, Con-

TALCOTT (continued)
necticut GSL
TANNER, Rosalie P w/o Dorsey, d/o James T & Frances Lewis d 27 July 1921 ae: 50y SD J:240
TAPLEY, Joshua d 15 Apr 1843 ae: 67y GSL
TAPSCOTT, Hannah M w/o Martin d 12 June 1857 ae: 38y GSL
TARR, Alice A d/o David A d 27 Apr 1867 ae: 6y 1m GSL
Delight w/o Richard d 13 Feb 1852 ae: 62y J:137
Susan d 22 May 1858 ae: 36y GSL
TAYLOR, Andrew L d 9 July 1871 ae: 78y 4m GSL
Charles R d 5 Sept 1890 ae: 57y Civ/War: 5th Reg Maine Inf Co D SD B:1
Edward Payson s/o Capt William & Mary d 31 Mar 1856 ae: 20y 9m B:1
Francis E s/o William A d 22 June 1860 ae: 2m 22d GSL
Gertrude no burial record SD B:1
Joshua L b 1850 d 1921 B:5
Lena d w/o Joshua L, d/o Capt Randall Doyle d 6 June 1866 ae: 19y B:5
Lizzie Gertrude d 22 Aug 1888 B:1
Maggie A w/o Joshua L, d/o Capt Randall Doyle d 2 Feb 1873 ae: 21y. B:5
Mary w/o William d 14 Nov 1871 ae: 73y 6m B:1
Mary R wid/o James d 19 Oct 1865 ae: 69y GSL
Payson no burial record SD B:1
Sally H d/o Andrew L d 12 Aug 1854 ae: 10y GSL
Capt William b 4 Jan 1804 d 20 Dec 1887 B:1
TEMLEN, Mary w/o John d 5 Aug 1844 ae: 36y Catholic GSL
TenBROECK, Lucretia w/o Rev Petrus S d 12 Oct 1861 Clinton, Iowa ae: 64y TenBroeck tomb A:11
Mary Octavia w/o Peter S d 24

TenBROECK (continued)
Sept 1919 New York City ae: 85y TenBroeck tomb A:11
Peter S s/o Petrus S d 19 Dec 1867 ae: 46y Civ/War: Maj; Surgeon, Med Dept USA Ten-Broeck tomb A:11
Rev Petrus S d 21 Jan 1849 Danvers, Massachusetts ae: 57y TenBroeck tomb A:11
William C s/o Petrus S d 28 Dec 1865 ae: 36y 11m TenBroeck tomb A:11
TENNENT, George d 28 Dec 1863 ae: 38y GSL
George s/o George d 22 May 1850 ae: 1y GSL
Henry M s/o George d 8 May 1863 ae: 8m 16d GSL
Margaret d 5 July 1843 ae: 25y GSL
TERRY, Enoch L d 27 Sept 1873 ae: 72y GSL
THATCHER, Amelia H d 15 May 1899 Ayer, Massachusetts ae: 72y 5m 15d I:104
Sarah B d 12 Oct 1876 ae: 57y SD I:104
THAYER, Clinton d 11 Mar 1835 ae: 50y D:39
Margaret wid/o Clinton d 12 Aug 1855 Waterville, Maine ae: 66y D:39
Sophia A d/o William d 18 Aug 1856 ae: 8y 7m GSL
William s/o William d 18 Aug 1856 ae: 6y 1m GSL
THOITS, Ralph A d 29 Jan 1892 ae: 4w G:42
Samuel Gould s/o Ferdinand d 22 Aug 1897 ae: 2y 19d SD G:42
Willie Franklin d 11 Aug 1877 ae: 7w GSL
THOMAS, Charles B s/o Bradford d 1 Sept 1851 ae: 2y GSL
Harriet L d/o Charles H & Octavia d 1 Dec 1854 ae: 9y Buried beside mother GSL
Octavia w/o Charles H d 20 Nov 1854 ae: 27y GSL
THOMES, Dolly T wid/o Capt William d 31 Mar 1887 ae: 75y

**THOMES** (continued)
H:44
Elizabeth Ann d/o Capt Wiliam & Dolly T d 15 Dec 1846 ae: 5y 9m H:44
Sarah L w/o Benjamin d 3 Nov 1870 ae: 85y 4m SD D:69
Capt William d 16 Feb 1842 ae: 40y SB H:44
William Edward s/o Capt William & Dolly T d 15 Aug 1834 ae: 2w H:44
**THOMPSON**, Edward F s/o Jacob d 8 Nov 1853 ae: 13m GSL
Frankie M d 5 Nov 1872 ae: 9m J:117
Hannah d 18 Aug 1876 ae: 87y GSL
Helen d/o Joseph & Sarah d 14 Nov 1852 ae: 7w J:259
John s/o Charles d 15 Sept 1855 ae: 1y GSL
John F d 25 May 1854 ae: 22y SBE C:1
Joseph F d 27 Nov 1870 ae: 38y 6m J:117
Joseph W d 18 Nov 1876 ae: 44y Civ/War: 5th Reg Maine Inf Co F J:259
Langdon d 1 Oct 1869 ae: 45y GSL
Louisa d 25 Oct 1873 ae: 51y GSL
Nellie N d/o Christopher d 29 Feb 1864 ae: 5m GSL
Rhoda C wid/o Edward d 25 Mar 1870 ae: 75y H:100
Sarah wid/o Joseph b 1829 d 1902 Former wid/o J F Hutchinson J:259
Sarah E w/o William d 15 Mar 1869 ae: 31y GSL
Willie no dates on stone; no burial record J:117
**THORN**, Harriet d 23 Jan 1853 ae: 50y Strangers' Ground GSL
**THORNDIKE**, Arvilla Jordan w/o John B d 2 Nov 1880 ae: 52y J:84
Charles s/o John & Lizzie d 26 Nov 1896 ae: 3-1/2m SD J:84
George B s/o John B & Arvilla J

**THORNDIKE** (continued)
d 12 Jan 1863 ae: 3y J:84
George W s/o John W d 17 Aug 1884 ae: 1m SD J:84
John B d 6 May 1893 ae: 68y J:84
Lizzie E w/o John W d 12 Oct 1896 Biddeford, Maine ae: 38y SD J:84
Lizzie M d/o John & Arvilla J d 15 Dec 1862 ae: 9y SD J:84
Margery d 8 Jan 1874 ae: 78y SBE J:84
Martha Ann d/o William & Margery d 14 Nov 1832 ae: 3y 6m SBE J:84
Mercy Ann d 11 Apr 1884 ae: 62y SD J:84
Ralph G s/o John W d 12 Apr 1893 ae: 1y 4m 24d SD J:84
Robert s/o William & Margery d 7 June 1833 ae: 2m SBE J:84
William s/o Robert d 20 Apr 1868 ae: 69y 4m SBE J:84
William H s/o William & Margery d 4 Nov 1832 ae: 2y SBE J:84
William H s/o William & Margery d 29 Jan 1835 ae: 6w SD J:84
William H s/o William & Margery d 29 Jan 1886 J:84
**THORNTON**, Martin s/o Martin d 19 Sept 1853 ae: 9m GSL
Martin s/o Martin d 13 Mar 1855 ae: 2d GSL
**THRASHER**, Maria W d/o John A d 4 Oct 1857 ae: 5m 11d GSL
**THULL**, Alice E d/o Edward S d 2 May 1854 ae: 16m SD B:14
**THURLOW**, Royal s/o John d 17 June 1855 ae: 5y SD F:29
**THURSTON**, Abbie J d/o Capt Henry & Jane P b 30 Aug 1851 d 5 Feb 1862 G:46
David F s/o Brown d 7 Dec 1857 ae: 4y 6m GSL
Elizabeth C d/o Edward d 17 May 1853 ae: 7y GSL
Ezekiel d 3 Dec 1859 ae: 73y SB I:126

THURSTON (continued)
Hannah w/o Ezekiel d 29 Nov 1881 ae: 93y 8m SB I:126
Harriet w/o John d 13 Jan 1887 ae: 72y SBE I:126
Henrietta M d/o Capt Henry T & Rhoda d 10 Sept 1849 ae: 13y 13d SD G:46
Henrietta M d/o Capt Henry & Jane P d 28 Sept 1870 ae: 22y 2m G:46
Henry s/o John & Harriet d 26 July 1864 ae: 21y 3m SBE I:126
Capt Henry b 1 Dec 1808 d 9 Feb 1860 SD G:46
Henry Jr s/o Capt Henry & Jane P b 2 Nov 1857 d 22 Aug 1859 SD G:46
Jane P wid/o Capt Henry, d/o Moses & Abigail Plummer d 31 May 1898 ae: 83y 9m 16d "Empress of America." G:46
John d 10 Apr 1869 ae: 56y SBE I:126
Margaret d/o Capt Henry & Jane P no burial record SD G:46
Marion d/o Capt Henry & Jane P no burial record SD G:46
Mason s/o Capt Henry & Jane P no burial record SD G:46
Nathaniel s/o John & Harriet d 29 Apr 1842 ae: 2y 5m SD I:126
Nathaniel S s/o John & Harriet d 12 Oct 1853 ae: 5y 8m SD I:126
Rhoda K w/o Capt Henry d 11 May 1845 ae: 30y G:46
William Edward s/o Capt Henry & Rhoda K b 29 Mar 1840 d 20 Feb 1858 Lost at sea G:46
TIBBETTS, Annie L d/o George H & Sarah E b 20 June 1859 d 12 Feb 1860 H:5
George H d 10 May 1895 ae: 67y 9m H:5
Ira B d 9 Sept 1872 ae: 79y G:32
Joanna B d/o Ira & Sarah d 29 Aug 1849 ae: 24y G:32
Lewis D s/o Bradbury & Mary d 7 Dec 1843 ae: 7y F:6

TIBBETTS (continued)
Lydia O wid d 20 Apr 1853 ae: 78y GSL
Mary wid/o John d 29 July 1853 ae: 78y G:32
Mary F d/o Ira B & Sarah d 3 Oct 1844 ae: 15m G:32
Rufus Edwin s/o Rufus d 17 Oct 1853 ae: 10m GSL
Sarah w/o Ira B d 9 Mar 1846 ae: 44y G:32
Sarah w/o Ira B d 1 Oct 1885 ae: 86y G:32
Sarah E d/o Ira B & Sarah d 26 Mar 1838 ae: 2y 3m G:32
Sarah E Patch w/o George H d 2 Apr 1895 ae: 64y 8m 16d H:5
Sarah J d/o Ira B & Sarah d 30 Sept 1830 ae: 13m G:32
Sarah J d/o Ira B & Sarah d 27 Nov 1831 ae: 7w G:32
TIERNEY, Maurice s/o Matthew d 25 Feb 1853 ae: 3y Catholic GSL
TIMMONS, Horatio H s/o Henry & Mary d 22 Feb 1854 ae: 13y Stone on D:72 C:15
Jabez D s/o Henry & Mary d 22 July 1910 ae: 31y SD C:15
TINKER, Adeline wid/o John d 17 June 1889 ae: 67y 8m SD I:82
John d 24 Sept 1888 ae: 76y Civ/War: 7th Reg Maine Inf Co I, US Navy I:82
John M s/o John d 26 Oct 1849 ae: 1m SD I:82
TINKHAM, Franklin d 15 Mar 1857 ae: 59y GSL
Susan wid d 21 June 1842 ae: 62y GSL
TITCOMB, Abigail S w/o William B b 1799 d 1885 G:23
Augusta H d/o William B & Abigail S d 1 Aug 1899 ae: 66y G:23
Julia Ann d/o William B & Abigail S d 5 Apr 1844 ae: 22y SBE G:23
Maria S d/o William B & Abigail S d 23 Aug 1899 ae: 77y G:23
William Henry s/o William B & Abigail S d 8 Apr 1844 ae: 6y

TITCOMB (continued)
SBE G:23

TOBIN, Ann d/o James & Ann d 19 Apr 1856 ae: 5d Catholic SD J:31

John E s/o James & Ann d 17 May 1850 ae: 3m 2d Catholic SBE J:31

Margaret d/o James & Ann d 3 June 1855 ae: 3m Catholic SD J:31

Mary Ann d/o James & Ann d 29 May 1852 ae: 10m 24d Catholic SBE J:31

TODD, Catherine w/o James A d 27 Mar 1857 ae: 26y GSL

Isaac d 24 Apr 1850 ae: 43y GSL

Isaac d 17 May 1864 ae: 22y GSL

TOMPKINS, Carrie T w/o Theophilus d 26 Dec 1866 of chloroform ae: 28y GSL

TOOMEY, Catherine d/o Matthew d 17 Aug 1853 ae: 10m Old Catholic Ground GSL

Ella d/o John d 27 Sept 1857 ae: 1y 8m Catholic GSL

Ellen d/o John d 25 Nov 1850 ae: 7w Catholic GSL

Jeremiah s/o John d 9 Sept 1855 ae: 9m Catholic GSL

John s/o John d 3 Oct 1848 ae: 12d Catholic GSL

Mary Carty w/o Edward d 26 Nov 1855 ae: 22y Catholic GSL

TORREY, Edward d 8 Mar 1843 ae: 20y GSL

Joshua d 5 Sept 1847 ae: 25y Drowned at Lewiston Falls, Maine Catholic GSL

TOTMAN, Horace s/o Horace d 5 Apr 1854 ae: 4y GSL

TOWLE, David s/o Peter d 4 Dec 1856 ae: 1y 5m Strangers' Ground GSL

TOWNSEND, Amelia H w/o Dr H G d 29 Jan 1864 ae: 27y GSL

George O s/o Ezra d 18 Aug 1848 ae: 6y GSL

James d 10 Dec 1842 ae: 52y GSL

John H s/o John R d 18 June 1853 ae: 9y GSL

TOWNSEND (continued)
John R s/o Franklin d 4 July 1849 ae: 2y GSL

Lysander P d 9 Feb 1867 ae: 35y Civ/War: 3rd Reg Maine Inf, 17th Reg Maine Inf Co I, 1st Reg Maine Heavy Art F:80

Malvina H d/o Abram d 30 Sept 1848 ae: 20m GSL

Martha A w/o Lysander P d 21 Mar 1911 ae: 80y SD F:80

Mary w/o Joseph d 21 Mar 1838 ae: 34y SD E:5

Olive d 29 Feb 1864 ae: 89y GSL

TRACY, Margaret wid/o James d 13 Dec 1857 ae: 57y Catholic GSL

Richard s/o Thomas & Mary b 6 Feb 1834 d 13 Feb 1841 Catholic I:25

TRAFTON, Catherine d/o Edward d 13 Sept 1856 ae: 13m GSL

Rufus d 19 Aug 1852 ae: 63y Strangers' Ground GSL

TRAIN, John s/o Thomas d 16 July 1857 ae: 4y GSL

TRASK, Abbie P d 16 Sept 1900 ae: 60y 6m SD I:148

Augusta M d 27 Mar 1881 ae: 43y GSL

Charles H b 1844 d ---- Civ/War: 29th Reg Maine Inf Co E I:148

Clara C d/o John & Martha d 3 Aug 1850 ae: 16m SBE I:148

Clarissa A d/o John d 3 Aug 1850 ae: 15m GSL

George F d 17 Apr 1882 ae: 42y Civ/War: 3rd Batt Maine Lt Art, 10th Reg Maine Inf Co B I:148

John E d 28 Apr 1853 ae: 9m SBE I:148

TRINOLINE, Margaret d/o John d 21 Aug 1841 ae: 13m Catholic GSL

TROWBRIDGE, Eunice wid/o John d 26 Oct 1852 ae: 76y GSL

John M d 30 May 1871 ae: 62y 7m GSL

Judith w/o Nathan N d 8 June

TROWBRIDGE (continued)
1850 ae: 48y H:51
Margaret S d 8 Mar 1851 ae: 11d
H:51
Nathan d 11 Aug 1865 ae: 65y SD
H:51
Sarah A w/o Nathan d 19 Mar
1854 ae: 38y H:51
Sarah D d/o Charles d 22 Oct
1862 ae: 5m GSL
TRUE, Charles s/o Samuel d 7
Sept 1843 ae: 14m GSL
Edwin H s/o Solomon d 14 Apr
1857 ae: 2y 3m GSL
Frederick M s/o David Jr & Har-
riet d 4 Apr 1851 ae: 7y SD
B:14
G F M s/o David T d 4 Apr 1851
ae: 6y GSL
Mary w/o Samuel d 25 July 1843
ae: 32y GSL
Samuel d 27 June 1855 ae: 46y
GSL
TUCKERMAN, Olvier P d 26 Jan
1868 ae: 50y 11m GSL
TUKESBURY, Capt Leonard M d
18 Dec 1852 ae: 44y GSL
TURNER, Frances L d 20 July
1853 ae: 28y G:36
Henry K b 23 Mar 1826 d 21 May
1899 Civ/War: 5th Batt Maine
Lt Art SBE J:82
James d 17 Nov 1852 ae: 21y
Catholic GSL
John s/o Hugh d 18 Aug 1856 ae:
20y GSL
Karl buried 13 Jan 1934, no death
record J:82
Margaret d/o James d 18 Dec
1857 ae: 2y GSL
Mary E Johnson w/o Henry K b
23 Mar 1826 d 7 Mar 1885 J:82
Moses d 18 May 1875 ae: 78y 6m
SBE J:36
Nellie H d/o Henry K & Mary E b
8 Apr 1852 d 13 Feb 1859 SBE
J:82
TUTTLE, inf c/o Edward & Ann d
15 Jan 1835 F:98
Ann d w/o Edward d 16 May 1841
ae: 43y SD F:98
Clinton s/o Edward d 21 June

TUTTLE (continued)
1872 ae: 21y SD F:98
Edward d 3 Oct 1850 ae: 29y SD
F:98
Edward d 2 June 1884 ae: 85y SD
F:98
Esther d/o Edward d 27 Sept
1844 ae: 15y SD F:98
Harriet L d/o Edward d 12 June
1849 Boston, Massachusetts
ae: 16y SD F:98
Mary w/o Edward d 3 Feb 1864
ae: 54y 7m SD F:98
Samuel s/o Edward & Ann b 14
Dec 1827 d 6 Sept 1832 F:98
Sarah A wid/o Edward d 18 Sept
1851 ae: 23y SD F:98
TWOMBLY, Julia d/o John d 27
Sep 1852 Saco, Maine ae: 11y
Catholic GSL
TYLER, James d 17 July 1849
ae: 67y I:73
Sarah w/o James, d/o Benjamin
Jordan d 20 Sept 1870 ae: 87y
8m I:73
ULRICK, Harriet N d/o John &
Sally no burial record SBE
I:63
John b 4 Oct 1784 Hamburg,
Germany d 10 Aug 1849 Bid-
deford, Maine I:63
Capt John Jr s/o John & Sally d
25 Feb 1847 Port Nova, Africa
ae: 29y 5m SBE I:63
Sally w/o John d 5 Mar 1849 ae:
58y 4m SBE I:63
Susan Ellen d/o John & Sally d
13 Sept 1855 ae: 22y 6m I:63
USHER, Jefferson B d 29 Apr
1867 ae: 67y GSL
Justa L d 3 Aug 1864 ae: 5m
GSL
VAIGLEY, Mary d/o James d 29
Apr 1858 ae: 1y 9m 10d GSL
VanBUSKIRK, Lawrence d 3 Sept
1856 Thomaston, Maine ae:
75y SB D:19
Maria d 11 May 1891 ae: 77y SD
D:19
Mary Ann w/o Lawrence d 7 Nov
1841 ae: 56y D:19

VARDICK, Lizzie no burial record, no dates on stone G:15
Zilpha d 5 Sept 1871 ae: 70y 6m G:15
VARNUM, John s/o Joseph d 12 Oct 1844 ae: 3m GSL
John L s/o Joseph D d 17 Jan 1849 ae: 1y GSL
Thomas s/o Joseph d 14 Feb 1846 ae: 4m GSL
VAUGHAN, Elizabeth Jordan w/o William d 5 Apr 1811 SBE E:1
Elizabeth Jordan d/o William & Elizabeth J no burial record SD E:1
Maria d/o William T & Eliza M d 23 Dec 1830 SD E:1
Olivia S d 27 Apr 1871 ae: 80y SD E:1
Richard N s/o William T & Sally S d 27 Sept 1813 SD E:1
S E s/o William T & Sally S d 10 July 1815 SD E:1
Sally S Barrett w/o William T b 29 July 1781 d 10 July 1815 SD E:1
Sarah Eleanor d/o William & Elizabeth d 20 Dec 1852 ae: 65y SD E:1
William b 13 Mar 1745 d 19 June 1826 SBE E:1
William T d 5 May 1845 ae: 62y Clerk of Court, Cumberland Co E:1
VEASIE, George W d 1 Mar 1850 ae: 39y GSL
VERRILL, Hannah M d/o John d 1 Sept 1847 ae: 17m Catholic GSL
VILES, Harriet C w/o Joseph d 27 May 1855 ae: 36y GSL
VINCENT, T E s/o John Pascal d 30 Apr 1853 ae: 11m GSL
WADE, Almira Isabelle w/o L Clifford d 27 Sept 1890 ae: 50y 10m Safford-Hall tomb A:20
L Clifford d 6 July 1899 ae: 59y 7m 3d Safford-Hall tomb A:20
WADSWORTH, Lucia d/o Peleg d 18 OCt 1864 ae: 81y Longfellow tomb A:12

WAITE, Annie M w/o Samuel B d 7 Mar 1906 ae: 66y 11m SD J:83
Augustus E s/o Charles W & Sarah S d 5 May 1831 ae: 9m I:131
Capt Charles W d 19 June 1853 ae: 57y I:131
John d 16 Mar 1838 ae: 87y F:1
Eliza w/o Capt John d 27 Oct 1854 ae: 45y GSL
John d 13 July 1857 ae: 29y Suicide by hanging SD F:1
Louise d/o Charles & Sarah S no dates on stone, no burial record I:131
Louise d 3 Feb 1853 ae: 80y F:1
Mary A b 17 Apr 1839 d 7 Mar 1906 J:83
Sally N w/o John d 3 Feb 1853 ae: 80y SD F:1
Capt Samuel B s/o John & Sally d 23 Apr 1826 ae: 23y SBE F:1
Sophronia S d/o Charles W & Sarah S d 12 July 1842 ae: 9y I:131
Sarah S w/o Charles W d 23 June 1873 ae: 68y 2m I:131
WALCH, Patrick d 6 Mar 1883 ae: 67y Catholic GSL
WALDEN, Nathaniel d 10 Mar 1870 ae: 66y GSL
WALDRON, Albertina d/o Silas H & Mary Ann b 1852 d 1854 F:78
Alzina d/o Silas H & Mary Ann b 1852 d 1865 F:78
Anna Q d/o Silas H & Mary Ann d 18 July 1909 Augusta State Hospital ae: 55y SD F:78
Franklin s/o Silas H & Mary Ann d 24 Dec 1848 ae: 5w F:78
Hannah E d/o Silas H & Mary Ann b 22 Sept 1840 d 17 Oct 1841 F:78
Helen d/o F A d 18 Sept 1858 Westbrook, Maine ae: 3m 16d GSL
Josephinie d/o Silas H & Mary Ann b 1849 d 1865 F:78
Lucy Ellen d/o Silas H & Mary

WALDRON (continued)
Ann b 18 Mar 1835 d 5 Apr 1843 F:78
Mary Ann Hamilton w/o Silas H d 5 June 1901 ae: 83y 10m F:78
Richard d 13 Jan 1857 ae: 75y GSL
Silas H b 1806 d 1878 F:78
William E s/o Silas H d 19 Dec 1856 ae: 1w SD F:78
William H s/o Silas H & Mary Ann d 11 Mar 1848 ae: 6m F:78
WALKER, Augusta d/o Samuel S d 20 Aug 1841 ae: 2y 6m GSL
Daniel b 1783 d 1880 F:77
Dexter d 8 Oct 1846 ae: 67y H:7
Eben S s/o Daniel & Sally b 1820 d 1847 F:77
Edward s/o Daniel & Sally b 1822 d 1835 F:77
Eleanor wid/o Gardner d 12 May 1846 East Boston, Massachusetts ae: 61y B:63
George s/o Samuel d 11 Jan 1863 ae: 17y 4m GSL
John d 25 Nov 1855 ae: 59y 8m GSL
Capt Joseph d 6 Jan 1861 ae: 86y 6m Walker tomb D:36
Kilby S s/o Daniel & Sally b 1812 d 1841 F:77
Mary d 14 May 1862 ae: 78y GSL
Mary d/o Daniel & Sally b 1785 d 1860 F:77
Mary w/o Capt Joseph d 21 Jan 1856 ae: 78y Walker tomb D:36
Mary A d/o Daniel & Sally b 1814 d 1833 F:77
Mary Caroline d/o William d 11 Feb 1846 ae: 6m GSL
Rebecca d/o Daniel & Sally b 1814 d 1833 F:77
Sally w/o Daniel b 1785 d 1856 F:77
Samuel A s/o late Samuel S d 11 Sept 1861 ae: 19y GSL
Samuel T d 30 Jan 1853 ae: 39y GSL
Thomas s/o Thomas d 31 May

WALKER (continued)
1858 ae: 5y GSL
Capt William d 25 Jan 1849 Matanzas, Cuba ae: 38y GSL
William S s/o Daniel & Sally b 1824 d 1843 F:77
WALL, Bessie d/o John E & C M d 26 Sept 1885 ae: 1y 8m SD B:67
Ellen d/o Thomas d 30 Oct 1857 ae: 17y 25d GSL
John E d 29 Dec 1885 ae: 29y B:67
Rosa d/o John E & C M d 7 Jan 1886 ae: 3y 11m SD B:67
WALLACE, Harriet w/o William B d 11 June 1872 ae: 71y I:75
Henrietta R d/o William B & Harriet d 1 July 1860 ae: 11y 8m SD I:75
Mary S d 8 June 1885 Brooklyn, New York ae: 39y 4m 17d GSL
Sarah A d/o James A d 17 Dec 1847 ae: 1y GSL
Sarah B d/o James d 10 Sept 1846 ae: 18m GSL
Sarah E w/o James A d 15 Oct 1868 ae: 28y GSL
Wiliam B d 3 Sept 1887 ae: 85y I:75
WALLS, Dorcas W b 8 Dec 1833 d 27 Feb 1897 Somerville, Massachusetts I:118
Martin Lewis s/o Nathaniel & Lucy d 12 Sept 1908 ae: 72y 3m 12d SD I:118
WALLEY, James s/o William d 11 Sept 1854 GSL
Mary w/o William d 13 Sept 1854 ae: 32y GSL
WALSH, Edward s/o Patrick & Joanna d ae: 10m no burial record Catholic SD J:209
Hannah d 24 Mar 1850 ae: 70y Catholic GSL
Hattie d 31 Oct 1919 Taunton, Massachusetts ae: 61y GSL
Johanna w/o Patrick d 1 Aug 1900 ae: 82y Catholic SD J:209
John s/o Samuel d 20 Sept 1867 ae: 2y 10m GSL

**WALSH** (continued)

Katie d/o Patrick & Johanna d ae: 15m no burial record Catholic SD J:209

Margaret d/o Patrick & Johanna d ae: 6w no burial record Catholic SD J:209

Mary d/o Patrick & Johanna d ae: 13m no burial record Catholic SD J:209

Nancy w/o Michael d 30 Oct 1842 ae: 38y Catholic SBE I:10A

Patrick d 6 Mar 1883 ae: 66y Native of Co Cork, Ireland Catholic J:209

Peter s/o Patrick & Johanna d ae: 2y no burial record Catholic SD J:209

Raphael s/o John d 26 Jan 1868 ae: 8m Catholic GSL

Robert s/o Patrick & Johanna d ae: 13m no burial record Catholic SD J:209

Robert s/o Robert d 13 Oct 1855 ae: 1y Catholic GSL

**WALTON**, Sarah E d/o Simeon & Mary d 20 Jan 1852 ae: 6m Unusual brownstone tombstone H:75

**WARD**, Bridget w/o Neal d 7 Feb 1851 ae: 39y Native of Co Tyrone, Ireland Catholic J:145

Bridget d/o Patrick d 4 Sept 1855 ae: 6m Catholic GSL

Catherine d/o John d 15 Nov 1855 ae: 10m GSL

Celia d/o Patrick d 7 Sept 1860 ae: 5m Catholic GSL

James s/o Patrick d 17 Feb 1857 ae: 8m Catholic GSL

Patrick s/o Michael d 21 Aug 1855 ae: 5w Catholic GSL

Richard d 7 May 1842 ae: 45y Catholic GSL

Sarah d 17 Sept 1857 ae: 76y GSL

Sarah Jane d/o Neal & Bridget d 23 Dec 1850 ae: 9d Catholic J:145

**WARNER**, Annie d/o David G d 13 Aug 1864 ae: 4m SD G:89

Susan C H Gates w/o David G d

**WARNER** (continued)

16 Mar 1864 ae: 20y 6m "Erected by her mother." G:89

**WARREN**, Charles B d 4 Sept 1839 Matanzas, Cuba ae: 21y D:42

Edward s/o George & Pamela d 15 May 1842 ae: 10y D:42

Elizabeth d/o George & Pamela d 15 May 1842 ae: 10y D:42

George H s/o Charles B & Sarah E b 1816 d 1872 D:42

Henrietta M w/o Calvin d 28 sept 1870 ae: 22y 2m GSL

John w s/o George & Pamela d 17 Jan 1845 ae: 23y D:42

Pamela Ann d/o George & Pamela d 20 July 1840 ae: 14y D:42

Sarah E w/o Charles B b 1846 d 1865 D:42

**WASHBURN**, Sylvia b 1774 d 1858 D:42

**WATEMAN**, Dorcus w/o Ebenezer d 8 Nov 1854 ae: 54y SD C:23 (See Addendum)

**WATERHOUSE**, Albert M d 2 Nov 1867 ae: 36y B:57

Alexander d 1 Apr 1869 ae: 75y F:55

Betsy d 31 May 1858 ae: 65y GSL

Charles A d 13 Nov 1853 ae: 21y SD B:57

Charlotte T w/o David b 1808 d 1880 B:57

Clara d/o Samuel T d 21 Nov 1861 ae: 1y 8m GSL

David d 1 Nov 1878 ae: 77y SD B:57

Eben N d 28 Jan 1882 ae: 64y SD B:70 (See Addendum)

Edward K d 1 July 1862 Richmond, Virginia ae: 24y B:57

Eliza d 3 Feb 1885 ae: 82y GSL

Elizabeth B w/o Josiah d 2 Sept 1854 ae: 25y SB B:49

Ethel d/o Leonard d 10 May 1868 ae: 1y 9m GSL

Eunice C w/o Alexander d 8 Apr 1869 ae: 72y F:55

George L d 19 Feb 1853 San

**WATERHOUSE** (continued)
Francisco, California ae: 24y
SD B:57

Hannah d 5 Mar 1865 ae: 87y 6m
SD B:57

Harriet d 8 Feb 1885 ae: 74y GSL

Helen M w/o Samuel d 15 June
1841 ae: 21y GSL

Jacob d 12 Aug 1850 ae: 82y GSL

Jane d 13 Jan 1862 ae: 53y GSL

John no burial record SD B:57

Josephine d/o Alexander d 25
June 1842 ae: 1y SD F:55

Joshua d 28 Dec 1814 ae: 37y SD
B:57

Joshua d 1 Feb 1869 ae: 72y GSL

Josiah d 23 June 1855 ae: 34y SB
B:49

Lydia B w/o Josiah d 30 July
1848 ae: 18y SB B:49

Sarah F d/o Alexander d 31 Oct
1847 ae: 20y SD F:55

William s/o Jacob d 21 Sept
1841 ae: 32y GSL

**WATERMAN**, Dorcas w/o Eben d
8 Nov 1851 ae: 65y SBE C:23

Ebenezer d 7 Oct 1863 ae: 68y
Dyer tomb A:15

Rachel D d 20 May 1875 ae: 79y
GSL

**WATERS**, Harriet P w/o John T d
30 Jan 1875 ae: 55y GSL

John d 19 Sept 1894 Greely
Hospital ae: 79y GSL

**WATSON**, John Edward s/o
George E d 13 Aug 1858 ae:
4m GSL

William J s/o John & Mary d 15
Oct 1869 ae: 1y 5-1/2m SD
F:26

**WATTS**, John S s/o John d 30
Feb 1858 Cambridgeport, Massachusetts ae: 26y GSL

**WEBB**, Benjamin d 28 May 1847
ae: 35y Wilson tomb D:33

Frances P d 1 Nov 1845 ae: 26y
Wilson tomb D:33

Sarah d/o Seth & Hannah d 21
June 1851 ae: 62y Native of
Deer Isle, Maine F:26

**WEBBER**, Charlotte T w/o David
d 26 Oct 1876 ae: 64y GSL

**WEBSTER**, Eben H s/o Otis d 7
Jan 1862 ae: 7y GSL

Mary M w/o Carl D d 6 Dec 1903
Greely Hospital ae: 68y SD
G:39

**WEED**, Benjamin F d 1 May 1852
ae: 24y SD J:115

**WEEDMAN**, James P s/o J R d
27 Nov 1857 ae: 10m GSL

**WEEKS**, Abby Louise d/o Joseph
& Elizabeth d ae: 22y no burial
record SBE I:133

Elizabeth w/o Joseph d 5 Sept
1863 ae: 73y I:133

Philip d 6 Mar 1829 ae: 79y GSL

Samuel Alton s/o Joseph & Elizabeth d 20 Aug 1850 ae: 1y
SBE I:133

**WELCH**, Agnes d/o John d 12
May 1869 ae: 7m GSL

Anne w/o Michael d 27 Oct 1842
ae: 38y Catholic GSL

Bartley d 18 Sept 1854 ae: 40y
GSL

Bridget d/o John d 5 July 1855
ae: 29y 9m Catholic GSL

Caroline T d/o Mark L d 13 Sept
1849 ae: 2y GSL

Catherine d/o Charles d 16 Nov
1856 ae: 2y Strangers' Ground
GSL

Catherine d/o Michael d 26 July
1850 ae: 16m Catholic GSL

Edward s/o Patrick d 1 Sept 1859
ae: 10m Catholic GSL

Edward s/o Thomas d 14 July
1858 ae: 3m GSL

Hannah d/o Michael d 12 Aug
1850 ae: 1y Catholic GSL

James s/o John d 8 Jan 1862 ae:
13m GSL

James E s/o Michael d 28 Sept
1857 ae: 9m Catholic GSL

Joseph s/o Edward d 17 May
1850 ae: 6m Catholic GSL

Mark E s/o Sarah F d 15 Apr
1858 ae: 7y 3m 10d "Drowned
in the canal." GSL

Mary d/o Patrick d 10 Sept 1852
ae: 1m Catholic GSL

Mary d/o Patrick d 17 June 1858
ae: 14m Catholic GSL

WELCH (continued)

Olive w/o Nathaniel B d 2 Oct 1858 ae: 27y GSL

Olive A G w/o Noble d 5 Oct 1858 ae: 27y GSL

Thomas d 18 Apr 1849 ae: 30y "Killed in fall from building." Native of Co Galway, Ireland Catholic J:187

WELDON, Bridget wid/o Patrick d 26 Aug 1856 ae: 41y Catholic GSL

Patrick d 10 Oct 1855 ae: 23y Catholic GSL

WELLS, Lucy Mrs d 16 Oct 1844 ae: 45y "Teacher in South Street Block." GSL

Martin d 18 Feb 1851 Cape Elizabeth, Maine ae: 68y Jordan tomb D:28

WENBERG, Fritz Herman s/o John F & Hannah H d 20 May 1842 ae: 22m SBE F:60

Helena Daiken d/o John F & Hannah H d 29 Apr 1831 ae: 10m SBE F:60

James C Jordan s/o John F & Hannah H d 2 Feb 1838 New Orleans, Louisiana ae: 2m SBE F:60

WENTWORTH, Jeremiah R s/o William d 25 Aug 1841 ae: 1y GSL

Margaret d/o E d 12 Dec 1844 ae: 10y 4m GSL

Mary d/o Ephriam d 7 Sept 1843 ae: 4y GSL

WESCOTT, Alice C w/o Eliott d 20 Jan 1872 ae: 37y GSL

Louise Alma d/o F R & A L d 8 July 1888 Cambridge, Massachusetts ae: 13d SD F:13

Robert d 16 May 1852 ae: 55y GSL

Susan d/o Robert d 16 May 1852 ae: 3y 5m GSL

WEST, James C s/o Frederick d 14 Oct 1872 ae: 3m Old Catholic Ground GSL

John d 19 Aug 1881 ae: 4y GSL

Manuel d 13 Sept 1877 ae: 49y GSL

WEST (continued)

Sophia R w/o Manuel d 23 Mar 1866 ae: 32y GSL

S Stillman d 19 July 1881 ae: 72y GSL

WESTON, Eugene E s/o H H & A M d 2 Feb 1852 ae: 12w SBE I:92

WETMORE, Lucas W s/o Ward C d 17 Oct 1853 ae: 2m 2d GSL

WHEATON, Patrick s/o Michael & Margaret d 7 Apr 1856 ae: 11y Catholic J:38

WHEELER, Annett d/o Samuel & Elizabeth d 7 Sept 1856 ae: 22m SD F:111

Mary wid/o Henry d 26 Jan 1851 ae: 83y I:116

Mary L d 29 Oct 1869 ae: 71y SBE I:116

WHEELIN, Ellen d/o John d 6 Aug 1854 ae: 9m Strangers' Ground GSL

WHEELOCK, Ann Eliza d/o A P & Catherine d 24 Apr 1837 ae: 6w SD J:267

Charlotte B w/o John A d/o John A & Mary J Balkam d 27 Dec 1851 ae: 25y J:233

George Prentiss s/o A P & Catherine d 5 Sept 1838 ae: 5y 6m SD J:267

Laura J d/o A P d 24 Feb 1851 ae: 1y SD J:267

Marcia H d/o Alonzo P d 5 May 1852 ae: 15y 10m GSL

WHIDDEN, Amelia B d/o A D d 7 Oct 1849 ae: 16m GSL

WHITE, Addie G d/o D d 21 July 1862 ae: 15y GSL

Alma d/o Daniel d 30 July 1868 ae: 6y GSL

Ann M d/o Frank B d 26 Nov 1866 ae: 13y 9m GSL

Charles E s/o Capt Daniel & Martha d 30 Sept 1848 ae: 7w SD H:84

Clara B d/o Robert A d 14 Sept 1888 ae: 15y 2m SD J:202

Daniel d 6 Dec 1863 ae: 64y Civ/War: 2nd Reg Maine Inf

WHITE (continued)
Co I SD H:84
Edward s/o Horace d 28 July
1857 ae: 18m GSL
Ellen A d/o David Jr d 25 Set
1852 ae: 1y 8m GSL
Henry s/o Richard d 10 Nov 1842
ae: 14m Catholic SBE J:200
Ida d/o Capt Daniel & Martha d
29 July 1868 ae: 7y SD H:84
Joseph H d 31 Oct 1869 ae: 49y
SBE F:36
Josephine C d/o Joseph H d 1
Nov 1863 ae: 7y 3m SD F:36
Martha w/o Capt Daniel d 4 Oct
1864 ae: 35y SD H:84
Mary E d/o Stephen d 10 Aug
1864 ae: 11m GSL
Richard H s/o Richard d 30 Aug
1864 ae: 7w GSL
Robert A d 12 Jan 1890 ae: 58y
SD J:202
Rufus J s/o Harriet d 15 May
1862 ae: 2y GSL
Sarah F w/o David Jr d 23 OCt
1853 ae: 23y GSL
Susan T w/o Joseph H d 6 Dec
1868 ae: 45y F:36
William d 11 Aug 1853 ae: 24y
Catholic SBE J:200
William s/o Michael d 25 Sept
1857 ae: 1y Old Catholic
Ground GSL
William A s/o Joseph d 19 Dec
1850 ae: 7m SD F:36
Wiliam H s/o Daniel d 8 Apr
1857 ae: 19y GSL
WHITEHOUSE, Eben N d 2 Jan
1882 ae: 63y 11m B:70
Emily A w/o Eben N d 21 Aug
1861 ae: 46y SB B:70
Ida E d/o Eben N & Emily A d 3
Feb 1857 ae: 4y 10m 8d B:70
John W s/o Benjamin F & Mar-
garet d 5 Sept 1858 ae: 7m 21d
SBE F:6
WHITGHER, Molly d 6 May 1851
ae: 66y C:10
WHITLY, Eliza P d/o Thomas b
9 Oct 1825 d 19 May 1896 D:14
Sarah W "Mother" w/o Thomas d
1 July 1864 ae: 70y 4m D:14

WHITLY (continued)
S Y H "Sister" no dates on stone;
no burial record D:14
WHITMAN, Josiah d 17 Sept
1848 ae: 56y GSL
Mary H wid/o Benjamin d 30 Nov
1860 ae: 81y 8m GSL
WHITMORE, Benjamin d 7 Oct
1850 ae: 72y GSL
Charles d 16 Mar 1871 ae: 22y
3m GSL
WHITNEY, Charlotte wid/o Na-
thaniel d 20 July 1850 Sears-
port, Maine ae: 48y GSL
Eunice W b 7 July 1817 d 15 Nov
1869 B:42
WHITTEMORE, Albertine w/o E
W, d/o S G & L A Patterson d
27 Jan 1864 Boston, Mas-
sachusetts ae: 21y C:55
Charles B d 16 Mar 1871 ae: 71y
C:55
WHITTEN, Fannie A d/o Newton
d 27 Apr 1865 Sanduskey, Ohio
ae: 6y 2m GSL
Mary H w/o Nathan d 17 Apr
1874 ae: 66y GSL
WHITTIER, inf s/o Alvan G d 25
June 1859 ae: 10d GSL
WHITTUM, Elizabeth S w/o Al-
bert C, d/o Michael & Cath-
erine Somers d 26 Mar 1932
Braintree, Massachusetts ae:
58y NS D:83
WIGGIN, George A d 28 Oct 1880
ae: 37y 4m F:139
Hannah S d 21 July 1861 ae: 56y
GSL
Julius d 10 Oct 1856 ae: 13y GSL
Martha w/o David d 24 Nov 1853
ae: 35y SD H:2
Sarah d 8 Aug 1866 ae: 23y 8m
GSL
WIGGINS, Addie B d/o Alfred d 9
Oct 1876 ae: 15m SD J:114
Annie w/o Reuben M d 23 Nov
1881 ae: 39y 11m SD B:6
Eddie E s/o Mark d 27 Dec 1869
ae: 6m 9d GSL
George L s/o Mark d 14 Apr 1861
ae: 2y 4m GSL
Greenleaf d 30 Sept 1856 ae: 23y

WIGGINS (continued)
GSL
John s/o Hannah d 1 Sept 1856
ae: 9m GSL
Mary W d 24 Nov 1856 ae: 21y
GSL
Moses s/o David d 17 Feb 1859
ae: 15y GSL
Nellie Eva d/o Alfred d 20 Aug
1861 ae: 2y SD J:114
WIGMORE, Clements s/o H d 14
Aug 1869 ae: 10m GSL
WILBORN, Patrick s/o Michael d
7 Apr 1856 ae: 11y Catholic
GSL
WILBUR, Jacob d 10 Dec 1854
ae: 55y GSL
WILCOX, Mary d/o George H d
17 July 1855 ae: 2w GSL
WILKINSON, Varnum d 18 May
1861 ae: 84y GSL
WILLARD, Myra d/o George d 24
June 1852 ae: 2y 4m GSL
WILLEY, Ella S d/o Phineas &
Hannah d 6 Sept 1850 ae: 4m
GSL
Hannah w/o Samuel d 22 June
1875 ae: 76y 4m F:125
Lizzie B w/o J H, d/o John &
Sarah A Edmunds d 26 May
1876 ae: 19y C:74
Lucy E d/o Samuel & Hannah no
burial record SBE F:125
Olive d/o Samuel & Olive d 29
Mar 1843 ae: 6y 8m F:125
Samuel d 9 Apr 1853 ae: 43y 8m
SB F:125
Samuel S s/o Samuel & Hannah b
20 July 1842 d 29 Oct 1879
F:125
William s/o Samuel & Hannah
no burial record SD F:125
WILLIAMS, Alden P s/o John &
Frances C d 3 Dec 1848 ae:
5m SD H:78
Catherine w/o Elijah H d 18 Apr
1858 ae: 37y 5m GSL
Charles H s/o Elijah H d 28 Jan
1849 ae: 16m GSL
Elijah H d 13 June 1859 ae: 40y
GSL
Elizabeth L w/o John A d 25

WILLIAMS (continued)
July 1917 ae: 65y 11m 9d H:78
Elizabeth M d 8 Dec 1903
Augusta State Hospital ae: 75y
3m SD J:121
Elizabeth S Furlong w/o Josiah b
13 Aug 1800 d 11 Nov 1860
J:121
Francis A s/o Elijah d 9 June
1854 ae: 9y GSL
Frances C Cash w/o John d 2
Mar 1906 ae: 90y 10m H:78
George S s/o Royal d 6 Oct 1852
ae: 5y 4m GSL
Hannah Y w/o William H d 3
Sept 1864 ae: 31y 8m GSL
Harriet E Emery w/o W H d 30
Mar 1855 ae: 24y J:121
Henry d 18 Nov 1862 ae: 38y Hil-
born tomb A:10
Henry w/o Royal buried 4 Aug
1854 ae: 21y d Cuba GSL
Isabella w/o Levi d 20 May 1845
ae: 42y GSL
James R S d 20 Oct 1878 ae: 51y
GSL
Janes S d/o Royal d 12 Nov 1851
ae: 8y GSL
Josiah b 6 Apr 1793 d 25 Jan
1872 SD J:121
John b 24 Sept 1817 d 21 Dec
1852 France G:21
John b 1810 d 1850 at sea H:78
John A d 7 June 1909 ae: 66y 8m
16d Civ/War: 6th Reg New
Hampshire Inf Co E, 10th Reg
Maine Inf Co C H:78
Lizzie C d/o Charles F d 21 Apr
1890 Boston, Massachusetts
ae: 21y 4m 3d Safford-Hall
tomb A:20
Margaret d 26 May 1857 ae: 30y
Old Catholic Ground GSL
Mary Louisa d/o William H d 28
Aug 1851 ae: 13m GSL
Melden P s/o John d 3 Dec 1848
ae: 5m GSL
Melissa J d/o John A & Frances
C d 25 May 1926 ae: 81y 27d
H:78
Susan w/o John A d 22 July 1865
ae: 39y GSL

WILLIS, Rebekah d 23 Apr 1841 ae: 50y F:8

Thomas s/o Thomas d 2 Sept 1843 ae: 6m GSL

WILLSEY, Arvilla d/o Seland & Rhody d 26 May 1847 ae: 23y C:94

Seland d 20 May 1851 ae: 49y C:94

WILSON, Alonzo s/o William L d 29 June 1849 ae: 3y GSL

Anna M d/o R d 12 Oct 1857 ae: 3y 9m GSL

Charles E s/o Charles O d 15 Sept 1847 ae: 14m Wilson tomb D:33

Charles F s/o Charles O d 24 July 1850 ae: 15m Wilson tomb D:33

Dorcas wid/o Joshua d 27 Dec 1856 ae: 79y Wilson tomb D:33

Eleanor d/o Archibald d 26 June 1857 ae: 3y 10m Catholic J:130

Ellen R d/o Archibald & Hannah d 26 June 1854 ae: 3y 10m Catholic J:130

Emmaline H wid/o Americus, d/o Thomas Powell d 8 Dec 1858 ae: 26y 7m GSL

George d 24 Apr 1842 ae: 40y Catholic GSL

Hannah wid/o Joseph d 10 July 1847 ae: 84y Wilson tomb D:33

Henry S s/o John S d 17 Mar 1877 ae: 6w GSL

James d 2 Sept 1899 ae: 81y SD H:50

WINCHESTER, Charles Edwin s/o William B d 27 Dec 1858 ae: 5m GSL

Ernest E s/o Augustus D d 27 June 1868 ae: 2y 6m GSL

WINNEY, Margaret d/o Stephen d 7 Aug 1848 ae: 18m Catholic GSL

WINSHIP, Canselo d 22 Oct 1890 ae: 66y 6m SD C:11

Charlotte L w/o Canselo d 13 Sept 1876 ae: 50y SD C:11

WINSHIP (continued)
Cynthia A wid/o Canselo d 28 Apr 1907 ae: 82y 3m 6d SD C:11

Granville s/o Jonas & Sarah d 26 July 1841 ae: 20y F:90

James d 26 Aug 1855 ae: 78y GSL

Sarah w/o Jonas d 11 Oct 1850 ae: 68y SD F:90

WINSLOW, Amanda w/o Charles, d/o Alexander Milliken d 17 Apr 1848 ae: 32y GSL

Ann w/o Moses d 26 Sept 1848 ae: 52y D:25

Charles H s/o Charles d 13 Jan 1846 ae: 8y GSL

Charlotte w/o George d 10 May 1854 ae: 52y SBE SB D:25

Elizabeth w/o Capt Thomas d 13 Apr 1909 ae: 85y 2m 5d Hilborn tomb A:10

Emily w/o Franklin d 16 Jan 1872 ae: 58y GSL

George s/o Henry d 29 Feb 1844 ae: 8m GSL

George H d 30 July 1859 ae: 60y SBE SB D:25

Harriet d/o Hezekiah d 3 July 1842 ae: 18m GSL

Helen A d/o Nathan d 4 Dec 1849 ae: 3y SD E:1

Honora d/o Franklin d 1 Sept 1851 ae: 13m GSL

Hezekiah d 16 Nov 1849 ae: 66y GSL

Horace S s/o Franklin C d 19 Aug 1856 ae: 1y GSL

Jane T d/o Moses & Ann d 20 Mar 1838 ae: 14y 6m D:25

Joseph s/o Charles d 12 Sept 1844 ae: 15m GSL

Joseph A s/o Charles d 12 Aug 1847 ae: 18m GSL

Josephine d/o Charles d 13 Sept 1852 ae: 9m GSL

Lorinda w/o Capt Nathan d 24 Oct 1863 ae: 50y GSL

Mary w/o Joeph d 3 Dec 1844 ae: 53y GSL

Mary B w/o Nathan d 12 Apr 1871 ae: 78y SB E:1

**WINSLOW** (continued)

Moses b 6 June 1799 d 5 Feb 1887 D:25

Nathan d 9 Sept 1861 ae: 76y E:1

Pauline wid d 16 Dec 1843 ae: 68y GSL

Samuel d 30 Aug 1842 ae: 35y GSL

Sarah d/o Nathan 2nd d 31 May 1842 ae: 3y GSL

Sumner C s/o George & Charlotte d 4 Oct 1839 ae: 15m SBE D:25

Sylvia N w/o Moses b 14 Nov 1815 d 2 Oct 1881 D:25

Wellington s/o Moses & Sylvia d 13 Nov 1855 ae: 2y 8m SD D:25

**WITHAM**, Abial d 27 Mar 1842 ae: 30y GSL

Albion s/o Benjamin d 28 Dec 1864 ae: 4m GSL

Eunice d/o John d 9 Oct 1842 ae: 6w GSL

Frederick M d 5 Feb 1881 ae: 6w GSL

Hannah L w/o Dunham d 30 Feb 1847 ae: 25y G:13

Joseph A s/o Joshua & Nancy d 29 Sept 1839 ae: 7y 6m SD F:8

William H s/o Dunham & Hannah L d 20 Oct 1843 ae: 1y 10m G:13

William Welch s/o John B d 31 Aug 1841 ae: 10m GSL

**WITHINGTON**, James Edwin s/o James d 12 Aug 1851 ae: 15m GSL

**WITTSEY**, Arvilla d/o Leland d 24 May 1847 ae: 23y GSL

**WOOLEY**, Cachurier d/o William d 9 Dec 1848 ae: 2y Catholic GSL

**WOOD**, Ann d 28 May 1874 ae: 72y GSL

Anna C w/o Henry C d 17 Sept 1859 ae: 21y GSL

Francis s/o Daniel d 27 Dec 1841 ae: 2y 9m Catholic GSL

Harriet M w/o Rufus H d 9 July 1852 ae 26y SBE C:24

James s/o Daniel d 2 Nov 1845

**WOOD** (continued)

ae: 1y 9m GSL

John E s/o John P & Jannette d 21 Apr 1851 ae: 14m 10d SD J:125

Mary E d/o Rufus & Harriet M d 6 Sept 1852 ae: 5m SD C:24

Mary J w/o John G d 18 Oct 1903 ae: 69y 10m SD F:18A

Samuel d 1 Jan 1848 ae: 61y 11m SD H:105

Wihelmina d/o Samuel d 27 Feb 1857 ae: 10y 5m GSL

**WOODARD**, Mary T Graffan d/o Enos d 8 Nov 1845 ae: 2y GSL

**WOODBURY**, ---- d/o Joel d 10 Sept 1854 GSL

Eliza F wid/o Ira P d 15 Oct 1854 ae: 50y GSL

Franklin P s/o William H d 21 Mar 1853 ae: 2m SD F:116

George s/o William H d 27 Aug 1856 ae: 7y 6m SD F:116

Helen M d/o William H d 19 Nov 1852 ae: 1y SD F:116

Henrietta C w/o Charles E d 9 July 1924 ae: 72y 1m 15d GSL

Ira P d 9 Apr 1851 ae: 48y GSL

**WOODMAN**, Eunice d/o late Josiah d 7 Nov 1862 ae: 7y GSL

Harriet d 2 Sept 1869 ae: 79y GSL

Jabez C d 8 Nov 1869 ae: 65y GSL

Jeremiah d 13 Dec 1855 ae: 86y GSL

Josiah d 18 May 1861 ae: 60y GSL

Julia Ann w/o Joseph W d 22 Dec 1851 ae: 58y I:130

Louisa w/o J C d 26 May 1856 ae: 50y GSL

Lydia d 18 Aug 1851 ae: 27y C:57

**WOODS**, Jane w/o James d 31 July 1853 ae: 31y GSL

Mary d/o Daniel d 6 June 1843 ae: 6y Old Catholic Ground

**WOODSIDE**, Fanny d/o William d 2 Jan 1852 ae: 3m GSL

**WOODWORTH**, Susan J w/o Syms d 12 Oct 1864 ae: 32y

**WOODWORTH** (continued)
8m SB H:49
**WORCESTER,** Albert E s/o
Thomas d 9 Dec 1844 ae: 2y
9m GSL
Thomas s/o Thomas d 7 Sept
1850 ae: 1y GSL
**WORMWOOD,** Anna wid/o John
b 10 Nov 1803 d 26 Mar 1890
Greely Hospital F:38
Clarence s/o Ansel d 5 Oct 1856
ae: 2m GSL
John b 9 Aug 1801 d 2 Feb 1881
F:38
Lendall s/o John & Phylena d 7
Nov 1840 ae: 5y F:38
Phylena w/o John d 20 Dec 1841
ae: 40y F:38
Sarah w/o John d 22 Dec 1841
ae: 37y SD F:38
**WORTHLEY,** Julia Ann w/o
Samuel d 11 Dec 1850 ae: 30y
6m SB C:3
**WRIGHT,** Cornelia E d 17 June
1857 ae: 18y GSL
Ellen d/o John & Ann d 7 Nov
1852 ae: 3y 8m J:189
Richard s/o John & Ann d 3 June
1849 ae: 7y 7m SD J:189
**WYER,** Ann w/o Martin d 27 Dec
1834 ae: 27y Native of Lim-
erick, Ireland Catholic E:7
Sarah Waterhouse d 9 May 1871
ae: 78y SB F:138
**WYMAN,** Edward no burial record
SD I:166
Harriet Frances d/o Seward &
Louisa b 17 Mar 1840 d 2 Oct
1904 I:166
Henrietta B d 22 Oct 1924 New
York City ae: 82y SD I:166
Louisa F w/o Edward d 21 Feb
1885 Washington DC ae: 75y
4m I:166
Mary Louisa d/o Edward & Lou-
isa F d 10 May 1839 New York
City SBE I:166
Mary Skelton d/o Seward & Lou-
isa b 25 Jan 1846 d 8 June
1885 SB I:166
Seward d 3 May 1860 ae: 56y 7m
SD I:166

**WYMAN** (continued)
William s/o Edward & Louisa F
no burial record SBE I:166
William S s/o Seward d 9 Oct
1849 ae: 1y SD I:166
**YEATON,** Delana w/o John W d
27 Aug 1853 ae: 31y GSL
Harriet w/o John Jr d 25 Mar
1852 ae: 25y C:94
Lewis s/o Richard d 5 Aug 1846
ae: 2y 6m GSL
Mary E wid/o John d 17 June
1899 ae: 86y SD J:36
Sarah d/o John Jr d 21 Oct 1855
ae: 15m C:94
Sarah S w/o John Jr d 22 Mar
1865 ae: 42y SD C:94
**YORK,** Eliza d/o John W d 18
Feb 1845 ae: 16y GSL
Ezekiel w/o William R & Rachel
d 19 Aug 1816 ae: 2y F:63
George H s/o William R & Ra-
chel d 19 Feb 1853 ae: 22y
Lost at sea F:63
Harriet buried 28 Nov 1928 no
burial record NS C:55
Harriet E Radcliffe w/o Philip O
b 1853 d 1928 C:55
Capt John C d 27 July 1855 ae:
60y GSL
Margaret wid/o Joseph d 24 Nov
1843 ae: 84y F:63
Mary d 7 Mar 1855 ae: 55y Hil-
born tomb A:10
Mary d/o Patrick d 14 Apr 1856
ae: 15m Old Catholic Ground
GSL
Mary Ellen d/o John & Mary d 6
Aug 1848 ae: 9y F:50
Mary J w/o George d 31 Aug
1854 ae: 26y Strangers' Ground
GSL
Mary M d/o David d 1 Nov 1846
ae: 1y 11m 3d SD G:88
Philip O s/o Abram C & Soph-
ronia d 14 Sept 1912 ae: 66y
5m 11d C:55
Rachel w/o William R d 28 Sept
1871 ae: 69y SD F:63
Capt William R d 24 Mar 1860
ae: 56y F:63
**YOUNG,** Charles G d 26 July 1861

**YOUNG** (continued)

Alexandria, Virginia ae: 40y GSL

Eleanor C d/o George d 6 Nov 1853 ae: 19m GSL

Eliza C d/o Charles d 11 July 1849 ae: 1y GSL

Lucy A w/o George d 22 Oct 1853 ae: 27y GSL

Mary F w/o A C d 13 June 1861 ae: 27y Dyer tomb A:15

# LOTS ASSIGNED BY THE SUPERINTENDENT OF BURIALS

ADAMS, Joseph 6 Jan 1850 I:105
Capt William 10 May 1854 B:3
ADDITON, Joseph 28 May 1850 Unknown
ALLEN, Mary Ann 23 Oct 1850 H:36
Moses 26 June 1852 F:43
APPLETON, John 6 Jan 1851 B:22
AYERS, John 22 July 1857 A:6
BACON, Dr Elbridge 26 Sept 1848 Unknown
BARNES, Nathan 2 Sept 1848 D:26
BARSTOW, George S 6 Aug 1851 Tomb - Unknown
BATES, Nathaniel 14 Sept 1850 J:74
BECKETT, Charles E 25 Mar 1850 Unknown
BELL, John 23 May 1849 Unknown
BERRY, Ira 18 Mar 1852 Unknown
BICKFORD, Joseph H 9 Feb 1853 C:15
BINGHAM, John 29 May 1857 Unknown
John A 11 Aug 1857 Unknown
BIRD, Seth 10 Oct 1849 Unknown
BLAKE, Charles H 28 May 1853 Unknown
BOLLIN, John 30 Apr 1851 Unknown
BOODY, Henry H 6 Jan 1851 Unknown
BRADFORD, Freeman 8 Nov 1848 Unknown
BRAGDON, John G 10 Nov 1857 G:96

BRESLIN, Thomas 4 Apr 1851 Unknown
BROWN, Alvira 10 Oct 1849 Unknown
BRYANT, Samuel 27 Aug 1850 B:39
BUDD, William 12 May 1851 C:7
BUNCE, Lewis & Thurston Unknown
BURKE, James W 28 May 1853 Unknown
BURNS, Matthew 3 Aug 1849 Catholic
CARTER, Caleb S 6 Jan 1851 Unknown
CHANEY, Deacon Benjamin 7 June 1853 Unknown
CHASE, William 8 Oct 1848 J:249
CHURCHILL, Edwin 6 Jan 1851 Unknown
CLARK, Dr E 28 Dec 1850 Unknown
Freeman S 15 June 1852 Unknown
Jabez 15 Aug 1850 Unknown
CLIFFORD, Nathan 6 Jan 1851 Unknown
CLOUDMAN, David P 28 Apr 1849 Unknown
COLBY, Samuel 12 June 1852 Unknown
COLE, Henry 17 Nov 1850 Unknown
Lorenzo D 16 Oct 1849 H:69
COLLEY, Albert A 28 Dec 1850 Unknown
Charles 15 June 1852 H:70
Joseph 9 Oct 1852 Unknown
CONLEY, John 10 June 1851 Catholic

147

COVELL, Hiram 28 Dec 1850 Unknown

CROCKER, Ira 6 Jan 1851 Unknown

CROCKETT, Leonard 27 Aug 1850 Unknown

Nathaniel 17 May 1849 Unknown

Richard 25 June 1850 Unknown

CUMMINGS, Rev Cyrus 1 Sept 1852 J:228

Daniel 5 June 1850 Unknown

Richard 15 Nov 1850 Catholic

DANA, Luther 20 Aug 1850 Unknown

DAVEIS, Charles S 26 Feb 1861 E:2

DAVIS, ---- 13 Oct 1850 Unknown

Charles 6 Jan 1851 Unknown

Thomas G 13 Aug 1850 B:66

DEAN, Samuel 25 May 1852 Unknown

DEEHAN, Charles 30 Apr 1849 Catholic

DEERING, Mary Ann 15 June 1849 Tomb - Unknown

DENNISON, Charles W 28 May 1849 H:103

DIXON, Thomas 8 Aug 1849 Catholic

DONAVAN, John 11 June 1851 Unknown

DOW, Josiah 28 Dec 1850 Unknown

Neal 28 Dec 1850 Unknown

DRESSER, Alfred M 18 Mar 1852 Unknown

Robert 9 July 1850 Unknown

DRINKWATER, William 22 Apr 1851 Unknown

DYER, Alvin 6 Aug 1851 Unknown

Nathan 12 OCt 1853 Tomb - A:15

EDMUNDS, John 3 Nov 1853 C:74

EMERSON, Erasmus 15 May 1851 C:5

ERSKINE, Mrs Submit 13 Apr 1849 Unknown

EVANS, William & Daniel 1 Aug 1849 Unknown

FAHEY, Michael P 2 Sept 1856 Unknown

FARRINGTON, Mary K 28 Sept 1848 Unknown

FEENEY, Timothy 30 Apr 1853 Unknown

FERNALD, James E 28 Dec 1850 Unknown

FESSENDEN, William P 6 Jan 1851 Unknown

FICKETT, Henry 2 Dec 1852 C:27

FITZGERALD, Mrs Ann 23 May 1850 Catholic

FLANNAGAN, James 23 May 1850 Catholic

FLAVEN, Thomas 19 May 1857 1/2 lot - Unknown

FOSS, Alpheus 26 May 1851 Unknown

FOSTER, Bowen L 28 May 1849 Unknown

FOX, Daniel Jr 11 Dec 1850 J:103

FOYE, Henry 15 June 1849 Tomb - D:29

FRENCH, William 20 July 1856 I:140

FREEMAN & HUNT 24 Apr 1851 Unknown

GAMMON, Ezekiel D 26 Sept 1848 D:27

GARDNER, John 25 May 1851 & 6 May 1856 C:84

GERRISH, Oliver 28 Dec 1850 Unknown

William 23 Aug 1852 Unknown

GETCHELL, Augustus 21 June 1852 Unknown

GILSON, Calvin 4 May 1850 Unknown

Calvin R 16 May 1851 I:95

GODDARD, Henry 6 Jan 1851 Unknown

GODDING, Capt Edward 3 Nov 1853 Unknown

Richard 7 Oct 1850 Unknown

GORE, Nancy 18 Nov 1848 Unknown

GORMLEY, Patrick 10 Sept 1856 Catholic

HALEY, James 1 July 1850 Unknown
HAMILTON, Capt Charles B 13 Apr 1849 B:44
HAMLIN, Edward Unknown
HANNA, Peter 22 June 1849 Unknown
HARFORD, Ezra 11 June 1850 Unknown
HARMON, Ebenezer 3 Oct 1850 Unknown
W T 19 Sept 1848 Unknown
HASKELL, Josiah M 16 Apr 1853 Tomb - Unknown
HASTY, John 3 Sept 1850 & 14 Oct 1850 Unknown
Capt John 24 Apr 1850 I:110
HATCH, Frederick 27 Aug 1850 Unknown
Jacob L 10 June 1858 Unknown
William 24 Apr 1851 Unknown
HAWES, Charles 18 Nov 1848 D:56
HAY, George S 4 May 1850 Unknown
HAYES, Thomas R 20 Aug 1850 Unknown
HIGGINS, Capt 16 July 1852 Unknown
Patrick 17 May 1850 Catholic
HILBORN, Erastus 21 June 1852 & 5 Sept 1853 Unknown
Seth B 5 June 1851 Tomb - A:10
HOBBS, Joshua 18 Aug 1849 Unknown
HOLBROOK, Widow 28 Oct 1852 Unknown
HOLMES, Eleazer 14 June 1849 H:88
HORN, William 2 June 1857 Unknown
HUCKINS, Capt J H 19 Aug 1853 D:45
HUMPHREY, A 11 May 1853 Unknown
HUNT, Israel 17 Sept 1856 Unknown
HUSTON, Paul 22 Apr 1851 Unknown
ILSLEY, Henry 18 Sept 1850 Unknown
Parker 1 May 1851 C:8

INGERSOLL, Isaac 10 Apr 1848 Unknown
JACKSON, Alden 19 June 1853 Unknown
JEWETT, Luther & George 8 Nov 1848 Unknown
JOHNSON, Andrew 6 Sept 1848 Unknown
Deering 8 May 1849 Unknown
Ephraim 8 Apr 1848 C:63
JONES, Daniel S Unknown
William 23 Apr 1851 J:61
JORDAN, William 12 Oct 1852 J:106
JOSE, Horatio N 8 May 1850 Unknown
Mark E Unknown
KEAZER, Capt David 14 Dec 1848 Unknown
Capt Reuben 14 Dec 1848 H:41
KELLOGG, Elijah 21 Oct 1850 J:108
KIMBALL, Amos 15 May 1853 Unknown
KNIGHT, James 26 Apr 1850 Unknown
Thomas E 20 June 1850 I:124
LANDERS, Richard 11 June 1849 Catholic
LARKIN, Andrew 11 May 1857 Catholic
Patrick 17 July 1856 Catholic
LARRABEE, William d 25 Oct 1849 Unknown
LAUGHTON, Mary 9 Oct 1848 Catholic
LEAVITT, John 16 Sept 1850 H:56
Joseph 25 June 1850 H:56
LEONARD, Patrick Unknown Catholic
LIBBY, Capt Thomas 5 Sept 1851 Unknown
LING, L DeM 26 May 1851 Unknown
Sylvanus Unknown
LORD, ---- 4 Sept 1849 Unknown
George 31 Aug 1853 Unknown
LORING, Capt John 21 June 1851 Unknown
LOTHROP, Ansel 12 July 1852

LOTHROP (continued)
Unknown
LOVEJOY, Wiliam H 8 May 1850
F:34
LYNCH, Thomas 29 Aug 1849
Catholic - J:178
MARK, Bartholomew 5 June 1849
Catholic
MARTIN, Robert 23 Apr 1851
Unknown
MARQUIS, George 7 May 1852
Unknown
McCALLAN, Hugh 12 Oct 1849
Catholic
McGLINCHY, Patrick 18 June
1849 Catholic
McLONE, James 28 May 1850
Catholic
MITCHELL, Charles C 18 Oct
1851 Unknown
Rev D M 19 Nov 1851 J:235
Capt Lewis 19 Nov 1851 Unknown
MORRILL, Jedediah 8 Oct 1850
Unknown
MORSE, Jonathan K 25 May 1850
Unknown
MOULTON, William 8 Nov 1848
Unknown
MUGFORD, Ezra 12 Oct 1849
I:165
MURCH, John 28 May 1851 C:82
MURPHY, Joanna 11 July 1856
Catholic
Timothy 31 Oct 1849 Catholic
MURRAY, Michael 17 May 1850
Catholic
NASON, Richard 23 Apr 1849 & 24
Apr 1850 Unknown
NEAL, Parmeneo 25 Sept 1849
Unknown
NOBLE, Isaac 9 Sept 1852 Unknown
Rufus W 10 Apr 1849 Unknown
O'BRIEN, Patrick 8 May 1856
Catholic
O'DONNELL, James 14 Sept 1858
Catholic
ORGIN, Patrick 5 June 1850
Catholic
OSGOOD, A L 24 Aug 1851 Unknown

OXNARD, Edward 6 Nov 1848
B:27
John 6 Nov 1848 Unknown
William 6 Nov 1848 B:27
PARKER, Kingsbury 28 Oct 1852
H:42
Nathaniel 28 Oct 1852 Unknown
PARKS, Asa 1 July 1852 G:90
PARSONS, Joseph U 5 June 1850
I:122
PEARSON, Charles 25 Oct 1850
Unknown
PETERSON, John 7 Aug 1849
Unknown
POOR, Joseph 26 Nov 1849 B:31
PONES, Daniel S 28 May 1850
Unknown
PORTER, Seward H 6 Jan 1851
B:55
PRAY, Francis E 7 Oct 1850
Unknown
PREBLE, William P 25 Aug 1848
Unknown
PRIOR, Wiliam M 6 Sept 1848
Unknown
QUINN, Philip 11 Apr 1849
Unknown
RACKLYFT, Mary Ann 27 July
1851 Unknown
RAMSEY, Edward B 3 Apr 1852
C:21
RAND, Samuel F 13 Apr 1849
Unknown
RAYMOND, Charles N 25 June
1857 Unknown
READ, Gilman H 2 Aug 1858 Unknown
REED, Rhilemon 11 June 1850
Unknown
RICE, Mrs 26 June 1852 Unknown
Thomas 3 Aug 1849 Unknown
RICHARDS, Harris 24 June 1851
Unknown
Joshua 18 Nov 1848 J:251
ROBERTS, Aaron 17 May 1848
D:79
Henry B 17 May 1848 Unknown
William H 10 Apr 1849 Unknown
ROBINSON, David 25 Aug 1848
B:21
ROGERS, John 6 May 1856 Un-

ROGERS (continued)
known
ROSS, Duncan Unknown C:91
James M 11 Apr 1849 C:89
John 11 Apr 1849 & 8 Aug 1850
I:144
Manuel 30 May 1849 Unknown
Walter Jr & John 11 Apr 1849
I:145
ROUNDS, Charles 24 May 1851
C:83
John 24 June 1851 & 25 Nov 1851
Unknown
RUSSEL, Ezra 21 Apr 1849 Un-
known
SAFFORD, William F 22 Sept
1851 Unknown
SAMPSON, Micah 21 Apr 1849
Unknown
SAWYER, D W 20 Nov 1851 Un-
known
Thomas L 11 June 1858 C:81
SENTER, William 28 Dec 1850
Unknown
SHACKFORD, Jesse 8 Sept 1852
Unknown
SHAW, Luther H 25 May 1852
J:265
SHELDON, Rev Nathan W 20 Aug
1850 B:7
SHEPERD, O P 6 June 1853 Un-
known
SHERWOOD, Mrs Unknown
Tomb - D:30
SINCLAIR, John 25 May 1852
Unknown
SMITH, John T 19 Nov 1850
Unknown
Robert S 28 Aug 1850 Unknown
Susan 27 June 1851 Unknown
SOMERBY, Abiel 10 Sept 1850
Unknown
SPARROW, William 21 July 1851
Unknown
SPRINGER, Joseph F 19 June
1853 I:75
STANWOOD, Gideon L 29 Mar
1850 I:103
STAPLES, James 27 Aug 1850
Unknown
STARBIRD, Thomas 31 Aug 1853
C:73

STEVENS, Benjamin J 24 Aug
1851 Unknown
Peter 15 May 1853 Unknown
STINSON, William & Alexander
26 Aug 1858 J:226
STORER, Woodbury 18 Oct 1851
Unknown
SULLIVAN, Mark 25 Sept 1849
Catholic
Timothy 7 July 1853 Catholic
SWEETSIR, John 29 May 1849
Unknown
Thomas B 18 Mar 1852 Unknown
TARBOX, Newell 19 Nov 1851
J:129
THOMPSON, ---- 20 July 1856
Unknown
THURSTON, John 11 June 1850
I:126
TIMMONS, H G 14 May 1858
Unknown
TONA, Mat 7 May 1856 Unknown
TRACY, Thomas 25 June 1849
I:25
TRUE, David T 18 Mar 1852
B:14
TUKESBURY, Benjamin 22 June
1852 Unknown
VAILL, John 16 Aug 1849 Cath-
olic
VERRILL, D R 21 July 1851
Unknown
WAITE, Charles W 8 July 1850
I:131
WARREN, John G 17 Aug 1850
Unknown
WATERHOUSE, John 11 June
1850 B:57
Sewell 11 June 1850 Unknown
WELCH, Mary 10 May 1849
Catholic
WEST, Manuel 10 Nov 1857 Un-
known
WETMORE, Ward C 28 Nov 1853
Unknown
WHEELER, Samuel 14 Sept 1856
F:111
WHITE, Darius 13 June 1851
Unknown
John B 19 May 1852 Unknown
Joseph 19 May 1851 F:36
WHITING, Calvin 13 Nov 1850

WHITING (continued)
Unknown
WHITNEY, Nathan 9 Aug 1852
Unknown
WHITTIER, Samuel A 23 Oct
1850 Unknown
WILLIAMS, Josiah 12 Oct 1852
J:121
WINSLOW, Charles 9 May 1856
Unknown

WOOD, John 2 Sept 1851 J:125
WOODMAN, George H 18 Mar
1852 Unknown
Jabez 28 Dec 1850 Unknown
WOODS, Daniel 11 June 1849
Catholic
YOUNG, Jesse 18 Oct 1851 Un-
known

An Ordinance in addition to an Ordinance entitled
*An Ordinance to regulate the Interment of the Dead*

Be it ordained by the Mayor, Aldermen, and Common Council of the City of Portland in City Council Assembled as follows:

Section 1. It shall be the duty of the Superintendent of Burials, under the direction of the Committee on Burying Grounds for the time being to assign to each and every family of the City, on application thereof, such space in the Western Cemetery, as may be deemed necessary and proper for a family burying-ground not exceeding one lot or plat to a family, of dimensions not exceeding fifteen feet front, agreeable to the plan of said Cemetery made by James Hall.

Section 2. It shall be the duty of said Superintendent to record in a book to be kept for that purpose, the number of the plat, and of the range where situated, which may be assigned to any family as aforesaid, together with the full name of the head of the family, and the time when it is so assigned.

Section 3. In all cases of interments not made in family plots or tombs or where less than a whole plat shall be considered sufficient and proper for a family as aforesaid, it shall be the duty of said Super-intendent to make such interments and assignments in the southerly and easterly portion of said Cemetery in the ranges appropriated there-for, agreeable to the plan aforesaid.

Section 4. That so much of section third of the Ordinance to which this is an addition, passed April 7, 1841, as relates to the size of spaces and the assignment thereof to families be and the same is hereby repealed.

In Board of Aldermen, July 1, 1846.  This ordinance having had two several readings, passed to be ordained.  Eliphalet Greely, Mayor. July 1, 1846.  City Of Portland Records, 6:128-129.


An Ordinance relating to Western Cemetery

Be it ordained by the Mayor, Aldermen, and Common Council of the City of Portland in City Council assembled as follows:

Section 1. From the date of the approval of this Ordinance all interments of the dead in the Western Cemetery in Portland are hereby expressly forbidden, except upon the special written permit of the Board of Commissioners of Cemeteries and Public Grounds, first obtained therefor.

Section 2. No such permit shall be granted by said Board nor be valid, except for the burial of those who were natives, or who died residents, of Portland, and who were at their deaths the owners, or members of the immediate families of owners, of private lots in that Cemetery.

Section 3. The Board of Mayor and Aldermen, acting with the Trustees of Evergreen Cemetery, are hereby authorized at any time, free from cost or upon such terms as they may determine, to exchange any lot to which the City has free title in Evergreen Cemetery for any lot in the Western Cemetery now held by a private owner, upon condition of the immediate removal of the remains of the dead from such lot in the Western Cemetery.

Section 4. Any undertaker, or other person, who violates the provisions of the first section of this ordinance shall be liable to a fine of one hundred dollars for each offence.

Section 5. This ordinance shall take effect when approved.

Approved by the Mayor, March 5 1888. City Of Portland Records, 23:211-212.

Interments in Western Cemetery

The Ordinance relating to interments in the Western Cemetery, recently amended, forbids the burial there of all except immediate members of families owning private lots in said Cemetery.

Since the destruction of the plan of the Western Cemetery in the fire of 1866 (A plan made from surveys of James Hall made in 1846) there has been no certain method of knowing who are owners of lots, a thing which is very essential if the above Ordinance is to be enforced.

I am informed that at an expense of thirty dollars, expended by the City Civil Engineer, a new plan of said Cemetery can be made, and I respectfully suggest that the Engineer be authorized to expend said sum for said purpose and have a plan of said Cemetery made, in order that the Ordinance relating thereto may be properly enforced. James S. Gould, Superintendent of Burials.

Referred to Comm. on Engineers Depart. Sent down concurred. October 7, 1889. City Of Portland Records, 24:110.

## Ownership of lots in Western Cemetery

Ordered: That the City Solicitor be and hereby is requested to give an opinion relative to the ownership of lots, and the restrictions of burials in the Western Cemetery. Read twice, passed and sent down for concurrence. Concurred. Approved by the Mayor April 5, 1904.

### Letter concerning ownership of lots

Portland, Maine, June 1, 1904

To the Honorable City Council:

In reply to your request for information as to the ownership of lots and the restriction of burials in Western Cemetery, permit me to say: That the land now known as Western Cemetery was purchased by the City of Portland of William Vaughan, et.als. by several deeds between the years 1829 and 1841.

The statutes of this state, from very early times authorized towns and cities to purchase and hold lands for public burial places.

In 1846 the City Council by ordinance provided for the assignment of lots in the Western Cemetery to every family in the city, of which assignment a record should be made and kept with the full name of the head of the family.

In a book of records of burials in the City Clerk's office are found at varying intervals reference to assignments of lots in Western Cemetery to certain persons, which was presumably done under the ordinance of 1846. At all events it is the only official record of assignment of lots of which I have been able to learn.

By a recent ordinance burials in Western Cemetery have been restricted to natives of Portland or to those who died residents of Portland, and who at their deaths, are lot owners or the members of immediate families of owners of private lots in that cemetery.

The right of the city to make reasonable restrictions as to burials in public cemeteries under its police powers seems to be well settled.

The only points, as I understand it, about which uncertainties have risen are how are the owners of lots to be determined, and who are included within the restrictions "members of immediate families?"

Undoubtedly, a very large proportion if not nearly all the persons to whom the lots were originally assigned, have already died, and owing to the meagre records we have, ownership in many cases may be difficult of proof.

All that can be said in this particular is, that the persons to whom the lots were originally assigned thereby acquired the right or license, exclusive of every other person to bury dead upon the plot assigned to them, a license which was irrevocable so long as the land continued to be used as a place of burial. (Gowen vs. Bessey 94 Maine 116; 6 Cyc 717; Sohier vs. Trinity Ch., 109 Massachusetts.)

While not settled by any decided case in this state, the preponderence of authorities seem to hold that rights of burial in a public cemetery in a particular plot partake of the nature of real property, and

155

like the rights of pews in houses of worship descend to the heirs of the deceased owner. (6 Cyc 718 note 54 and cases cited Washburn on Real Property v. 1, p. 31.)

It would seem therefore that the original assignees or holders of the lots in Western Cemetery, whither acquired by deed or recorded assignment in a book kept for that purpose, obtained an interest in their respective lots which would descend to their heirs, who would then become owners with the same rights of burial as their ancestors.

A present claimant of the right of burial should therefore be required to trace his title to his lot by descent or assignment before being allowed to inter therein.

To lay down the exact limit of the restriction "members of the immediate family" is not wholly free from difficulty.

The term "family" may include a man's household, consisting of himself, his wife, children, and servants; it may mean his wife and children, or his children, excluding his wife, or in the absence of wife and children it may mean his brothers and sisters, or next of kin, or it may mean the genealogical stock from which he may have sprung. (2 Story Eq. Juirs 13 Ed. Sec. 1065 b.)

Its ordinary meaning when standing alone includes parents, children, servants, all whose domicile or home is ordinarily in the same house under the same management or head.

If a child on becoming of age marries and leaves the parental roof and sets up a family of his own, he no longer in the popular sense is a member of the father's family.

In the ordinance, however, we have another qualifying word which considering the obvious purpose of the ordinance would seem to me to limit the term "family" to narrow confines. Members of the immediate family. I cannot conceive that the word "family" in this ordinance was intended to include servants of the lot owner or other members of the household besides his wife and children, who, if that word had been used alone and in its ordinary sense, might be also included among those who could be interred in Western Cemetery and the use of the word "immediate" would seem to indicate that the City Council used the term "family" in a more restricted sense. Immediate, when used to qualify relationship or dissent, refers to those descendents who are only one step removed from the common ancestor, as children, in distinction from mediate descendents who are more remote. (Levy, et. al. vs. McCarber, 6 Peters (U.S.) 102.)

I am unable to conclude, however, that it was intended to restrict burials to the children of the lot owners alone, to the exclusion of the lot owners wife, but taking the two terms together and the purpose and context of the ordinance, I am of the opinion that it was the intention to restrict burials to the family of the lot owner, consisting of husband and wife and children, so long as they remained under the parental roof, or until they have gone forth and established or set up a family of their own.

I, therefore, most respectfully submit that according to my interpretation of the ordinance in the light of such facts as I have been able to obtain in the matter, which is not wholly free from obscurity, is that a person to have the right of burial there should first be able to establish his ownership by descent or assignment; second, that he is a native of Portland, or a resident thereof, at the time of decease; and third, that he is either a lot owner or a member of the family of a lot owner, to wit, either the wife, husband, or child who still forms a part of the household of his parents. Respectfully submitted, Scott Wilson, City Solicitor. 6 June 1904. Portland City Records, 33:2-5.

# ADDENDUM

The following list of names were recorded incorrectly:

Basford should read Rasford.
Bonayne should read Ronayne.
Brucy should read Bracy.
Brvad should read Broad.
Connor should read O'Connor.
Fay should read Frye.
Huff should read McDuff.

Inos should read Innes.
Kash should read Cash.
Lyman should read Wyman.
McGuire should read Megquire.
McNerney should read McVarney.
Mellen should read Mullen.
Russell should read Buzzell.
Wateman should read Waterman.
Waterhouse should read Whitehouse.

# INDEX

This cross-index lists names buried in the text.

BURKE, Barbara Abbie 125
Michael 125 Sarah 125
BURNHAM, Martha 28 Mary 28
Mary A 33
BURNS, Frances 127
BURR, Mary 43
CARRUTHERS, Charles H 67
Elizabeth M 67 Greta E 67
CARTY, Mary 134
CASH, Frances C 142
CHAMBERLAIN, Edith 83 John
83 Rhebe R 83
CHANDLER, Mary 56
CHAPMAN, Minerva D 17
CHICK, Amos 128 Amy 128
Elizabeth H 128
CHICKERING, John W 5
CLAPHAM, Mary 99
CLARK, George 3 Harriet 70
Sarah Ann 3
CLEAVES, Sarah 113
CLIFFORD, Carrie 93
COBB, Cynthia M 3 Mary C 118
Matthew A 3 Sarah L 3
Thomas 118
CODMAN, Kate S C 120 Randolph
A L 120
CONNOR, Maria 101
COOLBROTH, Betsy 82 Frances
E 82 Lemuel 82
CRESSY, Noah 12 Sophia C 12
Sophia S 12
CROSSMAN, Elizabeth 64 Joseph
A 64 Sarah E 64
CROWTHER, Sarah 44
DANIELS, 32
DAVEIS, Elizabeth Taylor 1
Frances E 1 John T G 1 Mary
Cogswell 63
DAVIS, Maria E 68
DAY, Henrietta 126
DEAN, Eliza 36 Elizabeth 36
Robert 36
DEEHAN, Mary J 100
DEGURO, Harriet G 106 John 106
Sophia 106
DONLEY, Mary J 95
DOW, Jane 108
DOYLE, Lena 131 Maggie A 131
Randall 131
DURGIN, Elizabeth 71
DYER, 7 Caroline 130 Ebenezer

DYER (continued)
73 Eleanor 73 Sarah Ellen 73
EDMUNDS, John 5 142 Lizzie B
142 Sarah A 5 142 Sarah C 5
ELWELL, Julia A 76
EMERY, Ann T 12 Harriet E 142
Nicholas 12 Theresa Orne 12
EVANS, Elizabeth 37
EVELETH, Charles E 84 Sarah 84
Sarah E 84
EWING, Annie 123 Margaret E
123 William B 123
FAIRBANKS, Levi 39 Sybil 39
FESSENDON, Nathan 102
FIELD, Elias 116 Lucinda F 116
FLING, Ella J 130 Henry 130
Jane N 130
FOBES, Hannah 39
FOLLETT, Mary A 55
FOLSOM, Clarissa 5
FOY, Catherine 95
FREEMAN, Jane 128
FRENCH, Elizabeth 122 William
122
FROTHINGHAM, Mary 113
FULLER, Mary A 14
FURLONG, Elizabeth S 142
GARLAND, Ann Louise Virginia
106 Elizabeth K 106 John 106
GAY, Betsy 123 124
GILMAN, Anne Emery 32
Caroline 97 Elizabeth T 32
Elizabeth Taylor 32 Frances E
32 John T G 32 John Taylor 97
Mary 33 Mary H 97
GILSON, Calvin 64 Josephine 64
GOODING, Sarah A 43
GORDON, Frances 32 Frances E
32 Frances Ellen 32 John T G
32
GRAFFAN, Mary T 144
GRAVES, Sarah B 16 Sarah M 16
William 16
GREEN, Charles M 48 Eunice A
69 Lizzie F 48 Martha Q 83
GREENE, Eliza A 25 John 25
GRIFFIN, Timothy 116
HAMILTON, Mary Ann 137
HASKINS, David 102 Frances
Green 102 Mary A 102
HAZELTINE, Amanda 77 Nancy
D 77 Samuel 77

HEARD, Mary B 3
HEDMAN, Charles 106 Sarah 106
    Sarah E 106
HERSEY, Ann A 29
HILBORN, Ann S 111 Seth B 111
HILL, Clara 69
HOLBROOK, Sarah R 79
HORSLEY, Blanche 107
HORTON, Elizabeth 74
HUCKINS, John R 13 Mirmorah 13
HUFF, Ella A 42
HUNT, Daniel 74 Rebecca 74
    Sarah 74
HUTCHINSON, J F 132 Sarah 132
JACKSON, 24 Jeanette 126
JOHNSON, Mary E 135
JORDAN, Arvilla 132 Benjamin
    135 Elizabeth 56 136 Henrietta
    56 Sarah 135 Seth 56
KALLARD, T 3
KEAZER, Clarissa D 81 Joseph
    81 Mary 81
KEENE, Diana 41 Joshua 41
KELLOGG, Eunice M 5
KNIGHT, Martha 45 Sarah 114
LAKEMAN, Elizabeth 81
LEWIS, Frances 131 James T
    131 Rosalie P 131
LIBBY, Ellen 93 Lorenzo Dow 93
    Nellie A 93
LITTLE, Laura 46
LOCKE, Mary 73
LYONS, Mary Ann 124
MANCHESTER, Elizabeth B 63
    Joseph 63 Lydia J 63
MANGE, Mary 89
MANN, Esther 126 Rachel M 126
    Sarah J 62 Thomas 126
MARR, Helen 79
MCDONALD, Catherine 16
MCLAUGHLIN, Ellen 108
MCLEAN, Mary 53
MCLELLAN, Arthur 101 Eunice
    75 Joseph 5 Mary 75 101
MEANS-CUMMINGS, 7
MERRILL, Jennie 71
MILLIKEN, Alexander 143
    Amanda 143 Sarah 71
MORRISON, John 22 Sophia M 22
NASON, Mary 73
NEAL, Eleanor 60
NEWALL, Eliza 105

NUTTER, Mary A 114
O'NEAL, 32
PAINE, Mary 57
PATCH, Sarah E 133
PATTERSON, Albertine 141 L A
    141 S G 141
PETERSON, Amelia 25 Otto 25
    Thilda 25
PHILLIPS, Cora 113 Sabina I 113
    William H 113
PICKETT, Isaac 127 Mary 127
    Sarah C 42
PINSON, Deborah 81
PLUMMER, Abigail 133 Jane P
    133 Moses 133
POMEROY, Hannah Pearson 75
POOLE, Georgianna A 72
POWELL, Emmaline H 143
    Thomas 143
PRINCE, Harriet 100 Matilda 100
PROCTOR, Harriet M 53
RADCLIFFE, Harriet E 145
ROBINSON, Caroline A 118
    Charles P 118 Gertrude R 83
    Jacob W 83 Lydia G 118 Mar-
    tha A 83
SARGENT, Ruth 130
SAVILLE, Mary N 47
SAWYER, Elizabeth B 84
SCOTT, Mary B 12
SEWALL, Anne 100
SHANKS, Julia 7
SHATTUCK, Mary 46
SHURTLEFF, Almira 116
SIMONTON, Eliza 126 Mary 126
    Thomas 126
SKILINGS, Ellen K 15 Hannah 15
    Simeon 15
SKILLINGS, Nancy Preble 81
SMALL, Rozella R 103
SMITH, Chloe 64 J 24 Myra
    Adams 56 Sarah 130 William
    128
SOMERS, Catherine 141 Elizabeth
    S 141 Michael 141
SPELLMAN, Jeremiah 114
STAPLES, Mary E 53
STETSON, Harriette 104 Helene
    107
STIMSON, Etta M 92 Nathaniel 92
    Sarah M 92
STOVER, Annie 106 Frances L

STOVER (continued)
114 Samuel S 114
STROUT, George 54 Mary 54
Rosanna 54
STUART, Mary 19
SWANTON, Rachel 113
TANNER, Mabelle Scott 120
Sarah 120 William H 120
TARR, Martha A 71
THOIR, Mary L 45
THOMPSON, Mary H 74
TITCOMB, Eliza Sherburn 104
TOBIE, Mercy 46
ULRICK, Harriet 12 John 12 Sally
12
VANBUSKIRK, Lawrence 36 Mary
36 Susan S 36

VAUGHAN, Anne G 56 William
56
WALKER, Elizabeth 128 James
128 Sarah 128
WATERHOUSE, Anna 126 Sarah
145
WATERMAN, Ruth 67
WHITE, Martha 125
WHITNEY, Susan 50
WILLARD, Annis 114
WINSLOW, Amanda 92
WOODBURY, Asa 3 Nancy 3
WYER, Ruth 49
YORK, Charles 114 Mary C 114
Mary O 114